LEARNING FROM THE SAGES

Other Books by Roy B. Zuck

LEARNING FROM THE SAGES

SELECTED STUDIES ON THE BOOK OF PROVERBS

EDITED BY

ROY B. ZUCK

Baker Books
A Division of Baker Book House Co
Grand Rapids, Michigan 49516

© 1995 by Roy B. Zuck

Published by Baker Books
a division of Baker Book House Company
PO Box 6287, Grand Rapids, MI 49516-6287

Printed in the United States of America

Library of Congress Cataloging-in-Publication Data

Learning from the sages : selected studies on the book of Proverbs / edited by Roy B. Zuck.
    p.   cm.
    Includes bibliographical references.
    ISBN 0-8010-9941-2
    1. Bible. O.T. Proverbs—Criticism, interpretation, etc. I. Zuck, Roy B.
BS1465.2.L43   1994
223'.706—dc2094-9653

                                                   94-9653

CONTENTS

5

ABBREVIATIONS

AB	*Anchor Bible*
AEL	*Ancient Egyptian Literature,* M. Lichtheim
AfO	*Archiv für Orientforschung*
AJSL	*American Journal of Semitic Languages and Literature*
ANET	*Ancient Near Eastern Texts,* ed. J. B. Pritchard
ASV	American Standard Version
AV	Authorized Version
BAGD	W. Bauer, W. F. Arndt, F. W. Gingrich, and F. W. Danker, *Greek-English Lexicon of the New Testament*
BDB	F. Brown, S. R. Driver, and C. A. Briggs, *Hebrew and English Lexicon of the Old Testament*
BH(S)	*Biblia Hebraica*
Bib, Bibl	*Biblica*
BTB	*Biblical Theology Bulletin*
BWL	*Babylonian Wisdom Literature,* W. G. Lambert
CAD H	*The Assyrian Dictionary of the Oriental Institute of Chicago*
CBQ	*Catholic Biblical Quarterly*
CSR Bulletin	*The Council on the Study of Religion: Bulletin*
ET	English translation
EV	English Version
EvTh	*Evangelische Theologie*
HAT	Handbuch zum Alten Testament
HKAT	Handkommentar zum Alten Testament
HSM	Harvard Semitic Monographs
HUCA	*Hebrew Union College Annual*
ICC	International Critical Commentary
IDB	*Interpreter's Dictionary of the Bible,* ed. G. A. Buttrick
Int	*Interpretation*

IOT	*Introduction to the Old Testament,* R. K. Harrison
ITC	International Theological Commentary
JANES	*Journal of the Ancient Near Eastern Society*
JAOS	*Journal of the American Oriental Society*
JBL	*Journal of Biblical Literature*
JCS	*Journal of Cuneiform Studies*
JNES	*Journal of Near Eastern Studies*
JPS	Jewish Publication Society
JQR	*Jewish Quarterly Review*
JTS	*Journal of Theological Studies*
KB	L. Koehler and W. Baumgartner, *Lexicon in Veteris Testamenti libros*
KJV	King James Version
LB	Living Bible
LSJ	H. G. Liddell, R. Scott, and H. S. Jones, *Greek-English Lexicon*
LXX	Septuagint
MT	Masoretic Text
NAB	New American Bible
NASB	New American Standard Bible
NBD	*New Bible Dictionary*
NEB	New English Bible
NIV	New International Version
NJV	New Jewish Version
NT	New Testament
OIP	Oriental Institute Publications
OLZ	*Orientalistische Literaturzeitung*
OT	Old Testament
OTL	Old Testament Library
PSBA	*Proceedings of the Society of Biblical Archaeology*
RB	*Revue Biblique*
Rev d'Eg	*Revue d'égyptologie*
RSV	Revised Standard Version
SAOC	Studies in Ancient Oriental Civilizations
SBLDS	SBL Dissertation Series
SBT	*Studies in Biblical Theology*
TEV	Today's English Version

TDOT	*Theological Dictionary of the Old Testament*
ThWAT	*Theologisches Wörterbuch zum Alten Testament,* ed. G. J. Botterwick and H. Ringgren
TRE	*Theologische Realenzyklopädie*
UF	*Ugarit-Forschungen*
UT	*Ugaritic Textbook,* C. H. Gordon
VT	*Vetus Testamentum*
VTS, VTSup	*Vetus Testamentum Supplements*
WMANT	Wissenschaftliche Monographien zum Alten und Neuen Testament
ZAS	*Zeitschrift für Ägyptische Sprache und Altertumskunde*
ZAW	*Zeitschrift für die alttestamentliche Wissenschaft*
ZkTh	*Zeitschrift für katholische Theologie*

CONTRIBUTORS

Kenneth T. Aitken
Lecturer in Old Testament, University of Aberdeen, Scotland
Robert L. Alden
Professor of Old Testament, Denver Seminary, Denver, Colorado
Gleason L. Archer, Jr.
Professor Emeritus of Old Testament and Semitic Languages, Trinity Evangelical Divinity School, Deerfield, Illinois
C. Hassell Bullock
Associate Professor of Biblical Studies, Wheaton College, Wheaton, Illinois
Sid S. Buzzell
Academic Dean, Seminary of the East, Ambler, Pennsylvania
Kathleen A. Farmer
Professor of Old Testament, United Theological Seminary, Dayton, Ohio
Duane A. Garrett
Professor of Hebrew and Old Testament, Canadian Southern Baptist Seminary, Cochrane, Alberta
Ted Hildebrandt
Professor of Biblical Studies and Philosophy, Grace College, Winona Lake, Indiana
Kenneth G. Hoglund
Associate Professor and Director of Graduate Studies, Department of Religion, Wake Forest University, Winston-Salem, North Carolina
David A. Hubbard
President Emeritus and Professor of Old Testament Emeritus, Fuller Theological Seminary, Pasadena, California

Murray H. Lichtenstein
Associate Professor, Department of Classical and Oriental Studies, Hebrew
Division, Hunter College, City University of New York, New York City,
New York
Bruce V. Malchow
Professor of Hebrew Bible, Sacred Heart School of Theology, Hales Corners,
Wisconsin
Thomas P. McCreesh
Associate Professor of Scripture, Dominican House of Studies, Washington,
D.C.
William McKane
Professor of Hebrew and Old Testament, University of St. Andrews, Scotland
William E. Mouser, Jr.
Executive Director, International Council for Gender Studies, De Soto, Tex-
as, and former missionary to Austria
Roland E. Murphy
George Washington Ivey Emeritus Professor of Biblical Studies, Duke Uni-
versity, Durham, North Carolina
Greg W. Parsons
Professor of Biblical Studies, Baptist Missionary Association Theological Sem-
inary, Jacksonville, Texas
Allen P. Ross
Professor of Old Testament Studies, Trinity Episcopal School for Ministry,
Ambridge, Pennsylvania
John Ruffle
Keeper of the Oriental Museum, University of Durham, Durham, England
R. B. Y. Scott
Chairman, Department of Religion, Princeton University, Princeton, New
Jersey. Deceased.
Phyllis Trible
Baldwin Professor of Sacred Literature, Union Theological Seminary, New
York City, New York
Bruce A. Waltke
Professor of Old Testament, Regent College, Vancouver, British Columbia
R. N. Whybray
Professor Emeritus of Hebrew and Old Testament Studies, University of
Hull, England
James G. Williams
Professor of Religion, Syracuse University, Syracuse, New York
Eldon G. Woodcock
Professor of Bible, Nyack College, Nyack, New York

Gale A. Yee
Associate Professor, University of St. Thomas, St. Paul, Minnesota
Roy B. Zuck
Chairman and Senior Professor of Bible Exposition, and Editor, *Bibliotheca Sacra,* Dallas Theological Seminary, Dallas, Texas

INTRODUCTION

The Book of Proverbs tells us how to wise up and live. The appeal of this profound, down-to-earth book stems from its breadth of subject matter. It discusses everything from training a child to ruling a nation, from eating too much to talking too much, from how to succeed in life to how to live for God.

These pithy sayings comment on all kinds of people: the lazy person, the gossip, the liar, the drunkard, the prostitute, the false witness, and also the wise son, the just ruler, the honest businessman, the industrious worker—and many more.

What's more, like a magnet the book pulls readers to its pages because of its unique format and style. No other book of the Bible has such a collection of proverbs—hundreds of them, in fact—that state observations and admonitions so succinctly. Because of their terseness, they penetrate the soul like a sharp knife. They capture the reader before he has time to recoil. Their compact nature demands time for reflection, time for the thoughts "to ferment in the mind," as Hassell Bullock put it.

Numerous figures of speech, word pictures, puns, alliterations, synonymous and contrastive lines, and wit are among the rhetorical devices that add color to the book.

British Prime Minister Lord John Russell wrote that in proverbial sayings we have "the wisdom of many and the wit of one." Parents and other wise persons, including Solomon, the wisest of his day (1 Kings 4:29–31), wrote maxims that reflect concisely the accumulated experiences and observations of many. As Miguel de Cervantes, a Spanish novelist of the 1500s, put it, "Proverbs are short sentences, drawn from long experience."

But more than observations about life are to be found in the Book of Proverbs. Many verses present straightforward admonitions, hard-hitting commands on how to get the most out of life and how to avoid troublesome con-

15

sequences. And many of the directives include sensible reasons or goading motives.

A number of chapters in this anthology discuss issues pertaining to the Book of Proverbs including the book's style, theology, date, authorship, and hermeneutics. Other chapters present expositions of selected portions of Proverbs, key passages that call for exegetical expertise as well as personal application.

I appreciate the kind permission of the publishers to reprint from their works, and I am grateful for the fine contributions of the authors of these chapters. Obviously a work such as this calls for selectivity, which means that other equally outstanding writings could not be included because of lack of space. I trust this work will aid scholars and laypersons alike in their study of one of the Bible's richest—and most enriching—books.

Part 1

OVERVIEW AND THEMES IN THE BOOK OF PROVERBS

1

THE BOOK
OF PROVERBS

C. Hassell Bullock

Many persons who have become overwhelmed by a theoretical approach to Christianity have been able to get a handle on the faith by reading the Book of Proverbs. For this book represents the common-sense approach to life and faith. It touches the shared concerns of all who are given the gift of life and struggle with how to live it. For those who are recipients of the gift of faith, this book distills the theological substance of Old Testament religion into its practical essence.

In its basic form, the proverb is an ancient saying that takes wisdom and endows it with youthful vigor. In a few, piquant phrases the proverb capsulizes a practical idea or truth in such a way as to lift the commonplace to a new level of mental consciousness. It reweaves the threadbare idea and shows the ordinary to be quite extraordinary.

Yet the proverb is not the kind of form that one can assimilate in large quantities at once. W. A. L. Elmslie has astutely called it "compressed experience,"[1] and in this kind of literature overindulgence has its peculiar consequences. One needs time for some proverbs to ferment in the mind. Only contemplation will unfold the full meaning of:

> He who pursues righteousness and loyalty
> Finds life, righteousness and honor.
>
> [Prov. 21:21]

Although its face value is obvious enough, the meaning bears prolonged thought. Yet others are highly volatile and yield their content with a sudden burst, which is part of their appeal and power:

> Better is a dry morsel and quietness with it
> Than a house full of feasting with strife.
>
> [Prov. 17:1]

The face value is all that is intended. Still other proverbs convey their truth with a bit of humorous wit:

> Why is there a price in the hand of a fool to buy wisdom,
> When he has no sense?
>
> [Prov. 17:16]

Fundamental to the proverbial form is the fact that it bears a truth that has been tested by time. Fads have no place in proverbial literature, except as their shallow nature may need to be exposed. Time and experience have bestowed their blessing upon proverbial lore. They are the soil in which truth is germinated and sustained. But to that which does not possess the innate substance for life, they are stony ground.

Much more can be said on the nature of the proverb, or aphorism, that is the building block of the Book of Proverbs. Some of that will become obvious as the discussion proceeds, but much will depend upon time and experience to appropriate the magnitude of this book and the necessity of viewing life and faith from its practical perspective.

Title

"The proverbs of Solomon the son of David, king of Israel" (1:1) is very likely the original title of the book once the final edition was in place. The Septuagint has the slightly different title "Proverbs of Solomon son of David,

---

1. W. A. L. Elmslie, *Studies in Life from Jewish Proverbs,* 16. I acknowledge my indebtedness to Elmslie's excellent chapter entitled "The Characteristics of Proverbs," 13–27.

who ruled in Israel," whereas the Vulgate has simply "Liber Proverbiorum" (The Book of Proverbs). The abbreviated title "The Proverbs of Solomon" appears as the superscription heading up the section that begins at 10:1, and at 25:1 we have another variant, "These also are proverbs of Solomon." Many scholars assume that the title has been transplanted from one of these sections to the beginning of the book.[2] Actually the title may include verses 2–6, in which the author or editor sets forth his purpose for the entire collection. Although reasons may be advanced for the non-Solomonic nature of chapters 1–9, they are not substantive enough to give this conclusion finality, as we shall discuss later.

Nature and Purpose of Proverbs

Nature of Wisdom in Proverbs. The basic nature of wisdom as viewed by the author of Proverbs is summed up in his aphorism "The fear of the LORD is the beginning of knowledge" (1:7; cf. 9:10). Even though wisdom was associated very closely with craftsmanship and artistic ability (Exod. 35:30–35), the theological basis was still the Spirit of God. Thus in Proverbs the underlying basis of life and human experience is one's relationship to God. Out of that relationship grow moral understanding and the perception to judge what is right (2:6–22), a proper attitude toward material possessions (3:9–10) and industrious labor (6:6–11), the necessary equilibrium and sense of security for living in the world (3:21–26), and the right relationship toward one's neighbor (3:27–29), to mention only a few of the more practical benefits of that personal relationship.

The nature of wisdom in the book consists of a certain philosophic-theological approach to life that draws out the implications of worship and commitment to God. Whereas such an ethical document as the Ten Commandments puts the vertical dimension first (man's relationship to God) and the horizontal dimension second (man's relationship to his neighbor and his world), the Book of Proverbs capitalizes upon the practical implications of the horizontal perspective. The prophetic writings, to use a comparison, exhibit the same two-dimensional orientation, but the focus upon immediate divine revelation and its bearing upon life (which is predominant in the prophets) is a basic presupposition in Proverbs. The process has been taken one step further to the arena of daily life where no prophetic word persuades and exhorts. Rather the tone of Proverbs is affirmative and declarative,[3] seeking to answer the question "How ought we then to live?"

2. See "Date and Authorship," 164–68 [in my *Introduction to the Poetic Books of the Old Testament*].
3. R. B. Y. Scott, *Proverbs, Ecclesiastes,* 24.

The personification of wisdom in chapters 8–9 constitutes another dimension of wisdom in Proverbs that is more thought provoking. Although the descriptions in 1:20–22 and chapters 2–3 may be largely metaphorical, as in Job 28, we do have an example of personification in chapters 8–9, where wisdom is personified as a woman. She speaks, offers wealth and prosperity to her devotees (8:18, 21), existed before the creation of the world (8:22–23 . . .), assisted the Lord in creation (8:30), and possesses a house and servants (9:1–6). Yet wisdom does not have the ontological distinction that it does in the Wisdom of Solomon or that the Logos (Word) has in John's Gospel.

The purpose of personification in this instance is to help us understand God by abstracting one of his attributes and endowing it with personality and consciousness. The author wants to teach that wisdom is an attribute of God that is eternally related to him, understood only in relation to him, and is an extension of his dynamic Being to mankind. The method of personification is the means by which the practical perspective of wisdom is connected to God. It is the closest thing wisdom has to the prophetic formula "Thus says the Lord." By means of personified wisdom, the knowledge of God's nature is delivered to and integrated with man's everyday life.

Possibly based upon this method of personifying abstract ideas or divine attributes, later noncanonical authors emulated the method and developed it more fully. In Ecclesiasticus, wisdom is a direct emanation from God (24:3–5), was created before the world (1:4; 24:9), and has an eternal nature (1:1; 24:9). The most advanced level of this kind of thought is represented in the noncanonical Wisdom of Solomon, which R. H. Charles dates after 50 B.C.[4] There wisdom is hypostatized (cf. Wisd. 1:6–7; 6:12–24; chaps. 7–8), that is, endowed with a distinct essence and consciousness, much as the Logos is portrayed in the prologue to John's Gospel. Although scholars generally have viewed chapters 1–9 of Proverbs as a late composition, possibly even postexilic,[5] basing their conclusion in part upon the personification in chapters 8–9, the idea of unilinear development of concepts and institutions in the ancient East is dubious. In both Mesopotamia and Egypt, the personification of truth, justice, intelligence, understanding, and other abstract ideas are known from the third and second millennia B.C.[6] We shall discuss this matter further when we consider the authorship and date of Proverbs.

The word used to designate the contents of the book is *māshāl*, usually translated "proverb." Although the root is disputed among scholars, the general opinion is that it derives from the verb *māshal*, "to represent, be like."[7]

---

4. R. H. Charles, *The Apocrypha and Pseudepigrapha of the Old Testament in English*, 1:519.
5. E.g., Otto Eissfeldt, *The Old Testament: An Introduction*, 473.
6. K. A. Kitchen, *Ancient Orient and Old Testament*, 126–27.
7. Francis Brown, S. R. Driver, and Charles A. Briggs, *A Hebrew and English Lexicon of the Old Testament*, 605a.

Thus the meaning of the noun would be "likeness," and a *māshāl*, or proverb, would be a statement that seeks to reveal the true nature of one thing by comparing it to something else.[8] In the Old Testament generally the term is used variously. It may signify a simple folk saying (1 Sam. 10:12; 24:13), an allegory (Ezek. 17:2), an enigmatic saying (Ezek. 20:29), a taunt (Isa. 14:4; Hab. 2:6), a lament (Mic. 2:4), a prophetic discourse (Num. 23:7; 24:15), a didactic discourse (Ps. 49:4), or a plea (Job 29:1). In the Book of Proverbs it signifies either an aphorism (as in 10:1–22:16) or a discourse (as in chapters 1–9; 23:29–35; 27:23–27).[9]

The Didactic Nature of Proverbs. Whereas Job and Ecclesiastes are reflective wisdom, Proverbs and the Song of Songs are didactic. That is, they seek to teach rather than to argue or convince. The Book of Proverbs reiterates the necessity for instruction, provided by both father and mother (1:8; 6:20), and the urgency of the children's obedience. It is directed to young people (cf. 1:4) whose lives could still be shaped in the ways of wisdom. The products of both theory and experience are offered in short, pithy sayings that might be used as a rule of thumb for personal conduct. R. B. Y. Scott has identified seven proverbial patterns according to which these principles for living are expressed:

1. *Identity, or equivalence*
   "A man who flatters his neighbor
   Is spreading a net for his steps" (29:5).
2. *Nonidentity, or contrast*
   "A sated man loathes honey,
   But to a famished man any bitter thing is sweet" (27:7).
3. *Similarity*
   "Like cold water to a weary soul,
   So is good news from a distant land" (25:25).
4. *Contrariety to proper order indicative of absurdity*
   "Why is there a price in the hand of a fool to buy wisdom,
   When he has no sense?" (17:16).
5. *Classification of persons, actions, or situations*
   "The naive believes everything,
   But the prudent man considers his steps" (14:15).
6. *Valuation, or priority of one thing relative to another*
   "A good name is to be more desired than great riches,
   Favor is better than silver and gold" (22:1).
7. *Consequence of human character or behavior*

8. Scott, 13.
9. Crawford H. Toy, *A Critical and Exegetical Commentary on the Book of Proverbs*, 4.

"The sluggard does not plow after the autumn,
So he begs during the harvest and has nothing" (20:4).[10]

In addition to the aphorism, the book contains the longer, more reflective passages (e.g., 1:8–19; 5:1–23; 23:29–35; 27:23–27, etc.). We know that the wisdom schools, based upon the reflective, or higher, type of wisdom, involved more than just memorization of terse, practical sayings. And while some schools were likely inclined more toward the reflective than the pragmatic, some of both might very well have infiltrated the curriculum of any one school. Even in the highly reflective Book of Job we have brief proverbs imbedded in the discourses (e.g., Job 4:8; 12:11; 21:19). Therefore, we should not expect that the pedagogical methods in the wisdom schools were monolithic.

The Purpose of Proverbs. The didactic nature of the book is coincident with its purpose. In fact, the introduction to the book (1:2–6) sets forth the purpose: to initiate the reader into wisdom and instruction. The book then purports to be a primer of right conduct and essential attitudes toward life, aimed at producing lives in conformity to the divine will. The immediate object was to train and educate for the preservation of the family unit and social stability. Therefore, prominent in wisdom was the recognition that fulfillment of God's will is actualized in the personal and social conduct and institutions of his people.

Proverbs is an instructional manual that was put together largely out of Solomonic materials most probably during Hezekiah's reign (25:1), approximately 715–686 B.C. The collection of the book may have been associated with or may have followed upon Hezekiah's extensive religious reform early in his reign (2 Kings 18:1–6; 2 Chron. 29–31). The didactic purpose then assumed greater proportions as a religiously and socially decadent society began its arduous road back to spiritual health and social stability.

Literary Structure and Growth of the Book

For the most part, the literary structure of the book is indicated by the titles heading up each section. Although these are rather obvious in the Hebrew text, they are sometimes obscured in the English translations. Three times the title "the proverbs of Solomon" appears, the first time (1:1) applied to the entire book, and the other two occurrences (10:1; 25:1) applied to sections within the book. There is good reason to believe that the general editor(s) did not remove the last two headings because they signaled two distinct collections that were incorporated into the final edition. At the end of the section begun at 10:1, two shorter collections were inserted, simply titled "words of the wise" (22:17–24:22) and "Also these are for the wise" (24:23–34, author's trans.).

10. Scott, 5–8.

Although some scholars discount the historical value of the title that heads up chapters 25–29 ("These also are proverbs of Solomon which the men of Hezekiah, king of Judah, transcribed," 25:1),[11] we really have no substantial basis for rejecting its historical reliability.[12] The "men of Hezekiah" is a technical phrase for Hezekiah's scribes maintained under the auspices of the royal court (cf. "David's men" in 1 Sam. 23:3, 5 and "Abner's men" in 2 Sam. 2:31; 1 Kings 10:8). With the fall of the Northern Kingdom to the Assyrians in 733–722 B.C., a flurry of literary activity very likely occurred and involved not only wisdom writings but also prophetic literature. In the wake of the cataclysmic events in the North, the need for preserving the prophetic words, both fulfilled and unfulfilled, was impressed upon the southern counterpart, and a renewed practical emphasis received strong encouragement from the eighth-century prophets, who clearly perceived that the religiosity of both kingdoms was contradicted by unethical personal actions (cf. Isa. 1; Amos 8:4–6).

The last three sections of the book constitute an appendix, which may also have been a product of Hezekiah's school, although the evidence for dating both the composition of these documents and their addition to the book is inconclusive. The first two ("The words of Agur," chap. 30, and "The words of King Lemuel," 31:1–9) appear to be non-Israelite in nature.[13] The last section, "concerning praise of a virtuous wife" (31:10–31), is most likely Israelite in origin (cf. 31:30b) and functions as a theological equalizer for the last section of the appendix.

The growth of the book can be viewed in the stages shown on page 26.

Since Proverbs 25:1 states that Hezekiah's men compiled chapters 25–29 from Solomonic materials, the inference to be drawn is that the proverbs composing this section had not been collected into one single book until that time. These scribes likely had two Solomonic collections at their disposal. Note "These also" at 25:1, which would indicate that they were enlarging an existing book, the first consisting of 1:7–9:18 and the second of 10:1–24:34. The two brief appendixes following 22:16 ("words of the wise," 22:17–24:22, and "also these are for the wise," 24:23–34, author's trans.) may already have stood in the larger collection or been added by the Hezekiah scribes. This comprehensive collection is what Delitzsch called the older book

11. E.g., Toy, 457–58, contends that the Hebrew word for "transcribed" belongs to late literary vocabulary (in Gen. 12:8, KJV, it means "to remove"), and the time of Hezekiah was selected by the editor as an appropriate time for such literary activity, particularly in view of the activities of the prophets Isaiah and Micah and the tradition of Hezekiah's vigorous religious reform.

12. Scott, 17, finds no reason to disqualify the title. E. J. Young, *An Introduction to the Old Testament*, 317, cites the use of *'thq* in the Ras Shamra texts with the sense of "to pass" (of time) and suggests that the word may already have had a different nuance in earlier philological history.

13. See "Hermeneutical Considerations," 172–73 [*Introduction to the Poetic Books of the Old Testament*].

Stage 1	1:7–9:18 10:1–24:34	*First edition* of Solomonic proverbs, which may have already been a single unit or two separate units.	
Stage 2	1:7–9:18 10:1–24:34 +	*First edition*	*Enlarged edition* of Solomonic proverbs edited by Hezekiah's scribes, which may or may not have included chapters 30–31.
	25:1–29:27 + Superscription (1:1) and preface (1:2–6)	New Solomonic collection compiled by Hezekiah's scribes	

of Proverbs and proposed that it came into being during the reign of Jehoshaphat (870–848 B.C.), some seventy years after Solomon's death.[14]

To the two large collections, Hezekiah's scribes appended their recently edited book of Solomonic proverbs and superscribed this enlarged edition with 1:1 and a preface setting forth the purpose of the new edition (1:2–6). Since the new preface was non-Solomonic, the non-Solomonic appendix may have completed the literary symmetry (non-Solomonic–Solomonic–non-Solomonic).

We conclude that the final edition of Proverbs, possibly excepting chapters 30–31, was completed sometime in the first half of Hezekiah's reign, most likely by 700 B.C.

Literary Structure and Composition

Superscription	1:1
Introduction	1:2–6
Reflections on Wisdom	1:7–9:18
Miscellaneous Proverbs of Solomon	10:1–22:16
Words of the Wise	22:17–24:22
Also These Are for the Wise	24:23–34
Miscellaneous Proverbs of Solomon Collected by Hezekiah's Men	25:1–29:27
The Words of Agur	30:1–33
The Words of Lemuel	31:1–9
An Acrostic Celebrating a Virtuous Woman	31:10–31

14. Franz Delitzsch, *Commentary on the Proverbs of Solomon*, 1:29–30.

The Septuagint Order of the Text

Following Proverbs 24:22, the Greek textual order diverges markedly from the Hebrew. The two sections that we have recognized as non-Israelite (chap. 30; 31:1–9) have been inserted into the context of "words of the wise":

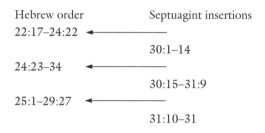

Hebrew order	Septuagint insertions
22:17–24:22 ←	
	30:1–14
24:23–34 ←	
	30:15–31:9
25:1–29:27 ←	
	31:10–31

Toy has seen in this different order the signs of an unsettled Hebrew text.[15] But in view of other difficulties associated with the Greek version of Proverbs, not the least of which is the translator's mistranslation of words and phrases,[16] caution must be exercised lest one put too much confidence in the Greek text. There is no reason whatsoever to distrust the Hebrew order. In fact the Greek order interrupts the long Solomonic sections. The probability is on the side of the Hebrew arrangement, although the Greek translator evidently had editorial reasons for his rearrangement.[17]

Date and Authorship

One must keep distinct the questions regarding date of composition and date of compilation of the book; the first relates to authorship and the second to editorship. Here we shall discuss the first of these; the second has already been discussed under "Literary Structure and Growth of the Book." Of course, it is not possible to keep the two matters entirely separated, but the distinction must be maintained.

The Jewish tradition preserved in the Babylonian Talmud (*Baba Bathra* 15*a*) recalled the role of Hezekiah's men and ascribed the writing of Proverbs to them, but this tradition more than likely referred to the editorship of the book rather than to its authorship. Among the early church fathers the opinion was expressed that the entire book was written by Solomon, but that was based upon the absence or obscurity of the titles of chapters 30 and 31 in the Greek and Latin manuscripts.[18]

---

15. Toy, xxxiii.
16. See comment on chapter 30, 185–86 [*Introduction to the Poetic Books of the Old Testament*].
17. Toy, xxxiii, in a footnote, remarks that Frankenberg observed that the Greek arrangement divides the material into two Solomonic collections with only two titles (10:1 and 25:1).
18. Young, 312.

The modern view generally represents 1:1–9:18 to be the latest collection. Eissfeldt concludes that it cannot be older than the fourth century B.C., a position based upon the long sentences in this collection and the personification of wisdom, both of which he attributes to Greek influence.[19] Yet Kitchen has observed that personification of abstract ideas was widely known in the ancient Near East as early as the third and second millennia B.C.[20] The implications of this, as Kitchen has remarked, are that "the first few chapters of Proverbs (cf. 1:1–7) is [sic] something more than just the idle fancy of some late scribe."[21] Young, responding to Eissfeldt's opinion, has assented to the position expressed by Kitchen on the basis of another contention, that the length of the passages in 1:1–9:18 is due to the subject matter and not to Greek influence.[22]

Delitzsch, in his thorough and helpful commentary, set forth the position that the allegorizing author of chapters 1–9 probably belonged to the beginning of Jehoshaphat's reign,[23] and that he based his composition on the Solomonic proverbs.[24] Delitzsch based his opinion upon the intensive teaching activities of Jehoshaphat's officials and Levites (2 Chron. 17:7–9), that king's reform (2 Chron. 17:3–6; 19:4), and the fondness for allegorical forms during this general period (2 Kings 14:8–11; 2 Chron. 25:17–21).[25]

The reasons for attributing chapters 1–9 to an author other than Solomon are understandable and somewhat attractive to the occidental mind, but the presupposition that Solomon could not have written the longer, more reflective proverbs, even utilizing the method of personification, is not justified. As we have already observed, our knowledge of ancient Near Eastern literature reveals both the reflective and the pragmatic curricular models in the wisdom schools.

Further, that the general editor(s) of the book believed Solomon to be the author of the bulk (1:7–9:18) of this section is beyond doubt. We do not question the fact that this document was involved in the editorial process during Hezekiah's reign, but the compelling reasons for postexilic dating or even post-Solomonic dating have been generally struck down by archaeological and textual research.

The second major section (10:1–24:34), which includes two appendixes (22:17–24:22 and 24:23–34), is generally acknowledged to contain old material. Based upon Aramaisms in 14:34; 17:10; 18:24; 19:20, and so forth,

19. Eissfeldt, 473.
20. Kitchen, 26, 126–27 and fn. 56.
21. Ibid., 26.
22. Young, 313.
23. Delitzsch, 1:29.
24. Ibid., 34.
25. Delitzsch, 1:29.

Eissfeldt maintains that 10:1–22:16 is not preexilic material.[26] Toy, following the method of dating by the presence or absence of certain concepts and social institutions, suggested that 10:1–22:16 and chapters 25–29 received substantially their present form between 350 and 300 B.C., the second collection a little later than the first.[27] Delitzsch, on the other hand, maintained that this section originated in the time of Jehoshaphat,[28] and Harrison has more recently proposed the Solomonic era.[29]

In response to these positions, it is more generally recognized today that the presence of Aramaisms in a document does not conclusively establish date, and certainly does not support the older scholarly opinion that Aramaisms were indicative of postexilic dating.[30] Further, there are no compelling reasons to doubt the truth of the tradition preserved in 1 Kings 4:29–34, which associates Solomon with the authorship of 3,000 proverbs and 1,005 songs, whose subject matter was taken from the flora and fauna of Palestine. Solomon may have popularized a couplet form of the proverb, but we should not assume that he adhered to that form undeviatingly. Scott's proposal that the title "proverbs of Solomon" (10:1; 25:1) refers to the literary form of a two-line poetic parallelism (couplet, or distich)[31] is unconvincing, even though it offers an escape route out of the complex problem of authorship. We cannot agree, therefore, that the attribution of the major portions of the book to Solomonic authorship is mere literary convention on the part of the editor(s).

Delitzsch has done an analysis of proverbs that are repeated exactly or with slight changes in comparative sections and concluded that 10:1–22:16 and chapters 25–29 were not both the product of Hezekiah's scribes. They knew the first collection but did not borrow from it because they sought to produce another book to be placed alongside it without making it superfluous.[32] In part, at least, this conclusion seems justified by the few proverbs repeated identically in both sections:

Identical

21:9	25:24
18:8	26:22
22:3	27:12
20:16	27:13[33]

26. Eissfeldt, 474.
27. Toy, xxviii–xxx.
28. Delitzsch, 1:28–29.
29. R. K. Harrison, *Introduction to the Old Testament*, 1017.
30. See Young's brief discussion, 313.
31. Scott, 9, 13.
32. Delitzsch, 1:26–27.
33. The duplication in the Hebrew text is clearer in the RSV than in the NASB.

Identical meaning with altered expression

22:13	26:13
19:24	26:15
19:1	28:6
12:11	28:19
22:2	29:13

One line the same

17:3	27:21
15:18	29:22[34]

That Hezekiah's scholars worked with written sources already at hand is implied in the heading of 25:1, and that these sources were Solomonic is asserted. Although repetition of single proverbs within one section or from one section to another points to the process of compilation, it really does not affirm or deny Solomonic authorship. Affirmatively, however, the peaceful reign of Solomon was conducive to literary activity and the development of wisdom schools. And in view of the national and international fame this monarch achieved, there is no reason to disbelieve that his words and reflections were preserved in writing for posterity.

That these compositions were available to Hezekiah's scribes almost three hundred years after Solomon may be attributable to Solomon's continuing popularity in Judah and the literary activity associated with royal courts in the ancient Near East. During David's reign two scribes are mentioned, Seraiah (2 Sam. 8:17) and Sheva (2 Sam. 20:25), the latter mentioned in company with the priests and other court officials. Hezekiah's scribe, Shebnah, was a participant in the events associated with the Assyrian invasion of Judah in 701 B.C. (2 Kings 18:18), and Shaphan was Josiah's scribe when the scroll of the Law was discovered in the Temple in 621 B.C. (2 Kings 22:9). One cannot fail to see the implications of these literary figures and their maintenance under royal patronage. Moreover, scribes and wise men were essentially the same class, and within their circle the major literary movements and activities were sustained.

It may be concluded that 1:7–29:27 is Solomonic in authorship, although some allowance may be made for editorializing in the process of compilation and the issue of the final edition under Hezekiah.

The authors of 30:1–33 and 31:1–9, although known by name, are otherwise unknown. The date of their composition and the final acrostic poem in praise of the virtuous wife (31:10–31) cannot be definitely established; however, little convincing data can be presented against a preexilic date.

---

34. Delitzsch, 1:25. For a linguistic analysis of terms common to both 10:1–22:16 and chapters 25–29, see Delitzsch, 1:31–32.

Canonicity

Sparse information on the disposition of the Book of Proverbs in the can-
onization process is found in the Babylonian Talmud (*Shabbath* 30*b*). A question revolved around the alleged contradiction between Proverbs 26:4 and
26:5: "Do not answer a fool according to his folly. . . . Answer a fool according to his folly" (KJV; cf. the interpretative effort of NASB, "as his folly deserves"). The rabbinic resolution was to view the first as a reference to matters
of the Law and the second to secular affairs. The doubts about the book were
dispelled early in postexilic times, and Proverbs exercised a pervasive influence
upon Judaism and early Christianity.

Poetic Structure of Proverbs

The Book of Proverbs does not employ the one-line popular proverb (e.g.,
"A rolling stone gathers no moss") as the basic form but rather the two-line
proverb (*distich*), which was the basic form of *māshāl* poetry. The two-line
proverb takes four basic forms, the second line being the variant element.

The first form is that of *synonymous* meaning, where the second line repeats
the sense of the first line in slightly different words:

> Pride goes before destruction,
> And a haughty spirit before stumbling.
>
> [16:18; also 16:13, 16; 11:25, etc.]

This form follows the basic type of parallelism that was characteristic of Hebrew poetry.

The second form of the two-line proverb, and probably the predominant
one in the book, is that of *antithetical* meaning. The second line expresses the
antithesis or the contrary sense of the first line:

> The merciful man does himself good,
> But the cruel man does himself harm.
>
> [11:17]

The third form of the two-line proverb is that of *synthetic* meaning, which
extends the sense of the first line in an expanded, or amplified, form. Rather
than merely reiterating or contrasting in the second line the sense of the first,
the synthetic form adds to the primary idea:

> He who conceals hatred has lying lips,
> And he who spreads slander is a fool.
>
> [10:18]

The fourth form is that of *comparative* meaning, in which case some ethical point or practical truth is explained by an illustration from nature:

> Like cold water to a weary soul,
> So is good news from a distant land.

[25:25]

In the last form, the primary idea may occur in the first or second line.

The two-line proverb forms multiples that are based upon the structures discussed above. The four-line proverb (*tetrastich*) normally gives the variant element in the last two lines. Examples of the synonymous (e.g., 23:15–16; 24:3–4), synthetic (e.g., 30:5–6), and comparative (e.g., 25:16-17) may be cited among the four-line proverbs in the book.

The longer, more reflective proverbs sometimes take the six-line form (*hexastich*). Frequently, the first two lines compose a prologue, and the following four lines provide the substance (e.g., 23:19–21). The eight-line (*octastich*) proverb may also be identified (e.g., 23:22–25).

The longer proverbs may be called the *māshāl ode,* or song. Many of these are incorporated in 1:7–9:18 as well as elsewhere in the book (e.g., 22:17–21; 30:7–9).

All of these are variations of *māshāl* (proverb) poetry and were probably in vogue quite early in the history of wisdom literature. To confine Solomon to the two-line proverb, as some scholars are inclined, is to commit oneself to a monolithic process of literary development from the simple to the complex, a position that is too simplistic to be credible. Further, Solomon's literary activity was evidently intensive and required the use of a variety of proverb forms. For one man to write three thousand proverbs and never advance beyond the two-line form is in itself incredible, not to mention monotonous.

We may look briefly at the different sections of the book and observe the variety of forms that each incorporates.

1:7–9:18	The predominant form is the *māshāl ode.*
10:1–22:16	All are two-line proverbs, with the greatest number antithetic in form.
22:17–24:22	Most forms occur, although the four-line proverb is preferred.
24:23–34	The two-line as well as the four-line proverb is identifiable, along with one *māshāl ode.*
25:1–29:27	These are largely two-line proverbs, with the antithetic and comparative forms predominant.

30:1–33   This section contains the two-line, four-line, and numerical (*middāh*) proverbs.

31:2–9   The two and four-line proverbs are identifiable.

31:10–31   This is an alphabetic acrostic poem.[35]

---

35. I am indebted to Delitzsch's helpful discussion in 1:6–24 for the data in this section.

2

INTRODUCTION TO PROVERBS

Allen P. Ross

Background

The Book of Proverbs is a marvelous collection of wise sayings and instructions for living a useful and effective life. The collection forms part of the larger group of biblical writings known as wisdom literature. This literature gives instructions for living while pondering the difficulties of life. Proverbial wisdom is characterized by short, pithy statements; but the speculative wisdom, such as Ecclesiastes or Job, uses lengthy monologues and dialogues to probe the meaning of life, the problem of good and evil, and the relationship between God and people.[1]

The genre of wisdom literature was common in the ancient world, and a copious amount of material comes from ancient Egypt (see Bryce, *A Legacy of Wisdom*). From the Old Kingdom (2686–2160 B.C.) we find pieces of wisdom in the "Instruction of Kagemni" and the "Instruction of Ptah-hotep" (2450 B.C.), which advise the proper decorum for a court official. Like Proverbs, Ptah-hotep counsels on persuasive speech: "Good speech is more hid-

1. See D. A. Hubbard, "Wisdom Literature," *NBD*, 1334.

den than the emerald, but it may be found with maidservants at the grind-stones" (*ANET*, p. 412). He further warns against going after a woman like a fool, for "one attains death through knowing her" (*ANET*, p. 413). The "Instruction of Merikare" (2160–2040 B.C.) records a monarch's advice for his son on the wise qualities needed by a king, including this saying: "The tongue is a sword . . . and speech is more valorous than any fighting" (*ANET*, p. 415).

In the New Kingdom period (1580–1100 B.C.), the "Instruction of Ame-nemope" stands out. Amenemope instructs his son regarding proper conduct. This work, arranged in thirty sections, contains many instructions that resemble in form and content various laws of the Pentateuch and teachings of Proverbs. These instructions are generally seen as forming the background of Proverbs 22:17–24:22. Although the two collections are not identical, they are similar enough to attest direct influence. General knowledge of wisdom sayings across the ancient Near East as well as specific interchange between Egypt and Solomon's court make a literary connection likely. Because of the dates involved, it is unlikely that Amenemope borrowed from Solomon. Similar teachings in the Pentateuch might suggest a greater antiquity for biblical wisdom sayings, but there is insufficient material to draw a firm conclusion. Many ancient laws, sayings, songs, poetic couplets, and proverbs found their way into inspired Scripture. Inspiration does not exclude the divine use of existing material; but in Scripture it takes on a new force, a higher meaning, and becomes authoritative.

In the Instructions morality is defined as what is pleasing to the god, and it forms the basis for life and prosperity. For example, the instructions include these: "Do not associate to thyself the heated man,/Nor visit him for conversation" (*ANET*, p. 423; cf. Prov. 22:24); "Do not strain to seek an excess,/When thy needs are safe for thee./If riches are brought to thee by robbery. . . . /(Or) they have made themselves wings like geese/And are flown away to the heavens" (*ANET*, p. 422; cf. Prov. 23:4–5).

After Amenemope, wisdom literature again surfaces with the "Instruction of Ani" (c. 1100 B.C.). Here a father instructs his son about personal piety, ritual purity, and appropriate speech. He enjoins fulfillment of religious and filial obligations, good manners, generosity, and reserve in speech; and he warns against adultery, clamor, and presumption before the god. He says, "Be on your guard against a woman from abroad . . . a woman who is far away from her husband. . . . She has no witnesses when she waits to ensnare thee" (*ANET*, p. 420). And much later there is the "Instruction of 'Onchsheshon-qy" (c. 400–300 B.C.), a large collection of about five hundred sayings and precepts like those in the Book of Proverbs that reflect the practical and religious concerns of the community. But they do not have the poetic parallelism characteristic of Hebrew proverbs. For example, their instructions include:

"Do not go to your brother if you are in trouble, go to your friend" (cf. Prov. 27:10); and "Better [to have] a statue for a son than a fool" (cf. Prov. 17:21) (see Scott, *Proverbs/Ecclesiastes*, p. xlv).

Mesopotamia also had collections of proverbial material (see Lambert, pp. 92–117). The "Instruction of Shuruppak" (c. 2000 B.C.) records the advice of a king to his son Ziusudra, the hero of the flood in the Sumerian version. For example, it says, "My son, let me give you instructions, may you pay attention to them," and "[My] son, do not sit [alone] in a [chamber] with someone's wife."[2]

The "Counsels of Wisdom" (c. 1500–1000 B.C.) are a collection of moral exhortations about avoiding bad company and careless speech, being kind to the needy, and living in harmony with one's neighbor and in loyalty to the king. For example, it says, "Do not return evil to your adversary; Requite with kindness the one who does evil to you,/Maintain justice for your enemy" (*ANET*, p. 595).

The "Words of Ahiqar" (700–670 B.C.) is a collection of proverbs, riddles, short fables, and religious observations by a court official for the Assyrian kings Sennacherib and Esarhaddon, giving advice on disciplining children, guarding the tongue, respecting secrets, and being circumspect in dealing with the king. For example, it says, "Withhold not thy son from the rod" (*ANET*, p. 428; cf. Prov. 13:24); and "I have lifted sand, and I have carried salt; but there is naught which is heavier than [grief]" (*ANET*, cf. Prov. 27:3).

Thus Proverbs has affinities with literature from other countries, and the Bible itself alludes to the wisdom of Egypt and Mesopotamia (1 Kings 4:30; Dan. 1:4, 17, 20).

This literary background is helpful to understanding the biblical book. First, it provides help in understanding the forms of wisdom literature—proverbs, maxims, fables, riddles, allegories, and instructions. Second, it indicates the antiquity of the forms used in the Bible, especially Proverbs 1–9, which was once considered to be the latest form. But it now can be demonstrated that the literary proverb of two lines may be as old as the Sumerian proverbs, and that collected instructions may be as ancient as the Old Kingdom of Egypt.

In making these comparisons, commentators find help in dating the various collections within the Book of Proverbs. Kitchen, for example, has argued for the plausibility of the Solomonic date for Proverbs 1:1–24:34 on the basis of its similarities with the instruction genre demonstrated in the first part of the second millennium. This form includes a title (cf. 1:1); a statement of purpose (cf. 1:2–7); a lengthy prologue exhorting and encouraging compliance to instruction (cf. 1:8–9:18); and a collection of maxims, proverbs, precepts,

---

2. See B. Alster, *The Instructions of Shuruppak: A Sumerian Proverb Collection* (Copenhagen: Akademisk Forlag, 1974), 15, 37.

and admonitions (10:1–22:16). Kitchen also argues for the early inclusion of 22:17–24:34 based on the dating of the "Instruction of Amenemope."[3]

In addition to this comparison with the great collections of wise instructions, there is also value to be gained from tracing similar concepts. For example, paralleling the Hebrew concept of wisdom is the Egyptian presentation of *Maʾat*—a fixed, eternal religious order, manifested in the stability of nature, in justice in society, and in the integrity of the individual's life (see Crenshaw, *Old Testament Wisdom*, p. 214). Another concept found in the Hebrew and Egyptian literature is the rhetorical use of personification to convey abstract concepts such as intelligence, understanding, justice, and skill. The biblical figure of personified wisdom (Prov. 8) corresponds to the personification of *Maʾat* in Egyptian art and literature.

Finally, many specific emphases in Proverbs find parallels in the wisdom literature of the ancient Near East. But even though the collections share some of the same interests, the biblical material is unique in its prerequisite of a personal faith in a personal God. To the Hebrews the success of wisdom did not simply require a compliance with wise instructions but trust in, reverence for, and submission to the Lord (Prov. 1:7; 3:5–6; 9:10), who created everything and governs both the world of nature and human history (3:19–20; 16:4; 21:1). Any ancient wisdom used by the Hebrews had to harmonize with this religious world view, and any ancient wisdom used in this collection took on greater significance when subordinated to the true faith.

The biblical writers occasionally used literary forms and expressions that were common to their culture. While the fullness of the Yahwistic faith in all its distinctions came by direct revelation, God did include Semitic customs, standard laws, treaty forms, poetic expressions, and wise sayings that were compatible with the truth and useful in the communication of the divine will. One may speculate how and when concepts such as wisdom, justice, and holiness, or sacrifice, sanctuary, and priesthood—to name but a few—found their place in primitive societies. But apart from that, to recognize the biblical texts as divine revelation does not necessarily mean that all its contents had to be previously unknown information. On the contrary, before many of these facts and concepts were written down, they were passed on verbally from generation to generation and consequently could have circulated over vast distances and found their way into many diverse cultures. Therefore, whatever the Spirit of God inspired the ancient writers to include became a part of the Word of the Lord. Such inclusions then took on a new and greater meaning when they formed part of Scripture; in a word, they became authoritative and binding, part of the communication of the divine will.

3. Kenneth A. Kitchen, "Proverbs and Wisdom Books of the Ancient Near East: The Factual History of a Literary Form," *Tyndale Bulletin* 28 (1977): 69–114.

Very likely the writers deliberately used well-known concepts and expressions from the pagan world to subordinate them to the true religion. For example, while *Maʾat* was a deity of justice and order in Egypt, no such deity existed in Israel. Rather, *ḥokmāh* ("wisdom") was personified and spoke its message in the first person—something *Maʾat* did not do. By incorporating wise sayings and motifs (in addition to producing new and unparalleled sayings) and investing them with the higher religious value, the Hebrew sages were in a sense putting new wine into old wine skins. They could forcefully teach, then, that true wisdom was from above and not from below.

Authorship and Date

The traditional view that Solomon wrote the entire Book of Proverbs is supported by the titles in 1:1; 10:1; and 25:1. Moreover, Solomon was a wise man, writing proverbs and collecting sayings from other wise men (see 22:17–24:34). Proponents of this view have also frequently assumed that Agur (30:1) and Lemuel (31:1) were pseudonyms of Solomon.

This general view, however, stands in need of some revision. It is now recognized that Agur and Lemuel were probably not pseudonyms for Solomon and that 22:17–24:34 forms a separate collection of proverbs because it has a distinct form, separate title and purpose, and seems to be directly related to the "Instruction of Amenemope." It would be impossible to determine who added this material to the collection of Proverbs. Furthermore, on closer examination the title of 1:1, which has generally been taken to head up 1:1–9:18, may not actually refer to these chapters; it may simply be the heading of the whole book in its final form and may not necessarily indicate that the first nine chapters are from Solomon.

It would be unreasonable, however, to deny that the largest portion of the proverbs were Solomon's, as older critical scholars often did. Otto Eissfeldt is only willing to say that "one or another of the sayings" are Solomon's and that "one or another of the quite small collections" go back to Solomon.[4] More and more scholars, however, acknowledge that the earlier period is an appropriate setting for the composition and collection of such wisdom sayings. The age of Solomon was characterized by national consolidation, the organization and development of the temple staff, and the collection of traditional literary works, including wisdom sayings. It was also a period of broad international exchange; for through his many alliances and trade contacts, Solomon would have had scribes of foreign lands in his courts. It is easy to see how similarities between Proverbs and other ancient Near Eastern literature could have developed.

4. *The Old Testament: An Introduction,* trans. P. R. Ackroyd (New York: Harper and Row, 1965), 476.

Yet it is not possible to date the Book of Proverbs only on the basis of literary style or content. All the literary forms and perhaps the overall structure can be demonstrated in early parallels as well as late parallels (see Waltke, pp. 223–26). In addition, the same sociological, theological, and educational background can be demonstrated for much of the wisdom literature in the ancient Near East. The instruction frequently came from a royal father concerned with preparing his son to replace him in court and teaching self-control in temperament, speech, and action so that his son might be successful. Also, the theology of Proverbs is consistent with the theology of the Law and the Prophets, making parallel references as a basis for dating rather difficult.[5] Moreover, even the earlier attempts to parallel motifs such as the personification of wisdom with the later Greek philosophical thought are no longer definite, for examples of such personification have been discovered all over the ancient world.[6]

An examination of the titles in the book is important to the study of its authorship. The heading in 10:1 clearly credits Solomon for the subsequent material. In 10:1–22:16 there may be two collections (chaps. 10–15; 16:1–22:16) due to the difference in style, the second collection having greater variety of parallelism. The heading in 25:1 also affirms that Solomon was the author (or editor) of a larger collection from which the scribes of Hezekiah's court excerpted the proverbs in chapters 25–29. Once again there are differences of style between chapters 25–27 and chapters 28–29, the former having more illustrative parallelism and more grouping by topics.

The title in 1:1 has been taken variously as the heading (1) to the book as a whole, (2) to 1:1–9:18, and (3) to other delimited sections such as 1:1–24:34.[7] The title probably cannot be limited to 1:1–9:18, for then we might have expected the heading in 10:1 to be like that in 25:1—"these *also* are the Proverbs of Solomon" (Kidner, *Proverbs*, p. 22). In addition, the term *mišlê* ("proverbs") does not describe any of the sayings in 1:8–9:18; so the title would be inappropriate if specifically introducing just that section. Finally, 1:2–7, which belongs with the heading of 1:1 by its grammatical construction, best expresses the general purpose of the whole collection of the Proverbs; as an introduction it forms part of the prologue (1:8–9:18) to the major collection of 10:1–24:34.

This introductory section (1:1–7), however, could have functioned as the introduction to an earlier collection as well. Since the expression "the proverbs of Solomon" fits the dominant form found in the collections of 10:1–22:16 and 25:1–29:27, the introduction of 1:1–7 could have for-

5. Ibid., 302–17.
6. See Kenneth A. Kitchen, "Some Egyptian Background to the Old Testament," *Tyndale Bulletin* 5–6 (1960): 4–6.
7. Kitchen, "Proverbs and Wisdom Books," 98–99.

merly introduced a collection now found in 10:1–31:31. And yet, since there seems to be no reason for dating 1:8–9:18 any later than the first Solomonic collection, this prologue could have been written for the core collection.

There are also titles in the book that are non-Solomonic. Any borrowing that took place might have been based on firsthand knowledge of the Egyptian material.[8] This dependence, confined to similarity of concepts and similarity of figures and not to precise wording, seems to be limited to 22:17–23:11. Since Amenemope dates from at least as early as 1000 B.C., the time could fit the Solomonic era. Scott thinks the "Instruction of Amenemope" was still being copied centuries later and "may well have been studied during his training by an Israelite scribe of the prophetic period" (*Proverbs/Ecclesiastes*, p. xxxv).

The title in 31:1 credits Lemuel with the sayings that follow. Although the NIV translates *maśśā'* as "an oracle," it may be that this refers to a kingdom named Massa that is attested in the annals of the Assyrian kings from the time of Hezekiah (roughly 715–687 B.C.). The poem in 31:10–31 has no heading and cannot be readily connected with Lemuel. The heading in 30:1, "The sayings of Agur son of Jakeh—an oracle ['*of Massa*,' NIV mg.]," is also obscure. . . .

In conclusion, then, Solomon is responsible for 10:1–22:16 and perhaps all or part of chapters 25–29. Most scholars, including many conservatives, see some dependence of 22:17–24:34 on the Instruction of Amenemope. The nature of this dependence is debatable, but it may be that Israel knew these sayings by the time of Solomon. Most scholars also see chapters 30–31 as non-Solomonic and from a later date, perhaps from a time contemporary with Hezekiah.[9] The prologue to the book (1:8–9:18) would have been added to form an introduction, certainly by the time of Hezekiah, and possibly in Solomon's time. The old title and introductory purpose (1:1–7) then headed up the final collection.

Literary Forms

A casual reading of the Book of Proverbs reveals the general form of a proverb. A proverb, as Scott says, is a short, pregnant sentence or phrase whose meaning is applicable in many situations (*Way of Wisdom*, p. 58). A thorough analysis of the Proverbs reveals that these short sayings follow many patterns and constructions that have bearing on the meanings.

8. For the connection of "the sayings of the wise" (22:17; 24:23) to the "Instruction of Amenemope," see J. Ruffle, "The Teaching of Amenemope and Its Connection with the Book of Proverbs," *Tyndale Bulletin* 28 (1977): 65.
9. Kitchen, "Proverbs and Wisdom Books," 100–102.

As with all Hebrew poetic discourse, the Proverbs use the different types of parallelism. *Synonymous* parallelism expresses one idea in parallel but slightly different expressions: "A fool's mouth is his undoing,/and his lips are a snare to his soul" (18:7). In *antithetical* parallelism the second line contrasts with the first: "The plans of the righteous are just,/but the advice of the wicked is deceitful" (12:5). This is the most common type of parallelism in the book; in 12:5 it sets before the reader the choice between the wise and profitable way and the foolish and disastrous way. *Emblematic* parallelism uses a figurative illustration as one of the parallel units: "As vinegar to the teeth and smoke to the eyes,/so is a sluggard to those who send him" (10:26). Another helpful category is the general one of *synthetic* parallelism. This is used for passages where the second line amplifies the first in some way: "The LORD works out everything for his own ends—/even the wicked for a day of disaster" (16:4). Lastly, proverbs whose second line simply completes the idea begun in the first are said to exhibit *formal* parallelism. One part may contain the subject and the second the predicate (15:31); the first line may state a condition and the second its consequences (16:7), its cause (16:12), or its purpose (15:24); and one part may state a preferred value or course over the other: "Better a little with the fear of the LORD/than great wealth with turmoil" (15:16).

Proverbs are essentially didactic, whether they follow the pattern of a formal instruction using imperatives or prohibitions (16:3; 23:9), are expressed in didactic sayings that observe traits and acts that are to be followed or avoided (14:31), tell an example story (7:6–23), make a wisdom speech (8:1–36), or develop numerical sayings (6:16–19).

Instructions, whether commands or admonitions, use motivations—reasons for complying. The most common form of motivation is a subordinate clause stating the purpose, result, or reason for the instruction: "Listen to advice and accept instruction,/and in the end you will be wise" (19:20). Sometimes the motivation is implied in a general observation: "My son, do not despise the LORD's discipline/and do not resent his rebuke,/because the LORD disciplines those he loves,/as a father the son he delights in" (3:11–12).

In general proverbs draw lessons by reflecting on the way things are in relation to right values and right conduct. Scott lists seven ways that this is done in the book: proverbs may present (1) things that appear distinct but are similar (14:4a), (2) things that seem the same but are different (27:7b), (3) things that are similar (using similes as in 25:25), (4) things that are absurd or futile (17:16), (5) sayings that classify types of people (14:15), (6) sayings that indicate relative values (27:3), and (7) sayings that set forth consequences (27:18) (*Way of Wisdom*, pp. 59–63).

Finally, it should be noticed that the structure of the entire book uses different forms. Proverbs 1:8–9:18 appears to be an organized introduction to the book with many admonitions and prohibitions as well as example stories and personified wisdom-speech. This section runs in cycles: the purpose of Proverbs is to give wisdom (1:1–7), but folly may interrupt this purpose (1:8–33); there are advantages to seeking wisdom (2:1–4:27), but folly may prevent one from seeking it (5:1–6:19); there are advantages to finding wisdom (6:20–9:12), but folly may prevent this too (9:13–18).

Proverbs 10:1–22:16 is a collection of some 375 unrelated proverbs. Then, after the sayings patterned after the "Instruction" (22:17–24:22), another collection of proverbs is included (chaps. 25–29). The last two sections include among other things the numerical sayings of the wise (30:10–33) and the acrostic poem on wisdom (31:10–31).

Theological Values

This collection of wise sayings is not exclusively religious; its teachings apply to human problems in general and not primarily to the problems of the religious community or to major theological themes such as election, redemption, and covenant. Rather the teacher of wisdom "concerns himself with people as plain, ordinary individuals who live in the world, and with the wisdom and folly of their attitudes and actions in the common things of life" (Aitken, p. 4). Accordingly, the sayings exhibit several distinctive characteristics. First, they focus attention on individuals rather than on the nation, setting forth the qualities needed and the dangers to be avoided by people seeking to find success with God. Second, they are applicable to all people at any period in history who face the same types of perils and have the same characteristics and abilities (1:20; 8:1–5). Third, they are based on respect for authority, traditional values and teachings, and the wisdom of mature teachers (24:21). Fourth, they are immensely practical, (1) giving sound advice for developing personal qualities that are necessary to achieve success in this life and to avoid failure or shame and (2) warning that virtue is rewarded by prosperity and well-being but that vice leads to poverty and disaster.

It would be wrong, however, to conclude that Proverbs is a secular book; its teachings are solidly based on the fear of the Lord (1:7), making compliance with them in reality a moral and spiritual matter. In fact, the book teaches that this fear of the Lord is the evidence of faith; for the wise teacher enjoins people to trust in the Lord whose counsel stands (19:21) and not their own understanding (3:5–7). The purpose of proverbial teaching, then, is to inspire faith in the Lord (22:19). Such reverential fear requires a personal knowledge of the Lord ("fear" and "knowledge" are parallel in 9:10)—to find this fear is to find knowledge (2:5), a knowledge that comes by revelation (3:6). Ultimately, however, the fear of the Lord is manifested in a life of obedience, confessing and forsaking sin (28:18), and doing what is right (21:3), which is the believer's task before God (17:3). Since the motivation for faith and obedience comes from the Scripture, Proverbs relates the way of wisdom to the law (28:4; 29:18). In the final analysis we must conclude with Plaut, "There are no 'secular' proverbs which can be contrasted with 'religious' ones; everything on earth serves the purposes of God and is potentially holy" (p. 7).

According to Jeremiah 18:18, prophets, priests, and sages molded the cultural life of Israel, the sages being an ancient and influential group (Isa. 29:14). In the early days their wisdom was probably declared in the gates for all to hear (Job 29:7–25). Their teachings were preeminently concerned with truth that had stood the test of experience—it had to ring true (Crenshaw, *Old Testament Wisdom,* pp. 68–69). They classified people into two groups—those who were wise, who possessed moral qualities to which wisdom makes her moral appeal, and those who are deficient in the same (R. K. Harrison, *IOT,* p. 1019). Accordingly, the teachings of Proverbs are of the highest ethical quality, relating virtue to the will of God. The disaster that comes to folly and vice is part of divine retribution—a more immediate concern than the question of immortality.

Finally, it may be observed that the religious value of the book is endorsed by its being in the canon. Furthermore, Jesus' recognition of the wisdom of Solomon recorded in Scripture was further evidence of its place in the developing plan of redemption.

Canon and Text

The Book of Proverbs is in all the Jewish lists of the books of the canon. It is quoted in the NT ten times (Rom. 3:15 [1:16]; 12:16 [3:7], 20 [25:21–22]; Heb. 12:5–6 [3:11–12]; James 4:6 [3:34], 13 [27:1]; 1 Peter 2:17 [24:21]; 4:8 [10:12], 18 [11:31]; 2 Peter 2:22 [26:11]). So the book is unquestionably an integral part of the Holy Scriptures. It was placed in the last section of the Hebrew canon, the *Kethubim* (the "Writings"), but it occupies different positions in different lists. According to Rabbinic literature, Proverbs follows Psalms and Job (*Baba Bathra* 14b, 15a); but the LXX grouped Proverbs, Ecclesiastes, and Song of Solomon on the basis of their authorship.

The Hebrew text is arguably in fair condition. Where the LXX differs in a number of places, the MT is usually far more satisfying. Harrison estimates that there are about twenty-five difficult readings in the Hebrew, along with some obscure words (*IOT,* p. 1018). But the LXX has greater problems. It is fairly close to the Hebrew in chapters 1–9, but in 10–31 the differences are great. The LXX retained the title in 1:1, omitted the title in 10:1, and changed the titles in 30:1 and 31:1. Throughout the book the LXX adds proverbs (which may be from a different Hebrew *Vorlage* [underlying text]) but deletes others. Moreover, the position of 30:1–31:9 differs in the Greek. Proverbs 30:1–14 is placed after 24:22, and 30:15–33 and 31:1–9 are placed after chapter 24. Possibly separate traditions of these chapters were in existence with differing orders; but it is also possible that the arrangement was the resolution of the LXX to show the Solomonic authorship (see Toy, pp. xxxi–xxxiv).

Bibliography

Commentaries

Alden, Robert L. *Proverbs: A Commentary on an Ancient Book of Timeless Advice*. Grand Rapids: Baker, 1984.

Alonso Schökel, Luis, and J. Vilchez Lindez. *Proverbios*. Nueva Biblia Española. Madrid: Ediciones Cristiandad, 1984.

Aitken, Kenneth T. *Proverbs*. Philadelphia: Westminster, 1986.

Cohen, A. *Proverbs: Hebrew Text and English Translation with Introduction and Commentary*. Soncino Bible. London: Soncino, 1946.

Delitzsch, Franz. *Biblical Commentary on the Proverbs of Solomon*. 2 volumes. Reprint. Translated by M. G. Easton. Grand Rapids: Eerdmans, 1970.

Greenstone, Julius H. *Proverbs with Commentary*. Philadelphia: The Jewish Publication Society of America, 1950.

Kidner, Derek. *The Proverbs: An Introduction and Commentary*. Tyndale Old Testament Commentary. Downers Grove: InterVarsity, 1964.

McKane, William. *Proverbs: A New Approach*. Old Testament Library. Philadelphia: Westminster, 1970.

Martin, G. Currie. *Proverbs, Ecclesiastes, and Song of Songs*. The New Century Bible. Edited by Walter F. Adney. New York: Henry Frowde; Edinburgh: T. C. and E. C. Jack, 1908.

Oesterley, William Oscar Emil. *The Book of Proverbs*. The Westminster Commentary. London: Methuen, 1929.

Perowne, T. T. *The Proverbs*. Cambridge Bible for Schools and Colleges. Cambridge: Cambridge University Press, 1899.

Plaut, W. Gunther. *Book of Proverbs*. Jewish Commentary for Bible Readers. New York: Union of American Hebrew Congregations, 1961.

Plöger, Otto. *Sprüche Salomos (Proverbia)*. Biblischer Kommentar Alten Testament. Volume 17. Neukirchen-Vluyn: Neukirchener Verlag, 1984.

Ringgren, Helmer. *Sprüche Salomos*. Das Alte Testament Deutsch. 16/1. 3d edition. Göttingen: Vandenhoeck und Ruprecht, 1981.

Scott, Robert Balgarnie Young. *Proverbs/Ecclesiastes*. The Anchor Bible. Volume 18. Garden City: Doubleday, 1965.

Stuart, Moses. *A Commentary on the Book of Proverbs*. Andover: Warren F. Draper, 1852.

Toy, Crawford Howell. *A Critical and Exegetical Commentary on the Book of Proverbs*. The International Critical Commentary. Edinburgh: T. and T. Clark; New York: Charles Scribner's Sons, 1899.

van Leeuwen, Raymond C. *Context and Meaning: Proverbs 25–27*. Atlanta: Scholars, 1988.

Selected Studies on the Book of Proverbs

Dahood, Mitchell. *Proverbs and Northwest Semitic Philology*. Scripta Pontificii Instituti Biblici. Volume 113. Rome: Pontifical Biblical Institute, 1963.

Gerlemann, Gillis. *Studies in the Septuagint, III: Proverbs*. Lunds Universitets Arsskrift, 52:3. Lund: C. W. K. Gleerup, 1956.

Gladson, Jerry A. "Retributive Paradoxes in Proverbs 10–29." Ph.D. dissertation, Vanderbilt University, 1978.

Kayatz, Christa. *Studien zu Proverbien 1–9*. Wissenschaftliche Monographien zum Alten und Neuen Testament. Volume 22. Neukirchen-Vluyn: Neukirchener-Verlag, 1966.

Nel, Philip Johannes. *The Structure and Ethos of the Wisdom Admonitions in Proverbs*. Beihefte zur Zeitschrift für die alttestamentliche Wissenschaft. Volume 158. Berlin: Walter de Gruyter, 1982.

Postel, Henry John. "The Form and Function of the Motive Clause in Proverbs 10–29." Ph.D. dissertation, University of Iowa, 1976.

Schachter, J. *The Book of Proverbs in Talmudic Literature*. Jerusalem, 1963.

Thompson, John Mark. *The Form and Function of Proverbs in Ancient Israel*. The Hague: Mouton, 1974.

Waltke, Bruce K. "The Book of Proverbs and Ancient Wisdom Literature." *Bibliotheca Sacra* 136 (1979): 221–38.

Whybray, Roger N. *The Book of Proverbs*. Cambridge Bible Commentary on the New English Bible. Cambridge: Cambridge University Press, 1972.

———. *The Intellectual Tradition in the Old Testament*. Beihefte zur Zeitschrift für die alttestamentliche Wissenschaft. Volume 135. Berlin: Walter de Gruyter, 1974.

———. *Wisdom in Proverbs: The Concept of Wisdom in Proverbs 1–9*. Studies in Biblical Theology, I/45. London: SCM, 1965.

Williams, James G. *Those Who Ponder Proverbs: Aphoristic Thinking and Biblical Literature*. Sheffield: Almond, 1981.

Selected Studies on Wisdom Literature

Beaucamp, Evode. *Man's Destiny in the Book of Wisdom.* Staten Island: Alba House, 1970. A translation by J. Clarke of *La Sagesse et la Destin des Elus.* Paris: Editions Fleurus, 1957.

Bergant, Dianne. *What Are They Saying about Wisdom Literature?* New York: Paulist, 1984.

Blenkinsopp, Joseph. *Wisdom and Law in the Old Testament: The Ordering of Life in Israel and Early Judaism.* The Oxford Bible Series. Oxford: Oxford University Press, 1983.

Bryce, Glendon E. *A Legacy of Wisdom: The Egyptian Contribution to the Wisdom of Israel.* Lewisburg, Penn.: Bucknell University Press; London: Associated University Presses, 1979.

Camp, Claudia V. *Wisdom and the Feminine in the Book of Proverbs.* Bible and Literature Series. Volume 11. Sheffield: Almond, 1985.

Crenshaw, James L. *Old Testament Wisdom: An Introduction.* Atlanta: John Knox, 1981.

———, ed. *Studies in Ancient Israelite Wisdom.* The Library of Biblical Studies. Edited by Harry M. Orlinsky. New York: KTAV, 1976.

Cross, Thurman L. "The Fear of the Lord in Hebrew Wisdom." Ph.D. dissertation, Drew University, 1957.

Gammie, John G., et al., eds. *Israelite Wisdom: Theological and Literary Essays in Honor of Samuel Terrien.* Missoula, Mont.: Scholars, 1978.

Gordis, Robert. *Poets, Prophets, and Sages: Essays in Biblical Interpretation.* Bloomington: Indiana University Press, 1971.

Gordon, Eckmund I. *Glimpses of Everyday Life in Ancient Mesopotamia.* Westport, Conn.: Greenwood, 1969.

Kevin, Robert Oliver. *The Wisdom of Amen-em-apt and Its Possible Dependence Upon the Hebrew Book of Proverbs.* Volume 14, Number 4. Reprint. Philadelphia: Journal of Society of Oriental Research, 1931.

Kidner, Derek. *The Wisdom of Proverbs, Job, and Ecclesiastes: An Introduction to Wisdom Literature.* Downers Grove, Ill.: InterVarsity, 1985.

Lambert, Wilfred G. *Babylonian Wisdom Literature.* London: Oxford University Press, 1960.

Langdon, Stephen. *Babylonian Wisdom.* London: Luzac, 1972.

Lange, H. O. *Das Weisheitsbuch des Amenemope: Aus Papyrus 10, 474 des British Museum.* Copenhagen: Andr. Fred. Høst and Son, 1925.

Morgan, Donn F. *Wisdom in the Old Testament Traditions.* Atlanta: John Knox, 1981.

Murphy, Roland E. *Introduction to the Wisdom Literature of the Old Testament*. Collegeville, Minn.: Liturgical Press, 1965.

Noth, Martin, and David Winton Thomas, eds. *Wisdom in Israel and in the Ancient Near East. Supplement to Vetus Testamentum*. Volume 3. Leiden: E.J. Brill, 1955.

Perdue, Leo G. *Wisdom and Cult: A Critical Analysis of the Views of Cult in the Wisdom Literature of Israel and the Ancient Near East*. Society of Biblical Literature Dissertation Series. Volume 30. Missoula, Mont.: Scholars, 1977.

Rad, Gerhard von. *Wisdom in Israel*. Neukirchen-Vluyn: Neukirchener Verlag, 1970.

Scott, Robert Balgarnie Young. *The Way of Wisdom in the Old Testament*. New York: Macmillan, 1971.

Simpson, W. K., ed. *The Instruction of Amenemope: The Literature of Ancient Egypt*. New Haven: Yale University Press, 1972.

Williams, Ronald J. "The Alleged Semitic Original of the Wisdom of Amenemope." *Journal of Egyptian Archaeology* 47 (1961): 100–106.

3

THE BOOK OF PROVERBS AND
ANCIENT WISDOM LITERATURE

Bruce K. Waltke

The comparison made in 1 Kings 4:29–34 between Solomon's
wisdom and that of the ancient Near Eastern sages strongly implies that his proverbs were a part of an international, pan-oriental, wisdom
literature. During the past century archaeologists have been uncovering texts
from Solomon's pagan peers, and scholars have been using them to further
the understanding of the Book of Proverbs. The purposes of this chapter are
to examine the ways in which this ancient literature has advanced the understanding of "the proverbs of Solomon, son of David, king of Israel" (Prov.
1:1 NIV), and to demonstrate how these texts help answer introductory questions (date; authorship; literary forms, structure, and arrangement; textual
transmission; and history of the wisdom tradition) and how these texts help
interpret the content of the book (the meaning of wisdom, its theological relevance, and the resolution of some exegetical problems).

From *Bibliotheca Sacra* (July–September 1979): 221–38. Used by permission of Dallas Theological Seminary.

Date and Authorship

Before the discovery and decipherment of these extrabiblical texts, scholars who applied to the Old Testament a historicocritical method (which presupposed the evolutionary development of religion) concluded that the biblical witnesses to Solomon's contribution to wisdom could not be taken at face value.[1] Instead, they argued, the postexilic Jewish community under Grecian influences must be credited for these literary achievements. Even as late as 1922, Hoelscher still placed the so-called older proverbial literature in the Persian period.[2] But the many pagan sapiential texts, found around the broad horizon of the Fertile Crescent, and confidently dated to the time of Solomon and centuries before him, have called their presupposition into question and have refuted their skepticism toward the biblical witness.

Giovanni Pettinato, in his preliminary report on the thousands of tablets unearthed in the royal archives at Tell-Mardikh (Ebla), alerted biblical scholars that some of those tablets contain collections of proverbs.[3] The precise dating of the royal palace at Ebla poses some difficulties, for the artifactual evidence points to a date between 2400 and 2250 B.C., while the paleography of the literary texts points to a period around 2450 B.C.[4]

Gordon has published two collections of Sumerian proverbs out of the fifteen collections he pieced together from the hundreds of clay tablets dug up from the scribal quarters at Nippur, Susa, and Ur.[5] These two collections containing about 200 and 165 proverbs respectively have a strikingly similar form to the Solomonic collections of 375 and 124 proverbs in 10:1–22:16 and 25:1–29:27 respectively. Gordon dates both of these Sumerian collections to the Old Babylonian period (ca. 1700 B.C.).

Lambert has published bilingual proverbial texts containing both Sumerian proverbs and their Akkadian translations.[6] Six of these fragments, dating

---

1. These biblical witnesses are 1 Kings 4:29–34; Proverbs 10:1; 25:1; and Matthew 12:42. Proverbs 1:1 is best taken as a title for the work and not a designation of the authorship of the whole book because the internal evidence of the book itself clearly shows that the book achieved its final form after the time of Hezekiah (25:1) and that others besides Solomon contributed to this anthology of wisdom material (cf. 30:1; 31:1). There is no evidence, however, that the book in its present form should be dated later than the time of the monarchy.

2. Gustav Hoelscher, *Geschichte der israelitischen und jüdischen Religion* (Giessen: A. Topelmann, 1922), 148.

3. Giovanni Pettinato, "The Royal Archives of Tell Mardikh-Ebla," *Biblical Archaeologist* 39 (May 1976): 45.

4. Paolo Matthiae, "Ebla in the Late Early Syrian Period," *Biblical Archaeologist* 39 (September 1976): 94–113.

5. Edmund I. Gordon, *Sumerian Proverbs: Glimpses of Everyday Life in Ancient Mesopotamia* (Westport, Conn.: Greenwood, 1969), 24, 152. Gordon also noted that "it is quite reasonable to assume a considerably older date for the origin of at least a great number of the proverbs included in them."

6. W. G. Lambert, *Babylonian Wisdom Literature,* 3d ed. (Oxford: Clarendon Press, 1975), 92, 97, 222.

from the Middle Assyrian times and later, overlap or can be placed in relation to each other, and thus provide a considerable part of one group of proverbs known as the *Assyrian Collection*. He also published an Akkadian translation from Middle Assyrian times of a Sumerian original entitled *The Instructions of Shuruppak* as well as the famous Akkadian work, *The Counsels of Wisdom*, which he dates to the Cassite period (1500–1200 B.C.).

Aramaic proverbs are given in a collection known as the *Words of Ahiqar*. Ahiqar was a sage in the court of the Assyrian kings Sennacherib (704–681 B.C.) and Esarhaddon (680–669 B.C.).[7]

Instructional literature from Egypt has close affinities to the admonitions found in Proverbs 1:2–9:18 and 22:17–24:34 and are dated from the Old Kingdom right on down to the Late Dynastic Period and Hellenistic Rule. The following is a list of those texts belonging to the Egyptian instruction literature.[8]

The Old Kingdom (2686–2160 B.C.)
  The Instruction for Ka-gem-ni
  The Instruction of Prince Hor-dedef
  The Instruction of Ptah-hotep
The First Intermediate Period (2160–2040 B.C.)
  The Instruction for King Meri-ka-Re
The Middle Kingdom (2040–1558 B.C.)
  The Instruction of King Amen-em-het
  The Instruction of Sehetep-ib-Re
The New Kingdom (1558–1085 B.C.)
  The Instruction of Ani
  The Instruction of Amen-em-Ope[9]
The Late Dynastic Period and Hellenistic Rule
  The Instruction of 'Onchsheshonqy (fifth or fourth century B.C.)
  The Instruction of the Papyrus Insinger (304–30 B.C.)

---

7. James M. Lindenberger, "The Aramaic Proverbs of Ahiqar" (Ph.D. diss., Johns Hopkins University, Baltimore, Md., 1974).

8. Leo G. Perdue, *Wisdom and Cult* (Missoula, Mont.: Scholars, 1977), 28–61.

9. The date of the *Instruction of Amen-em-Ope* is hotly disputed and deserves a separate study. The issue is of some importance because this text most closely resembles the Book of Proverbs. A date for this text shortly before the time of Solomon has received new support through the discovery by Černy of a broken (yet unpublished) ostracon in the Cairo Museum. See Ronald J. Williams, "The Alleged Semitic Original of the Wisdom of Amenemope," *Journal of Egyptian Archaeology* 47 (1961): 100–106.

In short, wisdom literature existed around the Fertile Crescent not only before Solomon but even before the Hebrews appeared in history!

Literary Forms

Like the wisdom sayings in the Book of Proverbs, these texts of varying provenience are composed in poetic form, that is, they are cast in parallelisms. Herder praised this form as "thought rhyme" and von Rad aptly likened it to expressing truth stereophonically. For example, the familiar antithetical parallelism of Solomon's proverbs finds its counterpart in this Sumerian proverb: "Of what you have found you do not speak; [only] of what you have lost do you speak."[10] In his "rhetorical analysis" of Sumerian proverbs, Gordon calls attention to antithetical, synonymous, climactic, and more complicated types of parallelism.

Most instructive here is the *Instruction of Amen-em-Ope*, preserved in a British Museum papyrus and on tablets in Turin and Paris. On these documents the parallelism is written stichically, that is, in lines that show the metrical scheme. Furthermore, the lines are grouped into chapters.

The Egyptians had the specific term *sboyet* ("instruction" or "teaching") for their literary genre[11] that closely approximates the precepts and maxims collected in Proverbs 1:2–9:18 and 22:17–24:34. On the other hand, the pithy Solomonic sentences designated "proverbs" in 10:1 and 25:1 resemble in the strictest sense the apothegms, adages, and bywords of the Sumerian collections.

But in contrast to the Solomonic collections, the Sumerian collections and the *Assyrian Collections* contain coarse and vulgar proverbs. Here are some edited samples: "[A low] fellow/[An A] morite speaks [to] his wife, 'You be the man, [I] will be the woman.'"[12] "A mother of eight [grown] young men who is [still capable of] bearing [more children] lies down [for copulation] passively [?]!"[13] "A thing which has not occurred since time immemorial: a young girl broke wind in her husband's bosom."[14] Such proverbs bear more kinship to the Arabic, Turkish, and other modern Near Eastern proverbs than to the known proverbs from the rest of the ancient Near East.

10. Gordon, *Sumerian Proverbs*, 47.

11. William Kelly Simpson, ed., *The Literature of Egypt* (New Haven, Conn.: Yale University Press, 1972), 6.

12. Lambert, *Babylonian Wisdom Literature*, 230. Lambert comments: "The section apparently refers to transvestite practices, which are first known in the ancient near East from their condemnation in Deuteronomy xxii.5. Later references to these rites in Syria and Asia Minor are more abundant (see S. R. Driver, *Deuteronomy*, p. 250), though there seems to be no clear evidence for them at any period in Mesopotamia. Thus the alternative 'Amorite' could be supported on the assumption that these people were notorious for this perversion, as were the men of Sodom, Corinth, and Bulgaria, and the women of Lesbos, for other things" (ibid.).

13. Gordon, *Sumerian Proverbs*, 273.

14. Lambert, *Babylonian Wisdom Literature*, 260.

Literary Structure and Arrangement

The literary structure of the Egyptian *sboyet* genre includes three elements: (a) a title—"the beginning of the instruction of X which he composed for his son Y"; (b) a prose or poetic introduction—the setting forth of the details of why the instruction is given; and (c) the contents—the linking together of admonitions and sayings in mutually independent sections of very diverse nature.

Aside from the omission of the first section, this is precisely the structure exhibited in the "Thirty Sayings of the Wise" (Prov. 22:17–24:22). The motive behind the collection is given in 22:17–21 which is followed by the diverse collection of admonitions in 22:22–24:22.

Compare, for example, the first two chapters of the *Instruction of Amen-em-Ope* with Proverbs 22:17–23.

Chapter 1

He says:
Give your ears, hear the sayings,
    It profits to put them in your heart,
    Woe to him who neglects them!
Let them rest in the casket of your belly,
    May they be bolted in your heart;
When there rises a whirlwind of words,
    They'll be a mooring post for your tongue.
If you make your life with these in your heart,
    You will find it a success;
You will find my words a storehouse for life,
    Your being will prosper upon earth.

Chapter 2

Beware of robbing a wretch,
Of attacking a cripple . . . .[15]

If those who divided the Bible into its chapters had been aware of these literary forms and structures found in the pagan sapiential texts, they no doubt would have made a chapter break between Proverbs 22:16 and 22:17.

The literary structure of the Egyptian "teaching" genre also enables one to detect better the structure undergirding the Book of Proverbs. After the prose introduction in 1:1 and before the collection of sayings in 10:1–31:31, the editor included a collection of admonitions and econiums to wisdom, setting forth in detail the value of the instruction (1:2–9:18).

The biblical student may find small comfort in learning that the sages throughout the ancient Near East essentially arranged their material in the

---

15. Miriam Lichtheim, *Ancient Egyptian Literature: A Book of Readings*, 2 vols. (Berkeley, Calif.: University of California Press, 1976), 2:149–50.

same baffling manner found in the Book of Proverbs. Is there any logic to the arrangement? Perhaps some help is found in the Sumerian collections which fall, with few exceptions, into groupings which have in common either the initial signs of each individual proverb or the subject matter of the proverbs in the group. The "key sign" may also occur in the second place or even further on in the proverb.[16] Moreover, the "key signs" also alternate occasionally. Gemser also notes rudiments of similar groupings in the *Instructions of 'Onchsheshonqy*.[17] Possibly the proverbial sentences and the admonitions in the Book of Proverbs are connected in this so-called anthological style whereby sayings are strung together by certain catchwords as in the more obvious key *king* in 16:12–15 and *Yahweh* in 16:1–7 which follows an alternating pattern in 16:7–11 (note *king* in 16:10).

It is also surprising to find lofty precepts mixed with more "trivial" apothegms. Of course, this is a misconception based on the modern-day viewpoint of life. From the sages' perspective each proverb is an expression of "wisdom," which is, as will be seen, the fixed order of reality. Viewed from this perspective no sentence is trivial, as Frankfort notes.

> But when a predestined order is recognized in so many quasi-permanent features of society . . . all rules of conduct become practical rules. There can be no contrast between *savoir-faire*—worldly wisdom—and ethical behavior. Conceptions which we distinguish as contrasts thus turn out to be identical for the Egyptian; statements of his, which have for us a pragmatic ring, appear to be transfused with religious reverence.[18]

Elsewhere Frankfort expanded on the traditional character of the wisdom literature.

> Such an inconsequential arrangement characterizes many books of ancient "wisdom"; the books of Proverbs and Ecclesiastes are cases in point. The absence of a systematic arrangement is due to the traditional character of the contents. There is no need of a closely knit argument; striking images, incisive wording are all that is required to give a fresh appeal to the truth of familiar viewpoints.[19]

Transmission of the Text

First Kings 4:29–31 suggests that the sages and their writings were held in high esteem in Solomon's world. The texts confirm this impression. One hi-

16. Gordon, *Sumerian Proverbs*, 24, 156.

17. B. Gemser, "The Instructions of 'Onchsheshonqy and Biblical Wisdom Literature," *Supplement to Vetus Testamentum*, vol. 7 (1960), 113.

18. Henri Frankfort, *Ancient Egyptian Religion*, 2d ed. (New York: Columbia University Press, 1961), 65.

19. Ibid., 61.

eratic papyrus put the value of wisdom literature this way: "Books of instructions became their [the learned scribes'] pyramids. . . . Is there another one like Ptah-hotep and Kaires?"[20] A wall of a New Kingdom tomb at Sakkara has representations of mummiform statues of important officials. Among the viziers are Imhotep and Kaires. Their inclusion is certainly partly to be explained on the basis of their reputations as sages.

Not surprisingly, then, their works seem to have enjoyed a canonical status. "Take no word away, add nothing thereto, and put not one thing in place of another," cautions Ptah-hotep with reference to his own work. His mentality corresponds to the godly Agur's admonition: "Every word of God is flawless; He is a shield to those who take refuge in Him. Do not add to His words or He will rebuke you and prove you a liar" (Prov. 30:5–6). Meri-ka-Re was told, "Copy thy fathers, them that have gone before thee. . . . Behold, their words endure in writing. Open [the book] and read, and copy the knowledge, so that the craftsman too may become a wise man [?]."

The conservative scribes by and large followed these admonitions. The Turin tablet contains the portion of the *Instruction of Amen-em-Ope* which corresponds to 24:1–25:9 in the complete British Museum papyrus. The tablet attests the same line arrangement and the extract copied on the tablet begins precisely at the beginning of a page in the complete papyrus.

The colophon to the *Counsel of Wisdom* reads, "Written according to the prototype and collated." Lambert commented on a bilingual tablet from Ashurbanipal's library, of which no duplicate or early copy has yet been found.

> Either this tablet, or an antecedent copy on which it is based, was copied from a damaged original, and the scribe very faithfully reproduced this. When he wrote on one line what was split between two in his original, the dividing point on the original was marked with the pair of wedges used in commentaries to separate words quoted from the comments on them. . . . Where the original was badly damaged, the scribe copied out exactly what he saw, and left blank spaces marked "broken" where nothing remained.[21]

But the evidence also shows that some changes were made. The comparison between the late bilingual tablets with their old Babylonian unilingual Sumerian material is proving to be a most helpful lesson in literary history. Gordon turned up thirty-four individual proverbs common to both the earlier unilingual material and the later bilingual texts. Lambert observed instances where no change occurred. "What is more significant is that whole groups of proverbs in the same sequence are carried over from the unilinguals to the late bilinguals."[22] But he also noted that one tablet of the late period has a proverb

20. From *Papyrus Chester Beatty* IV, following the translation of A. H. Gardiner.
21. Lambert, *Babylonian Wisdom Literature*, 239.
22. Ibid., 223.

not in the earlier collection. This shows that while collections were transmitted conservatively, yet choice proverbs could be added to the collection. In the same way, the editor of the Book of Proverbs felt free to bring together material from diverse sources. Lambert also found another tablet which added a variant from one in the earlier period. The circulation of variant forms of the same proverb is also well known in the Hebrew collection (cf. Prov. 11:14 with 24:6).

History of Wisdom Tradition

Many attempts have been made to trace in one way or another an evolutionary development in the history of the wisdom tradition. Richter,[23] for example, advanced the notion that the motive clauses in the admonitions were late, postexilic additions to the imperative statements.[24] But more recently Kayatz carefully documented the remarkable parallelism between the syntactic forms of these admonitions in both the Egyptian and Hebrew instructions.[25] Albright had earlier shown their close affinities with Ugaritic and Phoenician texts and on this basis had argued for their antiquity.[26]

Hermisson[27] and Murphy[28] have proved wrong the thesis of Schmid[29] that popular sayings (*Volksprüche*) developed into artistic sayings or aphorisms (*Kunstsprüche*).

Many today still attempt to date profane and secular wisdom with the early period and the more religious and ethical wisdom with a later period. According to this view Israelite Yahwism, with its strong religious stamp, was laid over an older pragmatic wisdom inherited from Egypt. But Frankfort and others have refuted this thesis recently propounded by McKane[30] and Whybray.[31]

It would seem that we have here material (from texts from the third millennium extending to the late dynastic times) for a history of ideas, and modern scholars have sometimes used these texts to describe a development of social and ethical thought in Egypt. I do not think that such an interpretation is tenable if we

23. W. Richter, *Recht und Ethos. Versuch eitner Ortung des weisheitlichen Mahnspruches* (Munich: Kösel-Verlag, 1966).

24. Compare the imperative statements in the odd-numbered verses and the motive clause in the even-numbered verses in 3:1–12.

25. Christa Kayatz, *Studien zu Proverbien 1–9* (Neukirchen-Vluyn: Neukirchener Verlag, 1966).

26. W. F. Albright, "Some Canaanite-Phoenician Sources of Hebrew Wisdom," *Supplement to Vetus Testamentum,* vol. 3 (1955), 4.

27. H. J. Hermisson, *Studien zur israelitischen Spruchweisheit* (Neukirchen-Vluyn: Neukirchener Verlag, 1968).

28. Ronald E. Murphy, "Form Criticism and Wisdom Literature," *Catholic Biblical Quarterly* 31 (1969): 477.

29. H. H. Schmid, *Wesen und Geschichte der Weisheit* (Berlin: Alfred Topelmann, 1966).

30. William McKane, *Proverbs: A New Approach* (Philadelphia: Westminster, 1970).

31. R. N. Whybray, *Wisdom in Proverbs* (Naperville, Ill.: A. R. Allenson, 1965).

study the evidence without prejudice—that is, without an evolutionary bias. The differences between the earlier and the later texts seem largely to have been caused by accidents of preservation, while their resemblance consists, on the contrary, in a significant uniformity of tenor.[32]

Erman concurs: "It ['Onchsheshonqy] is far removed from the pious quietism of the *Instruction of Amenemope* and in fact seems closer to some of the Old Kingdom practical instructions, those of Ptahhotep and Kegemni. . . ."[33] Whedbee addressed himself directly to McKane's view.

McKane does not deal with the basic concept of an order in the world, which seems to have formed a crucially important presupposition in the wise man's approach to reality. The wise man took this order—created and guaranteed by God—as the starting point in his attempt to master life. . . . To say that the wise man was completely an independent, empirical operator, as McKane does, is to misread the data of the ancient wisdom and view it through the lens of a modern construct. The wise man always reckoned with God. . . .[34]

Murphy holds the same opinion. "No distinction of 'profane' or 'sacred' is applicable here; God was considered the guardian of the social order. . . ."[35]

Hubbard concludes that no evolution in the history of the wisdom tradition can be discerned. "Simple evolutionary approaches ought to be *passé* in studies of wisdom as they are in those of prophecy or cultus."[36]

The Setting

For whom were the proverbial sentences and admonishing sayings originally composed? How should one interpret the frequently recurring expression, "my son"? For lack of space the theories given in answer to these questions cannot be discussed here. But it is this author's conviction that the wisdom material had its original setting in the home of the courtier.

At least that seems to have been the case for the Egyptian teachings. As noted earlier, the titles of these works uniformly follow the form: "The instruction of X . . . for his son Y." As Frankfort observed, "The authors of the 'teachings' do not present themselves as priests and prophets. They appear as aged officials at the end of active and successful careers, desirous to let their

---

32. Frankfort, *Ancient Egyptian Religion*, 59. Fr. R. W. von Bissing finds a constant spiritual and moral stance throughout the history of the sapiential genre (*Altaegyptische Lebensweisheit* [Zurich: Artemis-Verlag, 1955]).

33. Simpson, *The Literature of Egypt*, xxi.

34. J. William Whedbee, *Isaiah and Wisdom* (Nashville: Abingdon, 1971), 118–19.

35. R. E. Murphy, "Assumptions and Problems in Old Testament Research," *Catholic Biblical Quarterly* 29 (1967): 103.

36. David A. Hubbard, "The Wisdom Movement and Israel's Covenant Faith," *The Tyndale Bulletin* 17 (1966): 18.

children profit by their experience."[37] Here, for example, are the introductions to Ptah-hotep and Ka-gem-ni, respectively:

> The Instruction of the Mayor and Vizier Ptah-hotep. . . : "O Sovereign, my lord: Oldness has come; old age has descended. . . . Let a command be issued to this servant to make a staff of old age (that is, the son as the support of his father), that my son may be made to stand in my place. Then may I speak to him the words of them that listen and the ideas of the ancestors. . . ."[38]

> The vizier had his children called after he had completed (his treatise) on the ways of mankind and on their character as encountered by him. And he said unto them: "All that is in this book hear it. . . ."[39]

Amen-em-Ope, a high official in the administration of royal estates, wrote expressly for his own son, Hor-em-maa-kheru, a young priestly scribe. Erman points out that the content of these texts supports this alleged setting: "What King Amenemhet committed to his son far exceeds the bounds of school philosophy, and there is nothing whatever to do with schools in the great man warning his children to be loyal to the king."[40]

The expression "my son" also appears to have its face value in the Akkadian *Counsel of Wisdom*. Lambert makes the following comment on the use of the term in this text:

> The advice given in the section "My son" can have had relevance for very few people. . . . This suggests that we are to construe the text as being in the form of admonitions of some worthy to his son who will succeed him as vizier to the ruler.[41]

Ahiqar, the vizier to the Assyrian king Sennacherib, wrote his words for his nephew Nadin.[42] He too uses the recurrent parental address, "my son."

Thus across many cultures through centuries of history these admonitions are those of a high court official addressing his son.

The admonitions and proverbs in the biblical text also appear to have originated in courtiers' homes. In addition to Solomon's proverbs, other literary achievements collected in the Book of Proverbs are attributed to King Lemuel's mother (31:1) and to the copying of Solomon's proverbs by the men of Hezekiah (25:1).

---

37. Frankfort, *Ancient Egyptian Religion*, 60.
38. James B. Pritchard, *Ancient Near Eastern Texts Relating to the Old Testament* (Princeton, N.J.: Princeton University Press, 1955), 12.
39. Simpson, *The Literature of Egypt*, 178–79.
40. Ibid., 54.
41. Lambert, *Babylonian Wisdom Literature*, 96.
42. The story is set during the reign of Esarhaddon.

Moreover, the subject matter of Proverbs best suits this setting. Some of them are most appropriate for kings and for those associated with him, for example, proverbs pertaining to the nation (11:14) or the king (16:10; 20:2); dining with royalty (23:1–3); behaving in a way worthy of a king (31:4); etcetera. Here too it should be noted that court wisdom in Egypt also focused on the king's responsibilities as guarantor of justice.[43] In addition, the Book of Proverbs, like the Egyptian literature, includes a mingling of urban and agricultural concerns, particularly those of the wealthy plantation owner.[44] Such a breadth of interest and perspective on life admirably suits the position of courtiers.

But these kings and high officials in Israel are writing for their sons. There is no reason not to take the reference to "my son" in any other way than in its normal significance. Elsewhere in the Old Testament the father is held responsible for his child's social, moral, and religious training (Gen. 18:19; Exod. 12:24; Deut. 4:9–11). Furthermore, it is certain that skills and trades were passed down from father to son without recourse to schools. But above all, the references to the mother in 1:8; 4:3; 6:20; 31:1, 26 clinch the argument. Whybray argued cogently:

> Here the father and mother are placed on exactly the same footing as teachers of their children. . . . The phraseology of these sentences corresponds almost exactly to that of their Egyptian counterparts . . . ; and this throws into greater relief the one feature which is entirely unique in them: the mention of the mother. It is difficult to avoid the conclusion that this feature is an example of the adaptation of the Egyptian tradition to the peculiar situation in which the Israelite instructions were composed: a domestic situation in which the father and mother together shared the responsibility for the education of the child.[45]

But while these sayings originated in the courtiers' homes, they seem to have been disseminated in Mesopotamia and Egypt through the schools for most of these texts have been unearthed in scribal schools. The *Satire on the Trade Winds* reads, "The beginning of the instruction which a man of the ship's cabin, whose name was Duauf's son Khety, made for his son, [whose] name was Pepy, as he was journeying upstream [to] the Residence City, to put him into the Writing School among the children of officials. . . ." Indeed, many of the extant copies of these texts are obviously schoolboy efforts to reproduce what their instructors were teaching them. In Israel the sayings of its

43. H. Brunner, "Gerechtigkeit als Fundament des Throns," *Vetus Testamentum* 8 (1958): 426–28; cf. H. Schmid, *Gerechtigkeit als Weltordnung* (1968).

44. R. Gordis, "The Social Background of Wisdom Literature," *Hebrew Union College Annual* 18 (1943–44): 77–118.

45. Whybray, *Wisdom in Proverbs*, 42.

courtiers were democratized for the improvement of all Israel through such a work as the Book of Proverbs.

The Meaning of Wisdom

Crenshaw justly complained that "the many attempts to define wisdom have not been altogether successful."[46] He is well aware, however, that efforts to understand this term so central to the teaching of the Book of Proverbs have been greatly advanced through an understanding of its Egyptian equivalent *Maʾat*. The Egyptian term, like Hebrew חָכְמָה ("wisdom"), lies at the heart of its wisdom teaching. A section in the *Instruction of Ptah-hotep* presents *Maʾat* in these terms:

> Maʾat is good and its worth is lasting. It has not been disturbed since the day of its creator, whereas he who transgresses its ordinances is punished. It lies as a path in front even of him who knows nothing. Wrongdoing [?] has never yet brought its venture to port. It is true that evil may gain wealth but the strength of truth is that it lasts; a man can say: "It was the property of my father."[47]

From this statement Frankfort made the following conclusion:

> The Egyptians recognized a divine order, established at the time of creation; this order is manifest in nature in the normalcy of phenomena; it is manifest in society as justice; and it is manifest in an individual's life as truth. Maʾat *is* this order, the essence of existence, whether we recognize it or not.[48]

This notion of a fixed, eternal righteous order does compare favorably with the biblical meaning of "wisdom." The figures of speech used in the first section of the Book of Proverbs (1:2–9:18) suggest that it is Yahweh's eternal and righteous order granting life to those who walk in it. In 1:20–33 wisdom is likened to a street preacher (Lady Wisdom) who laughs at the calamity of the fools who ignored her or disdainfully rejected her, that is, it is an inviolable righteous order. In 3:18 it is referred to as a tree of life in the midst of time. According to 3:19–20 it was God's instrument for creating the cosmos. The point of this statement seems to be that wisdom is the principle that accounts for order and life found in creation. In 4:10–27 in a series of poems it is designated "the way," that is, it is an ordered realm without imperfections. In 8:1–11 an evangel proclaims that righteousness, justice, and truth are the way to lasting well-being. In 8:22 wisdom is likened to a craftsman at Yahweh's side delighting above all in man at the time of creation. The point of this comparison seems to be that it is an eternal order existing for man's good. Finally in 9:1–18 Dame Wisdom contends with Dame Folly in their rival invitations

---

46. James L. Crenshaw, *Studies in Ancient Israelite Wisdom* (New York: KTAV, 1976), 3.
47. Frankfort, *Ancient Egyptian Religion,* 62.
48. Ibid., 63.

for the soul of the simpleton. In a word, wisdom is a potent righteous force opposed by a potent unrighteous force.

The Egyptian concept of *Ma'at* has helped gain from these metaphors the meaning that wisdom is God's fixed order for life, an order opposed by chaos and death. But man must choose by faith to trust the Lord who stands behind this created order.

The Theology of the Book of Proverbs

The Egyptian sages seem to have discerned values in *Ma'at* similar to those affirmed in Israel for "wisdom." Since the pioneering efforts of Budge[49] and Gressmann,[50] it has been clear that the *Instruction of Amen-em-Ope* most closely approximates the teachings of the Book of Proverbs, especially the "Thirty Sayings of the Wise" in Proverbs 22:17–24:22.

Simpson called attention to the following parallels, among many others, between the Hebrew and Egyptian works.[51]

1. "Better a little with the fear of the Lord
 than great wealth with turmoil.
Better a meal of vegetables where there is love
 than a fattened calf with hatred."

[Prov. 15:16–17 NIV]

Better is poverty at the hand of God
 than riches in the storehouse.
Better is bread with happy heart
 than riches with vexation."

[Amen. 9:5–8]

2. "In his heart a man plans his course,
 but the Lord determines his steps."

[Prov. 16:9 NIV]

"The words which men say are one thing.
 The thing which God does is another."

[Amen. 19:16]

3. "Do not say, 'I'll pay you back for this wrong!'
 Wait for the Lord, and he will deliver you."

[Prov. 20:22 NIV]

49. E. A. W. Budge, *The Teaching of Amen-em-apt, Son of Kanekht* (London: M. Hopkinson and Co., 1924).

50. Hugo Gressmann, *Israels Spruchweisheit im Zusammenhang der Weltliteratur* (Berlin: Karl Curtius, 1925).

51. D. C. Simpson, "The Hebrew Book of Proverbs and the Teaching of Amenophis," *Journal of Egyptian Archaeology* 12 (1926): 232–39.

"Say not, 'Find me a redeemer,
    for a man who hateth me hath injured me' . . .
Sit down at the hand of God;
    your tranquility will overthrow them."

[Amen. 22:3–4, 7–8]

4. "Do not make friends with a hot-tempered man,
    do not associate with one easily angered,
or you may learn his ways
    and get yourself ensnared."

[Prov. 22:24–25 NIV]

5. "Do not wear yourself out to get rich;
    have the wisdom to show restraint.
Cast but a glance at riches, and they are gone,
    for they will surely sprout wings
    and fly off to the sky like an eagle."

[Prov. 23:4–5 NIV]

"Labor not to seek increase . . .
[perchance] they have made themselves wings like geese,
    they have flown to heaven."

[Amen. 9:14–10:4]

These individual sayings not only agree in form and sometimes even in wording, but when viewed collectively they share the same ethical and social ideals. Lichtheim summarizes the ideal man, "the silent man," in this Egyptian text in this way:

> [He] is content with a humble position and a minimal amount of material possessions. His chief characteristic is modesty. He is self-controlled, quiet, and kind toward people, and he is humble before God. This ideal man is indeed not a perfect man, for perfection is now viewed as belonging only to God.[52]

Here again space does not permit discussion of a much-debated issue related to these sapiential texts, namely, how this striking relationship between the Bible and these pagan texts is to be accounted for. Suffice it to say here that Oesterley seems to have the best of the arguments in his contention that both go back to a common stock of international, pan-oriental, proverbial literature.[53]

But the question still remains, In what way is the theology of Proverbs unique? Indeed, anyone familiar with studies comparing other literary forms

52. Lichtheim, *Ancient Egyptian Literature,* 146.
53. W. O. E. Oesterley, "The 'Teaching of Amen-em-Ope' and the Old Testament," *Zeitschrift für die alttestamentliche Wissenschaft* 45 (1927): 9–24.

of the Bible with their counterparts in the ancient Near East will immediately grasp the point that the question needs to be expanded: In what way is the Old Testament unique? The theological significance of the Book of Proverbs does not depend on the originality of its individual sentences or sayings any more than the theological significance of the so-called Book of the Covenant rests in the originality of its individual commandments. These can be paralleled at point after point in the Babylonian, Assyrian, and Hittite laws, and they clearly reflect a common body of ancient Near Eastern legal tradition. The same is true of Israel's hymns; they are stamped by a hymnology common to the ancient Near East. The theological significance of the Old Testament rests rather on the connection of all this literature with Yahweh, the God of Israel. The theological significance of the Book of Proverbs rests in its clear affirmation that Yahweh brought "wisdom" into existence, revealed it to man, and as Guarantor upholds this moral order.

Hubbard pointed in this direction when he wrote, "Pagan wisdom though it, too, may be religious has no anchor in the covenant-God. . . ."[54] The pagan sages do not even know the name of the God who created and sustains the fixed moral and ethical order that their consciences bore witness to. Frankfort rightly observed this lack in the Egyptian texts: "But is it not remarkable that none of the gods are mentioned by name in any of the 'teachings'? When the Egyptians appeal to 'God,' . . . they impart to the divine interest in man's behavior a distinctly impersonal character."[55]

Keimer put it this way: "All in all, one has the impression that there is for Amenemope but one God; it remains open to the individual, however, to represent this highest being as he will."[56] Paul's famous sermon to the Athenians, in which he related their unknown god with the Creator and the God who raised Jesus Christ from the dead, springs immediately to mind (Acts 17:22–31).

Since the Egyptians did not know the name of this "urgott," with whom they had no personal relationship, they do not attribute their understanding of the fixed order to him. Of course, this is strikingly different from the claim made in Proverbs 2:6: "For the LORD gives wisdom, and from his mouth come knowledge and understanding" (NIV).

Finally, it should be noted that the Egyptian fathers did not call on their sons to trust an impersonal, unnamed God. By contrast the godly Hebrew

---

54. D. A. Hubbard, "Wisdom," in *The New Bible Dictionary* (Grand Rapids: Eerdmans, 1962), 1333.

55. Frankfort, *Ancient Egyptian Religion*, 76. While most scholars think *Amen-em-ope* has an "urgott" in view, both Frankfort and Hellmut Brunner suppose that Egyptian *netjer* ("god") designates an individual's personal god, *his* god ("Der Freie Wille Gottes in der aegyptischen Weisheit," *Sagesses*, 103–20). Joseph Vergote believes that a distinction can be made between the mention of "specified gods" and the anonymous "unique" god ("La notion de Dieu dans les Livres de sagesse égyptiens," *Sagesses*, 159–90).

56. Ludwig Keimer, "The Wisdom of Amen-em-ope and the Proverbs of Solomon," *American Journal of Semitic Languages and Literatures* 43 (1926–27): 11.

courtiers realized that ultimately the son must trust in Yahweh who founded, revealed, and upheld this fixed moral order. Its promises were only as sure as he is trustworthy.[57] It is instructive to note that in the introduction to the "Thirty Sayings of the Wise," which bears such a strong resemblance to chapter 1 in the *Instruction of Amen-em-Ope,* the Israelite sage uniquely adds that his purpose is that his readers' "trust may be in the LORD" (Prov. 22:19 NIV). In that unique addition the essential theological relevance and distinctiveness of the biblical book stands out. That demand for faith informs the whole book (cf. Prov. 3:5–6 and the recurrent expression, "Fear the LORD" [1:7], which is the motto of the book).

Some Exegetical Problems

On the basis of the similarity between the sayings collected in Proverbs 22:17–24:22 and the *Instruction of Amen-em-Ope* and the fact that both works contain thirty sayings—a point stated explicitly in Amen-em-Ope 27:7—most modern versions emend the obscure *Kethibh* readings שָׁלְשׁוֹם "day before yesterday" = "heretofore" (?), and the Qere reading, שָׁלִישִׁים, "officer" = "excellent" (?), to שְׁלֹשִׁים, "thirty."

In Proverbs 24:12 Yahweh is represented as one "who weighs the heart." This figure goes back to the Egyptian god Thoth, who is often represented as standing at the judgment of the dead beside the scales with the human heart.

The Septuagint and some ancient versions have rendered the ambiguous אֲשֶׁר of Proverbs 23:1 by "note well *what* is before you," while other versions have "note well *who* is before you." The parallel in *Amen-em-Ope,* "Look at the cup that is before you," suggests that the Septuagint and those versions agreeing with it have the better translation.

Conclusion

The contribution of the ancient Near Eastern sapiential literature to biblical studies is apparent. It helps to establish the plausibility of a position contending for the preexilic date of the content of the Book of Proverbs and for the historical credibility of those texts which attribute their authorship to Solomon. A "proverb" can now be defined more accurately and confusion with other literary forms in the book can be avoided. There is firm reason to think that the text of the Book of Proverbs was transmitted conservatively, and that the attempt to arrange its sources chronologically by distinguishing so-called earlier, profane texts from later, sacred texts is wrong-headed. The structure of the literary forms within the book and of the book itself, along with its anthological arrangement, no longer appears so disconnected as it once did. As

---

57. Gerhard von Rad, *Wisdom in Israel* (Nashville: Abingdon, 1972), 193.

the sayings and poems within the book are read, one now envisions a godly, noble couple instructing their children. No longer can wisdom be defined simplistically as "the practical application of knowledge." Instead wisdom must be thought of as a broad, theological concept denoting a fixed, righteous order to which the wise man submits his life. Also commentaries should appeal to ancient sources to clarify obscure texts where that is possible.

These sources also provide data for the systematic theologian. The shape and form of the Word of God was popular in its own time and even some of its material is similar to that found in the pagan world. The way in which these inspired sages integrated contemporary literature with their faith provides a model for the saint today. Moreover, one is forcibly reminded that while the Word of God is unchanging, his understanding of it is progressing.

4

THE PROVERBS
OF ANCIENT ISRAEL

R. B. Y. Scott

The Proverbs of Ancient Israel

If Francis Bacon was right, that "the genius, the wit and the spirit of a nation are discovered in its proverbs," the Book of Proverbs should be one of the most interesting parts of the Bible. It is not, of course, simply an anthology of wise sayings commonly heard in ancient Israel, though many of these are included in it, especially in the two collections entitled "Proverbs of Solomon" which begin at chapters 10 and 25. Rather, it is a source book of instructional materials for use in a school or in private study, for the cultivation of personal morality and practical wisdom. It opens with a series of ten admonitory discourses, interspersed with some poetry and some proverbs. It includes in 22:17–24:22 a distinct work, "Thirty Precepts of the Sages," modeled on an Egyptian composition; and in chapters 30–31 four distinctive appendixes. Yet the two collections of sentence-proverbs under Solomon's name comprise the major part of the book, and give it its distinctive tone.

What, then, is a proverb? The Oxford English Dictionary defines it as "a short, pithy saying in common use." Archer Taylor[1] says that the typical proverb is anonymous, traditional, and epigrammatic, and quotes the observation that it is characterized by "shortness, sense and salt." In Lord John Russell's oft-quoted epigram, a proverb contains "the wisdom of many and the wit of one." It sums up in compact and easily remembered form an observation or judgment which is widely held to be true. Hence the frequent use of proverbs by a speaker to illustrate a statement, to clinch an argument, or to lend authority to an admonition. The teaching function is especially evident in the biblical Book of Proverbs.

Strictly speaking, an epigram, an aphorism, or a maxim does not qualify as proverbial unless it has passed into common use. An epigram like Lord John Russell's is a perceptive observation wittily expressed, but no one would quote it unless he were discussing the present subject. An aphorism like "Beauty is truth, truth beauty" is philosophical in tone and lacks the common touch. A maxim is an axiom or rule of conduct which may or may not gain widespread acceptance, such as "Knowledge is power." The homeliness of the truth expressed and the simplicity, conciseness, and picturesqueness of its expression characterize the anonymous familiar popular saying. "Dead men tell no tales." "A new broom sweeps clean." "Chickens come home to roost."

A good many biblical proverbs have passed into current use in Europe and America, and more might have done so had the terms in which they are put been less strange to our ears. We say, "Hope deferred makes the heart sick" (Prov 13:12); "The way of transgressors is hard" (Prov 13:15); "A soft answer turns away wrath" (Prov 15:1); "Pride goes before destruction" (Prov 16:18). We are less likely to quote: "Better is a dinner of herbs where love is, than a stalled ox and hatred therewith" (Prov 15:17); "The beginning of strife is as when one lets out water" (Prov 17:14); "Seest thou a man diligent in his business? He shall stand before kings" (Prov 22:29).

Folk sayings gleaned from the pages of the Old Testament are . . . concise, picturesque, thought-provoking, and sometimes witty and amusing comments on men and their behavior, and on common experience. Not infrequently their tone is scornful or sarcastic, as in 1 Kings 20:11, "One who is girding himself [for battle] should not boast like one who is ungirding himself [afterwards]." Some sound a warning based on unfortunate experience, for example, Prov 13:20, "The fellow of fools will fare ill." They carry their own note of authority, that of the obvious truism, or the social authority of general consent; cf. "In all toil there is profit" (Prov 14:23), and "Without [his] people, a prince is nothing" (Prov 14:28).

---

1. *The Proverb*, 1931, pp. 7–8, 95.

Deep in this folk wisdom may be discerned something that becomes more explicit in the words of the later teachers of practical and speculative wisdom: *the idea of order,* of norms, rules, right values, and due proportions. This is expressed in proverbs which bring to light the identity or equivalence of some things and the non-identity of others, the distinction of the appearance from the reality, common factors and characteristics, cause and consequence; and also what is *contrary to right order:* the irregular, absurd, paradoxical, and impossible. This underlying idea and the proverbial patterns which it creates may be observed in the folk wisdom of many peoples, ancient and modern.

The first of these patterns points to *identity, equivalence,* or *invariable association:* "This is really [or, always] that"; "Where [or, when] this is, that is"; "Without this, there is no that." Familiar examples in English are: "Business is business" (in which the tautology is apparent only); "A friend in need is a friend indeed" (which exhibits the fondness of the proverb maker for alliteration and rhyme); "Easy come, easy go"; "A penny saved is a penny earned"; and (from Aesop's fables), "One man's meat is another man's poison." Among biblical proverbs of this type may be cited: "As the man, so his strength" (Judg 8:21); "The man who cajoles his companion is spreading a net for his feet" (Prov 29:5); "Without [the labor of] oxen, the manger is bare" (Prov 14:4); "What a man sows is what he will reap" (Gal 6:7).

The second proverb pattern is that of *non-identity, contrast,* or *paradox:* "This is not really that"; "Not every this is that"; "This, yet paradoxically that." Examples are: "All that glisters is not gold"; "Not all are hunters, who blow horns"; "Much noise, few eggs"; "A cobbler's wife is always ill-shod"; "Good fences make good neighbors." Examples from the Bible are: "What has straw in common with wheat?" (Jer 23:28); "A soft tongue can break a bone" (Prov 25:15); "To the hungry man even the bitter tastes sweet" (Prov 27:7); "He who loves money never has enough money" (Eccles 5:10 EV); "Can anything good come from Nazareth?" (John 1:46).

The third proverb pattern is that of *similarity, analogy,* or *type:* "This is [or, "acts like"] that"; "As this, so that"; "This is [metaphorically] that"; "Like so-and-so, who. . . ." Here we have: "A chip off the old block"; "Time and tide wait for no men"; "He who keeps company with a wolf learns to howl"; "Like master, like man." The last corresponds exactly with the biblical "Like people, like priest" (Hos 4:9); "Like mother, like daughter" (Ezek 16:44). Striking similes are frequent: "Like arrows in the hands of a warrior are the sons of one's youth" (Ps 127:4); "Like the coolness of snow in the heat of harvest time is a reliable messenger to him who sends him" (Prov 25:13); "It is like having a loose tooth or a palsied foot to rely on a deceiver in time of trouble" (Prov 25:19); "Singing gay songs to a heavy heart is like disrobing a man on a cold day, or adding sour wine to soda" (Prov 25:20); "Good news from a distant land is like a drink of cold water to a weary man" (Prov 25:25). Persons who have become types or standards for comparison are illustrated in: "Like Nimrod, a mighty hunter before the Lord" (Gen 10:9); "Like Rachel and Leah, who built up the family of Israel" (Ruth 4:11); "No prophet like Moses" (Deut 34:10).

The fourth proverb idiom focuses on what is *contrary to right order*, and so is *futile* or *absurd*. It employs the mocking comparison, for example, "A whistling woman and a crowing hen are liked neither by God nor men"; the rhetorical question: "What's the use of running when you are on the wrong road?"; and the maxim, as in "Don't count your chickens before they are hatched."

The Hebrews were especially fond of the taunt or mocking question. When Jeremiah said "Every wine jar shall be filled with wine" (Jer 13:12), he was mocking drinkers, not talking about wine jars. "As a door turns on its pivot, so a lazy man turns on his bed" (Prov 26:14) sounds like a favorite sarcasm of the early risers. "Do horses run on a cliff [i.e., like insects]? Do you plow the sea with an ox?" cried the prophet Amos in derision (Amos 6:12). Jeremiah's challenge is perhaps more familiar: "Can an Ethiopian change his [black] skin, or a leopard his spots?" (Jer 13:23). In Prov 17:16 a teacher of privileged youth reflects ruefully, "What good does it do a fool to come fee in hand to buy wisdom, when he has no mind?" In Prov 1:17 another instructor clinches his warning of the dire results of associating with thieves, by quoting the proverb, "It's no use setting a net so the birds can see it."

A fifth type of proverb *classifies* and *characterizes* persons, actions, or situations: "Children and fools speak the truth"; "A rolling stone gathers no moss"; "He that steals an egg will steal an ox"; "There are three things which drive a man out of the house—smoke, rain [which gets in], and a scolding wife." The Book of Proverbs has many examples of such characterizations of the fool, the scoffer, the sluggard, and the shrewish wife; for instance, "The simpleton believes everything he hears" (14:15); "The insolent will not listen to rebuke" (13:1); "The lazy man puts his hand into the dish, but he is too weary to raise it to his mouth" (26:15); "A wife's grumbling is a continual dripping [of water]" (19:13). The most famous of several examples in Prov 30:15–31 of the numerical proverb of classification is: "Three things astonish me, there are four I cannot fathom—how an eagle soars in the sky, how a snake glides across a rock, how a ship moves over the sea, and how a man wins his way with a girl." What might be called a "progressive classification" appears in Prov 27:3: "A stone may be heavy, or a load of sand, but a provoking fool is harder to bear than both together."

The sixth identifiable idiom or pattern is that of *value, relative value* or *priority, proportion* or *degree*: "This is worth that"; "The more [or less] this, the more [or less] that"; "Better this than that"; "First this, then that"; "If this, how much more that!" Familiar examples come to mind: "A bird in the hand is worth two in the bush"; "Better late than never"; "The nearer the bone, the sweeter the meat"; "Out of the frying pan into the fire"; "Cut your coat according to the cloth." This is a common biblical type: "A good name is more to be desired than great riches" (Prov 22:1); "Better to be poor than a liar" (Prov 19:22); "Better the end of something than its beginning" (Eccles 7:8); "The more he talks, the more meaningless it becomes" (Eccles 6:11); "To obey [God] is better than [to offer] sacrifice" (1 Sam 15:22). "A sacrifice offered by wicked men is an abomination, all the more so if one brings it with a shameful purpose" (Prov 21:27).

A seventh proverb pattern in folk wisdom turns on the *consequences of human character and behavior:* "Nothing venture, nothing win"; "Give him an inch and he'll take an ell"; "Don't bite off more than you can chew!" The most famous biblical example of this is quoted by both Jeremiah and Ezekiel: "[When] the fathers have eaten unripe grapes, the children's teeth are set on edge [or "blunted"]" (Jer 31:29; Ezek 18:2). Others are: "They are sowing the wind, they shall reap the whirlwind" (Hos 8:7); "A happy heart lights up the face" (Prov 15:13); "He who digs a pit [for another] will fall into it [himself]" (Prov 26:27); "At the onset of winter the idler does not plow, so at harvest time he looks for [a crop] and finds none" (Prov 20:4).

These are by no means all the proverbs patterns which can be traced in the Bible and in the sayings of other peoples, ancient and modern. To be on the lookout for them will add interest to the reading of the Book of Proverbs, where the long sequences of unconnected sayings and precepts all too easily fail to hold the attention. As W. A. L. Elmslie remarks truly in his delightful *Studies in Life from Jewish Proverbs,*[2] "Proverbs cannot be absorbed in quantity," and "Many proverbs speak truth, but a true word can be spoken too often." We must remember, in any case, that the Book of Proverbs is not intended to be an anthology of folk sayings, but a source book of materials for instruction in religious morality. It is deliberately didactic, and its air of somewhat ponderous authority and complacent moralizing reflects the schoolmaster, not the village wit. Even the literary form of these proverbs is changed in the interests of instructional method. In place of short, pointed, and picturesque sayings, often characterized by alliteration, we find formal couplets in poetic parallelism. The second line may point a contrast,

> A wise son makes a happy father,
>   But a foolish son is a grief to his mother (10:1).

Or it may say the same thing in different words, as in

> Vile men will be made to bow before the righteous,
>   And the wicked at the gates of the just (14:19).

2. London, 1917, pp. 15–16.

Sometimes the second line simply carries forward what is said in the first:

> Religious belief is a well of life
>   By which one avoids deadly snares (14:27).

At some points it seems very evident that a banal second line has been added to a picturesque folk saying, as in

> "The toiler's appetite toils for him,"
> For his hunger drives him (16:26).

What explains this form is almost certainly an instructional method in which a teacher spoke the first line and was answered in chorus by the class (or an individual pupil) responding with the appropriate second line. We have a glimpse of such a method in operation in Isa 28:9–10: "Whom will he teach knowledge? . . . precept upon precept, line upon line," and again in Isa 29:13: "Their fear of me is a human commandment learned by rote." Since the two collections of such two-line parallel in didactic sayings are designated, "Proverbs of Solomon" in the titles at Prov 10:1 and 25:1, it is reasonable inference, that *this literary form* is primarily what is meant by the designation, rather than an affirmation of Solomon's authorship.

5

THE POWER OF FORM: A STUDY OF BIBLICAL PROVERBS

James G. Williams

Abstract

This study seeks to show that biblical proverbs are not least among the poetic varieties of aphoristic speech. The thesis informing this study is that there are definite artistic forms and methods in the sentence literature of the Book of Proverbs. Recognizing these forms and methods may contribute to a renewed literary and religious appreciation of the proverbs. After a discussion of terminology and of some of the basic features of aphoristic speech (assertiveness, insight as process, paradox, brevity and conciseness, word play, subjective energy, comparison), reflections on the relation of "aphorism" to "proverb" are presented. The next major section is a discussion of three aspects of artistic form and method in Proverbs: (1) The juxtaposition of images and sentences is the basic formal pattern of the proverbs studied. (2) The patterns of sound are involved in the dynamic play of language that both correlates sounds and perceptions to key images and evokes the capacity to cor-

From *Semeia* 17 (1980): 35–58. Used by permission.

relate them. (3) The expansion of folk sayings into literary proverbs discloses a skillful artistry and suggests that the world of the popular proverb and the world of the intellectual proverb shared certain basic assumptions; the former could serve as the text for the latter.

The first two parts of the chapter give examples showing that aphoristic speech poses particularly acutely the problem and potential of all metaphorical language: more than one, perhaps many, meanings. The semiotic model sketched by Susan Wittig is employed to gain a more focused view of the problem. Two proverbs, Proverbs 18:21 and 26:27, are discussed and interpreted by means of the model.

Introduction

> To the ethical by way of the esthetic,
> as Juan de Mareina said. . . . [Machado, 16]

One common assumption about biblical proverbs, especially those in the Book of Proverbs, is that they are dry, stale, and hackneyed. Many readers have certainly had an initial experience of Proverbs as a rather boring collection of sayings. The translations tend to concentrate on rendering the *content* of the proverbs, and the commentaries deal more with *concepts* and philological information than with their aesthetic dimension.

The fault lies with all of us—teachers, scholars, translators—who have nourished such judgments with poor translations, literary insensitivity, and stereotyped assumptions that are read into the proverbs. The energizing perspective of this essay is that the proverbs will disclose their riches and stir our imagination when they are read with an informed, sympathetic sensitivity; they are trite and stereotypical only when read tritely and stereotypically.

"Stirring our imagination" would not matter, of course, *if we knew for sure* what the proverbs meant. We are now in a situation in which such certainty of meaning is problematic. Traditional forms of criticism stemming from historiography seem to worry the text as though there is some definite content there to find. I believe that the content is there to find only through the *form*, and that one must attend carefully to this form in a new era for biblical studies when a shift is occurring from historical to literary criticism (see Miles; Robertson chap. 1). I agree with Miles that literature can never be an effective substitute for religion; it can however, be a *way in* to religion. Thus, "to the extent that a fierce and compelling religion is *in* the Bible and not alone in those institutions which assign the Bible a religious meaning, to that extent an aesthetic reappropriation of biblical sensibilities will be a religious experience" (Miles, 6).

In the hope that a new aesthetic appreciation of biblical proverbs will contribute to religion and theology by way of literature, I present the following study as a set of reflections on the various facets of the formal dimension of the proverbs:

1. Their character as a variety of aphoristic speech.
2. Their formal construction, which comprises juxtaposition of images (2:1), patterning of sounds (2:2), and literary expansions (2:3).
3. The use of a semiotic model to clarify the source of ambiguity in proverbs as metaphorical speech.

The basic thesis of the chapter is thus that there are fine artistic forms and methods in the sentence literature of the Book of Proverbs. The implication of the thesis is that, if these artistic forms and methods are recognized, a renewed literary and perhaps religious appreciation of proverbs may be possible.

Most of the translations of proverbs will be offered in two modes: "literal" and "poetic." The literal translation is an attempt to give the reader a sense of the brevity and syntax of the original Hebrew and to show how much is "filled out" in most translations. The poetic translation, though perhaps wanting in true poesy, seeks to give the reader some sense of the poetic form, tone, and play of images in the original.

Aphoristic Speech and the Character of Biblical Proverbs

[The aphorism] wants to be heard and enjoyed *en passant*, it seeks to flash into conversation and disappear before it stands in the center of attention. . . . It doesn't allow itself to be taken alive. And dead it is no longer the same as it was in its liveliness. [Asemissen, 176]

The immediate problem is to name the subject. This is not easy. The word we commonly use is "proverb." As a noun denoting the short forms in the biblical book and in various biblical passages, it is supported by long usage in the Western languages. The Hebrew word is *māšāl*, which has been translated in various contexts as proverb, parable, allegory, riddle, taunt-song, etc. The core idea of *māšāl* may be that of "likeness" and "comparison." McKane argues for "model" (22–33), which is often fitting. However, "model" requires the basic ideas of comparison and likeness, and it would be off the mark to understand certain instances of *māšāl* as model. Do singers sing models? (Num. 21:27). Is one nation ridiculed by another as a model? (Deut. 28:37). Is an enigmatic song a model? (Ps. 49:5). One strains to catch a likeness, a hidden comparison therein—but it is not a model. Insofar as consideration of the etymology or root idea of *māšāl* is pertinent to its meaning and function in specific instances, I would see it as likeness/comparison.

The history of short forms of speech in Western cultures does not disclose compelling reasons to prefer one term over another (Schalk, 75–89). Proverb, aphorism, sentence, gnome, maxim, *pensée*: all have their attractions and connotations. Perhaps the most appealing word is aphorism. From the Greek *aphorismos,* its root idea of delimiting (Latin *definitio*) experience through language would place our reflection and study on a broad base. Yet the base is too broad: the word lacks specificity and has been used in numerous ways (Asemissen, 160).

In this chapter the noun employed most often will be "proverb." It is part of our religious and literary heritage, and, as applied to biblical short forms, it signifies sayings that are usually viewed as the articulation of experience accepted by people generally (Grenzmann, 195), both during and since the biblical period. There is no other word that obviously commends itself. However, since aphorism has had a long literary usage and bears an etymology that interests me, I shall frequently employ the adjective "aphoristic," as in "aphoristic speech." The use of adjectives derived from aphorism helps to counteract some of the stereotypes imposed on the Hebrew *māšāl.*

Biblical proverbs can be expected to exhibit many of the features of aphoristic speech as noted by modern literary historians and critics. A first characteristic is that aphoristic speech is assertive, apparently self-explanatory; it says something as though it is *a priori,* though it is not (Asemissen, 163; Grenzmann: "It does not develop, it asserts"—196). An example is the dictum of Heidegger (21):

> Nie ist das Gesprochene und in keiner Sprache das Gesagte.
> Whatever the form of speaking, the spoken is never what is said.

A second characteristic is that of insight, insight as process. The aphoristic saying is a delimitation that invites its hearer to move beyond limits, to go beyond fixed boundaries. It starts a journey of thought. As Marie von Ebner-Eschenbach says (cited in Grenzmann, 197):

> Ein Gedanke kann nicht erwachen, ohne andere zu wecken.
> One thought cannot awake without waking others.

There is a sense in which the aphoristic thought "arrives" or occurs to the subject as though at the end of a journey, yet it starts another series of reflections. This is articulated by Heidegger (11):

> Wir kommen nie zu Gedanken. Sie kommen zu uns.
> We never come to thoughts. They come to us.

A third feature is paradox. Reversing expectations, provoking surprise, ex-aggeration: these are manifestations of the very *raison d'être* of aphoristic speech. Why? As Grenzmann indicates, aphoristic thinking and speech is en-gendered by *revaluation* (*Umwertung*); it both feeds upon and encourages a different way of looking at things (Grenzmann, 194). Such revaluation was Pascal's project as he sought to understand his religious experience *vis-à-vis* the life of a scientist:

> Le coeur a ses raisons que la raison ne connaît point.
> The heart has reasons reason has not heard.

A fourth feature is brevity and conciseness. This may vary somewhat, but it doubtless bestows on aphoristic speech much of its force and appeal. There is, on the one hand, a great deal of tension in the saying that is just at the point of being unleashed. On the other hand, there is a certain sharpness which comes with brevity and conciseness and which enables the speaker and hearer to "cut through" some tangles of experience. The importance of brevity and conciseness is indicated by the terms employed in the various languages: *aph-orismos, definitio, Sentenz, pensées,* etcetera. The point is a maximum of mean-ing in a minimum of words. Hippocrates sets a good example: *vita brevis— ars longa.* How ironically interesting to be told by the briefest of art forms that art is long (enduring? immortal?) and life is brief!

A fifth feature of aphoristic speech is the attempt to bring sound and sense as closely together as possible. Certain ideas, images, situations, and persons are shown to belong together or to be antithetical by the combination of sound, image, and referent. Pascal's famous line, quoted previously, tells the hearer effectively that "COeuR" and "COnnaîtRe" are inseparable, whereas "la raison ne connaît point." The "heart hears." Von Ebner-Eschenbach says two things with her onomatopoeia in the aphorism cited: (a) The denoted, namely, a thought not only "awakes" but "wakes up" other thoughts. (b) The connoted, namely, thinking and waking go together.

All of the features—assertiveness, insight as process, paradox, brevity, play on word and sound—have two more basic characteristics in common. One pertains to the subject who speaks or composes, the other to the formal struc-ture of aphoristic speech. Aphoristic speech stems from the dynamic of a searching subject. Grenzmann calls this "being full of subjective energy" (195). Aphoristic speech forms and expresses the desire to be original, to set aside certain limits and prejudices, to prepare the way for spontaneous recog-nitions. The situation of the aphorist, claims Grenzmann, is usually that of in-tellectually uncertain times (207). Of course, the topic here is biblical prov-erbs, so we must ask whether these features of aphoristic speech are applicable to biblical proverbs. My response is that the various facets of the presentation in parts 2 and 3 of this chapter point to the conclusion that most of the sentence and expanded sentence forms in Proverbs 10–31 were highly original and experientially oriented. Such matters must be judged from case to case, but I disagree with McKane's sweeping contention that the sentence literature of the Book of Proverbs "is devoid of the imaginative constituents of the popular proverb" (32).

Basic to the structure of aphoristic speech is comparison, whether overt or concealed. This basic structure is a factor in all gnomic utterances. The structure of comparison sometimes suggests itself in the *tertium comparationis,* which exemplifies the riddle that is often lurking in aphoristic speech. For example: "The kingdom of God is like treasure hidden in a field" (Matt. 13:44). What do the kingdom of God and treasure have in common? That they are hidden? So it seems. That they are precious? Yes again, but here one touches upon the hidden comparison: they are valuable to the extent that they are valued above all things by a *valuer.* The tertium is the valuer, the investor. The second part of the saying is thus an interpretive expansion that spells out the *tertium comparationis* as understood by the speaker or Evangelist: "The man who found it buried it again; and for sheer joy went and sold everything he had and bought that field." This interpretive expansion changes the saying from a *māšāl* which is a simile into *māšāl* which is the basic plot of a story.

If proverbs may be viewed as instances of aphoristic speech, how is "aphorism" related to "proverb"? It would appear that if the aphorism or gnomic utterance is hallowed by long usage, certain of its features are accentuated and the character of the short form is changed. "Subjective energy" may become the force of tradition, especially if the short form is put to didactic use in a traditional society. Paradoxes can lose their surprise and become nonparadoxical, especially if a tradition transmits a "right" interpretation of the paradox. The qualities of assertiveness and insight can come to be understood or felt as that which is given "in the beginning." Proverbs usually have the air of the archaic; they may originate in sayings that are deliberately archaizing (Greimas, 311, 313). One can imagine, for example, the aphoristic appeal of a saying like this:

> Hope drawn out drains the heart,
> but a desire fulfilled is paradise. [Prov. 13:12]

But within the literature of the Bible as canon, and thus drawn into the network of the Israelite story of origins, the form becomes a brief communication of the mythical (this would be the ironic point of the quotation of the first line in Beckett's *Waiting for Godot*). Its authority is that of a reality placed outside of time. Greimas (313) has said that, "The archaic character of proverbs constitutes, therefore, a *placement outside of time* in their meanings. This is a method comparable to the 'once upon a time' of the fairy tales and legends that is intended to situate the truths revealed by the narrative in the time of 'the gods and heroes.'"

This archaic character of the proverb is thus no more and no less positive than that of myth and fairy tale. The question is whether the aphoristic quality of the proverb can be appreciated anew.

The Construction of Biblical Proverbs

JUXTAPOSITION OF IMAGES

Artistic method and understanding of existence can be distinguished: they cannot be separated. In working with the short "sentence" proverbs, translating them, attempting to render them as I find them in the Hebrew text, I have begun to understand something of the strategy of juxtaposition. Its basic form is simple: whether it is a matter of synonyms or antithetical parallelism, two sentences are juxtaposed. These sentences contain words and images which play off against each other. They do not "define" each other, but they suggest a web of meanings.

Furthermore, within each sentence there is a juxtaposition of images which are projected stroboscopically: they are seen quickly side by side, then they are shut off. For example:

bāz-lĕrēʿēhû	*ḥăsar-lēb*
wĕʾîš tĕbûnôt	*yaḥărîš* (11:12)
despiser of his neighbor	lacking of mind
and man of discernings	keeps still

Who reviles another lacks sense,
but who understands keeps silent.

hôlēk rākîl	*mĕgallĕh-ssôd*
wĕneĕmān-rúaḥ	*mĕkassĕh dābār* (11:13)
goer as gossip	revealer of counsel
and faithful of spirit	concealer of word

The gadding gossip gives away confidence,
but the faithful confidant keeps counsel.

yôdēʿa saddíq	*nĕpĕš bĕhĕmtô*
wĕraḥămê rĕšāʿim	*akzāri* (12:10)
knower is the righteous	of life of his beast
and compassion of wicked	cruel

The good person perceives his beast's fatigue,
but the bad man's mercies are mean.

tôḥĕlĕt mĕmūššākā   *maḥălâ-lēb*
weʾṣ ḥayyîm   *taʾăwâ bāʾâ* (13:12)

hope drawn out   sickens mind
and tree of life   desire come

Hope drawn out drains the heart,
but a desire fulfilled is paradise.

pôrēʿa mûsār   *môʾēs napšô*
wĕšômēʿa tôkaḥat   *qônĕh lēb* (15:32)

rejecter of discipline   despiser of his soul
and hearer of reproof   acquirer of mind

Who rejects discipline despises his life,
but who accepts criticism acquires a mind.

kĕbôd ʾĕlōhîm   *hastēr dābār*
ûkbôd mĕlakîm   *ḥāqōr dābār* (25:2)

glory of God   to conceal word
glory of kings   to search word

Godly glory conceals meaning;
kingly glory unseals meaning.

šamaîm lārûm   *wāʾāreṣ lāʿōmĕq*
wĕlēb mĕlākîm   *ʾên ḥēqĕr* (25:3)

heaven for height   and earth for depth
and mind of kings   no searching

As the sky is high and the earth is deep,
so the mind of kings is sought in vain.

These aphoristic assertions are made as though something is evident, but it is not. "A priori sentences say something obvious in the broadest sense. . . . Aphorisms say something not obvious. But they say it in such a way that it seemingly goes without saying" (Asemissen, 163).

It seems obvious that a hope that is prolonged without actualization is depressing, that is, it makes the heart/mind (*lēb*) sick. But is it obvious? Doesn't hope keep one going? Is not the anticipation of fulfillment a support of the *lēb* that is more significant than any realization?

The connection of the juxtaposed sentences is by means of the simple *waw*, "and," the basic conjunction in Hebrew. We supply the "but" for English minds in cases of antithetical parallelism. There are proverbs, of course, which have no conjunction of the sentences. For example:

nĕzĕm zāhāb	*bĕ°ap ḥăzîr*
°iśśāh yāpá	*wĕsārat ṭā°am* (11:22)
gold ring	in nose of wild pig
pretty woman	and lacking taste

A pig with a pearl necklace is like
a woman pretty but reckless.

The character of conjunctions and their omission is important in understanding aesthetic form and strategy in biblical proverbs. Comprehending this importance is not only a matter of translating but of becoming aware of what the translator supplies with respect to words and suppositions. A statement by Friedrich Hauck in the *Theological Dictionary of the NT* (Friedrich-Bromiley, 5.748) is indicative of the problem: "Formally many of [the proverbs] use the comparative 'as' (25:11–13; 26:18f.; 27:15). In others a 'but' is used, esp[ecially] 10:3–14:23." The "but" is always the *waw*. And two of the cited instances of the comparative "as" have no comparative particle at all in the Hebrew text (25:11–12).

In many of the examples we encounter play: word play, image play. This playful element is an important feature of wisdom reflection and expression. Images rebound off each other. We find that the discerning person is basically different from one who reviles his neighbor, though we are not told that they are categorical opposites. We hear that one who lacks "mind" or "sense" (*lēb*) is not like one who keeps still. In an instance of synonymous parallelism we observe that *nĕpĕš* (soul, life, appetite, etc.) is in the semantic range of *lēb*, mind, yet the two are not synonymous. (The beast, too, has a *nĕpĕš*.) A "tree of life" has something to do with being wise and is a metaphor of "desire (*ta°ăwāh*) fulfilled." The latter is probably a learned allusion to the story wherein the fruit of the tree was for Eve "a desire (*ta°ăwāh*) to the eyes" (Gen. 3:6). And this is another facet of play: clever allusions. We really do not know how many allusions there may be to images and stories both extant and extinct.

In allowing oneself to enter into this kind of "proverb-play," one can begin to feel as though a discovery is being made. As Asemissen says concerning the aphorism: "It mediates insight as process, but it does not allow itself to call attention to this" (163).

There are occasionally sayings that are enigmatic in their compactness. A whole mythology may be compressed within 25:2–3. One senses that if one were to "crack these nuts" it would be like splitting an atom. An entire world ready to explode from a proverb.

Position and opposition of images result in frequent paradox of thought (cf. Grenzmann, 194; Asemissen, 165–66). At the conceptual level certain assertions appear to be contradictions; in fact, they are unexpected (paradoxical). Does one who "spares the rod" love his child? Or does the "disciplinarian" hate his child? "No," one might say, "not necessarily." Someone else may say "probably not" or even "of course not." The qualifications are possible when the insight is expressed as a question, or in any fashion which allows for discussion. In aphoristic form, however, the insight takes on the style of a paradox which commands assent:

hóśēk šibṭô	*śônēʾ běnô*
wĕʾōhăbô šiḥărô	*músār* (13:24)

sparer of rod	hater of his son
and who loves him	applies to him discipline

Save your strap and spoil your son;
if you love him let him learn discipline.

Not infrequently there is humor, especially of the ironic sort. The "mercy" of the wicked is "mean"! And:

ṭāman ʿāṣēl yādô baṣṣallāḥat
gam-ʾel-pîhû lōʾ yĕšîběnnâ (19:24)

the sluggard hides his hand in the dish
even to his mouth; he returns it not

The lazy one leaves his hand in the dish,
he won't even lift it to his mouth!

šûḥâ ʿămuqqâ pî zārôt
zěʿûm yhwh yippol-šām (22:14)

deep pit	mouth of a stranger woman
abhorred by Yahweh	will fall therein

A terrible trap is a seductress's mouth;
those despised by Yahweh will trip into it.

These observations suggest much concerning the intellectual situation of the wise and of the wisdom tradition—that is, the creation they conceived, the world in which they understood themselves to be participating. The method of juxtaposing images, the word play, the frequent humor are intimations of the experience of life as a dynamic reality. Many of the proverbs show signs of having been the fresh, original aphoristic speech of those who were seeing the world in new ways.

PATTERNS OF SOUND IN PROVERBS
māwĕt wĕḥayyîm bĕyad- lāšôn
wĕ'ōhăbêhā yō'kal piryá (18:21)

death and life in hand of tongue
and her lovers will eat her fruit

Life and death are held by Dame Tongue,
and her devotees will taste her fruit.

Aesthetic strategy and understanding of existence come closest to merging in the method of structuring sounds. The music of poetry emits a message from its interior. This quality prevents the proverb or aphorism from degenerating into staleness.

One way of making words sing is through the use of consonants. Kenneth Burke, in a suggestive little essay, has dealt with his use of consonants (296–304; cf. Hartman, 339ff.; and Fokkelman). Burke discusses repetition of cognate consonants concealed in variations, acrostic combinations, chiasmus, and augmentation and diminution. In doing this he takes all his examples from Coleridge.

An example of concealed alliteration is "bathed by the mist." In English *b* and *m* are close phonetic relatives. So also are *th, s,* and *t.*

An example of acrostic structure: "A damsel with a dulcimer."

d-m-s-l
d-l-c-m (plus r)

A chiasmus is a "cross" (X) arrangement, either A, B, B', A', or A, B, C, B', A'. So in "beneath the ruined tower":

Augmentation involves expansion by stretching sounds or placing them further apart. Diminution involves bringing the sounds closer together than they were:

Augmentation:
> She sent the gentle sleep from Heaven,
> That slid into my soul.

Here *sl-* and *sl-* (sleep and slid) are made into a longer note (soul).

Diminution:
> But silently, by slow degrees.

Here the time between *s* and *l* is collapsed in "slow."

Before giving examples of these patterns in biblical proverbs, I think it important to point out that the principles involved are basically aesthetic. Ideas are not lacking in the sentences to be considered, but they are incorporated into the context of spoken and heard language. The order of pleasing sounds is more important than analytic thought. Thought, in turn, is given power by being profoundly rooted in concrete and vivid expressions of language. For aphoristic speech is an expression of the human capacity to correlate sounds and perceptions and it evokes this capacity. This is why it is able to "generalize concretely," to be extremely concrete or very general, sometimes simultaneously (see Neumann, 6ff.).

It is a simple matter to find the repetition of sounds in cognate variations. For instance:

| *ʾōgēr baqqayiṣ* | *bēn máskîl* |
| *nirdām baqqāṣîr* | *bēn mēbîs* (10:5) |

| gatherer in summer | son who proves prudent |
| sleeper in harvest | son who shames |

> A sensible son makes hay while the sun shines;
> a shameful son sleeps in the hay through harvest.

There is an alliterative play on *qayiṣ* and *qāṣîr*, and a repetition of palatal sounds in the first sentence: *g, q, k*. Also noteworthy is the frequency of the labial *b*.

Another interesting example is 15:23.

simḥâ lāʾîš bĕma ʿăneh-pîw
wĕdābār bĕittô mah-ṭôb

| joy to one | in response of his mouth |
| and word in its season | how good |

> A person gets pleasure from an apt reply,
> and how salutary is a word in season!

This proverb is punctuated by nicely spaced labials: *b*, *p* in the first sentence, *b*, *b*, *b* in the second. One could add an *m* in both lines if the Hebrew *mem* be counted as a labial sound (but see Blau, 4–5).

Acrostic patterns are fairly frequent. A simple example is the antithetical pair in 11:12: *ḥsr*/ *ḥrš* (lacking/to keep still). Acoustic plays on *kĕsîl*, "fool," occur often. "In the ears of the senseless (*kĕsîl*) do not speak, for he will refuse the sense (*śēkĕl*) of your words" (23:9). In the same proverb there is an acrostic combination contained in *bĕ°oznê* ("in ears of") and *yābûz* ("he will refuse").

A pattern of alliteration, though not a full acrostic, is to be observed in 26:11: *kĕlēb* (dog)/*kĕsîl*. In the same vein, with palatal sounds, is 27:14:

bĕqôl	*gādôl*	("with loud voice")
	qĕlālâh	("curse")

He who "blesses" his neighbor early in the morning brings a curse on himself! "Loud voice" and "curse" are thus associated by means of assonance and alliteration.

Chiasmus is not rare. To dip into Qohelet, the popular saying in Qohelet 7:1a provides a good instance:

ṭôb	*šēm*	*miššĕmĕn* *ṭôb*	
A	B	C B′	A′

better a name than fine ointment
Prefer fame to fine perfume.

Its literary continuation (7:1b) is nicely arranged:

wĕyôm hammāwĕt miyyôm hiwālĕdô
A B B A B B A A

and the day of death than the day of one's birth
And the day of death to the day of delivery.

A nice chiasmus of initial sounds occurs in Proverbs 22:14:

šûḥâh ʿămuqqâh pî zārôt   *š* ⟍   *z*
zĕʿûm yhwh yippol šām   *z* ⤫ *š*

This proverb leaves no doubt that those hiring and those seduced by sirens are abhorred by Yahweh!

It is more difficult, I find, to locate good examples of augmentation and diminution such as Burke illustrates in Coleridge. An instance of diminution is 16:26, where the ʿ and *l* of ʿ*āmēl*/*omlâ* are brought together in ʿ*ālāyw*. More examples may be found upon further investigation. Augmentation and diminution depend on clusters of consonants in a language. Biblical Hebrew, following as it does a pattern of consonant-vowel in words, may not have many such combinations in comparison to English. However, there are frequent consonant clusters in the transition from one word to the next (e.g., *bĕrēʾšît bārāʾ*). Such links between words may be worth investigating. An instance which does not show augmentation or diminution, but which is interesting, is 18:4:

> *mayim* ʿ*ămuqqîm dibrēy pî-ʾîš*
> *naḥal nōbēaʿ mĕqôr ḥokmâ*

> deep waters   words of a man's mouth
> rushing torrent   source of wisdom

> The words of the mouth are deep waters;
> a surging stream is the source of wisdom.

The translation is disputed; some translators think "source of wisdom" belongs with "deep waters" and "words of one's mouth" goes with "rushing torrent" (so NEB). But if one rearranged the sentences notice how the play on ʿ-*m*-*q* would be lost:

> ʿ*ămuqqîm*
> *nōbēă ʿ mĕqôr*

    Did the investors of proverbs self-consciously employ principles of musicality? Perhaps at times. Probably, however, they usually followed their "ear." Poets usually do the latter, although they may tend toward either pole of the ear-principles spectrum. As Burke suggests concerning modern poets, many poets are very much aware of *method,* but it would not be wise to attribute *methodology* unless we had the poet's own statement (301–2). Or at least there should be firm evidence of a self-conscious use of principles and procedures. But if one has no evidence of definite methodology per se, yet it is clear that sounds are patterned in definite and often complex ways, this becomes another interesting source of reflection in the human mind: are there similar patterns and structures to be discerned at every stage from sound to story, from combinations of phonemes to combinations of mythemes?

    At any rate, one cannot assume a disjunction of sound and sense in proverbs. Aphoristic speech and thinking strive to bring onomatopoeia, concept, and referent as closely together as possible. Thus in the tongue that is like a woman who offers fruit to her friends, the labial sounds (§2.2) reinforce the images of "tongue" and "eating fruit."

> *Mā Wĕt WĕḥayyîM Bĕyad-lāšôn*
> *WĕʾōhăBéhā yōʾkal Piryá*

THE LITERARY EXPANSION OF PROVERBS

Ancient Israelite Folk Sayings

If we can isolate folk proverbs in the Bible and relate these to the literary proverbs of the Book of Proverbs, it may shed light on some literary questions, with important implications for phenomenology of religion and theology.

R. B. Y. Scott has done as much as anyone, at least in scholarly writings published in English, to investigate folk sayings in biblical and ancient Near Eastern literature (1961; 1971, 63–70). Some of the characteristics he points out are terseness, compactness, and occasional alliteration and assonance (1971, 63–64).

> *mērĕšācîm yēṣēʾ rĕšac* (1 Sam. 24:14)
> From those evil evil comes.

> *ʾal-yithallēl ḥōgēr kimĕpatēaḥ* (1 Kings 20:11)
> let not the girder boast as the ungirder
> Boast not before the battle's won.

A folk saying is one that is not only anonymous, but appears always to have been, is easy to remember and repeat, and seems "just right" in contemplating a given situation. Its vocabulary is from a common stock of words, though the proverb may put the words to uncommon use.

Scott has also sought to isolate originally nonliterary proverbs within the sentences of Proverbs and Qohelet. For example:

> *bāʾ -zādôn wayyābōʾ qālôn* (Prov. 11:2a)
> comes insolence and comes disgrace
> Haughtiness comes and honor leaves.

> *wĕrōʿeh kĕsîlîm yērôac* (13:20b)
> companion of fools will be hurt
> Fellow of fools fares ill (Scott's trans.)

> *šōmēr miṣwâh šōmēr napšô* (19:16a)
> keeper of command keeper of his soul
> Who keeps the law keeps his life.

On the basis of the known colloquial sayings (see citations in Scott), I would make the following tentative observations.

Literary and folk proverbs both presuppose the principle of retributive justice (e.g., 1 Sam. 24:14; Prov. 22:8a). In one instance a well known proverb expresses inherited retribution which is superseded by the prophetic word:

> The fathers have eaten sour grapes
> and the sons' teeth grate together. [Jer. 31:29 = Ezek. 18:2]

In the folk sayings we occasionally find a nice alliteration (1 Sam. 24:14), a clever assonance (2 Sam. 20:18), and sometimes both.

> *yādô bakkōl wĕyad kōl bô* (Gen. 16:12)
> His hand held against all, all hands held against him.

Both literary and folk expressions share fondness for word play (e.g., Prov. 13:20b; Qoh. 7:1a).

A very brief, compact image or flash of insight is expressed in both types.

Folk Proverbs Expanded Literarily

Colloquial sayings do not usually have the kind of complexity that results from deliberate composition. If I may offer an example from our English heritage: "Look before you leap." To fashion this into a literary proverb one could add a stich in this manner:

> Look before you leap,
> and listen to the learned.

Or:

> Birds of a feather flock together,
> and fools fare ill with the wise.

Of course, it is not always easy to discern whether or not one has a folk saying which has been expanded with the addition of a literary line, or whether it is a really clever folk saying or perhaps a literary creation which the composer has sought to make "folkish." To return briefly to an aphorism cited in the first part of this chapter, let us examine Pascal's famous line as though we knew nothing about its origin and literary character. The first part of the sentence sounds as though it could be a folk saying: "le coeur a ses raisons." This, or some similar saying, may have been known in French for a long period of time. But the continuation, "que la raison ne connaît point," would probably not have been part of a popular proverb for two reasons. First, the word "la raison" as the subject of a verb would not belong to the layperson's repertoire. As an abstraction *la raison* appears in French popular speech as it does in English. For example: "ramener quelqu'un à la raison"; "mettre à la raison"; "listen to reason." But this is different from personified reason speaking, knowing, et cetera. Second, the author has composed a clever alliteration of coeur/que/connaît. This is probably too clever for an originally popular saying, forming as it does a near chiasm (actually A/B/A /B /A if one counts the relative *que*). Such cleverness is not unknown in folk wisdom, although it usually takes simpler forms (e.g., the chiasmus of Qoh. 7:1a involves only *tôb šēm* plus *mi-* and *-en*). But the two reasons (sic!) taken together would weigh against its origins as a folk gnome.

Some of the sentences in Proverbs have the earmarks of popular sayings in both lines. Their subject, vocabulary, and play on sound show them to be cleverly constructed, but not literary compositions. For example:

> *ḥôaḥ ʿālâ bĕyad-šikkôr*
> *ūmāšāl bĕpî kĕsîlîm* (26:9)

> a thorn goes up into the hand of a drunk
> and a parable in the mouth of fools.

> A thorn that sticks in the hand of a sot:
> so a parable in the mouth of the senseless.

Also 19:24, previously quoted:

> The lazy one leaves his hand in the dish,
> he won't even lift it to his mouth!

On the other hand, I do not see how Proverbs 23:9 could be anything but a literary couplet:

> *bĕ'oznê kĕsîl   'al-tĕdabbēr*
> *kî-yābûz lĕśēkĕl millĕykā*

> in the ears of the fool do not speak
> for he will refuse the prudence of your words

> In the hearing of the witless do not speak,
> for he will hate the wisdom of your words.

The two acrostic pairs, *bĕ'oznê/yābûz* and *kĕsîl/śēkĕl*, have already been noted. This is a highly sophisticated literary device. And the syntax of the first line is too literary for colloquial usage. In biblical prose and in the commonly recognized folk sayings a verb would usually precede the governing phrase, and this holds for the imperative. For instance:

> šā'ōl yišā'ălû bĕ'abēl
> wĕkēn hētammú (2 Sam. 20:18)
> 'al-yithallēl ḥōgēr kimĕpattēaḥ (1 Kings 20:11)

This word order could be changed for reasons of emphasis or sound, for example, 1 Samuel 24:14. But departure from a standard prose syntax is usually a sign of literary usage.

Some of the most interesting proverbs for the study of the reflective literary process leading to "scripturization" of what was popular and oral are those in which one sentence was obviously colloquial, the latter serving as the text for a literary member. A good example of this is Proverbs 14:4:

> bĕ'ên 'ălāpîm 'ēbûs bār
> wĕrāb-tĕbû'ôt bĕkōaḥ šōr

| with no cattle | crib bare |
| and much income | by strength of ox |

No cattle and the grain is gone,
but great the income with the ox's might.

One feature of the literary expansion of the first line is the continuation of play on labial sounds in the second line (*b, p, b, b/b, b, b*). *tĕbû'ôt*, a plural noun from *bô'*, "come, enter," would not have been exactly an "intellectual" word, but it still seems a bit refined for a popular saying. In folk form one would expect *dāgān*, not "corn, grain," or some such word. Finally, the second sentence commences with a neat little acrostic of the last word of the first line: wĕRĀB/BĀR.

On the other hand, 19:16b provides a good case of poor literary expansion.

19:16a   *šōmēr miṣwâ šōmēr napšô*
          Who keeps the law keeps his life.

19:16b   *bôzēh dĕrākāyw yāmūt*
          who despises his ways shall die.

There is practically no alliteration or assonance. There is a bit of music in the labial-sibilant construction of naPŠô/BôZēh, but that is all. The referent of "his" in the second sentence is uncertain. It could be human subject or God, but probably the latter. Sometimes ambiguity increases the appeal of a proverb, but here it comes across as wooden.

Here are three examples of the skillful, sometimes profound way in which folk sayings are often expanded in Proverbs:

> *baᵓ-zādôn wayyābôᵓ qālôn*
> *wĕᵓēt-ṣĕnûᶜîm ḥokmâ* (11:2)

comes insolence and comes disgrace
and with the humble is wisdom

Haughtiness comes and honor leaves,
but wisdom is with the humble.

> *ᶜōbēd ᵓadmātô yiśbaᶜ-lāḥem*
> *ûmĕraddēp rēqîm ḥăsar-lēb* (12:11)

worker of the soil   sated of bread
and pursuer of empty things   lacking of mind

Who works his soil has his fill of food;
who goes gadding is full of folly.

> *nĕpeš ᶜāmēl ᶜomlâ llô*
> *kî-ᵓākap ᶜālāyw pîhû* (16:26)

appetite of the laborer labors for him
for urges upon him his mouth

The hunger of the laborer labors for him,
for his mouth lures him on.

Concerning 11:2, *ṣĕnûᵓîm* as the antithesis of *zādôn* plays nicely off the sound of the latter, sharing a sibilant (*s/z*) and the *n*. The image of the "humble" is a clever play on "disgrace" or "shame" (*qālôn*). Someone who is *qālôn* is little, light, lacking in esteem; he is the opposite of the honored, who is "weighty" (*kābôd*). But the weighty person, it turns out, is one who does not push his weight around, who does not boast and advertise himself (see McKane's note, 428). There is a world of ironic play in the interstices of this proverb!

The literary stich added to 12:11a skillfully juxtaposes an image of satisfied hunger to that of an undernourished mind. The worker of his soil will be full (*yiśbaᶜ*): how different is the one who chases things that lack substance (*rēqîm*). Correspondingly, this pursuer of folly is empty in the head (*ḥăsar-lēb*)! His poor hungry mind will not be satisfied.

We can observe here also the retributional character of the world. The worker of his soil (ʿōbēd ʾadmāto—an allusion to Adam who was created to till the ground?) is intelligent and his stomach is satisfied. The soil responds to him. And the pursuer of vain things gets what he is after, too: nothing!

The expansion involved in 16:26 is an example of another sort. There is no word play in the second stich, although ʿalāyw in response to ʿāmēl ʿomlâ is a nice touch. What is significant is the fruitfulness of this proverb. It has any number of intellectual seeds. As McKane says, "It has allusiveness and openness to interpretation . . ." (491). Does it refer to the human need for incentives, the struggle of the toiler, the great capacity of the human nĕpĕš (appetite/soul/desire/life)? Or is the mouth a metaphor of "appetite" and "speech" combined and interrelated? The LXX expanded the two stichs and turned them into a contrast of the silent industrious person and the person who busies himself with misrepresentations (deceitful mouth).

A Semiotic Interpretation of Biblical Proverbs

A Semiotic Model

The aphoristic saying and the proverb are often enigmatic and open to many interpretations. Why is this? Obviously they share certain features of metaphorical speech, which has a built-in ambiguity by virtue of being metaphorical. But can we get a more precise sighting of the ambiguity of the metaphor? I think that Susan Wittig has contributed to clarification of this problem by sketching an interesting semiotic model for comprehension of the multiple meanings of the parabolic sign. "Parabolic sign" means practically the same thing as "proverbial sign" or "aphoristic sign," so her theory can be appropriated for this study and for any analysis of metaphor.

Wittig's model begins with the basic semiotic relationship:

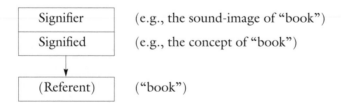

I have here modified her model a little by putting "referent" within parentheses. This is in order to indicate that the referent is not simply out there, a *Ding an sich* that exists apart from the sound and concept that make it what it is for the perceiver.

Wittig points out that the parabolic structure has two orders of signification: a stated signified (*denotatum*) and an unstated signified (*designatum*). The latter is provided by the hearer or perceiver in the context of the constraints imposed by the *denotatum* within a given first order and the other of the second order. A diagram of the model (Wittig, 85):

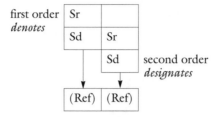

The levels of the parabolic construct may be viewed in the following manner (Wittig, 85–86). (I have modified Wittig's diagram only by placing the second Sd directly under the second Sr.)

$$\text{first order} \begin{bmatrix} \text{linguistic} & (\text{Sr}) \\ \text{conceptual} & (\text{Sd}/\text{Sr}) \\ \text{parabolic} & (\text{Sd}) \end{bmatrix} \quad \text{second order}$$

This model will now be used to interpret two proverbs and to show their polyvalence.

MULTIPLE MEANINGS IN PROVERBS 18:21 AND 26:27

The translations of Proverbs 18:21 are an interesting case for illustrating the various meanings and connotations of translations, which in turn are efforts to wrestle meaning out of complex signs that have a double structure.

LXX: Death and life are in the hand of the tongue; and those who rule her (*kratountes autēs*) will eat her fruits.

JPS: Death and life are in the power of the tongue; And they that indulge in it shall eat the fruit thereof.

NEB: The tongue has power of life and earth; make friends with it and enjoy its fruits.

RSV: Death and life are in the power of the tongue, and those who love it will eat its fruits.

Three of these translations are within the same range of meaning, although their connotations are different. The LXX tells us to control the tongue, NEB tells us to befriend it (in other words, "grasp the opportunity") and RSV recommends loving it. JPS differs in presenting an implied warning against indulging in the tongue's power.

The focal word is *lāšôn,* tongue. The idea denoted is "tongue, speaking, speech." *lāšôn* is here and usually a feminine noun. Death and life are *běyad lāšôn,* "in the hand of *lāšôn,*" and "her lovers/friends will eat her fruit." The image of *ʾōhēb,* "lover, friend," is reminiscent of adherents of *ḥokmâ,* Dame Wisdom (see Prov. 8:17, 21; cf. 8:36). Fruit comes from a tree, *ʿēṣ,* but tree is masculine; so also are death and life, so there is no doubt that the possessive pronouns in the second line refer to the tongue.

The image of the tongue holding—offering?—fruit which is death and life suggests to me an image of the woman in the garden of Eden offering fruit to the man. This particular image that gives rise to the second order is not a *necessary* step. The point of the semiotic model is to clarify the possibility of multiple meanings. The system has "dynamic, unstable *indeterminacy* which invites, even compels, the perceiver to complete the signification" (Wittig, 87). The four translations . . . indicate the many connotations that the same saying may have for different interpreters. The dominant image that is sought by the hearer functions like the *tertium comparationis* in simile proverbs. The hearer's mind must go to work at the second level to infer the signified and referent of the second order.

My own reading of the proverb is as follows. The image of the tongue-as-speech, represented as a figure holding fruit, is that of the woman in the garden of Eden. She is the unspoken comparison, the one who transmits knowledge of good and evil. The signified of the second order is thus Dame Speech whose lovers eat her fruit. Is the fruit "good," that is, the fruit *ḥayyîm,* life? The proverb is very ambiguous in this regard. The image of eating the fruit in paradise intimates the ingestion of the knowledge of both good and evil, which apparently includes sexual differentiation and death. There is also another tree, the tree of life. Be this as it may, the proverb itself gives no sure clue as to whether one eats "life" *instead* of "death," or "life" *and* "death." The connotation may be that Dame Speech offers fatal fruit, but that some fates are better than others.

A diagram of the interpretation offered here:

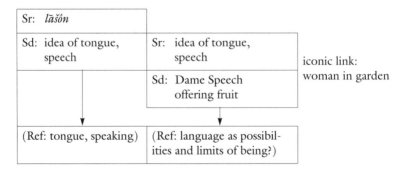

To turn to 26:27, "digging a pit" obviously has a conventional signified. But "digging a pit," in the sense of digging a pit for someone else to fall in, is one figure of plotting against others (Ps. 7:16; Jer. 18:20, 22). The image is complicated by another connotation: the "pit" (*šaḥat*) is also the place of the dead as the grave or Sheol (Job 17:4; 33:22, 24, etc.) The second sentence multiplies the possibilities of meaning geometrically, for "roller of a stone" could reinforce the image of plotting or of death (ignominious death: Josh. 7:26; 10:27; 2 Sam. 18:17). It implies, as does digging a pit, a demanding project which requires all one's effort. If this project is one in which one "falls," the web of imagery would then seem to suggest that in plotting against others one is unknowingly working out one's own death. We thus find images with a suggestive openness to numerous interpretations. The meaning that I find is illustrated in the semiotic model:

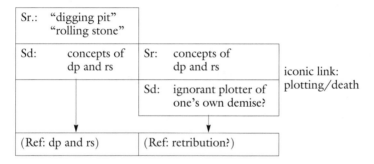

These interpretations of the two proverbs are not presented as the "correct" ones. The very point of the semiotic model is that multiple meanings are possible for the doubled parabolic structure. My reading is informed by the constraints of my cultural setting, conscious and unconscious concepts, and knowledge of biblical literature. Whether or not the interpretations are true to the *intention* of the aphorists is difficult if not impossible to say, although probably the constraint of my specialized knowledge gives some sort of *entrée* into their patterns of thinking.

The possibility of multiple meanings may be viewed as unfortunate or as a way of weaseling out of the interpreter's responsibility. I view it as a challenge to the interpreter to allow the proverb to provoke and challenge his mind.

Bibliographical Note

I have frequently consulted the commentary by McKane. McKane's research and reflections are very helpful, although the philological pull of his work prevents him from attaining a fuller literary appreciation of proverbs. G. von Rad's *Wisdom in Israel* has been a source of insight. Many of Gordis's writings have affected my perspective on wisdom literature (1939–40, 1965, 1968). An anthology of important essays, with a helpful introduction and a valuable bibliography, is Crenshaw, ed., *Studies in Ancient Israelite Wisdom*. Essays by Asemissen, Grenzmann, and Schalk have enhanced my theoretical understanding. These essays and others are in a book edited by G. Neumann, whose introduction to the collection is useful. Professor Donald Morton of the English Department at Syracuse University has made available to me his rough draft translations of the essays by Asemissen, Grenzmann, and Schlak, and he has read two earlier drafts of this chapter. Professor Matitiahu Tsevat of Hebrew Union College read an earlier version of "Patterning of Sounds in Proverbs," and made important critical comments. Dominic Crossan . . . has contributed much to the final form of the chapter. I thank them for their assistance, and I accept full responsibility for all errors and deficiencies. Other sources drawn upon are adequately indicated in the text of the article and the "Works Consulted." All translations from foreign languages are my own.

Works Consulted

Asemissen, H. U. 1976. "Notizen über den Aphorismus," in Neumann, *Aphorismus*, 159–76. (Originally published in *Trivium* 7 [1949].)

Blau, Joshua. 1976. *A Grammar of Biblical Hebrew*. Wiesbaden: Harrassowitz.

Burke, Kenneth. 1957. "On Musicality in Verse," in *The Philosophy of Literary Form*, rev. and abr., 296–304. New York: Vintage.

Crenshaw, J. L., ed. 1976. *Studies in Ancient Israelite Wisdom*. New York: KTAV. (Abbreviated as *SAIW*.)

Fokkelman, J. P. 1975. *Narrative Art in Genesis*. Assen/Amsterdam: van Gorcum.

Friedrich, G., and G. W. Bromiley. 1967. *Parabolē*, in *Theological Dictionary of the NT*, vol. 5, 744–61. Grand Rapids: Eerdmans.

Gordis, Robert. 1939–40. "Quotations in Wisdom Literature." *JQR* 30:123–47. (Reprinted in Crenshaw, *SAIW*.)

———. 1965. *The Book of God and Man*. Chicago: University of Chicago.

———. 1968. *Koheleth: The Man and His World*. New York: Schocken.

Greimas, A. J. 1970. *Du Sens: essais sémiotiques*. Paris: Editions du Seuil.

Grenzmann, Wilhelm. 1977. "Probleme des Aphorismus," in Neumann, *Aphorismus*, 177–208. (Originally published in *Jahrbuch für Aesthetik und Allgem. Kunstwissenschaft*, 1951.)

Hartman, Geoffrey H. 1970. *Beyond Formalism*. New Haven, Conn.: Yale University Press.

Heidegger, Martin. 1965. *Aus der Erfahrung des Denkens.* 2 Auflage. Pfullingen: Neske.

Machado, Antonio. 1963. *Juan de Mairena.* Edited and translated by Ben Bellit. Berkeley/Los Angeles: University of California.

McKane, William. 1970. *Proverbs: A New Approach.* Philadelphia: Westminster.

Miles, John A., Jr. 1976. "The Debut of the Bible as a Pagan Classic," *CSR Bulletin* 7/1:3–6.

Neumann, Gerhard, ed. 1976. *Der Aphorismus: zur Geschichte, zu den Formen und Möglichkeiten einer literarischen Gattung.* Darmstadt: Wissenschaftl. Buchgesellschaft. Einleitung: 1–18. (Abbreviated as *Aphorismus.*)

Rad, Gerhard von. 1962. *Old Testament Theology.* Vol. 1. New York: Harper and Row.

——— 1972. *Wisdom in Israel.* New York/Nashville: Abingdon.

Robertson, David. 1977. *The Old Testament and the Literary Critic.* Philadelphia: Fortress.

Schalk, Fritz. 1976. "Das Wesen des französischen Aphorismus," in Neumann, *Aphorismus,* 75–111. (Originally published in *Die neuere Sprachen* 41 [1933].)

Scott, R. B. Y. 1961. "Folk Proverbs of the Ancient Near East." *Transactions of the Royal Society of Canada* 15:47–56. (Reprinted in Crenshaw, *SAIW.*)

——— 1971. *The Way of Wisdom in the Old Testament.* New York: Macmillan.

Wittig, Susan. 1977. "A Theory of Multiple Meanings." *Semeia* 9:75–103.

6

A Theology of Proverbs

Roy B. Zuck

The Doctrine of Wisdom

Wisdom and creation order. Wisdom means being skillful and successful in one's relationships and responsibilities. It involves observing and following the Creator's principles of order in the moral universe. This order manifests God's wisdom, which is available to man. So to the extent man follows this order, he is wise. Heeding the wisdom of the Book of Proverbs, then, brings harmony to one's life. By contrast, failure to heed God's divine design results in disorder. Lack of compliance with God's wise ways brings unpleasant and disastrous consequences on oneself and others.

In identifying the wise with the righteous, and the unwise with the foolish, the Book of Proverbs demonstrates that wisdom is more than intellectual. It encompasses the moral and the religious. Two paths are set before the reader: the path (or conduct and character) of the righteous/wise, and the path (or conduct and character) of the wicked/foolish. Each path bears certain consequences. The path of wisdom leads to life, and the path of folly leads to death.

The value of wisdom. Because of its value to the character of the wise person, wisdom is likened to silver and hidden treasure (2:4). In fact its value exceeds that of gold, silver, or rubies (3:14–15; 8:10–11, 19; 16:16). The wise person understands what is right, just, and fair (2:9; 8:15–16), is protected from harm (2:8, 11–12, 16; 4:6; 6:24; 7:5; 14:3), and has prosperity and wealth (3:2, 16; 8:18, 21; 9:12; 14:24; 16:20; 21:20–21; 22:4), health and nourishment (3:8; 4:22), favor and a good reputation (3:4; 8:34–35; 13:15), honor (3:16, 35; 4:8–9; 8:18; 21:21), security and safety (1:33; 3:22–23; 4:12; 12:21; 22:3; 28:26), peace (1:33; 3:17–24), confidence (3:25–26), guidance (6:22), life (3:2, 16, 18, 22; 4:10, 22; 6:23; 8:35; 9:11; 10:16–17, 27; 11:19; 16:22; 19:23; 22:4),[1] and hope (23:18; 24:14).[2]

Others also benefit from an individual's wisdom. For example the wise person brings joy to his parents (10:1; 15:20; 23:15–16, 24–25; 27:11; 29:3). Righteous/wise living results in a tree of life (11:30; 13:12; 15:4; cf. 3:18), that is, like a tree it is a source of benefit to others. And wisdom is also a fountain of life (10:11; 13:14; 15:27; 16:22), bringing rejuvenation to others.

No wonder wisdom is to be sought after (2:3–4), attained (4:5, 7), loved (v. 6), chosen (v. 8), grasped and guarded (v. 13), heard (vv. 32–34), and found (v. 35). Wisdom is to be valued like a necklace (1:9; 3:3, 22; cf. 6:21) and a garland or crown on one's head (1:9; 4:9).

Similarly *Ma'at*, the Egyptian goddess of justice, order, and truth, is presented in ancient Egyptian literature as providing protection,[3] giving a garland or wreath of victory to the gods,[4] and is pictured as a chain around the neck of judges and the vizier.[5] In addition *Ma'at* carries an *ankh*, as the sign of life, in one hand and a scepter, as a symbol of riches and honor, in the other hand (cf. 3:16).[6]

---

1. "Life" may refer to length of years, the continuation of life, as in 3:2, 16; 9:11; 10:27, or to quality of life, as in 11:19; 19:23; 21:21. Walter Brueggemann refers to life in Proverbs as "all the assets—emotional, physical, psychological, social, spiritual—which permit joy and security and wholeness" (*In Man We Trust* [Richmond: John Knox, 1972], 15). Death, by contrast, may refer to physical loss of life (10:27), or figuratively to the loss of blessing in life.

2. These benefits of wisdom do not suggest so-called prosperity theology, which teaches the way to become wealthy and healthy is to serve God. The Book of Proverbs points up, instead, the normal though not guaranteed consequences of wisdom. Exceptions may occur, but these are not stated. Furthermore, wisdom was to be pursued for its own sake, not for the sake of its benefits. The benefits were bestowed as a by-product of acquiring wisdom. In addition, as Scott points out, other motivations for conduct, besides material rewards and punishments, are mentioned in Proverbs. These include the pleasure or displeasure of the Lord (12:22), honor or shame brought to one's parents (10:1), effect on others (10:12, 21; 11:10), and the desire for wisdom (12:1; 13:14) (R. B. Y. Scott, *Proverbs, Ecclesiastes,* The Anchor Bible [Garden City, N.Y.: Doubleday, 1965], 25).

3. Christa Kayatz, *Studien zu Proverbien 1–9* (Neukirchen-Vluyn: Neukirchener Verlag, 1966), 103.

4. Ibid., 112, n. 1.

5. Ibid., 108.

6. Ibid., 104.

Does wisdom always result in these and other blessings? The experience of many people seems to present a challenge to these assurances of long life, well-being, and prosperity. Three answers to this problem may be suggested. First, these statements present what is usually and normally true. Though not everyone who is "upright" (2:7) is protected from harm (vv. 7–8, 11), physical protection *is* often experienced more by the wise, godly person than the foolish, wicked person. Living wickedly leads to risk-taking, which often results in harm, a sense of insecurity, restlessness, and/or lack of honor. Even casual observations of wicked people confirm this fact. True, some exceptions may be noted, but the proverbs are pointing to what is normal and usual, what is recurring enough to be considered normative.

Second, many proverbs are intentionally written in contrastive modes to underscore the vast differences of conduct and consequences. This teaching device is designed to motivate toward proper action and away from improper action.

Third, circumstances may introduce exceptions to the statements otherwise seen as absolutes. Or one's own conduct may alter the outcome. The self-will or disobedience of a child may alter what would otherwise appear to be the statement of guarantee in Proverbs 22:6, "Train a child in the way he should go, and when he is old he will not turn from it." While this verse is *generally* true, folly, which "is bound up in the heart of the child" (v. 15), may introduce a situation which is an exception to the norm.

The personification of wisdom. Ascribing personal traits to inanimate objects or to abstract ideas is common in the Old Testament. Mountains singing and trees clapping their hands (Isa. 55:12), truth stumbling (59:14), and the tongue hating (Prov. 26:28) are examples of personification. It is not surprising to see wisdom personified in Proverbs. The fact that wisdom is personified as a woman is partly explained by the fact that the noun *ḥokmāh* is feminine. Another reason is that wisdom, like a woman, is said to be attractive. Just as a man may be attracted to and desire a woman's beauty, so he should respond to and desire wisdom. The personified figure of wisdom also heightens the contrast between wisdom and folly. Folly, also personified as a woman (9:13–18), seeks to attract male followers. Just as immoral women can lead men into illicit conduct and dire consequences ("death"), so folly can lead people to pursue improper conduct that results in defeat and death.

Wisdom is presented as a prophetess (1:20–23; 8:1–21), a sister (7:4), a child (8:22–31), and a hostess (9:1–6). As a prophetess, she cries out in the streets, where people are traveling, public squares, where people are buying and selling, and gateways, where business is transacted (1:20–21). She admonishes "simple ones" and "mockers" because of their love for naive ways and mockery of others, and "fools" because of their hatred of knowledge (v. 22). Because they fail to heed her rebuke and to learn from her (vv. 23–

25), she will ignore their cries for help when they are overtaken by calamity and distress (vv. 26–27). Their ignoring her cry will result in her ignoring their cry. Refusing to fear the Lord and spurning wisdom's advice (vv. 28–30), they will suffer the consequences of their actions ("the fruit of their ways," v. 31), including death (v. 32).

An intimate relationship with wisdom is suggested by wisdom's being personified as a sister (7:4). Being closely related to wisdom is a means of protection from the adulteress (v. 5). As one enjoys wisdom like a sister, he is deterred from the allurement of adultery. Wisdom, accompanied by godliness, is contrasted to adultery, the height of folly and wickedness.

Proverbs 8 is the classic chapter on personification of wisdom. Again wisdom, like a prophetess, calls out to the "simple" and the "foolish" (8:5), urging them to heed her words, which are true, just, and right (vv. 7–9), and priceless in value (vv. 10–11). She gives discretion (vv. 12–14), hatred of evil (v. 13), justice for rulers (vv. 15–16), and wealth, honor, and righteousness (vv. 17–21). Wisdom is to be loved (vv. 17–21), again suggesting the appropriateness of personifying wisdom as a woman.

Wisdom had a special role in God's creative work (8:22–31). She existed before the creation of the world (vv. 22–26), and she rejoiced as she by his side beheld him create the world (vv. 27–31). The fact that wisdom preceded the creation of the universe is shown by a plethora of phrases: "At the beginning of his work" and "before his deeds of old" in verse 22, and "from eternity," "from the beginning," and "before the world began" in verse 23. Wisdom existed when there were no oceans or springs, mountains or hills, or earth with its fields and dust (vv. 24–26). She was acquired (or created, v. 22), appointed (v. 23), and given birth (vv. 24–25).

Does the verb *qānāh* mean "to acquire" or "to create, to give birth to"? Elsewhere in Proverbs the verse means to acquire or possess ("get," 1:5; 4:7; 16:16; 23:23; "gains," 15:32; "get," 19:8). On the other hand the verb in Genesis 4:1 and Psalm 139:13 does seem to mean "to create." These two passages use this verb in a context of birth, which aligns with the references to wisdom being given birth in Proverbs 8:24–25. Therefore it may be preferable to render the verb *qānāh* by the word "create." Metaphorically, then, God "created" wisdom. It did not exist apart from him.

Continuing to speak in the first person, wisdom stated that, having existed *before* creation (8:24–26), she was present *at* creation (vv. 27–31). Wisdom witnessed the Lord's making the heavens (v. 27; Gen. 1:1–5) and also the separating of waters on the second day of creation (Prov. 8:27b–28; cf. Gen. 1:6–8) and the forming of the land and sea on the third day of creation (Prov. 8:29; Gen. 1:9–10).

Being "at his side" (Prov. 8:30), wisdom was intimately associated with the Lord as an *ʾāmôn*. This word is rendered "craftsman" (or "master craftsman" or "workman") by some interpreters[7] and "nursing child" by others.[8] Several factors indicate a preference for the latter translation. (1) Verses 30–31 refer to wisdom rejoicing, not working. God did the creative work. (2) The context of childbirth (vv. 22–25) suggests the translation "nursing child." (3) A verbal form of this word is used in Lamentations 4:5 to refer to those "brought up" or nursed as children. (4) Ma'at, the Egyptian goddess, is likened to a child playing before Re–Atum.[9] In chiasm, wisdom is said to be (a) "filled with delight," (b) rejoicing in God's presence, (c) rejoicing in God's world, and (d) delighting in mankind, the apex of his creative genius. Cavorting as a child, wisdom is pictured as being overjoyed with all God made.

Because of wisdom's ancestry, existing before creation, and because she witnessed the creation of the world (cf. Eliphaz's taunt against Job in Job 15:7–8), wisdom has unequaled authority in appealing to men to follow her. Those who listen to her and heed her ways are blessed and become wise. In Proverbs 8:32–34 the words "listen" and "blessed" are used alternately ("listen," v. 32; "blessed," v. 32; "listen," v. 33; "blessed," v. 34; "listens," v. 34). Finding wisdom brings life (v. 35) and rejecting wisdom brings harm and ultimately death (v. 36).

When God created the world, wisdom was at his side, that is, his creative work was a wise work. There was nothing foolish about what he did. He made it all "in wisdom." This truth is also stated in 3:19–20. This again points to the fact, as stated earlier, that wisdom theology is creation theology. The created world was brought into existence by the wise God.

Not a separate, independent entity (hypostasis),[10] nor a mythical goddess,[11] nor an adumbration of Christ, wisdom in Proverbs 8 is best seen as a poetic personification of God's attribute of wisdom.[12]

In Proverbs 9:1–6 wisdom is personified as a virtuous hostess. Having built a house of seven pillars (v. 1), that is, a large, spacious house suggestive of prosperity, and having prepared a banquet (v. 2), she instructed her maids to call out (cf. 1:21; 8:1–3) to the naive to share her banquet (9:4–5). By doing so, they would live (enjoy life to the fullest) and have understanding (v. 6).

7. For example, Mitchell Dahood, "Proverbs 8:22–31: Translation and Commentary," *Catholic Biblical Quarterly* 30 (1968): 518–19. 'Āmôn is thought to be from an Akkadian loan-word *ummānu*.

8. For example, Crawford H. Toy, *A Critical and Exegetical Commentary on the Book of Proverbs*, The International Critical Commentary (Edinburgh: T. and T. Clark, 1899), 177–79.

9. Kayatz, *Studien zu Proverbien 1–9*, 93–98.

10. This view is proposed by Helmer Ringgren, *Word and Wisdom: Studies in the Hypostatization of Divine Qualities and Functions in the Ancient Near East* (Lund: Hakan Ohlssons Boktryekei, 1947).

11. This view is suggested by William F. Albright, "Some Canaanite-Phoenician Sources of Hebrew Wisdom," *Vetus Testamentum Supplement* 3 (1960): 8.

12. Von Rad, *Wisdom in Israel*, 144–70.

Three lines (vv. 7–8a) point up the dangers of rebuking sinners, whereas three lines (vv. 8b–9) point up, by contrast, the response of a wise person to rebuke and instruction. Wisdom's final words in 9:10–12 summarized several truths in chapters 1–9. (1) The essence of being wise is fearing the Lord. (2) Being wise results in blessings, including long life. (3) The opposite of being wise— actively rejecting wisdom as a mocker—brings suffering. Lady Wisdom is then contrasted with Lady Folly, who also invites men to her house but who is bois- terous, deceptive, and disastrous (9:13–18). Again death results from folly (v. 18), whereas life comes from wisdom (v. 6).

Some Bible students also see wisdom personified by the "wife of noble character" in Proverbs 31:10–31. This is based on statements made about this wife that are familiar to statements made earlier about wisdom.[13] The wife "is more precious than rubies" (31:10) as is wisdom (3:15; 8:11; cf. 8:10, 19; 16:16). The noble wife laughs (in confidence and security) at any future threat (31:25), and wisdom too laughs at disaster (1:26). Her lamp (*nēr*) does not go out at night (31:18), and the light (*nēr*) of the righteous continues to shine (13:9). In 31:10–31 she is a wife of virtue and industry, and in 9:1–6 wisdom is pictured as a young, virtuous woman preparing a banquet for young men. In 31:26 the noble wife gives instruction, and numerous passages in Proverbs 1–9 refer to wisdom giving instruction.

It is also argued that the position of the passage, at the end of the Book of Proverbs, suggests that the noble wife represents wisdom, the topic of the book. Because wisdom was personified in several other passages in Proverbs, it is argued that the woman here is also a personification of wisdom. And the position of the passage makes a fitting inclusio, it is suggested, with chapters 1–9, in which wisdom is personified as a woman. This view, however, has sev- eral problems. (1) The activities of the wife suggest more than wisdom. When wisdom is personified in chapters 1–9, she is not pictured as having a husband (31:11), or as one who sews (vv. 13, 19, 22), cooks (v. 15), purchases food and real estate (vv. 14–16), plants (v. 17), trades (v. 18), sells (v. 24), provides for the various needs of her husband, children, and servants (vv. 15, 21, 27), and helps the needy (v. 20). She is energetic, hard-working, well-to-do, com- passionate, strong, confident, and spiritual. (2) Wisdom in chapters 1–9 is not pictured as a mother, as is the woman in 31:15, 28. (3) The noble woman speaks with wisdom (v. 26). If this woman is wisdom, then the verse would be stating that "wisdom speaks with wisdom." This seems to make no sense.

Therefore it seems preferable to see the woman in 31:10–31 as a wife and mother. She is a *wise* woman, not wisdom personified. This finds support in verse 30, "a woman who fears the Lord is to be praised." Since fearing the Lord is the essence of wisdom, the ideal woman, the one who fears God, is

---

13. Thomas P. McCreesh, "Wisdom as Wife: Proverbs 31:10–13," *Revue Biblique* (1985): 41–43.

indeed wise. She is a model or example of a wise woman. In contrast to a foolish, adulterous woman (2:16–19; 5:20; 6:23–34; 7:4–27) this woman is faithful to her family and is therefore praised (31:30–31) by her children and her
husband (v. 28) and the public (v. 31). As a wise woman, she is in contrast to
"woman Folly" (9:13–18). Rather than a personification of wisdom, the
woman in 31:10–31 is an embodiment or model of wisdom, a woman who is
wise because she is living skillfully.

The Doctrine of God

His names. The name *Yahweh* is used of God in Proverbs eighty-seven
times, *ʾĔlōhîm* occurs only seven times (2:5, 17; 3:4; 14:31; 25:2; 30:5, 9)
and *ʾĔlôăh* occurs once (30:5). God is also called the Holy One (9:10; 30:3),
the Righteous One (21:12), the Defender (23:11), and the Maker (14:31;
17:5; 22:2).

His attributes. The attributes of God presented in the Book of Proverbs include his *holiness* ("the Holy One," 9:10; 30:3), *omnipresence* (5:21; 15:3),
omnipotence (as the Creator of the universe [3:19–20; 8:22–31; 30:4] and of
man's ears and eyes [20:12; 29:13], and the Maker of the poor [14:31; 17:5;
22:2] and the rich [22:2]), and *omniscience* (in examining and knowing death
[15:11], man's conduct [5:21; 21:2], man's motives [16:2], and heart [17:3;
20:27; 24:12], and in seeing good and evil [15:3], and those who gloat over
others' misfortunes [4:16–17]).

God also possesses *sovereignty,* working everything for his purposes (16:4;
19:21), even determining man's decisions (16:33) and course of action (v. 9),
directing the hearts (or interests and decisions) of kings (21:1), and superseding every plan of mankind (19:21; 21:30). God has *wisdom* (3:19–20) and
justice. In his justice (29:26) he is the Righteous One (21:12) who thwarts
and punishes the wicked (3:33; 10:3; 11:8; 21:12; 22:12), the crafty (12:2),
and the proud (15:25), and he upholds the poor and afflicted (22:22–23;
23:10–11). His justice is equitable for he repays man in accord with his conduct (20:22; 24:12), and rewards the righteous (19:17; 25:22).

In his justice God hates perversity (3:32; 11:20), pride (6:17; 16:5), lying
(6:17–19; 12:22), violence ("hands that shed innocent blood," 6:17), wicked
scheming and actions (v. 18), dissension (v. 19), dishonesty (11:1; 20:10,
23), hypocrisy ("the sacrifice of the wicked," 15:8; 21:27; the prayers of the
lawless, 28:9), and injustice (17:15).

God's *personality* is evident in that he loves and disciplines (3:12), hates
(6:16–19), delights (in honest business dealings, 11:1; in the conduct of the
blameless, v. 20 [cf. 16:7a]; in people who are truthful, 12:22; and in the
prayers and righteous conduct of the godly, 15:8–9).

His actions. The preceding paragraphs show that God's attributes reveal a
number of his actions. These include creating, seeing, examining, purposing,

influencing, directing, punishing, defending, rewarding, hating, loving, and delighting. Other actions include giving wisdom (1:7; 2:6), giving grace to the humble (3:34), protecting the righteous (2:7–8; 3:26; 10:29; 14:26; 15:25; 18:10; 19:23; 29:25; 30:5), providing for the righteous (10:3), delivering the righteous (20:22), blessing the righteous (3:33; 10:22; 12:2), giving life (10:27), giving men prudent wives (18:22; 19:14), directing those who trust him (3:5–6), giving people words to say (16:1), guiding man's ways ("steps," v. 9; 20:24) and decisions (16:33), and hearing the prayers of the righteous (15:29).

The Doctrine of Man

Proverbs frequently uses the metaphor of the way or the path, as already stated. By metonymy a way or path came to represent the conduct of the person walking in that direction or along that path.[14] This figure of speech suggests a choice, a decision as to which one of two kinds of life a person will lead. The two contrasting invitations—to follow wise conduct or to follow foolish conduct (8:1; 9:1–6, 13–18)—call for a choice. This figure also calls attention to the contrasting terminations of the paths, the resulting consequences of the two kinds of conduct.

The two paths are those of righteous living and wicked living, which are also identified as wise conduct and foolish conduct. All people are either righteous/wise or wicked/foolish. This path of righteousness or wisdom is the path of virtue, whereas the path of wickedness or folly is the path of vice. The lifestyle of the former leads to blessing, and the lifestyle of the latter leads to bane. Since wise living means following the principles or rules of God's order or pattern for life, harmony or blessing comes to the extent a person heeds the admonitions and observations in Proverbs pertaining to the path of wisdom. Conversely, as a person neglects or disdains wise living, pursuing the foolish path, he experiences disorder and chaos.

Wickedness takes a person on a path of darkness and crookedness (2:13–15; 4:19). It is a deviant path, leading to loss of blessing, including death (2:18; 8:36; 11:19; 14:12). Righteousness, however, takes a person along a path that is straight (2:13; 4:26) and bright (v. 18). It leads to fullness of life (2:20–21; 8:35).

Proverbs points out the many different circumstances and relationships of the righteous/wise course of action, and many different contrasting circumstances and relationships of the wicked/foolish course of action. The righteous/wise path begins with a right relationship and response to God. Fearing the Lord is the starting point of wisdom and also the controlling principle or

14. "Way" and "ways" occur sixty times; "path" and "paths," twenty-nine times; and "walk," "walks," and "walking," seventeen times.

essence and heart of wisdom. The righteous/wise way of life begins by fearing God, that is, recognizing his superiority, and responding in awe, humility, worship, love, trust, and obedience to God. Fearing God results in life (10:27; 14:27; 19:23; 22:4). Trusting God, part of the response in fearing him, is enjoined several times in Proverbs. It results in guidance (3:5), prosperity (28:25), and safety (29:25). Fearing God also involves committing one's conduct to the Lord (16:3), and in hating and spurning evil (3:7; 8:13; 16:6; cf. v. 17).

Several terms are used in Proverbs to describe the foolish person. *Petî,* used fourteen times in Proverbs,[15] means one who is naive, gullible, open to influence, easily persuaded. *Kᵉsîl,* used forty-nine times in Proverbs and twenty-one times elsewhere, means to be stupid or thickheaded. The word *ᵉwîl,* found nineteen times in Proverbs[16] and several times elsewhere, speaks of a fool who is coarse, hardened, or obstinate in his ways. *Nābāl,* used only three times in Proverbs (17:7, 21; 30:22) and nine times elsewhere, describes a person lacking ethical or spiritual perception, one who is morally insensitive. *Ḥăsar lēb,* "lacking in heart," means to be without any sense. It occurs only ten times, all of them in Proverbs,[17] where the NIV renders it "lacks judgment" or "lacking in judgment."

Moral uprightness, extolled in numerous ways in Proverbs, stems from being rightly related to God (by fearing, trusting, and obeying him) and being wise. Apart from a right relationship to God, moral excellence is not possible. One of the virtues commended in Proverbs is *diligence* (10:4–5; 12:24, 27; 14:23; 24:27), with its benefits of profit (10:4; 14:23), food (12:11; 20:13; 27:18; 28:19), responsibility (12:24), self-satisfaction (13:4), ease (15:19), and honor (22:29). Another quality commended in Proverbs is *humility,* which increases one's wisdom (11:2) and brings honor (15:33; 29:23), wealth and life (22:4), and grace (3:34). Being "lowly in spirit" is to be preferred to having wealth with proud people (16:19).

Patience and *self-control* are desirable virtues for they are associated with wisdom and understanding (14:29; 17:27; 19:11; 29:11), and they help calm quarrels (15:18). *Courage* (28:1); *love* (10:12; 16:6; 20:28); *reliability* (11:13; 25:13); *truthfulness* (12:17, 19, 22; 14:5, 25; 16:13); *kindness* (11:17) to animals (12:10) and to the poor and needy (14:21, 31; 19:17; 31:9, 20); *generosity* (11:25; 22:9); *honesty* in giving witness in court (12:17), in answering questions (24:26), and in business transactions (11:1; 16:11; 20:10, 23); *teachableness* (10:8, 17; 12:1; 13:1, 13, 18; 15:5, 31–32; 19:20);

15. 1:4, 22, 32; 7:7; 8:5; 9:4, 6, 16; 14:15, 18; 19:25; 21:11; 22:3; 27:12.
16. 1:7; 7:22; 10:8, 10, 14, 21; 11:29; 12:15–16; 14:3, 9; 15:5; 16:22; 17:28; 20:3; 24:7; 27:3, 22; 29:9.
17. 6:32; 7:7; 9:4, 16; 10:13; 11:12; 12:11; 15:21; 17:18; 24:30.

moderation in eating (23:1–3; 24:13; 25:16, 27), and *sobriety* (20:1; 23:20–21; 31:4)—all these are characteristics of the wise and godly person.

In addition, Proverbs says much about the proper use of one's *words*. Right words can encourage and uplift (10:11, 21; 12:18, 25; 18:21), impart wisdom (10:13; 15:7; 16:21, 23; 20:15), and protect (21:23). Words should be spoken with restraint (10:19; 11:12; 13:3; 15:28; 16:23; 17:27; 21:23; 29:20), and should be fitting or appropriate to the occasion (10:32; 15:1, 23; 16:24; 25:11, 15).

Many vices or undesirable qualities discussed in Proverbs present exact opposites of the foregoing virtues. For example, opposite to diligence stands *laziness*, which is strongly chided (22:13; 26:13–15) because it results in poverty (6:10–11; 10:4; 13:4; 20:13), disgrace to one's parents (10:5), frustration (v. 26), hunger (12:27; 19:15, 24; 20:4; 21:25–26; 26:15), problems (15:19; 24:33–34), and even death (21:25). *Pride* is condemned repeatedly as a sin (21:4). God hates pride (6:16–17; 16:5). It leads to disgrace (11:2), loss of one's possessions (15:25), one's downfall (16:18; 18:12; 29:23), quarrels and strife (13:10; 28:25), and punishment (16:5). Pride is foolish (14:16; 26:12; 30:32). Seeking one's honor or boasting of one's accomplishments is detestable (25:27; 27:2).

Anger and loss of temper are repeatedly denounced as foolish (14:16–17, 29; 15:18; 19:19; 22:24–25; 29:11, 22), for a person without self-control is vulnerable to many kinds of problems, much as a city without walls in Bible times was insecure and subject to enemy attacks (25:28).

The wrong uses of one's *words* include lying (26:28), which God hates (6:16–17; 12:22); slander (10:18; 30:10); gossip, which betrays confidences (11:13; 20:19), separates friends (16:28; 17:9), and is not easily forgotten ("they go down to a man's inmost parts," 18:8; 26:22); chattering (10:19; 19:7; 20:19); false witnessing (12:17; 14:5, 25; 19:5, 28; 21:8; 25:18); mocking (13:1; 15:12; 22:10; 24:9; 30:17); perverse or harsh talk (10:13, 31–32; 12:18; 13:3; 15:1, 28; 19:1, 28); boasting (17:7; 25:14; 27:2); quarreling (17:14, 19; 20:3); flattery (26:28; 28:23; 29:5); and foolish talk (14:7; 15:2, 14; 18:6–7).

Greed (15:27; 28:25; 29:4), *envy* and *jealousy* (3:31; 6:34; 14:30; 23:17; 24:1, 19; 27:4), *drunkenness* (20:1; 21:17; 23:20–21, 29–35; 31:4–7), *hypocrisy* (10:18; 12:20; 13:7; 21:27; 23:6–7; 26:18–19, 24–26; 27:6), *oppression* of the poor (3:27–28; 13:23; 14:31; 22:22–23; 28:3, 8; 29:7; 31:4–5, 9), *injustice* (10:2; 16:8; 17:15, 26; 18:5), *bribery* (6:35; 15:27; 17:8, 23; 21:14; 29:4), and acquiring money by *dishonesty* (10:2; 13:11; 28:20, 22) are all condemned.

The godly, wise person also honors God in societal relationships, including the family. Husbands and wives are to be faithful to each other (5:15–19; 31:10–11), assiduously avoiding sexual misconduct or immorality (2:16–19;

5:20; 6:23–29, 32–35; 7:4–27; 22:14; 23:27–28; 30:20). Wives are not to be contentious or quarreling (19:13; 21:9, 19; 25:24; 27:15–16). A disgraceful wife is a problem (12:4), but a prudent, noble wife is a blessing from God (12:4; 18:22; 19:14; 31:10). For a woman, being wise and fearing God is far more virtuous than possessing physical beauty (11:22; 31:30).

Sons are challenged to heed parental teaching (1:8–9; 4:1–9, 20; 5:11–12; 6:20–22; 13:1; 15:5, 32; 19:27; 23:22), including the instruction given by their mothers (1:8; 6:20; 31:1). Child discipline, while painful for parents to apply, benefits the child (3:12; 13:24; 19:18; 22:6, 15; 23:13–14; 29:15, 17). Wise, obedient sons brings joy to their parents (10:1; 15:20; 23:15, 24; 27:11; 29:3), whereas unwise, unruly children cause parental grief (17:21, 25; 19:13; 28:7; 29:15). Children who disregard or dishonor their parents will suffer serious consequences (11:29; 15:20; 19:26; 20:20; 28:24; 30:11, 17). Parents who live righteously give their children a sense of personal security (14:26; 20:7).

Grandparents who lead upright lives can be glad for long life and grand-children (13:22; 16:31; 17:6; 20:29). Even servants in the home can benefit from being wise (14:35; 17:2) and diligent (27:18). Outside the family, one must choose his friends carefully (12:26; 22:24). True friends are faithful (17:17; 18:24; 27:10), can give wise counsel (27:9), and even, when needed, reproof (27:6). Gossip, on the other hand, can spoil friendships (16:28; 17:9). Neighbors, too, should be treated properly, avoiding betrayal (25:8–10), false testimony (24:28; 25:18), deception (26:18–19), thoughtlessness (27:14), and flattery (29:5). Getting advice from others marks a person wise (12:15; 13:10; 19:20) for it can lead to success in one's endeavors (11:14; 15:22; 20:18; 24:6).

Friends and associates must be chosen carefully. The wise avoid being around fools (13:20; 14:7; 17:12; 23:9), the proud (16:19), talkers (20:19), the wicked (1:10–19; 22:5; 24:1–2), the rebellious (24:21) and violent (3:31; 16:29), drunkards (23:20), gluttons (28:7), thieves (29:24), and immoral women (2:16–19; 5:8; 6:24–26; 29:3).

Proverbs also includes standards for kings and rulers. Their qualifications include honesty (16:13), humility (25:6), justice (16:10, 12; 25:5; 29:4; 31:8–9), reliability (20:28), sobriety (31:4–5), and self-control (16:14; 19:12; 20:2; 28:15).

Any society must transact business using money as a means of exchange. Therefore it is not surprising that Proverbs, with its emphasis on interpersonal societal relationships, says much about business and finances. Hunger (16:26) and profit (14:23) motivate people to work. Money provides a degree of pro-tection (like a "fortified city," 10:15; 18:11), keeps one alive (10:16), attracts friends (14:20; 19:4), and grants a degree of influence (22:7). However, the power of money is limited, for it cannot divert God's wrath (11:4), and it is temporary (23:4–5), especially if it is gained dishonestly (10:2; 13:11; 20:17; 21:6) or foolishly (17:16). Money acquired by wicked means brings trouble (1:13–14, 18–19; 15:6), whereas money properly acquired brings long life.

Wealth is no substitute for integrity (10:9; 16:8, 19; 19:1, 22; 22:1; 28:6), fear of the Lord (15:16), or wisdom (16:16). True, using money to bribe others may be influential (17:8; 21:14), but bribery is wrong (15:27; 17:23; 29:14). Money should be shared with the poor and needy (11:24–25; 14:31; 19:17; 21:13; 22:9, 22; 28:27), for the one who does so honors God and in turn will be blessed. Get-rich-quick approaches are condemned (20:21; 28:20, 22), as is partiality (18:5; 24:23; 28:21), unfair pricing of products (11:1; 16:11; 20:10, 23), and providing guarantees for loans that have exorbitant interest rates (6:1–5; 11:15; 17:18; 20:16; 22:26–27).[18]

Emotions addressed in Proverbs include anxiety (12:25), disappointment (13:12), satisfaction from hopes fulfilled (13:12, 19), and joy and heartache (14:10, 13, 30; 17:22; 18:14; 25:20; 27:6). Man's heart (his inner being) is referred to seventy times in Proverbs. "Soul" is mentioned fourteen times; "spirit," ten times; and "body," four times.

In its theology, the Book of Proverbs, amazingly broad and inclusive in its topics, clearly delineates the two paths (kinds of conduct) of wisdom/righteousness and folly/wickedness.[19] And it does so with startling variety, intricately spelling out the characteristics and consequences of the two paths. No one can be truly wise (skillful in living) without fearing the Lord and heeding the direct commands, stern admonitions, keen observations, and probing maxims presented in the Book of Proverbs.

18. These verses against putting up "security" for someone else's loan do not say borrowing or lending is wrong. Instead they speak against being held accountable for others' loans with high interest rates. In Israel lending was a means of helping a fellow Israelite, but interest was not to be charged (Exod. 22:25; Lev. 25:35–37). Loans to non-Israelites could include interest (Deut. 23:19–20), but not with excessively high rates (Prov. 28:8; cf. Ezek. 22:12).

19. Other topics not mentioned in this chapter but discussed in Proverbs include, but are not limited to, death, encouragement, enemies, failure, prayer, purity, reputation, sacrifices, success, and worry.

7

BASIC TERMINOLOGY OF WISDOM, FOLLY, RIGHTEOUSNESS, AND WICKEDNESS

Eldon G. Woodcock

A major purpose of the Book of Proverbs is to motivate its readers to apply the ways and principles of wisdom to every dimension of their lives. Several terms describe different aspects of wisdom, folly, righteousness, and wickedness. Overlapping in meaning, some terms within each category are at times virtually synonymous. We shall examine for each word its basic range of meanings, distinctive nuances, and usage in Proverbs.

The Vocabulary of Wisdom

Wisdom

Several Hebrew words, *ḥākām* and cognates, describe being "wise," "skill-ful," "prudent." These words occur 101 times in Proverbs and define the central theme—wisdom.

Wisdom involves a right attitude and approach to all areas of life. In spiritual life, it includes a commitment to follow the teachings of the holy and righteous God who expects his people to reflect his qualities, and a moral commitment to do what is right and to avoid what is wrong. In secular life, wisdom involves prudence, skills in the arts and various types of work, administrative ability, and development of strong personal relationships. In all of these areas, wisdom enables us to adapt what we know so we can do effectively what we do.

Readers are often commanded to obtain wisdom as their top priority (4:7). One obtains wisdom by observing (6:6), associating with the wise (13:20), accepting instruction (19:20) and commands (10:8), being corrected by rebukes (15:31) and, if necessary, the rod of correction (29:15).

The Lord who used his wisdom in creation (3:19) gives wisdom, knowledge, and understanding (2:6). The fear of the Lord is the beginning of wisdom (9:10), teaches wisdom (15:33), and motivates one to wisely avoid evil (14:16). In fact, there is no mere human wisdom or plan that can succeed against the Lord (21:30).

The wise maintain a right attitude (23:19), seek knowledge (18:15), store it (10:14), commend it (15:2), and spread it (15:7). They are discerning (16:21), prudent (14:8), righteous (10:31), humble (11:2), understanding (10:23), and accept advice (13:10).

Wisdom is rewarding (9:12) and a fountain of life (13:14). It provides guidance (4:11), protection (28:26), and healing (12:18). It enables people to speak wisely (31:26) and to appease anger by keeping themselves under control (29:8, 11). The wise win people (11:30), obtain honor (3:35), wealth (14:24), and power (24:5). There is no material benefit or monetary value that can even begin to be comparable to the tremendous privilege of possessing wisdom (8:11; 16:16).

Virtually synonymous to these words for wisdom are the Hebrew words (*śekel*) and cognates. They picture a thorough understanding of how to integrate the relevant thoughts and facts to generate a wise, prudent, and successful course of action.

Understanding or Discernment

Several Hebrew words, *bîn* and cognates, include the ideas of "understanding," "discernment," "perception," and "insight." These words occur sixty-six times in Proverbs. Their key idea is to come to an understanding by discerning and choosing between such alternatives as good and evil, right and wrong, true and false. Understanding is received as a gift from God, yet it is to be diligently sought by those who would be discerning.

The Book of Proverbs was designed to motivate and to enable its readers to attain wisdom (1:2). Wisdom exhorts us to gain (understand) prudence (8:5), to obtain understanding (4:7), and to follow its ways (9:6).

Understanding or discernment is very closely related to wisdom. These terms overlap each other, at times being almost equivalent in meaning. The wise are called discerning (16:21). The discerning person perceives that the teachings of wisdom are right (8:9) and delights in them (10:23). He keeps wisdom in view (17:24), possesses it (14:33), expresses it in his conversation (10:13), and discerns human purposes (20:5). The discerning are urged to get guidance (1:5) and acquire knowledge when rebuked (19:25). Knowledge comes easily to the discerning who seek it (14:6).

Understanding has an important role in the spiritual, ethical, and social realms. Knowledge of God is understanding (9:10) which the Lord gives (2:6). By wisdom and understanding, the Lord created the heavens and the earth (3:19). There is no human wisdom or insight that can succeed against the Lord (21:30). Thus we are to trust in the Lord and not lean on our own understanding (3:5). The discerning understand the fear of the Lord (2:5).

The discerning keep the law (28:7) and understand justice (28:5b). Understanding involves a straight course (15:21), patience (14:29), and appropriate restraint (11:12). God discerns (or "weighs") the inner thoughts and motivations of a person (24:12). People with understanding are blessed (3:13) and protected (2:11). Understanding is far more valuable than vast riches (16:16). For he who cherishes understanding prospers (19:8).

Knowledge

The Hebrew words, *yāda* and cognates, occur over eighty times in Proverbs. They primarily mean "knowledge" but include "perception," "discernment," "wisdom," and "knowing people." They cover many facets of knowledge, especially those obtained through the physical senses and experience.

These words describe both knowledge by God and about God. The Lord used his knowledge in creation (3:20) and knows people's thoughts (24:12). The Lord gives knowledge to man (2:6). Fearing the Lord is the beginning of knowledge (1:7) and is equivalent to knowing the Lord (2:5). Those who know him are to acknowledge him (3:6). In some cases the verb may mean "cause to know"; for example, to "teach" (22:19).

Knowledge is often associated with similar and overlapping terms. Those who would be wise are urged to gain (know) understanding (4:1). Discerning people seek knowledge (15:14) and acquire it (18:15) easily (14:6), even occasionally from a rebuke (19:25). Wise men gain knowledge through instruction (21:11), store that knowledge (10:14), commend it (15:2), and spread it (15:7). The converse is also true. For knowledgeable people discern words of wisdom to be faultless (8:9). The Book of Proverbs enables people to attain (know) wisdom and discipline (1:2). Closely associated with knowledge are discretion (1:4), wisdom (8:12), discipline (12:1), and counsel (22:20). The prudent man possesses and uses knowledge (13:16). A righteous man learns when taught (made to know, 9:9). He uses his knowledge to avoid the destructive talk of the godless (11:9). He knows what is fitting (10:32). He cares (knows) about justice for the poor (29:7).

A man of knowledge increases his strength (24:5) and uses his words with restraint (17:27). A knowledgeable ruler maintains order (28:2). Zeal is undesirable without knowledge (19:2). Knowledge is pleasant (2:10) and more valuable than huge quantities of money (8:10) and rubies (20:15). Thus, knowledge is to be preserved (5:2). The ideas of wisdom and knowledge overlap because both concepts involve a person's effective functioning in relationships with God, family, and other people. In Proverbs, what a person knows generally produces knowledgeable behavior; what he does reflects what he knows.

Discretion

The Hebrew words, *mᵉzimmâ* and cognates, describe making plans—both good and evil. They often picture people with evil plans (30:32), evil intent (21:27), foolish schemes (24:9), and evil conduct, perhaps as a result of evil plans (10:23). They describe crafty men as condemned by the Lord (12:2), hated (14:17), and plotting evil (24:8).

The singular form of *mᵉzimmâ* pictures discretion, that is, being careful about what a person says and does, as a result of perceptive planning that lies behind wise actions. It is a quality of wisdom (8:12) that a person should maintain (5:2), since it provides protection (2:11).

Prudence

The Hebrew words, *ʾārum* and cognates, picture being prudent—using common sense and sound judgment. Prudence is closely associated with wisdom (8:12). A prudent man keeps his knowledge to himself (12:23) and is crowned with knowledge (14:18), which he uses (13:16). Giving thought to his ways (14:8), he takes refuge when he perceives danger (22:3). He overlooks an insult (12:16) and heeds correction (15:5). The words rendered "prudence" and "discretion" overlap in their meanings and are, at times, virtually synonymous.

Advice

The Hebrew words, *ʿēsâ* and cognates, convey the ideas of "advice" or "counsel" based upon a carefully developed plan. The Lord's purpose or plan must succeed (19:21). The earnest counsel of a friend is pleasant and valuable (27:9). Counsel is a property of wisdom (8:14). The wise listen to advice (13:10) on which they base their plans (20:18). Promoters of peace experience joy (12:20). Sound advice produces victory in battle (11:14) and success in other enterprises (15:22). That is why it is foolish to ignore wise counsel (1:30–31).

Discipline

The Hebrew words, *mûsār* and cognates, picture "corrective discipline" that results in instruction. This correction may include chastisement. They describe God's disciplining his children in their covenant relationship to him and parents' disciplining their children. Discipline lays the foundation for developing wisdom, knowledge, and understanding.

The fear of the Lord produces the disciplined instruction that leads a person to wisdom (15:33). Those who love discipline love knowledge (12:1). Readers are urged to listen to instruction (4:1), to accept it (19:20), and to apply themselves to learning through it (23:12). For following discipline is the way to life (6:23). The Book of Proverbs was written to enable people to acquire discipline (1:2–3). People need to acquire discipline (23:23) by giving it top priority, to hold on to it (4:13), and then to be sure to discipline their children (13:24). For the rod of discipline will remove folly from a child's heart (22:15).

The dangers of ignoring discipline include despising oneself (15:32), leaving the path of knowledge (19:27), and being led astray by one's folly (5:23), producing the results of poverty and shame (13:18). The wise do not despise the Lord's discipline (3:11).

Rebuke

The Hebrew words, *tôkaḥat* and cognates, mean "rebuke," "reproof," "correction." The purposes of a rebuke are to expose a person's sin, to bring that person to repentance, and to correct his ethical or social behavior to conform to the standards of wisdom and righteousness.

The wise teacher urges his readers not to resent the Lord's rebuke (3:11–12). One who heeds correction has honor (13:18), prudence (15:5), and understanding (15:32). For the rod of correction imparts wisdom (29:15) and makes wise those who listen (15:31). That is why the wise man loves the one who rebukes him (9:8) and the discerning man gains knowledge by it (19:25). Thus, it is valuable (25:12). An open rebuke is better than hidden love (27:5), for the corrections of discipline are the way to life (6:23).

Teaching

The Hebrew noun, *tôrâ,* means "teaching" or "instruction." God's revealed instruction for the lives of his people Israel governs every area—spiritual, moral, social, civil, political, financial—and is called the Law, which is recorded in Exodus through Deuteronomy. But in its broader sense of teaching, the *tôrâ* comprises the entire OT. Therefore, it includes not only the Law, but also history, illustrations, prophecy, and the sort of advice that is recorded in Proverbs. In the Book of Proverbs, *tôrâ* refers to the teachings of wisdom. It makes no specific reference to the law of Moses, although it may include it in such references as 29:18.

Wise teachings are described as a light (6:23) and as a fountain of life (13:14). The wise wife (31:26) consistently presents them. Readers are urged to guard wise teachings as their most valuable possession (7:2). Those who follow wise teachings are blessed (29:18), discerning (28:7a), and resist the wicked (28:4b). Readers are commanded neither to forget (3:1) nor to forsake (4:2) wise parental teachings. Those who do forsake them find even their prayers to be detestable to the Lord (28:9).

Command

The Hebrew noun, *miṣwâ,* means command. Although often used in the OT to refer to the commandments revealed by God to define Israel's covenant obligations, in Proverbs it involved the instruction given by the teachers of wisdom. It indicates the authority behind the command, whether that of God, parent, or teacher. The wise teacher urges his students to absorb and obey his commands (2:1; 6:20), which are a lamp (6:23). He who respects a command is rewarded (13:13); he who accepts commands is wise (10:8). He who obeys instructions is guarding his life (19:16).

The Vocabulary of Folly

Three Hebrew words are rendered "fool." We have distinguished among them by indicating in parenthesis the Hebrew root from which "fool" comes.

Fool or Foolish (kᵉsîl)

The Hebrew word, *kᵉsîl,* pictures one who is foolish, stupid, and inclined to make wrong choices. His decisions move him in a direction that may provide immediate pleasure, but will eventually lead to ruin and destruction. He is mentally dull, morally insensitive, arrogant, disrespectful, deceitful, and untrustworthy.

Fools lack knowledge (14:7), prudence, and understanding (8:5). They reject wisdom, knowledge, and discernment (1:22; 18:2; 23:9). Fools express their folly (12:23) repeatedly (26:11). Complacent (1:32), they trust in themselves (28:26). Money (17:16) and provisions (21:20) are useless to fools who consume them rapidly. Luxury (19:10) and honor (26:1, 8) are also inappropriate. Fools are useless as messengers (26:6) and are generally unemployable (26:10). Fools enjoy evil (10:23) and hate to turn away from it (13:19). Their folly is deception (14:8). Speaking in haste (29:20), they spread slander (10:18), speak perversely (19:1), express uncontrolled anger (29:11), and are hotheaded and reckless (14:16). Such talk is their undoing (18:7). It produces strife (18:6) and makes them dangerous (17:12). Fools are shamed (3:35) and suffer harm (13:20), including beatings (19:29) and destruction (1:32).

Folly, Fool, Foolish (ʾĕwîl)

The Hebrew words, ʾĕwîl and cognates, also convey the idea of being a fool or foolish. These words overlap kᵉsîl in meaning. The ʾĕwîl seems somewhat worse than the kᵉsîl, for it stresses spiritual and moral deficiency, even moral insolence more than stupidity. However, this distinction is a matter of emphasis rather than a major difference, since both terms include these qualities.

Fools are considered wise and discerning if they remain silent (17:28). But in reality wisdom is too high and unattainable for a fool (24:7), so he becomes a servant to the wise (11:29) because fools despise and reject wisdom and discipline (1:7). The way of a fool seems right to him (12:15). Lacking judgment, he delights in folly (15:21).

Folly is bound up in a child's heart (22:15). It is extremely difficult to remove from fools (27:22). Instead, fools feed on folly (15:14), produce it (14:24), expose it (13:16), gush it (15:2), and repeat their foolish acts (26:11). Fools are often quarrelsome (20:3), quick tempered (14:17, 29), and very burdensome (27:3). They answer before listening (18:13). The folly of fools is deception (14:8) that leads them astray (5:23). They develop sinful schemes (24:9) and mock at making amends for sin (14:9). Fools die as a result of their poor judgment (10:21). They are punished (16:22), ruined (19:3), and bring disaster (17:12).

Fool (nābāl)

The Hebrew words, nābāl and cognates, mean to be "foolish," "stupid," "senseless," and "disgraceful." They include the ideas of insensitivity to the Lord, moral apathy, and rejecting what is reasonable. They overlap the other Hebrew words for fool, ʾĕwîl and kᵉsîl. But the nābāl words emphasize strongly the disgraceful, boorish, and domineering aspects of the fool's behavior. Observe Nabal's behavior (1 Sam. 25). Arrogance is unsuitable to a fool (17:7). A fool exalts himself (30:32) and, when stuffed with food, is intolerable (30:22).

Simple

The Hebrew word, petî, means "simple" or "naïve." It describes one who is immature, foolish, naïve, inexperienced, excessively open, and thus easily enticed to do wrong. A simple person lacks the discernment needed to distinguish between right and wrong or wise and foolish behavior. He is often thoughtless and impulsive.

Gullible (14:15), the simple are easily led astray from what is right and into serious danger (1:32), which they neither detect nor avoid (22:3). For example, they are enticed into adultery (7:7ff). The simple need wisdom (9:4) and prudence (8:5) to motivate them to leave their simple ways (9:6), which they naïvely love (1:22).

Mocker

The Hebrew words, *lîs* and cognates, convey the ideas of mocking, scorning, deriding. They express an attitude of arrogance combined with an open contempt for what is good and righteous. They describe stubborn people who adamantly refuse to change their ways, aggressive free thinkers who scornfully push their ways on others.

Proud and arrogant (21:24), mockers delight in mockery (1:22b). A corrupt witness mocks at justice (19:28). Fools mock at making amends for sin (14:9). No wonder that mockers produce strife and tensions (22:10). Since mockers reject rebukes (13:1) and correction (15:12), they do not find wisdom (14:6). The Lord mocks mockers (3:34). They are detested (24:9), will suffer (9:12), be punished (21:11) and flogged (19:25).

A synonym is *laʿag*. It describes a fool who mocks the poor (17:5) and his father (30:17) just as wisdom mocks the foolish in their disaster (1:26).

Sluggard

The Hebrew words, *ʿāṣēl* and cognates, mean to be "sluggish" or "lazy." They describe people who have no ambitions and who avoid work. The sluggard does not satisfy his desires because he is unwilling to do the necessary work (21:25). He claims to be afraid to go outside to work because of a lion that may be prowling in the area (26:13). As a result, his way is blocked with thorns (15:19). Inclined to excessive sleep (6:9), he is intolerable to send on an errand (10:26).

Another Hebrew word, *rᵉmiyâ*, is a synonym. It pictures the results of laziness as not eating (12:27), hunger (19:15), poverty (10:4), and slave labor (12:24).

Deceitful

Three groups of virtually synonymous Hebrew words involve the ideas of lying and deceit. They picture a deliberate presentation of what is false or misleading for purposes of deception, fraud, dishonesty, or treachery.

For the Hebrew words, *mirmâ* and cognates: The folly of fools is deception (14:8). False witnesses (14:25) and malicious people who plot evil are deceitful (12:20). The Lord detests dishonest (or deceitful) scales (20:23). Deceitful behavior shrugged off as a joke is deplorable and potentially dangerous (26:18–19).

For the Hebrew words, *kāzāb* and cognates: God will rebuke and establish as a liar anyone who adds to his words (30:6). A person is not to crave a ruler's food because it is deceptive (23:3). Rather it is better to be poor than a liar (19:22b). Agur asked the Lord to keep falsehood and lies far from him (30:8a). A false witness in court deceives (14:25) and lies (14:5b). False witnesses will be punished by not going free (19:5b) and perishing (19:9b).

For the Hebrew words, *sheqer* and cognates: Lies and hatred are closely related (26:28). A liar pays attention to malicious talk (17:4). The Lord detests lying (12:22), especially from false witnesses (6:19). The righteous also hate what is false (13:5). Both lying (17:7) and listening to lies (29:12) are inappropriate and disastrous to a ruler. Gains obtained by fraud are temporary and unpleasant, whether food (20:17) or money (21:6). The wicked earn deceptive wages (11:18). For liars will not go unpunished (19:9a). Deceptive boasting is futile (25:14); charm, deceptive (31:30).

The Vocabulary of Righteousness

Righteous

The Hebrew words, *sedeq* and cognates, mean "righteous," "just," "correct," and "innocent." The Lord loves those who pursue righteousness (15:9). He considers righteousness to be better than sacrifice (21:3). He blesses and responds to the prayers of the righteous (10:6; 15:29).

Righteousness makes a straight path (11:5), guards integrity (13:6), and hates what is false or dishonest (13:5; 29:27). The righteous are committed to justice (29:7) and disapprove of any miscarriage of justice (18:5), as does the Lord (17:15). They give honest, accurate testimony (12:17). The wise speech (10:31) of the righteous is choice silver, nourishing many (10:20–21). They are generous (21:26), bold (28:1), and wise (8:20).

The righteous keep on getting up after falling (24:16). They display stability, standing firm (10:25) and not being uprooted (12:3). They are delivered from trouble (11:8). The righteous triumph over the wicked (29:16), experiencing great prosperity (13:21; 15:6). Their desires are fulfilled (10:24). Rewarded (11:18), they experience joy (10:28). The righteous attain life (11:19), living long and fruitful lives (16:31). Righteousness exalts a nation (14:34) and secures its government (16:12) through its commitment to justice (8:15).

Justice

The Hebrew words, *mishpāṭ* and cognates, indicate justice administered by all functions of government. The verb pictures going to court to obtain justice (29:9) and the importance of fairness in judging (29:14). In most of its occurrences in Proverbs, the noun means "justice" or "just." The Lord guards the course of the just (2:8) and provides justice in his judgment (29:26). It is important for kings to carefully maintain justice for their political stability (29:4). It is wrong to pervert justice through bribes (17:23) or partiality (18:5). The righteous plan what is just (12:5) and rejoice in justice (21:15). The Lord is the source of just (i.e., accurate) scales and balances (16:11).

Integrity

The Hebrew words, *tōm* and cognates, convey the idea of completeness, ethical soundness, especially integrity and uprightness. Since these words also picture those who are innocent of charges against them, they are often rendered "blameless" and even "perfect." They do not, however, convey the idea of sinless perfection. For the best of people are excellent without being perfect, generally blameless without being absolutely blameless or sinless.

The Lord delights in (11:20) and protects the blameless (2:7b). Their protection (28:18) by righteousness (13:6) enables them to prosper (28:10). The righteous (11:5) and the upright (11:3) have integrity, which is better than riches (28:6).

Upright

The Hebrew words, *yāshār* and cognates, have the central idea of "straight," from which the ethical meanings "upright," "right," "fair" developed. The upright do what is morally proper.

At times the physical and ethical nuances of being or going straight merge in the same text. Such are the exhortation to look straight ahead (4:25) and the seductive invitations of the woman Folly to those who go straight on their way (9:15). The Lord and the righteousness of the upright make straight paths for them (3:6; 11:5). The wise lead along straight paths (4:11) that the understanding keep (15:21).

The upright have integrity, righteousness, and innocence (11:3, 6; 21:8). Their paths avoid evil (16:17) while the wicked leave the straight paths (2:13). The upright fear the Lord (14:2) who gives them victory (2:7). Their prayers please him (15:8) as he takes them into his confidence (3:32). They express their upright ways in both their speech (8:6) and conduct (20:11). They prosper (14:11), express goodwill (14:9), and are appreciated by kings (16:13). The wicked detest them (29:27) and try to kill them (29:10). Thus, the words rendered "integrity" and "upright" overlap in meanings.

Good

The Hebrew words, *tōb* and cognates, designate many varieties of what is good.

They often convey an ethical sense of good. The Lord watches the good and the wicked (15:3). A good man obtains favor from the Lord (12:2). Evil men bow down in the presence of the good, who are righteous (14:19). Every good path involves what is right, just, and fair (2:9). To walk in the ways of good men is to follow the paths of the righteous (2:20).

They also picture what is beneficial. The wise secure a good reputation (3:4). He who seeks good finds good will (11:27). Those who plan what is good find love and faithfulness (14:22). A wise wife brings her husband good (18:22; 31:12), including profitability (31:18). Acquiring wisdom brings sound (good) learning (4:2) and good understanding (13:15). Those who follow instruction and cherish understanding prosper (literally, find good; 16:20; 19:8). And that prosperity produces affluence (13:21–22).

The words rendered "good" also portray a happy, positive, encouraging attitude. The cheerful (good) heart has a continual feast (15:15). Such a healthy attitude is good medicine (17:22). A good, encouraging word brings cheer (12:25), joy (15:23), health (15:30), and refreshment (25:25). Positive, encouraging talk produces good things (12:14). The wise use their knowledge competently (15:2). The generous (literally, with a "good eye") will be blessed (22:9). Honey is good to eat (24:13). "Good" is often used in comparisons that designate one thing as better than another (e.g., 15:16–17).

The Vocabulary of Wickedness

Wicked

The Hebrew words, *rāshāʿ* and cognates, mean "wicked," "evil," "wrong," "guilty." They are general terms for all that is contrary to God's character, attitude, and will. Covering virtually all categories of sin, "wicked" refers to both sinful acts and sinful people. Wicked people are often hostile to God, neighbor, and community. They do not hesitate to violate the financial and social rights of others through dishonest business practices, false testimony in court, and even violence.

The most basic characteristic of the wicked is their craving for evil (21:10), which they absorb (4:17; 19:28) and discuss incessantly (15:28). They are sinful (21:4), cruel (12:10), desire plunder (12:12), and speak destructively (12:6). Apathetic to justice (29:7), they accept bribes to pervert justice (17:23). When in power, their rule is irresponsible, often disastrous (28:15), and promotes sin (29:16). Giving deceitful advice (12:5), they lead people astray (12:26). They detest the upright (29:27) and abuse those who rebuke them (9:7).

The Lord detests the way of the wicked (15:9), especially their perversion of justice (17:15) and their hypocritical sacrifices (15:8). Thus, he remains far from them, rejecting their prayers (15:29). God's negative response is mirrored in the human realm where wickedness brings contempt (18:3). People groan (29:2) and become inconspicuous when the wicked rise to power (28:12).

The future for the wicked is bleak. For their wages are deceptive (11:18), bringing treasures without value (10:2). Their hopes come to nothing (10:28). What they dread will occur (10:24). The Lord thwarts their craving (10:3) and allows them to be hungry (13:25). He curses the wicked (3:33), who are ensnared by their evil deeds (5:22). They are humbled before the righteous (14:19), punished (10:16), overthrown (12:7), brought down by calamity (14:32). They experience trouble (11:8), ruin (3:25), disaster (16:4), violence (10:6), and premature death (10:27). As a result, they perish (11:10), being swept away (10:25), destroyed (14:11), snuffed out (24:20).

Evil

Two groups of Hebrew words, *ra*ᶜ, *ʾāwen* and their cognates, picture both what is morally evil and what is naturally bad without any moral connotation. In their moral sense, they are similar to "wicked." In their nonmoral sense, they mean "bad," "wrong," "poor quality," "trouble," "harm," "calamity," "ruin." The trouble may, at times, result from one's evil behavior. However, these are general terms that describe any sort of badness.

For the Hebrew words, *ra*ᶜ and cognates: The wicked crave evil (*ra*ᶜ; 21:10). Evil people listen to evil talk (17:4), plot evil (16:27), rush into evil (6:18), delight in doing evil (2:14), and gush evil (15:28). They do not understand justice (28:5).

It is inappropriate to sing to a heavy (*ra*ᶜ) heart (25:20). The oppressed are continually wretched (*ra*ᶜ; 15:15). The buyer complains that the merchandise is bad before he boasts about his purchase (20:14). The stingy (literally, with an "evil eye") are eager to get rich (28:22).

The wise avoid the ways of evil men (2:12) and immoral (*ra*ᶜ) women (6:24). This enables them to avoid danger (22:3), harm (1:33), trouble (19:23). The wise hate (8:13) and shun evil (14:16; 16:17). They are ordered not to avenge wrong (20:22) and not to envy wicked men (24:1). For the Lord detests the wicked's thoughts (15:26) and disapproves of gloating over one's enemy (24:17–18).

Those who search for evil will find it (11:27). Evil men are trapped by their sinful talk (12:13) and ensnared by their own sin (29:6). Their wickedness will be exposed (26:26) and not go unpunished (11:21).

A companion of fools suffers harm (13:20). For fools detest turning from evil (13:19). The wicked experience trouble (12:21), misfortune (13:21), stern discipline (15:10), ruin (21:12), calamity (24:16). Pursuing evil leads to death (11:19). The evil have no future hope (24:20).

For the Hebrew words, *ʾāwen* and cognates: The wicked gulp down evil (19:28). Evil people listen to evil talk (17:4) and devise wicked schemes (6:18). Nevertheless, an adulteress claims to have done nothing wrong (30:20). Justice brings terror to evildoers (21:15). The wicked (*ra*ᶜ) encounter trouble (22:8), but no harm comes to the righteous (12:21).

Sin

The word often rendered "sin" is a standard term for sin that means to "miss the mark or way" (19:2). More often it refers to sin as falling short of the standard set by the Law or by wisdom.

No one can make a valid claim to be without sin (20:9). Sinners entice (1:10) others to participate in foolish, evil schemes (24:9). Sin includes despising one's neighbor (14:21) and being haughty and arrogant (21:4). It is a disgrace (14:34) that will be punished (10:16). The cords of a man's sin hold him fast (5:22). Misfortune pursues the sinner (13:21). Wickedness overthrows the sinner (13:6) whose wealth is stored up for the righteous (13:22). Those who would be wise are urged not to envy sinners (23:17).

Transgression

The Hebrew words, peshaᶜ and cognates, mean "transgression," "rebellion," "sin," "offense." They picture a deliberate act of sin that expresses a person's rebellion against God. Such a person has rejected God's authority by doing what he has rightly prohibited. They also describe the breaking down of human relationships by disregarding the principles that define them.

Much talk includes sinful elements (10:19). It is wrong to conceal one's sins (28:13) and sinful to deny one's wrongs (28:24). Quarreling (17:19) and uncontrolled temper (29:22) produce sin. Sin or transgression thrives when the wicked thrive (29:16). An evil man is trapped by his sinful talk (12:13) and snared by his sin (29:6). An offended brother is more unyielding than a fortress (18:19). Love covers all wrongs (10:12). Overlooking an offense promotes love (17:9) and brings honor (19:11).

Perverse

Two synonymous Hebrew words, tahpūká and ᶜiqqēsh, picture a turning away from what is straight to what is crooked. Whether referring to attitudes, speech, or deeds, they portray them as crooked, twisted, distorted, perverted, deceptive.

For tahpūká: The wicked rejoice in the perversity of evil (raᶜ; 2:14). They produce perverse talk (10:32), which the Lord hates (8:13). They plot perversity (16:30) and are deceptive (6:14). The wicked are overthrown and are no more (12:7). When drunk, men become confused and imagine confused things (23:33).

For ᶜiqqēsh: The Lord hates perverse hearts (11:20), talk (6:12), and ways (28:6). The perverse may expect exposure (10:9), obstacles (22:5), trouble (raᶜ; 17:20), and a sudden fall (28:18).

For Further Study

1. This chapter discusses the vocabulary on the basis of their usage in Proverbs. Read discussions of these words in *The Zondervan Pictorial Encyclopedia of the Bible* for a broad, biblical perspective.

2. What are the relationships among wisdom, understanding, knowledge, discretion, and prudence? In what ways are these qualities important and desirable?
3. For acquiring wisdom, what is the significance of discipline and rebukes? Why should a person appreciate them?
4. What are the relationships among righteousness, justice, uprightness, and integrity? Why are these qualities important elements in biblical wisdom? How important are they to Christians?

8

THE VOCABULARY
OF WEALTH AND POVERTY
IN THE BOOK OF PROVERBS
(10:1–22:16 AND 25–29)

R. N. Whybray

Wealth, Power and High Social Status

ʿāšîr, "rich" (person), "the rich" as a class (10:15; 14:20; 18:11, 23; 22:2, 7, 16; 28:6, 11).

This term has no synonyms.[1]

Wealth, however, is denoted by a variety of abstract nouns:

ʿōšer, "wealth," 11:16, 28; 13:8; 14:24; 22:1, 4

hôn, "wealth," 10:15; 11:4; 12:27; 13:7, 11; 18:11; 19:4, 14; 28:8, 22; 29:3

môtār, "abundance, plenty," 14:23; 21:5

From *Wealth and Poverty in the Book of Proverbs* (Sheffield: JSOT Press, 1990), 11–23. Reproduced by permission of Sheffield Academic Press.

1. On *ʿāšîr* and the various terms for wealth in Proverbs see especially T. Donald, "The Semantic Field of Rich and Poor in the Wisdom Literature of Hebrew and Accadian" (1964).

ḥōsen, "wealth, treasure," 15:6; 27:24
taʿanûg, "luxury," 19:10
ʾôṣār, "treasure," 10:2; 15:16; 21:6, 20
ḥayil, "wealth" (elsewhere "strength"), 13:22

The following verbs denote the acquisition or possession of wealth:

ʿāšar, "to be or become rich," 10:4, 22; 13:7; 21:17; 28:20
dšn (pual), "to become prosperous," 11:25; 13:4; 28:25

Other expressions:

śābaʿ leḥem, "to have plenty of food," 12:11; 20:13; 28:19
śōbaʿ nepeš, "eating one's fill," 13:25
śôr ʾābûs, "a fat ox," 15:17
bayit mālēʾ zᵉbāḥîm, "a house full of feasting" (literally, "of sacrifices"),
   17:1

In addition to these there are numerous references to

kesep, "silver," 10:20; 16:16; 17:3; 22:1; 25:4, 11; 26:23; 27:21
zāhāb, "gold," 11:22; 17:3; 20:15; 22:1; 25:11, 12; 27:21

and to costly ornaments:

nezem zāhāb, "a gold ring," 11:22; 25:12
tappûḥê zāhāb bᵉmáśkiyyót kesep, "'apples' of gold in a silver setting," 25:11
ḥᵃlî ketem, "an ornament of Nubian (?) gold," 25:12
pᵉnînîm, "corals," 20:15
kᵉlî yᵉqār, "a costly ornament," 20:15

References to commercial activities do not necessarily imply wealth, but they
testify to a concern with its power and the temptations of its acquisition:

qānâ, "to buy," 17:16; 20:14
mākar, "to sell," 23:23
mᵉḥîr, "price," 17:16; 27:26
mōʾzᵉnayim, "scales," 11:1; 16:11; 20:23
peles, "balance, scale," 16:11

ʾeben, "stone, weight," 11:1; 16:11; 20:10, 23
ʾêpâ, "ephah," 20:10

The inheritance of property is represented by

nāḥal, "to inherit," 13:22; 28:10
naḥᵃlâ, "inheritance, property," 17:1; 19:14; 20:21
ṣāpan, "to store up (for an heir)," 13:22

A number of words denote income and profit:

yʿl (hiphil), "to profit," 10:2; 11:4
ysp (niphal), "to be increased," 11:24; (hiphil) "to increase," 10:22
pᵉʿullâ, "reward, wages," 10:16; 11:18
tᵉbûʾâ, "wages, income," 10:16; 14:4; 15:6; 16:8; 18:20
śeker, "hire, wage," 11:18
nešek, "interest," 28:8
tarbît, "increment, usury," 28:8
ʾîš malweh, "creditor," 22:7

References to lavish spending, generosity, and almsgiving imply some degree of wealth:

pzr, "to scatter, distribute," 11:24
šbr (hiphil), "to sell" (bār, "corn") (rather than withholding it to make a greater profit), 11:26
ḥānan, "to be kind, generous (to the poor)," 14:21, 31; 19:17; 28:8
nātan, "to give" (to the poor), 28:27
ʾîš mattān, "a generous man," 19:6
mattāt, "gift," 25:14
ṭôb ʿayin, "a generous man," 22:9

Meanness, on the other hand, is expressed by

ḥāsak, "withhold (one's wealth)," 11:24
mānaʿ, "hold back (grain)," 11:26

There are two words for bribery:

šōḥad, "bribe," 17:8, 23; 21:14

mattān, literally, "gift" (see above), but used in the sense of bribery, 18:16; 21:14

kōper, 13:8; 21:18 means "ransom"

Warnings against the folly of going bail for others presuppose the possession of property, though they also warn against the danger of losing it.

ʿārab, "to go bail," 11:15; 17:18; 20:16; 27:13

ʿᵃrubbâ, "security," 17:18

tāqaʿ, "to stand security," 17:18

It may be assumed that wealth, social status and power were closely associated. The following terms denote persons of high social status and power:

melek, "king," 14:28, 35; 16:10, 12, 13, 14, 15; 19:12; 20:2, 8, 26, 28; 21:1; 22:11; 25:1, 2, 3, 5, 6; 29:4, 14

śar, "official, nobleman," 19:10; 28:2

rāzôn, "ruler," 14:28

nādîb, "prince, nobleman," 17:7; 25:7; 19:6

qāṣîn, "ruler, prince," 25:15

nāgîd, "ruler," 28:16

mōšēl/mōšēl, "ruler," 28:15; 29:12, 26

gᵉdōlîm, "the great, nobles," 18:16; 25:6

yôʿēṣ, "counselor," 11:14; 15:22

mᵉšārēt, "courtier, royal official," 29:12

There are, then, more than 120 verses out of a total of 513 which refer to wealth, a comfortable existence, or positions of power and influence. The list does not include a number of words which refer only indirectly to the possession of wealth, for example, *gēʾîm*, "proud," 15:25; 16:19; *beṣaʿ*, "ill-gotten gains," 15:27; 28:16; or *rāšāʿ*, "wicked," a very frequent word in these chapters, which in some instances at least has such an implication.

Poverty and Low Social Status

The two most frequently occurring words meaning "poor" in these chapters are:

rāš, 13:8; 14:20; 17:5; 18:23; 19:1, 7, 22; 22:2, 7; 28:3, 6, 27; 29:13

dal, 10:15; 14:31; 19:4, 17; 21:13; 22:9, 16; 28:3, 8, 11, 15; 29:7, 14

Other words are:

ʿānî/ʿānāw, 14:21; 15:15; 6:19[2]
ʾebyôn, 14:31
ḥᵃsar-leḥem, "a person in want" (literally, "one who lacks bread"), 12:9
lōweh, "a debtor," 22:7
ʾalmānâ, "a widow," 15:25

Verbs denoting poverty are:

ḥāsar, "to be in want, go hungry," 13:25
rāʿēb, "to be hungry, starve," 10:3; 19:15; 25:21
yāraš (niphal), "to be dispossessed, become destitute," 20:13
rûš, "to be poor," 10:4; 13:7

The following nouns denote the state of poverty:

rēš/rîš, "poverty," 10:15; 13:18; 28:19
ḥeser, "want, poverty," 28:22
maḥsôr, "want, poverty," 11:24; 14:23; 21:5, 17; 22:16; 28:27
mᵉḥittâ, "ruin," 10:15 (also frequently in a less precise sense)

Several other words and expressions refer to various degrees of poverty:

ʾᵃruḥat yārāq, "a meal of vegetables, a poor meal," 15:17
mᵉʿaṭ, "a little," 15:16; 16:8
pat ḥᵃrēbâ, "a dry crust," 17:1
pat-leḥem, "a crust of bread," 28:21
ʾayin, "nothing," 13:4, 7; 20:4

A frequent cause of poverty is laziness, referred to in the following:

---

2. The question whether these are two separate words, *ʿānî,* "poor" and *ʿānāw,* "humble," or are variants of a single word is especially relevant to the interpretation of certain Psalms, but of little significance in Proverbs. *ʿānî* occurs in the singular in 15:15 and clearly means "poor." In 14:21 and 16:19, where the plural is used, Kethib has *ʿᵃniyyîm* but Qere *ʿᵃnāwîm.* In 14:21 the meaning is clearly "the poor." In 16:19 "humble" is a possible but not a necessary meaning.

ʿāṣēl, "lazy, feckless," 10:26; 13:4; 15:19; 19:24; 20:4; 21:25; 22:13;
  26:13, 14, 15, 16
ʿaṣlâ, "laziness," 19:15
rĕmiyyâ, "slackness," 10:4; 12:24, 27; 19:15

Laziness is also referred to in other words in 10:5; 27:23–27.

Diligence, on the other hand, is praised as a means by which a person may avoid poverty and become self-sufficient or even wealthy:

ḥārûṣ, "diligent," 10:4; 12:24, 27; 13:4; 21:5
ʿābad, "to work" (one's land), 12:11; 28:19

Low social status is denoted by the following words:

mas, "forced labor," 12:24
ʿebed, "slave," 11:29; 12:9; 14:35; 17:2; 19:10; 22:7; 29:19, 21
ʿāmēl, "laborer," 16:26

There are thus more than seventy verses which refer to poverty or low social status in these chapters. This list does not include a number of verses which refer to the small farmer who works for himself, such as 10:5; 14:4.

The frequency of references to wealth, poverty, and social status in these chapters may be summed up as follows:

Total number of verses   513
Verses in which such references occur   158
Number of relevant words   95
Total number of occurrences of these words   261

Some Features of the Terminology

"Poor" and "Poverty"

rāš and dal, together with the less frequent ʿānî and ʾebyôn, are the principal words generally rendered by "poor"; rēš and maḥsôr are the main words for "poverty." Are these words synonymous, or are there nuances which denote different types of poverty?[3] Or, again, do they all in fact mean "poor in the

---

3. Of the twenty-one occurrences of rāš in the Old Testament, sixteen are found in the wisdom literature: fourteen in the chapters of Proverbs under discussion here, and two in Ecclesiastes. Of the five remaining instances, three occur in Nathan's parable (2 Sam. 12:1–4), one in

purely economic sense"? These questions have been much discussed. They will be briefly examined here *purely from the point of view of the internal evidence of actual usage in these chapters.*[4]

In some verses two or more of these words occur together in ways which suggest synonymity:

---

1 Sam. 18:23 ... and one in Ps. 82:3. In this last passage (Ps. 82:3) all the main words for "poor" (*dal, ʿānî, rāš* and *ʾebyôn*) occur together in a way which suggests synonymity or at least close association. The fact that *rāš* occurs overwhelmingly in Proverbs led A. Kuschke ("Arm und reich" [1939], 47, 53) to suggest that *rāš* differs in meaning from the others and is used in Proverbs (together with the less frequent *ḥāsēr*, and in common with *miskēn*, which occurs only in Ecclesiastes) to express a theme peculiar to that book: the *rāš* was, according to him, the person who was responsible, through a defect of character, for his own misfortunes, and deserved no sympathy or help. There were thus two "classes" of poor in Proverbs, and it is only for the other class that sympathy is expressed. J. van der Ploeg, however ("Les pauvres d'Israël" [1950], 254–58), disputed this view: there are, he argued, differences between the various words used, but they are only minor ones. Van der Ploeg is correct. In fact none of the occurrences of *rāš* in Proverbs speaks of a poverty that is deserved, and several speak in quite different and positive terms of the *rāš*: his poverty may be accompanied by moral integrity superior to that of the rich (19:1, 22; 28:6); to sneer at him is to insult his Creator (17:5); Yahweh himself created both him and the rich man (22:2; 29:13). As for the other terms mentioned by Kuschke, *ḥāsēr*, "lacking," occurs in connection with poverty only in the phrase *ḥăsar-lāḥem* in 12:9 in the neutral sense of "lacking food." It is true that the cognate term *maḥsôr*, which occurs six times in these chapters, always refers here to deserved poverty; but the other occurrences in the Old Testament show it to have been a purely "neutral" word with no such implications (Deut. 15:8; Judg. 18:10; 19:19, 20). That it should have acquired a more specialized meaning in Proverbs is unlikely. There is in fact no evidence for Kuschke's thesis that there are two classes of poor in Proverbs.

4. That is, without recourse to etymological arguments, and with an awareness that it is misleading to assume a total uniformity of the meaning of a word throughout the Old Testament, irrespective of context. On the first point, J. Barr (*The Semantics of Biblical Language* [1961]) has exposed the "etymological fallacy" of assuming that the meaning of a word can be determined on the basis of a supposed "root meaning." The second point may be illustrated by referring to some recent discussion of the meanings of *dal* and *rāš*.

Elsewhere in the Old Testament *dal* often means "weak" rather than poor. Further, it has been pointed out (by van der Ploeg [1950], 251; Schwantes, 79–80; H.-J. Fabry, *ThWAT II*, col. 232; R. J. Coggins, "The Old Testament and the Poor" [1987–88], among others) that in some passages in the Old Testament laws the *dal* is not entirely impoverished: he is expected to be able to pay his half-shekel contribution like others (Exod. 30:15) and to contribute sacrificial offerings, even though less is required of him than of other citizens (Lev. 14:21). It has also been pointed out that the *rāš*, "poor man," in Nathan's parable (2 Sam. 12:1–4), though specifically contrasted with the ʿāšîr, has his own house and is the possessor of a lamb. Clearly in these contexts these words denote relative rather than absolute poverty.

These passages, however, do not justify the assertion (e.g., by Schwantes, 261–62) that this must also be true of the use of these words in Proverbs, for which the internal evidence is of a contrary nature. The laws of Exodus 30 and Leviticus 14—usually regarded as late—probably reflect quite different social and economic circumstances from those of Proverbs, in which these terms may well have somewhat different connotations. With regard to the term *rāš*, David's self-deprecating reference to himself as "poor and of no account" (*rāš wĕniqleh*) in 1 Sam. 18:23 shows that the term could in certain circumstances be used hyperbolically. Nathan's parable could well be another example of such hyperbolic usage: the author wished to stress the extreme contrast between the economic circumstances of the *rāš* and the ʿāšîr in the story—a contrast so frequently made that it seems to have been a cliché—but at the same time the need, also for the purposes of the story, to develop an analogy between David's action in taking another man's wife and that of the ʿāšîr made it essential that the "poor" man should have a prized possession which

dal/rēš

10:15   A rich man's wealth (*hôn ʿāšîr*) is his strong city;
        the ruin (*mᵉhittat*) of the poor (*dallîm*) is their poverty (*rêšām*).[5]

rāš/dal

28:3   A poor man (*rāš*) who oppresses the poor (*dallîm*)
        is (like) torrential rain which leaves no crop.

This proverb only makes sense if the two terms are virtually synonymous.

dal/mahsôr

22:16   He who oppresses a poor man (*dāl*) increases his wealth (*lᵉharbôt lô*):
        he who gives to the rich (*ʿāšîr*) will only come to want (*mahsôr*).[6]

dal/ʾebyôn

14:31   He who oppresses a poor man (*dāl*) insults his Maker,
        but he who is generous to a poor man (*ʾebyôn*) honors him.

rāš/mahsôr

28:27   He who gives to a poor man (*rāš*) will not come to want *(mahsôr)*,
        but he who turns a blind eye to him will get many a curse.

It appears from these instances that no distinction is made between the states of poverty denoted by *rāš/rēš, mahsôr, ʾebyôn,* and *dal.* A further indication of this is to be found in those proverbs in which either *rāš* or *dal* is contrasted with *ʿāšîr.*

ʿāšîr and its antonyms *ʿāšîr* and *rāš* are contrasted in several proverbs in a way which leaves no room for doubt that the author sees these two types as representing the extremes of economic status:

---

could be taken from him. The fairytale atmosphere of this story is shown by the curious detail that the poor man's lamb was not an ordinary farm animal but a household pet. The context is clearly not one from which a definition of *rāš* in its ordinary usages can be extracted. With regard to the meaning of *dal,* the definition in Jer. 39:10 of the *dallîm* as "those who owned nothing" (*ʾᵃšer ʾên-lāhem mᵉʾûmâ*) is likely to be realistic, at least for the period when it was written.

5. There is a kind of tautology here in both lines. But clearly in the first, *hôn* is regarded as that which characterizes the *ʿāšîr,* and similarly in the second line, although the syntactical arrangement is different, *rēš* is intended to denote what is characteristic of the *dal.* The meaning of this proverb is that wealth affords protection to its possessor, while poverty offers none and so is only one step away from total disaster.

6. The *lô* in *lᵉharbôt lô,* literally "to multiply for him," is ambiguous: the meaning might be either that the oppressor will increase his own wealth or that he will unwittingly increase that of the *dal* because the latter will receive a blessing to compensate for his ill treatment. There are also other problems of interpretation here: it is not clear why one should give to the rich, or what is the relationship between the two lines. Nevertheless the link between *dal* and *mahsôr* is clear.

14:20 Even by his neighbor the poor man is hated,
but many are those who love the rich man.
18:23 The poor man speaks deferentially,
but the rich man answers harshly.
28:6 Better is a poor man who walks in his integrity
than a rich man whose ways are perverse.
22:2 The rich man and the poor man meet one another (*nipgāšû*).
it is Yahweh who made them both.
22:7 The rich man rules over the poor,
and the debtor is slave to the creditor.

Yet *ʿāšîr* and *dal* are contrasted in exactly the same way. [Proverbs] 10:15 has already been considered. In 28:11 there can be no doubt that *dal* is the antonym of *ʿāšîr*:

A rich man is wise in his own eyes,
but a discerning poor man will see through him.

dal is also contrasted quite definitely with *hôn*, "wealth" in 19:4:

Wealth makes many friends,
but a poor man becomes estranged from his friend.

It is significant that this theme is identical with that of 14:20, where the contrast is between *ʿāšîr* and *rāš*.

A further test of the relative meanings of *rāš* and *dal* may be carried out by comparing what is said in these chapters respectively about the *characteristics and situations* of the types of person so designated.

It has already been pointed out that 14:20 and 19:4 speak respectively of the *rāš* and the *dal* in similar terms as being *friendless and disliked* in their communities. A further instance of this in the case of the *rāš* is 19:7:

All the poor man's brothers hate him;
how much more do his friends stay clear of him!

A further characteristic of the poor man is his *vulnerability to the depredations of the rich and powerful*. In the case of the *rāš*, 18:23 and 22:7 have already been referred to in this connection. There the *rāš* is treated with contempt by the rich man, who regards him as a dependent. The following proverbs refer similarly to the treatment by others of the *dal*:

14:31a He who oppresses a poor man insults his Maker.
22:16a He who oppresses a poor man increases his wealth.

21:13 refers to those who ignore the *dal's* cry for help:

> He who closes his ear to a poor man's cry of distress
> will himself get no answer when he cries for help.

29:7 refers to the inability of the *dal* to obtain justice:

> A righteous man recognizes the cause of the poor,
> but a wicked man does not pay attention to such knowledge.

From these proverbs it might be argued that the *dal* is not necessarily a poor person but rather a defenseless one. The verb $^c\bar{a}saq$, "oppress," is used in these chapters only with *dal* as its object (in 14:31; 22:16; 28:3), never with *rāš* or any other word meaning "poor." What kind of "oppression" is meant is not stated; but 29:7, with its reference to the denial of the *dal's* civil rights, and perhaps 21:13 with its reference to his cry for help, might suggest that *dal* here may be intended to convey the idea of a person helpless to defend himself either in legal disputes or accusations or from unscrupulous creditors, rather than simply one who is economically poor. Since, however, poverty and powerlessness were closely associated in ancient Israel, as often elsewhere, and in view of the contrast with *hôn* in 19:4, it is likely that the difference between *rāš* and *dal*, if any, is one of nuance or point of view rather than of substance. The *dal* was almost always *rāš*, and the *rāš* in certain situations was perceived as *dal*. They are not two distinct types of person. It may also be remarked that 14:31 regards the *dal* simultaneously from both angles: as oppressed, he is powerless; as set in parallelism with the *ʾebyôn*, he is poor.

A further theme in which the words for poor are used interchangeably is that of the blessing which will reward *kindness (ḥnn) or generosity (ntn) to the poor,* sometimes combined with a warning of those who ignore or are unconcerned with their plight. Of the six proverbs in question, three have *dal* as the recipient, one has *rāš*, one has $^c\bar{a}n\hat{i}/\bar{a}n\hat{a}w$, and one has *ʾebyôn*:

28:27a   He who gives to a poor man (*nôtēn lārāš*) will not come to want.
22:9b   For he gives of his food to the poor (*nātan millaḥmô laddāl*).
28:8b   Gathers it to give to the poor (*lᵉḥōnēn dallîm*).
19:17a   He who is generous to the poor (*ḥônēn dāl*) lends to Yahweh.
14:21b   And happy is he who is generous to the poor (*mᵉḥônēn ᶜᵃniyyim/ᵏᵃnāwîm*).
14:31   He who oppresses the *dal* insults his Maker,
          but he who is generous to a poor man (*ḥōnēn ʾebyôn*) honors Him.

This interchange of terms (*ḥnn* in these contexts is virtually synonymous with *ntn*) confirms the view that, even though *dal* may in some circumstances have a slightly different connotation from *rāš*, there was no significant difference between them in the speakers' perception of their economic status.

The same is true of both *ʾebyôn* and *ʿānî/ʿānāw*, which occur much less frequently: *ʿānî/ʿānāw* three times, *ʾebyôn* only once. With regard to *ʿānî/ʿānāw*, two more proverbs add further confirmation of this.

> 16:19 It is better to be humble (*šᵉpal-rûaḥ*) with the *ᶜⁱniyyîm/ᶜⁱnāwîm* than to divide the spoil with the proud (*gēʾîm*).

Here it has been supposed that *ᶜⁱniyyîm/ᶜⁱnāwîm* means "humble" as in some of the Psalms; but in view of the tautology which would then be created in the first line, and of the contrast with the "spoils" (or "gains"—*šālāl*) of the "proud" in the second, "poor" (with, perhaps, a small nuance) is to be preferred. The same applies to 15:15:

> All the days of the *ʿānî* are wretched,
> but a cheerful heart is a perpetual feast.

Here *ʿānî* can hardly mean "humble." It is the days of the poor which are miserable, but there can be an inner cheerfulness able to overcome the unpleasant circumstances.

The other words denoting poverty in these chapters speak for themselves. The noun *rêš/rîš* and the verb *rûš* are cognates of *rāš*, and it is clear that all these denote a state of poverty. The group of words from the root *ḥsr*, "lack, want" (*ḥāsēr*—in the phrase *ḥᵃsar-leḥem*—*ḥeser, maḥsôr*) all refer to a state of deprivation of the necessities of life. *rāᶜēb* means "to be hungry, to starve"; *yāraš* (niphal) "to be dispossessed, destitute." *mᵉḥittâ*, which occurs several times (10:14, 15, 29; 13:3; 14:28; 18:7; 21:15), means desperation or ruin, not necessarily in the economic sense; but in 10:15b it is the consequence of poverty.

Conclusion

It therefore appears probable that no significant distinction between the words for "poor" and "poverty" was intended by these speakers. The reason for their use of such an abundance of synonyms is not, however, apparent.

ʿāšîr, "Rich"

Of a total of twenty-three occurrences of *ʿāšîr* in the Old Testament nine are found in these chapters. In all these cases with one exception (18:11) *ʿāšîr* stands in opposition to either *rāš* or *dal*. In contrast with the plethora of words meaning "poor" it is remarkable that no other adjective or noun signifying "rich" occurs,[7] although a number of other words and phrases denoting wealth and its acquisition are used quite frequently.

It is important to note that the portrait of the ʿāśîr presented here is far from sympathetic. In contrast with the poor he has security, or believes himself to be secure (10:15; 18:11), and his wealth brings him many "friends" (ʾōhᵃbîm, 14:20—there is probably an ironical tone here: it is implied that they "love" him only for his wealth). The ʿāśîr lords it over the rāš (22:7; cf. 22:16) and gives a harsh reply to his entreaties (18:23). In 28:6 the dishonest or "crooked" (ʿiqqēš) ʿāśîr is contrasted with the honest and upright rāš; and in 28:11 it is the ʾîš ʿāśîr who is convinced of his own cleverness (ḥākām bᵉʿênāw), but the discerning poor man (dal mēbîn) who sees through him. The comment that the ʿāśîr and the rāš have a common Creator (22:2) and so a common humanity is susceptible of different interpretations, but does not suggest either approval or disapproval of the social and economic system which regards the former as innately superior to the latter.[8]

It is remarkable that not a single virtue is attributed to the ʿāśîr in these chapters. Yet other proverbs make it clear that generosity to the poor is well attested. It is equally clear that wealth is not despised by the speakers of these proverbs; it is often regarded as something positively desirable. This may suggest that ʿāśîr here has a special connotation: that it refers not simply to persons who have achieved or inherited greater prosperity than others, but to a particular kind of person who represents the exact opposite of the truly indigent, and who is regarded by the speakers with hostility. There is no suggestion, however, in these proverbs that the speakers envied the ʿāśîr or wished to attain his status or the position of power that went with it.

7. This is true of the Old Testament as a whole.

8. In fact poverty is virtually always taken for granted in the Old Testament in the sense that it is not regarded as an evil contrary to the will of God which can and must be abolished. However, G. von Rad (Weisheit in Israel [1970], 105; ET 76) correctly pointed out that the point of view expressed in the "sentence-literature" of Proverbs is "static" to an exceptional degree: it shows no awareness of the social problems and conflicts which are so evident in the teaching of the preexilic prophets. Although these speakers could experience a twinge of conscience over the sufferings of the poor, they did not call for a radical change in the social system, which they regarded as essentially stable. Poverty was, in their view, mainly the consequence of individual failures to conform to the norms of the established social order. See also D. Michel, TRE, IV (1979), 72.

9

FILLING IN THE BLANK: ASYMMETRICAL ANTITHETICAL PARALLELISMS

William E. Mouser, Jr.

One and one is more than two in Proverbs. By bringing two ideas together in a poetic parallelism, Solomon communicated more than the mere sum of the two ideas. The juxtaposition itself creates a puzzle. You must discern how the two ideas relate to one another, whether by contrast, comparison, or some other relationship. In a synonymous parallelism, the message of the proverb gets fuller expression by being stated twice; in antithetical parallelisms, both the message and its converse are displayed.

In most of the parallelisms in Proverbs, either idea will stand by itself and make good sense. When you discern the relationship between the two ideas, then that relationship becomes a device for making inferences *about* one idea *from* the other idea *through* the relationship between them. Many of the proverbs, especially those which display antithetical parallelism, seem deliberately crafted so as to invite the making of inferences from the materials provided in

From William E. Mouser, Jr., *Walking in Wisdom: Studying the Proverbs of Solomon* (Downers Grove, Ill.: InterVarsity, 1983), 35–52. Used by permission of the author.

the proverb. You must explicate what the proverb leaves unsaid through careful meditation on the elements of the proverb.

In order to recognize those proverbs which invite this kind of elaboration, you must first learn to identify those proverbs which invite no inferences at all—those antithetical parallelisms which display all their meaning on the surface. These proverbs are symmetrical contrasts and often are formally symmetrical as well.

Symmetrical Antithetical Parallelisms

A proverb exhibits symmetrical antithetical parallelism when the contrasts between the two ideas are all explicit in the words of the proverb. For example, consider Proverbs 10:1, the first proverb in Solomon's collection:

A wise son makes a father glad,
But a foolish son is a grief to his mother.

This proverb exhibits two kinds of symmetry which are clear from the following diagram:

10:1a	10:1b
a wise son	a foolish son
makes	is
a glad	a grief
father	mother

By means of a very slight paraphrasing of 10:1a, the formal symmetry can be seen in this diagram. Each line of the proverb follows the order of subject-verb-object; each subject is a noun modified by an adjective. The verbs are not precisely symmetrical, as one is transitive and the other intransitive; however, Proverbs often pairs transitive and intransitive verbs in both synonymous and antithetical parallelisms.

The other kind of symmetry displayed by Proverbs 10:1 involves the *sense* of each line. Each element in each line finds a precise lexical contrast in the other line. *Wise* and *foolish* contrast well with each other; *glad* and *grief* are opposite in sense even though they are not the same part of speech; even *father* and *mother* make an interesting counterpoint with one another even though they are not the same as the other contrasts in Proverbs 10:1. In both sense and form, Proverbs 10:1 is symmetrical.

Proverbs 15:1 is another symmetrical antithetical parallelism:

15:1a	15:1b
a gentle answer	a harsh word
turns away	stirs up
wrath	anger

The formal symmetry is evident in that each line follows the subject-verb-object pattern. The sense of Proverbs 15:1 is also symmetrical. *A gentle answer* is balanced with its contrast, *a harsh word,* and the verbs *turn away* and *stir up* also contrast well. *Wrath* and *anger,* of course, are synonyms. As we examine more antithetical parallelisms, it will become evident that they often contain synonymous elements on each side of the parallelism.

The symmetry of Proverbs 15:18 is easy to see when it is diagrammed:

15:18a	15:18b
a hot-tempered man	the slow to anger
stirs up	pacifies
strife	contention

The formal symmetry is not so rigid. The subjects, for example, are not the same form; 15:18a has a noun and an adjective for a subject, while the second line uses a substantive made from an adjective with an adverbial infinitive. Otherwise, the syntactical order of subject-verb-object is followed in each line of 15:18.

The sense of 15:18 is also symmetrical. Though the subjects are formally different, they are complete opposites in sense. *Stirs up* and *pacifies* make good contrasts as well. As we saw in the previous example, Proverbs 15:18 is an antithetical parallelism even though it contains the synonymous elements *strife* and *contention* paired in formal symmetry.

The formal symmetry which some antithetical parallelisms display can prove helpful in clarifying the sense of one or the other of the paired ideas. Consider, for example, the interpretive problem which pronouns pose in Proverbs 14:31:

> He who oppresses the poor reproaches his Maker,
> But he who is gracious to the needy honors him.

If the second line is considered in isolation from the first, *honors him* could mean "honors the needy" (the Hebrew does not indicate whether *him* should be upper or lower case). Pairing the formal elements of the proverb, however, makes it clear that the actual antecedent of "him" is in the first line:

14:31a	14:31b
he who oppresses	he who is gracious
the poor	to the needy
reproaches	honors
his Maker	him

As *him* in 14:31b formally pairs with *his Maker* in 14:31a, they are probably synonymous terms, one being the antecedent of the other.

Notice that recourse to formal symmetry in 14:31 does not clear up the ambiguity attached to *his* in the term *his Maker*. If the antecedent of *his* is *he who oppresses*, then the proverb is telling us that an oppressor of the poor is reproaching his own maker; if the antecedent of *his* is *the poor*, then an oppressor of the poor man is reproaching the poor man's maker. This kind of ambiguity appears frequently in Proverbs and begins to look suspiciously deliberate. If the ambiguity is deliberate, the point may well be that oppressing the poor reproaches God in two ways: it is a reproach to the Creator when his creation behaves unseemly, and it is a reproach to the Creator when his work is attacked or abused.

Asymmetrical Antithetical Parallelisms

The most transparent antithetical parallelisms are those which we have just examined, those which display a symmetry of both form and sense. All the meaning of such proverbs lies clearly exposed in the precisely paired contrasts of each idea. When this symmetry is disturbed in either form or sense, a more difficult proverb results. Such proverbs are called asymmetrical antithetical parallelisms. The difficulty of these proverbs, however, is also the source of their strength. The asymmetrical antithetical parallelism invites you to make various inferences from one idea to another in order to restore the symmetry which is lacking in the explicit words of the proverb. As you restore, to some degree, the balance which is lacking, meaning emerges from the proverb which was otherwise hidden.

A simple example of this kind of proverb is Proverbs 10:5, which is diagrammed below:

10:5a	10:5b
he who gathers	he who sleeps

in summer	in harvest
is	is
a son who	a son who
acts wisely	acts shamefully

The formal symmetry of this proverb is very precise. However, the sense of the various paired elements is asymmetrical. We apprehend almost immediately that Proverbs 10:5 is an antithetical parallelism, but some of the elements which are paired on opposing sides of the formal contrast are not really contrasts.

The subjects of each line do not contrast well on the surface; *gathering* is not the opposite of *sleeping*. However, the son who is sleeping is obviously not gathering during the harvest, and the son who gathers is evidently not asleep when he does so. Thus, even though there is some apparent asymmetry in the subjects, they are probably to be understood as loose contrasts.

The situation is different, however, in the last clause of each line. *Wisely* and *shamefully* are not contrasts at all. Throughout Proverbs the proper contrast with *wisdom* is *folly*, and the proper contrast with *shame* is *honor*. Though *wisely* and *shamefully* are paired formally in this proverb, their meanings have no explicit balancing contrast in the other line. To supply the balance of sense to Proverbs 10:5 we would need to make certain inferences. These inferences are based on contrasts which are implied but not stated:

10:5a	10:5b
he who gathers	he who sleeps
in summer	in harvest
is	is
a son who	a son who
acts wisely	(acts foolishly)
(acts honorably)	acts shamefully

The inferences are placed in parentheses in the diagram to distinguish them from the explicit statements of the proverb. When the sense of Proverbs 10:5 is fleshed out in this manner, still more lessons are suggested.

If gathering in summer is wise, then Proverbs 10:5 implies that sleeping in the time of harvest is folly. There is time enough to sleep when the conditions are not good for harvest, as in the autumn when the rains make harvesting an impossibility. Anyone who sleeps away the only opportunity to harvest the crops is a fool. On the other hand, there is more at stake than just the character of the worker; his actions also reflect upon the reputation of his parents. A son who acts wisely brings honor to the parents who reared him; conversely, the son who acts foolishly brings shame to his parents, who must claim a son who sleeps when he should be gathering.

Proverbs 11:1 is another antithetical parallelism with precise formal symmetry but some asymmetry in the sense of two elements which are paired:

11:1a	11:1b
a false balance	a just weight
is	is
to the LORD	His
an abomination	delight

In making this diagram, the word order is altered in order to pair the corresponding elements from each line with one another. The words *abomination* and *delight* are good contrasts. However, *false* and *just* are not contrasts; *true* is the proper contrast of *false*, and *unjust* is the proper contrast of *just*.

A diagram of Proverbs 11:1 with these contrasts supplied in their appropriate places would look like this:

11:1a	11:1b
a false	a (true)
(unjust)	just
balance	weight
is	is
to the LORD	His
an abomination	delight

When both the explicit and implicit ideas of this proverb are seen, they provide a needed corrective to modern American notions of justice. Modern conceptions of justice are apt to revolve around notions of legal courts or legislatures which mandate justice through statute. On the other hand, injustice is mostly thought of as a violation of rights which a government grants to its citizens. Proverbs 11:1 makes justice a crucial commodity of the marketplace, an issue between a buyer and a seller. Furthermore, God himself stands behind this union of truth and justice in business dealings. True balances and just weights delight the God of all justice; he whose name is Truth regards the false and the unjust as abominable. Service to such a God does not end in the temple or the church meeting. It extends to the market, trading floor, show-room, and board meeting.

In the previous examples, the proverbs displayed symmetry in form, and both symmetry and asymmetry in content. In Proverbs 10:5 and 11:1, the asymmetry arose from elements which were formally paired but were not precise contrasts. Proverbs contains many examples in which there is still symmetry of form but complete asymmetry in sense.

One example of this kind of proverb is 28:27:

28:27a	28:27b
he who gives	he who shuts
to the poor	his eyes
will never want	will have many curses

As it stands, there is a formal symmetry in the way the ideas of 28:27 are composed and paired; the subjects are formed in the same pattern, and each predicate expresses a consequence of the activity in the subject. However, the phrase *who gives to the poor* does not properly contrast with *who shuts his eyes;* similarly, the phrase *will never want* is not really the antithesis of *will have many curses.* Nevertheless, Proverbs 28:27 clearly displays antithetical parallelism, although precise contrasts are not expressed anywhere in the proverb.

When all the suppressed contrasts are exposed, several interesting traits of each character appear.

28:27a	28:27b
he who gives to	(he who withholds from
the poor	the poor)
(he who opens his eyes)	he who shuts his eyes
will never want	(will want)
(will have many blessings)	will have many curses

We discover that the one who is giving to the poor does so because he is alert to those in need, and as he finds them he helps them. On the other hand, the person who is withholding from the poor does so through willful ignorance of their plight. He refuses to look at them and so does not fill their needs. The alert giver will never lack anything, and the contrast suggests why this is so. He will reap many blessings which will supply his lack even as he has supplied the lack of others. The one who shuts his eyes and his hand will have many curses. Again, the contrast in this proverb indicates that this will result in his having want himself.

All these ideas are expressed in other parts of Solomon's proverbs (compare 17:5; 19:17; 21:13; 22:22–23). The asymmetry of Proverbs 28:27 permits many ideas to be compressed into few words. As you expose through inference what is latent in the proverb, the message of the proverb expands in surprising and unexpected ways.

Proverbs 28:27 is also a good example of the kind of problem which can arise as you attempt to balance the asymmetry of a proverb through inference. Consider, for example, the subject of 28:27a: "he who gives to the poor." Which idea shall we infer as the most proper contrast for 28:27b—he who does not *give* to the poor or he who *withholds* from the poor? Certainly, it would be safe and accurate to infer the former. However, in 28:27b we find a fellow who shuts his eyes, presumably a deliberate and purposeful activity. In the context of this proverb, such shutting of the eyes must be solely to avoid beholding the plight of the poor. Therefore, we conclude that the person who is shutting his eyes is not merely failing to give to the poor, he is actively withholding aid from them.

A similar problem arises in contrasting the predicates of 28:27. The stingy man is said to *have many curses.* Does this imply that the generous man will simply lack curses, or will he also have many blessings? It is hard to imagine that the mere lack of curses will result in lack of poverty, especially as the person who is giving to the poor is depleting his own resources to do so. If he is to escape poverty himself as a result of his own generosity, his resources must be replenished and enriched. From other proverbs it is clear that God is the one who enriches and restores what the generous person gives away (see Prov. 19:17). Several hundred years after Solomon collected this proverb, we find Paul encouraging the Corinthian church that God still supplies the resources for a ministry of giving (2 Cor. 9:10–11).

In all the previous examples the asymmetry in sense has been easy to recognize because the proverbs were symmetrical in form. When a proverb exhibits formal symmetry, it is easy to pair up the formal elements and then decide whether or not they constitute good contrasts with one another. When asymmetry in sense is discerned, then you can make whatever inferences are required to balance the sense of the proverb. This procedure becomes almost mechanical for proverbs which display formal symmetry. However, the process of inferring suppressed contrasts becomes more difficult as the asymmetry of the proverb's form increases.

Consider, for example, Proverbs 14:16: "A wise man is cautious and turns away from evil,/But a fool is arrogant and careless." Although this proverb is asymmetrical in form, it may be diagrammed in such a way as to expose the suppressed contrasts.

14:16a	14:16b
a wise man	a fool
is	is
cautious	careless
(and humble)	and arrogant
and turns away from evil	(does not turn away from evil)

Because of the obvious antithetical parallelism, it is not difficult to make the inferences which appear in the parentheses above. In this proverb, the inferences restore not only a balance of sense, but something of a balance in form as well.

Sometimes simple paraphrasing will transform formal asymmetry into formal symmetry so that easy diagramming is possible. Proverbs 11:6, for example, has verbs in different voices: "The righteousness of the upright will deliver them,/But the treacherous will be caught by their own greed." The verb in the first line is in the active voice, while the verb in the second line is in the passive voice. For this reason, it is impossible to pair formally the genuinely contrasting elements of this proverb in a diagram, for they appear in differing syntactical relationships in their own sentences.

If, however, the voice of either verb is altered to conform to the voice of the other verb and the necessary paraphrasing is done to maintain the sense, then the following diagram may be made:

11:6a	11:6b
(the generosity)	the greed
the righteousness	(the unrighteousness)
of the upright	of the treacherous
will deliver them	will capture them

In the diagram above the second line of 11:6 was rewritten in the active voice. If instead the first line is rewritten in the passive voice, the following diagram results:

11:6a	11:6b
the upright	the treacherous
will be delivered	will be captured

by their righteousness   (by their unrighteousness)

(by their generosity)   by their greed

Either way *upright* and *treacherous* are clear contrasts, as are the verbs *deliver* and *capture*. *Righteousness* and *greed,* however, are not good contrasts, even though we would understand greed to be a form of unrighteousness. Yet because of this contrast, we infer that the righteousness which the proverb has in mind is generosity. This same expressing of righteousness through generosity lies behind the preaching of John the Baptist. When the multitudes asked him what works he was speaking of which were befitting the repentance he demanded, John answered, "He who has two coats, let him share with him who has none; and he who has food, let him do likewise" (Luke 3:10–11 RSV). He further admonished the tax gatherers not to collect more than what was due, and the soldiers were exhorted to be satisfied with their wages and to avoid using their power to extort money (Luke 3:12–14). In John's day as well as in Solomon's, the righteous generosity of the upright would deliver them. The treacherous, who would profess repentance without any change of behavior, would be caught in their own greed.

Some proverbs are so asymmetrical in form that they cannot be easily rewritten. Others can still be diagrammed. Proverbs 11:2, for example, has no formal symmetry at all: "When pride comes, then comes dishonor,/But with the humble is wisdom." A diagram of this proverb, which exposes a suppressed contrast, looks like this:

11:2a   **11:2b**

when pride comes   with the humble

                           is

(folly)   wisdom

then comes dishonor   (honor)

In this diagram the phrase *with the humble* is paired with *when pride comes* because they are contrasts in sense. *Dishonor* and *wisdom* are not contrasts, so their contrasts are supplied in parentheses.

What this diagram exposes is the source of the dishonor for the proud person. Pride moves a person to behave foolishly so that he is dishonored. The genuinely humble person might be completely overlooked, except for the wisdom which comes with humility. Because of skill in living, the humble person attracts the honor of those who see his success. In a similar way, the folly which the proud person commits draws attention, though not the attention of esteem, but rather shame.

Some proverbs are so asymmetrical in form that no diagramming is possible. One such proverb is 12:15: "The way of a fool is right in his own eyes,/ But a wise man is he who listens to counsel." All efforts to paraphrase either side of the proverb in order to bring it into sufficient formal symmetry produces an extremely cumbersome result hardly worth the effort. Nevertheless, it is clear that a contrast is being made, even though it is suppressed.

The unraveling of this proverb commences when we merely infer the contrast of either line relative to its partner. If the wise man listens to counsel, then the fool does not. Therefore, the complete message of 12:15 concerning the fool is that he does not listen to counsel (implicit), and that his way is right in his own eyes (explicit). What is implied about the fool becomes the consequence of what is explicitly said about him. As the fool's way is right in his own eyes, he not only refuses to listen to counsel, he probably rejects whatever is offered to him (compare Prov. 1:7). On the other hand, if the fool's way is right in his own eyes, it is implied that the wise man's way is not right in his own eyes. The wise man does not trust his own perception of matters, but seeks out the viewpoints of others. He does not lean on his own understanding. What is implied about the wise man in 12:15 becomes the explanation for what is explicitly said about him.

Beginners' Blunders and Bungles

Before they ever learn to ride a bicycle themselves, little boys and girls see their friends cruising effortlessly. It looks so easy to ride on two wheels, or even one wheel if their older friends can do wheelies. When the bicycle arrives on Christmas morning or during a birthday celebration, hopes are fulfilled; when the first few rides are attempted, hopes are dashed. What looked so easy is found to be very hard.

Something very like this child's disappointment often settles over students as they begin to gambol through Solomon's proverbs, applying some simple technique or concept which unlocks some of their tightly held wisdom. Some of the proverbs, for example, are easily seen to be antithetical or synonymous parallelisms. Some of the antithetical parallelisms are easily seen to be symmetrical or asymmetrical. Some of the asymmetrical proverbs are easily balanced through simple inferences. But sooner or later—usually sooner—the eager student of wisdom finds a proverb which is not so easy. Then he or she happens upon some which are not easy at all or discovers those that are positively difficult. When the apparently simple procedure of diagramming asymmetrical parallelisms is attempted in order to balance the asymmetry, the results are either trivial or nonsensical. Disappointment and frustration rear their ugly heads.

The beginner has two problems: a misunderstanding of the method used in studying the proverbs, and a lack of experience in applying that method. The following warnings will help you to avoid these pitfalls.

Warning Number One: Each word on one side of an antithetical parallelism does not need to have a contrast on the other side of the parallelism. This is clear from those perfectly symmetrical antithetical parallelisms we examined early in this chapter. Consider again the diagram of Proverbs 10:1:

10:1a	10:1b
a wise son	a foolish son
makes	is
a glad	a grief
father	mother

Note the contrast between the subjects of each line: the contrast with *a wise son* is *a foolish son,* not something like *a foolish daughter* or *a foolish non-son.* On the other hand, *father* and *mother* are not intended to be contrasts in this proverb, but rather stylistic variants for *parents.*

You may sometimes misapply the relationship of contrast in an asymmetrical parallelism, thinking that each element on any side of the parallelism must find a contrast on the other side. A misguided student might take Proverbs 14:21, "He who despises his neighbor sins,/But happy is he who is gracious to the poor," and diagram it like this:

14:21a	14:21b
he who despises	he who is gracious
his (rich) neighbor	to the poor (stranger)
sins	(does righteousness)
(is unhappy)	is happy

This diagram goes astray in pairing *neighbor* and *poor.* Because the student misunderstood these terms to require contrasting elements, he provided *rich neighbor* to contrast with *poor stranger,* an odd contrast indeed. Actually, *neighbor* and *the poor* are synonymous elements in an antithetical parallelism. Proverbs 14:21 is speaking about behavior directed at *the poor* who are our *neighbors,* the poor in our midst.

Beginning students often have a misunderstanding about antithetical parallelisms. They suppose that every word in each line must have a contrast in the corresponding line. This almost never happens. In fact, antithetical parallelisms often contain elements which are synonymous or even identical. For example, a wise *son* is contrasted with a foolish *son,* or a sluggard's *work* with the *work* of a diligent man.

These examples also illustrate that proverbs tend to contrast wisdom and folly concretely rather than abstractly. People are wise or foolish in child raising, money management, personal relationships, their relationship to God, or dozens of other areas of living to which the proverbs speak.

Warning Number Two: When in doubt about what contrast to supply in balancing an asymmetrical parallelism, merely supply the negation of the element you are trying to balance. Searching for nonexistent antonyms is a waste of time.

For example, consider Proverbs 17:9: "He who covers a transgression seeks love,/But he who repeats a matter separates intimate friends." Against the background of interpersonal relationships, the phrase *seeks love* is perhaps a sufficient contrast with *separates intimate friends.* However, the words *repeats a matter* do not form a good contrast with *covers a transgression.* Proverbs 17:9, therefore, is making a suppressed contrast which is exposed in the diagram below:

17:9a	17:9b
he who covers	(he who does not cover
a transgression	a transgression)
(he who does not repeat	he who repeats
a matter)	a matter
seeks love	separates intimate friends

In making the inferences for this diagram, it is sufficient to infer that *he who does not cover* is a contrast for *he who covers.* Similarly, *he who repeats a matter* is sufficiently contrasted with *he who does not repeat a matter.* Indeed, by inferring these simple negations in order to balance the contrasts of each line, we learn what covering a transgression looks like in practice: merely refusing to repeat something which one has seen or heard is all that is required.

Warning Number Three: Beware of figures of speech, as these pose special problems in making inferences. Consider, for example, Proverbs 27:6: "Faithful are the wounds of a friend,/But deceitful are the kisses of an enemy." *Wounds* and *kisses* might be some sort of contrast, as they are opposite kinds of physical contact between persons. However, in this proverb friends are making wounds and enemies are giving kisses. Surely something other than concrete kisses and wounds are being considered here. How is it that faithfulness can be a property of a wound or deceitfulness a characteristic of kisses?

The answer lies in the figurative use of the words in Proverbs 27:6. Figures of speech and their proper interpretation must be taken into account in order to discern the parallelism of a proverb and to make any inferences necessary to balance its asymmetry. . . .

Warning Number Four: Do not become disillusioned if every proverb in Solomon's collection does not become transparent. Remember that wisdom comes by doing, not by reading a book. Some of the proverbs are simple, and they are designed for the simple, those who are just beginning to exercise their spirits to know wisdom. As skill is acquired through practice, more and more proverbs will begin to open up like rosebuds. "Knowledge is easy to him who has understanding," Solomon says in Proverbs 14:6. The beginner does not have the understanding to fathom more than a portion of the simpler proverbs.

Even those who are wise will not exhaust the proverbs of Solomon, though they can always hear and gain more wisdom. At the end of his life, Solomon himself confessed that his determination to be wise had ended in failure: "I said, 'I will be wise,' but it was far from me. What has been is remote and exceedingly mysterious. Who can discover it?" (Eccles. 7:23–24). Nevertheless, this was the same Solomon who praised wisdom repeatedly in Proverbs 1–9 and who was responsible for composing and collecting the wisdom contained in the rest of Proverbs. If we may never be wise, at least we can always be wiser. Faithful attention to Solomon's proverbs may never deliver us at a destination, but it will keep up walking in the path.

10

GUIDELINES FOR UNDERSTANDING AND PROCLAIMING THE BOOK OF PROVERBS

Greg W. Parsons

The Book of Proverbs includes many practical and down-to-earth sayings. Yet few sermons are preached from this book. For many preachers the Book of Proverbs apparently seems like "nothing more than a deserted stretch of highway between Psalms and Ecclesiastes" that appears "dry and barren."[1] Collins asserts that "the crisis of relevance" for the preacher is particularly acute for the Book of Proverbs since it provides little inspiration or excitement. He opines, "With the exception of Leviticus, it is doubtful that any biblical book is viewed with less enthusiasm by the preacher."[2] Why is it that, although Proverbs is a rich source of devotional reading, preachers and teachers normally bypass Proverbs for public presentation?[3]

From *Bibliotheca Sacra* 150 (April–June 1993): 151–70. Used by permission of Dallas Seminary Press.

1. Thomas G. Long, *Preaching and the Literary Forms of the Bible* (Philadelphia: Fortress, 1989), 53.
2. John J. Collins, *Proverbs Ecclesiastes,* Knox Preaching Guides (Atlanta: John Knox, 1980), 1.
3. David A. Hubbard, *Proverbs,* The Communicator's Commentary (Dallas: Word, 1989), 17.

Several problems face the expositor in seeking to understand and proclaim the Book of Proverbs. (1) Some proverbs seem to conflict with human experience (10:27; 22:4) or seem contradictory to one another (26:4–5; cf. 6:6–11 with 15:16).[4] (2) Many proverbs, on the whole, appear to be secular common-sense sayings, almost devoid of theological content. (3) Some proverbs seem excessively moralistic (20:13) or overly concerned with the status quo (24:21).[5] (4) Others seem totally amoral observations of society (14:20; 17:8). (5) Proverbs 10:1–22:16 and chapters 25–29 consist of hundreds of individual sayings seemingly unconnected with what comes before or after.[6] (6) Some proverbs may be culturally problematic. Can Proverbs 23:13 be utilized by the preacher who faces a society full of child abuse?[7]

How can the biblical expositor deal with such enormous obstacles to his understanding and proclaiming the Book of Proverbs? Are there any guidelines to assist him in running through this "obstacle course"? Few have written even minimal guidelines for either interpreting or preaching biblical poetry or the Book of Proverbs in particular.[8] Recently Hubbard has laid an excellent foundation for understanding the Book of Proverbs.[9] Other authors offer some insights for preaching from Proverbs but seldom in detail.[10] Collins gives a brief "preaching guide" to Proverbs from a neoorthodox perspective.[11] However, he offers no specific guidelines.

Therefore this chapter offers guidelines for both understanding and proclaiming the Book of Proverbs.

4. Elizabeth Achtemeier, *Preaching from the Old Testament* (Louisville: Westminster/John Knox, 1989), 171.

5. Long, *Preaching and the Literary Forms of the Bible*, 53–54.

6. Achtemeier, *Preaching from the Old Testament*, 171. However, chapters 25–29 sometimes have small clusters of proverbs on certain subjects (apparently the work of Hezekiah's scribes, 25:1). See Derek Kidner, *The Wisdom of Proverbs, Job and Ecclesiastes: An Introduction to Wisdom Literature* (Downers Grove, Ill.: InterVarsity, 1985), 32.

7. Long, *Preaching and the Literary Forms of the Bible*, 61–62.

8. For instance, the recent helpful book by Sidney Greidanus (*The Modern Preacher and the Ancient Text: Interpreting and Preaching Biblical Literature* [Grand Rapids: Eerdmans, 1988]) contains nothing on the poetic books or Proverbs in particular.

9. Hubbard lists six useful guidelines for interpretation and proclamation that the present author has adapted (*Proverbs*, 17–30). However, though Hubbard's guidelines rightly emphasize the hermeneutical, few remarks specifically interface with proclamation. Valuable hermeneutical "rules" for Proverbs have been suggested by Gordon D. Fee and Douglas Stuart (*How to Read the Bible for All Its Worth* [Grand Rapids: Zondervan, 1981], 195–203). See also the helpful work of C. Hassell Bullock, *An Introduction to the Old Testament Poetic Books*, rev. ed. (Chicago: Moody, 1988), 146–65, esp. 161–65.

10. See Long, *Preaching and the Literary Forms of the Bible*, 53–66. Achtemeier treats the Book of Proverbs in conjunction with her treatment of wisdom literature (*Preaching from the Old Testament*, 165–76).

11. Collins, *Proverbs Ecclesiastes*.

Suggested Hermeneutical Guidelines for Proverbs

Guideline One: Interpret Individual Passages in Light of the Overall Structure, Purpose, and "Motto" of the Book of Proverbs.

Overall context of the book as an anthology. The overall literary structure of Proverbs suggests that the book is not only an anthology of sayings but is also "a collection of collections of wisdom materials."[12] The headings that introduce its major sections at 1:1; 10:1; 22:17; 24:23; 25:1; 30:1; and 31:1 may indicate seven distinct collections that vary in form and content.

Therefore initially it seems prudent to interpret each individual proverb or wisdom unit primarily within the context of its own individual collection. Then one must consider the context of the Book of Proverbs as a whole. The use of a concordance is essential for the precise meaning of words in the wisdom (or proverbial) vocabulary.[13]

Purpose and setting. In contrast to many books of the Bible, the purpose for Proverbs is clearly stated in 1:2–6. As a primer of right conduct and proper attitudes, Proverbs gives the inexperienced youth (1:4)—or even the older immature person—wisdom and instruction necessary to conform to God's will.[14] A twofold emphasis is indicated: to give *moral* prudence and skillfulness for holy living (1:2a, 3–5); and to give *mental* discernment (1:2b, 6).[15] The latter includes discerning the meaning of various kinds of wisdom sayings such as proverbs, riddles, and figurative maxims or expressions (v. 6).[16] The proverb in the mouth of a fool is inappropriate and can even be hazardous (26:7, 9). Discernment may also refer to knowing the difference between sham and reality so as to sift out the satanic counterfeit of wisdom.[17]

Though the setting of Proverbs has been debated (whether it was the royal court or the home), the data seem to indicate that the Book of Proverbs in its canonical form was an "instructional manual"[18] designed "for use by the young men of Israel's society who were being groomed for positions of leadership."[19] However, the individual sayings reflect the family (or clan)

---

12. Hubbard, *Proverbs*, 18.

13. Ibid., 25–26.

14. Bullock, *Introduction to Old Testament Poetic Books*, 152–53.

15. Allen P. Ross, "Proverbs," in *The Expositor's Bible Commentary* (Grand Rapids: Zondervan, 1991), 5:904–6.

16. The precise interpretation of the Hebrew word מְלִיצָה, "parable" (NIV) or "figure" (NASB) is disputable.

17. Ross states that this involves insight concerning lessons of life "such as distinguishing permanent values from immediate gratifications" ("Proverbs," 905).

18. See Bullock, *Introduction to Old Testament Poetic Books*, 152–53.

19. Hubbard, *Proverbs*, 26. He cogently argues that the centralization of government under David and Solomon called for many administrators to be trained for positions of responsibility. Beginning in Solomon's day there may have been some kind of schooling system such as was known in Egypt, Assyria, and Babylonia. Hezekiah may also have had a similar system (Prov. 25:1).

wisdom of centuries past handed down from father to son throughout the generations (cf. Prov. 4:1–4).[20] As Johnson states, the Book of Proverbs is "the boiled-down summation of many generations of experience in living."[21]

Motto. The motto of the book is found in 1:7 and 9:10 ("The fear of the Lord is the beginning of knowledge/wisdom"). This serves not only as a literary *inclusio*[22] but also as the compass to give orientation to chapters 1–9.[23] This motto rectifies the view that Proverbs is basically secular in its orientation.[24] Proverbs is designed to teach people how to steer their lives properly (cf. 1:5)[25] under the command of Yahweh.

Guideline Two: Recognize the Various Literary Forms and Devices (the "Building Blocks" of the Individual Passages or Proverbs) as a Clue to the Context.

The purpose of Proverbs involves "the enhancement of understanding through an instrument of finely turned language that needs to be properly grasped" (see 1:2; 5–6).[26] The terms in verse 6 (especially מָשָׁל and מְלִיצָה) are preeminently literary terms that indicate that the reception of wisdom requires careful reading of Proverbs to determine its literary forms.[27] Consequently it is essential for the expositor to recognize its various literary forms and devices.

Two basic literary forms. In general there are two basic literary forms or types of proverbs: the wisdom sentence and the admonition. The wisdom sentence (or saying) is an observation based on experience which is stated in the indicative mood (e.g., Prov. 12:4). This type occurs primarily in 10:1–22:16

---

20. Hubbard, *Proverbs,* 26–27. However, at the same time, the frequent use of "my son" (or my child) in Proverbs apparently indicates that the wisdom teacher was a sort of substitute parent to the person seeking wisdom from him (Fee and Stuart, *How to Read the Bible for All Its Worth,* 190).

21. L. D. Johnson, *Israel's Wisdom: Learn and Live* (Nashville: Broadman, 1975), 30. Waltke says that the original setting of the wisdom material in Proverbs was the home of the courtier, a high court official addressing his son (Bruce K. Waltke, "The Book of Proverbs and Ancient Wisdom Literature," *Bibliotheca Sacra* 136 [July–September 1979]: 230–32).

22. "The woman who fears the Lord" (31:30) is part of an *inclusio* for the whole book. The technical term *inclusio* is the literary envelope structure whereby a unit begins and ends with the same or similar phraseology.

23. Bullock observes, "Thus in Proverbs the underlying basis of life is one's relationship to God. Out of that relationship grow moral understanding and the ability to judge what is right (2:6–22), a proper attitude toward material possessions (3:9–10), industrious labor (6:6–11), the necessary equilibrium and sense of security for living in the world (3:21–26), and the right relationship toward one's neighbor (3:27–29) to mention only a few of the more practical benefits of that relationship" (*Introduction to Old Testament Poetic Books,* 148; cf. 166).

24. Cf. Collins, *Proverbs Ecclesiastes,* 4:6–10.

25. The NIV translation "guidance" in 1:5 reflects the Hebrew term תַּחְבֻּלוֹת, an apparent nautical term cognate to חֹבֵל ("sailor") who is "the one who pulls the ropes" to guide a ship.

26. Robert Alter, *The Art of Biblical Poetry* (New York: Basic, 1985), 167.

27. Cf. ibid., 167–68, 175.

and chapters 25–29.[28] The admonition, which occurs in the imperative mood (in either the second or third person),[29] is found mainly in chapters 1–9 and 22:17–24:22.[30] It may be a positive instruction or command or a negative prohibition. The admonition may add the reason(s) or motivations(s) often introduced by "for" (see 3:1–2 and 1:15–16, which combine both negative and positive components). Frequently there are extended admonitions to the "son" (esp. chaps. 1–9).[31]

Basic types of poetic parallelism. Though all the basic types of poetic parallelism can be illustrated from the Book of Proverbs, the most significant are antithetic and emblematic parallelism.[32]

Antithetic parallelism is the most common category in Proverbs, particularly in chapters 10–15, in which about 90 percent of the proverbs are of this type.[33] This type emphasizes the importance of choosing correctly to avoid the fate of the fool. It contributes greatly to the teaching of "the two ways,"[34] setting "before the reader the choice between the wise and profitable way versus the foolish and disastrous way" (cf. 12:5).[35]

Emblematic parallelism is actually a type of synonymous parallelism in which one line is figurative and the other line is literal[36] (see 10:26; 25:25; and 26:20). Proverbs of this type may also qualify as riddles since every statement "A is like B" implies the question "How is A like B?"[37] Therefore one must determine the common denominators in the comparison, ascer-

28. The two main literary subtypes of the wisdom sentence are comparisons and numerical sayings (the latter being frequent in chapter 30 and sometimes involving several verses). See Hubbard, *Proverbs,* 20–21, for more details.
29. The Hebrew jussive (third person positive or second person prohibition) is featured in this type.
30. Hubbard, *Proverbs,* 21. His statement that both collections of the wise (22:17–24:22 and 24:23–34) feature the admonition is not precisely stated. Only a small part of the second collection (namely, 24:27–29) contains admonitions.
31. Ibid., 18. These extended wisdom speeches or poems of 10 or 20 lines make up roughly one-third of the Book of Proverbs, according to Alter (*The Art of Biblical Poetry,* 179).
32. Synonymous parallelism is fairly common (see Prov. 20:1a; cf. 17:4 and 18:7), especially in chapters 18 and 19. Synthetic parallelism, frequent in chapters 16–22, has two main variations—either completing the thought (16:3, 6–7, 10, 12) or advancing the thought (16:4) (Hubbard, *Proverbs,* 19, and Ross, "Proverbs," 888). Also see Greg W. Parsons, "Guidelines for Understanding and Proclaiming the Psalms," *Bibliotheca Sacra* 147 (April–June 1990): 179–81.
33. This estimate comes from Johnson, *Israel's Wisdom: Learn and Live,* 20.
34. Hubbard, *Proverbs,* 19.
35. Ross, "Proverbs," 888. However, as Hubbard observes, this type also plays a significant role in chapters 1–9 in numerous antithetic summaries where "two back-to-back verses or lines state the positive and negative outcomes of heeding or spurning wisdom" (*Proverbs,* 19). See 1:32–33; 2:21–22; 3:33–35; 4:18–19; 8:35–36; 9:12.
36. William S. LaSor, David A. Hubbard, and Frederick W. Bush, *Old Testament Survey* (Grand Rapids: Eerdmans, 1982), 308.
37. See William E. Mouser, Jr., *Walking in Wisdom* (Downers Grove, Ill.: InterVarsity, 1983), 60.

taining the main point of the comparison within its historical-cultural milieu.[38]

In analyzing the meaning of half of the parallelism, one must consider the proverb as a whole, utilizing both halves of the verse. For instance Proverbs 10:1 reads, "A wise son makes a father glad, but a foolish son is a grief to his mother." The two halves of this antithetic proverb must not be isolated so as to conclude mistakenly that a mother has no joy in a wise son or that the "macho" father shows no grief over a foolish son. Rather the parallelism of "father"/"mother" means "parents" who share emotions of joy or grief.[39] Thus the total message may be greater than the sum of its independent components; it emerges from the harmonious interaction between the two lines.[40]

The clues in the various English translations as to the probable kind of parallelism need to be observed carefully. Antithetical parallelisms normally use the word "but." Emblematic parallelisms have the word "like" or "as" at the beginning of one line. However, since a translator frequently has added these words from the context (as in 25:25–26, 28),[41] the reader must be cautious about the "announced" kind of parallelism. These clues may sometimes convey an incorrect message.[42]

Since so much of the Book of Proverbs consists of individual proverbs (which may be compared to color slides placed somewhat randomly in a projector tray), the hermeneutical caveat implied in the proverb, "A text without a context is a pretext," must be applied in a unique manner. (a) The internal context of each individual proverb is heightened. (b) Other verses in the immediate paragraph(s) or chapter(s) are not nearly so important as the literary and theological context of the whole collection. A topical study of the subjects and words will provide a perspective helpful in interpreting an individual proverb.[43] Proverbs employs the technical jargon of wisdom literature. Through the use of a good concordance (especially in Hebrew), the expositor can analyze the specialized meanings of such words as "way" (or "path") or

38. Cf. ibid., 60–64. The expositor must avoid the temptation to judge the significance of the parallelism from a modern Occidental perspective.

39. LaSor, Hubbard, and Bush, *Old Testament Survey*, 309, 316.

40. Alter notes that one problem for many readers is that much of Proverbs has indeed become proverbial in English with the result that only a portion of the individual proverb is quoted. This tends to divorce one half from its mate and distorts the proverb's meaning (*The Art of Biblical Poetry*, 164). Ronald Barclay Allen gives the analogy of stereophonic sound to illustrate the need to "hear" both lines of Hebrew poetry (*Praise! A Matter of Life and Breath* [Nashville: Nelson, 1980], 51).

41. Students of Hebrew realize that the conjunction ן may be translated "and" or "but" or "so" or a variety of other ways. Sometimes the two lines are connected in asyndetic fashion (a mere juxtaposition) with no conjunction at all.

42. Mouser, *Walking in Wisdom*, 32–33, 74.

43. Though all usages of a specific word or phrase in Proverbs are important, perhaps the first priority should be occurrences within the primary context of a specific subcollection (e.g., 10:1–22:16).

"law." A study of these words will reveal rich dividends.[44] Though a study of "way" (דֶּרֶךְ) in Proverbs 22:6 will not resolve all difficulties, the expositor may find help in coming to his own conclusions.[45] The word "law" (תּוֹרָה) usually does not mean the Law of Moses but the authoritative instruction of a parent or teacher (cf. Prov. 3:1).[46]

The theological context of the "motto" (1:7; 9:10) must always be considered.

In longer units in chapters 1–9 or 30–31, certain literary clues should be noted as evidence of structural links or grouping. The use of repetition, catchwords, and *inclusios* are some of the most prominent devices.[47]

Guideline Three: Beware of the Erroneous Assumption That Proverbs Are Unconditional Promises.

It is important for the expositor to become aware of the assumptions and nature of proverbial wisdom literature.[48]

Assumptions of proverbial wisdom. Bullock correctly observes that the Book of Proverbs as wisdom literature assumes "a fundamental relationship between the natural and social/moral order."[49] Proverbs 3:19–20, which states that Yahweh created the universe through wisdom, and the many references to His acts of creation (8:22–31) demonstrate that creation is viewed as the basis for order in the universe. The implication is that God through wisdom placed "order" in the very fabric of the cosmos. These verses set the stage for the whole book, which is designed to exhibit the order that holds together all

---

44. Proverbs uses several Hebrew words for "path" or "way." Proverbs 4:11–19, 25–26 illustrates most of them. Verse 11 refers to the "way" (דֶּרֶךְ) of wisdom and the right "paths" (lit., "wagon-tracks" [מַעְגַּל]) of uprightness. Verse 14 contrasts the "pathway" (אֹרַח) of the wicked with the "way" (דֶּרֶךְ) of the evil ones. Verses 18 and 19 contrast the "pathway" (אֹרַח) of the righteous as light and the "way" (דֶּרֶךְ) of the wicked as darkness.

45. The specific use of this word with the pronominal suffix suggests that the translation of "his way" may mean "his (own) way" (cf. 16:9; 11:5) in contrast to the traditional viewpoint of "the way he should go." Cf. Douglas Stuart, *Old Testament Exegesis: A Primer for Students and Pastors,* 2d ed. (Philadelphia: Westminster, 1984), 51–52. This may mean training should be given with consideration for his individuality (or habits). However, the context of 22:5 and 14:12 suggests that this meaning does not allow the child to have his own way (Derek Kidner, *The Proverbs: An Introduction and Commentary* [Downers Grove, Ill.: InterVarsity, 1964], 147). On the other hand, since Proverbs presents only two ways a child can go (the way of the righteous and wise or the way of the wicked and fool) there may be merit in retaining the traditional view (Ross, "Proverbs," 1061–62).

46. Hubbard, *Proverbs,* 25–26. However, Kidner argues that where the Hebrew תּוֹרָה occurs in the book unqualified (as in 28:9 and 29:18) it refers to divine law, but when qualified (as in 1:8; 3:1; and 13:14) it refers to home teaching (*The Proverbs,* 63). This conclusion should be evaluated in light of the specific data. Hubbard argues that a dogmatic position cannot be taken on 28:9 (*Proverbs,* 290–91).

47. See Hubbard, *Proverbs,* 23–24, for examples.

48. Cf. some general assumptions of wisdom literature as part of what Bullock calls "biblical humanism" (*Introduction to Old Testament Poetic Books,* 54, 63–65).

49. Ibid., 162.

of life.[50] Within this context there is a "solidarity" between all parts of God's creation, over which He is Ruler, from the universe itself down to a colony of ants (6:6). What one observes in the natural cosmos has implications for understanding the social and moral order.[51]

Proverbs assumes that the physical and moral universe operates by cause and effect. Therefore good behavior is rewarded and bad deeds are punished (e.g., 10:30). In Hubbard's words, the various "*analogies* and *comparisons* between animal life and human experience make sense (see chap. 30) because behind both stands the hand of the one Creator. It is that hand which underlies the *cause* and *effect* pattern of proverbs, where good conduct carries its own reward and bad behavior brings its own woe."[52]

The nature of proverbial wisdom. Because proverbs are wise observations based on experience, they must not be understood as unconditional promises but as pragmatic principles (or procedures) to follow.[53] Neither are the proverbs "legal guarantees from God" but rather "poetic guidelines for good behavior."[54] Thus the proverbs tell what generally takes place without making an irreversible rule that fits all circumstances. This is a key to understanding problematic proverbs such as 22:6.[55] This verse should not be considered a promise but a general "principle of education and commitment."[56]

Furthermore certain proverbs that make amoral observations (e.g., 14:20; 17:8) must not be seen as condoning or encouraging evil.[57] A distinction must be made between what is described and what is prescribed as proper.[58]

The proverbs are limited by the characteristics of brevity and catchiness. On the surface some proverbs read almost like an algebraic equation or mechanical law (22:4).[59] However, Fee and Stuart aptly state that proverbs are "worded to be memorable" rather than "technically precise."[60] The very lit-

50. Hubbard, *Proverbs*, 25. Also see Waltke, "The Book of Proverbs and Ancient Wisdom Literature," 233. For a helpful summary of those who view wisdom as basically "a search for creation's order so as to master life" and for those who reject this, see Roy B. Zuck, "A Biblical Theology of the Wisdom Books and the Song of Songs," in *A Biblical Theology of the Old Testament*, ed. Roy B. Zuck (Chicago: Moody, 1991), 211–13.

51. Bullock, *Introduction to Old Testament Poetic Books*, 162; Kidner, *The Wisdom of Proverbs, Job and Ecclesiastes*, 14.

52. Hubbard, *Proverbs*, 25 (italics his).

53. Cf. Bullock, *Introduction to Old Testament Poetic Books*, 162.

54. Fee and Stuart, *How to Read the Bible for All Its Worth*, 98–99, 203.

55. Walter C. Kaiser, Jr., *The Uses of the Old Testament in the New* (Chicago: Moody, 1985), 199.

56. Bullock, *Introduction to Old Testament Poetic Books*, 162.

57. Cf. Achtemeier, *Preaching from the Old Testament*, 171.

58. Walter C. Kaiser, Jr., *Toward Old Testament Ethics* (Grand Rapids: Zondervan, 1983), 66.

59. Alden observes that the verse seems to say, "Obedience plus humility equals riches, honor, and life" (Robert L. Alden, *Proverbs: A Commentary on an Ancient Book of Timeless Advice* [Grand Rapids: Baker, 1983], 160).

60. Fee and Stuart, *How to Read the Bible for All Its Worth*, 196, 201–3.

erary form necessitates that they overstate the case and oversimplify without including "fine print" or "footnotes" with "lists of exceptions."[61] So one must be alert to the following limitations implied from an overall study of the context of the Book of Proverbs.[62]

Examples of specific limitations stated or implied in the Book of Proverbs.

1. Proverbs 26:4–5 demonstrates limitations to certain circumstances. These side-by-side, opposite proverbs should not be considered as inconsistent or contradictory but as defining specific situations noted in the biblical text.[63]

Complementary proverbs imply that the application of a specific aphorism must be tempered by certain conditions. Proverbs 15:22 praises careful planning with the use of human counselors; however, this is balanced with the warning that while "man proposes, God disposes" (19:21; 16:9; cf. 20:24; 21:30–34).[64] Zuck suggests that folly, which according to 22:15 is "bound up in the heart of the child," may introduce a situation that is an exception to the general principle of 22:6.[65]

2. Proverbs may be limited to a certain tendency of things to cause a particular effect (see 15:1). A gentle answer may turn away wrath, but at times such an answer may have no positive effect on stubborn individuals.[66]

3. Proverbs may be limited to what ought to be done not (necessarily) what actually takes place (see 16:10).[67]

The literary context of wisdom literature as a whole. This brings a more balanced understanding to the Proverbs. The traditional wisdom of Proverbs, which deals with the "built-in regularities which make nine-tenths of life manageable," is challenged by Job and Qoheleth.[68] The message of these two books illustrates that the proverbs are ultimately limited by the mystery of Yahweh's sovereignty. The natural order God established in the universe cannot tell everything about God. Hubbard rightly concludes that fear of the Lord[69] should restrict self-confidence in using the various proverbs to determine how God will act.

61. Hubbard, *Proverbs,* 25.
62. Ironically the person who desires to use the Proverbs in the pursuit of wisdom must use wisdom in reading and employing the proverbial genre (Long, *Preaching and the Literary Forms of the Bible,* 58).
63. Kaiser, *Toward Old Testament Ethics,* 64.
64. Kidner, *The Wisdom of Proverbs, Job and Ecclesiastes,* 26. Cf. Hubbard, *Proverbs,* 25.
65. Zuck, "A Biblical Theology of the Wisdom Books and the Song of Songs," 234.
66. Kaiser, *Toward Old Testament Ethics,* 64. Cf. Kaiser, *The Uses of the Old Testament in the New,* 199.
67. Kaiser, *Toward Old Testament Ethics,* 65.
68. "Proverbs seems to say, 'Here are the rules for life: try them and see they will work.' Job and Ecclesiastes say, 'We did, and they don't'" (David A. Hubbard, "The Wisdom Movement and Israel's Covenant Faith," *Tyndale Bulletin* 17 [1966]: 6). These books operate in "creative conflict" with Proverbs. See Kidner, *The Wisdom of Proverbs, Job and Ecclesiastes,* 36, 116–24).
69. The fear of God is a common denominator in wisdom literature (see esp. Prov. 1:7; 9:10; Job 28:28; Ps. 111:10; Eccles. 12:13; and numerous other instances).

We cannot use proverbs like subway tokens, guaranteed to open the turnstile every time. They are guidelines, not mechanical formulas. . . . We heed them as best we can, try to gain the wisdom that experience can teach, and then leave large amounts of room for God to surprise us with outcomes different from what our plans prescribe.[70]

Guideline Four: Realize That Some Proverbs Are Unconditionally True (e.g., Prov. 16:2, 12, 33).

The recognition that the proverbs have limitations does not nullify the fact that some proverbs may always be true. Frequently these are connected to an attribute or action of God (11:1; 12:22; 15:3; 16:2, 33; 22:2). However, this does not mean that because the name of the Lord is used in the proverb there is a "blank check" to use in an unconditional fashion. For instance 15:25 and 16:7 must not be forced to apply to all situations. The experience of mankind will often alert the expositor to proverbs that have exceptions. However, ultimately the way to decide whether a proverb is always true or limited to certain circumstances is not by means of a subjective "vote" but by correlation with the rest of the biblical canon, beginning with the context of the Book of Proverbs and of wisdom literature as a whole and concluding with the New Testament evidence.[71]

Guideline Five: Interpret the Book of Proverbs in Light of the Historical-Cultural Context of Extrabiblical Wisdom Literature.

This is imperative for at least two reasons. First, Solomon was not the sole author of all the Proverbs but the inspired editor or collector of wise sayings from other cultures.[72] Second, the Book of Proverbs shares the literary forms of the proverbial and wisdom literature of the ancient Near

70. Hubbard, *Proverbs*, 25.

71. For instance the promises of long life, peace, riches, and honor to those who obey the commandments of parents or wisdom teachers in chapter 3 (see esp. vv. 1–2, 16) can be clarified by noting Jesus' life. Though he embodied wisdom and fulfilled all the requirements of Proverbs 3, he did not have a long life, riches, or much honor while on earth (in seeming contradiction to the text). This does not mean that these proverbs are inaccurate or uninspired; rather this illustrates that they are general precepts which describe the norm but are not without exception. Ephesians 6:1–4 includes a "promise" of blessing and long life on earth. Though the commandment to obey and honor parents must be considered as absolute (Exod. 20:12), the motivation or reward must not be interpreted as an unconditional promise. God in his sovereignty may make an exception as in the case of Jesus.

72. This is clear from the plain statement that Proverbs includes the words of King Lemuel (31:1), apparently a non-Israelite. Further support is derived from the possible translation of the word "oracle" in 30:1 and 31:1 as "Massa," which may identify Agur and Lemuel as Ishmaelite converts from northern Arabia (cf. Gen. 25:14). See Kidner, *The Wisdom of Proverbs, Job and Ecclesiastes*, 33 (also n. 1) and Bullock, *Introduction to Old Testament Poetic Books*, 164, 176. Furthermore the several parallels between Proverbs and Egyptian literature (esp. 22:17–23:14 and the Egyptian "Instruction of Amenemope[t]") demonstrates that the Book was not written in a vacuum. See Kidner, *The Wisdom of Proverbs, Job and Ecclesiastes*, 126–32, for some specific parallels, and Waltke, "The Book of Proverbs and Ancient Wisdom Literature," 234–35.

East.[73] This common literary background may help the interpreter achieve one of the purposes of the Proverbs, namely, to understand the various types of wisdom literature including proverbs, instructions, riddles, and fables (1:2b, 6.).[74]

An awareness of the historical-cultural and literary background of Proverbs minimizes the temptation to interpret Proverbs from the modern Occidental perspective. A common error is to forget that Proverbs is an ancient wisdom book. For example one would totally miss the meaning of Proverbs 26:17 if one envisioned a pet dog being taken by the ears. In the ancient world, dogs were wild scavengers similar to jackals.

Sometimes figures of speech complicate the problem of understanding the ancient text. The meaning of "you will heap burning coals on his head" (25:21–22; Rom. 12:20) is confusing to the modern reader. An awareness of Egyptian culture may provide the answer. One clue may be in the next verse (25:23), which has perplexed commentators because in Palestine the north wind does not bring rain.[75] However, since this statement is true for Egypt, it may suggest an Egyptian milieu for the proverbs in this section. One Egyptian text records that a penitent would go to the one he wronged carrying a clay dish on his head with burning coals. Thus the possible meaning of the proverb is that if one acts charitably he may bring his enemy to repentance.[76]

Suggested Homiletical Guidelines for Proverbs

Guideline One: In Seeking to Apply a Proverb, Be Sure to Validate the Application through the Context of the Bible.

Note the context of Proverbs and wisdom literature. A common error is to take the proverbs out of context and misapply them in a literalistic way. For instance, Proverbs 10:22, which speaks of God's blessing of wealth, is sometimes preached as a sign that God wants all believers to prosper materially.[77]

---

73. Chapters 1–9 and 22:17–24:22 share many of the same literary forms as the instruction genre of Egypt and Mesopotamia. For an extensive introduction to this extrabiblical literature including analysis of literary forms, see William McKane, *Proverbs,* The Old Testament Library (Philadelphia: Westminster, 1970), 51–208. Concerning the commonality of literary forms between Proverbs and the Egyptian literature, see the brief but beneficial remarks of Waltke, "The Book of Proverbs and Ancient Wisdom Literature," 223–26.

74. Ross, "Proverbs," 884–85, 906. It may assist the student in understanding various abstract concepts which are conveyed through figures of speech. For instance the personification of wisdom found in chapters 1–9 is similar to the personification of *maʾat,* the Egyptian term for wisdom. For implications of the concept *maʾat* for understanding biblical "wisdom," see Waltke, "The Book of Proverbs and Ancient Wisdom Literature," 232–34.

75. The KJV translation, "the north wind driveth away rain," is incorrect, perhaps being influenced by the translation of Jerome's Vulgate. Jerome's knowledge of the weather patterns of Palestine caused him to mistranslate the Hebrew word. See Mouser, *Walking in Wisdom,* 62–63.

76. See Peter Cotterell and Max Turner, *Linguistics and Biblical Interpretation* (Downers Grove, Ill.: InterVarsity, 1989), 302–5.

77. Grant R. Osborne, *The Hermeneutical Spiral: A Comprehensive Introduction to Biblical Interpretation* (Downers Grove, Ill.: InterVarsity, 1991), 192.

However, the immediate context is a contrast between the righteous who work diligently and the wicked who are negligent (10:3–5), both of whom the Lord will pay accordingly (10:16). The application must be tempered by the larger context of other verses which clearly imply that godly individuals may be poor[78] (see 15:16; 16:8; 19:1; 28:6).

Doing typical studies in Proverbs with the help of a good concordance provides an initial safeguard against using any single proverb as a "proof text."[79]

An awareness of the overall context of Proverbs may clarify certain passages (e.g., 31:10–31). To read this passage in a literal fashion and preach it as the pattern for women today may leave many wives and mothers feeling inadequate. As Fee and Stuart observe, this passage could seem to "the literalistic reader to be a pattern of life impossible for any mortal woman to follow."[80] But is this the purpose of the acrostic poem? The numerous parallels between the feminine imagery of chapters 1–9 and 31:10–31 suggest that the ideal woman embodies the essence of wisdom that has been espoused in the book.[81] Therefore it seems likely that hyperbole has been used to emphasize the joy a good wife and mother brings to her family.[82] These parallels plus the mention of the fear of the Lord in 31:30 serve as a literary *inclusio* to balance out the first main section (chaps. 1–9).[83] Through somewhat idealized language and the use of the alphabetic acrostic, the passage implies that the young man ought to marry someone like Lady Wisdom.[84] Since the description is couched in the language of ancient Israel's culture and may include hyperbole, one must exercise care in transferring this to today's society.

78. Ibid.

79. Kaiser argues cogently that the Bible "gives no aid to the view that poverty is in all its forms a result of the judgment of God and an evidence that the persons so afflicted are outside the will of God. Such a universal categorization is a caricature of the biblical position" (Walter C. Kaiser, Jr., "The Old Testament Promise of Material Blessings and the Contemporary Believer," *Trinity Journal* 9 [fall 1988]: 166). Though many have become poor through laziness (10:4–5; 12:24; 20:13), ignoring discipline (13:18), or through gluttony and drunkenness (23:20–21), others are impoverished only because of the providential will of God (29:13); therefore the poor must not be mocked (17:5).

80. Fee and Stuart, *How to Read the Bible for All Its Worth*, 201–2.

81. For a summary of the most significant parallels, see Claudia V. Camp, *Wisdom and the Feminine in the Book of Proverbs* (Sheffield: Almond, 1985), 188–89; also see Zuck, "A Biblical Theology of the Wisdom Books and the Song of Songs," 237–38.

82. Fee and Stuart, *How to Read the Bible for All Its Worth*, 202.

83. See Henri Blocher, "The Fear of the Lord as the 'Principle' of Wisdom," *Tyndale Bulletin* 28 (1977): 4–5.

84. Herbert Wolf, "Proverbs," in *The NIV Study Bible* (Grand Rapids: Zondervan, 1985), 945. This does not mean that the text has no application for today. By contrast Collins expresses doubt that this description can be used as a job description for the modern woman (*Proverbs Ecclesiastes*, 68–70). Zuck cites valid objections to the view that the ideal woman is merely the personification of wisdom ("A Biblical Theology of the Wisdom Books and the Song of Songs," 237–38). For instance, in contrast to personified wisdom of chapters 1–9, the woman of chapter 31 is described as having a husband (v. 11) and as a mother (vv. 15, 28). But the literary evidence implies that the poem describes not only a wise woman and mother. The portrait is idealized to remind the reader of Lady Wisdom.

Note the context of the Bible. Though Proverbs does not mention the "salvation history" of Israel as in the Pentateuch and the Prophets, the expositor must not ignore the implicit covenantal context of the book. The foundational motto concerning the fear of Yahweh, the covenant God of Israel, tied creation and covenant together.[85] The Proverbs were spoken in a culture in which the religious character of life permeated everything. Consequently Long argues, "To listen to a proverb without at the same time hearing its covenantal background is to pry a gem from its setting."[86] Therefore the "antecedent theology"[87] of the Pentateuch and other books may be important in interpreting some of the proverbs. For instance, the proverbs condemning dishonesty in business may be a poetic reflection of the legislation of the Torah. Those referring to false weights and measures as being abominable to the Lord (11:1; 20:10, 23; cf. 16:11) imply the commands of Leviticus 19:35–36 and Deuteronomy 25:13–16.[88] Kaiser suggests that the seemingly materialistic motivations of Proverbs may find clarification in Leviticus 26 and Deuteronomy 28.[89] As Hubbard wrote,

> This covenant setting is what keeps the proverbs from shriveling into legalism. Their ground rules for life are not a prescription for salvation. . . . The proverbs are not bite-size tablets of the law but neither are they sparkling tokens of grace. . . . They are designed to enable us to live out the full meaning of the life that springs fresh daily from the hand of the Creator and Savior.[90]

Thus the expositor must consider the impact of the coming of Christ and the New Covenant in seeking to understand and apply proverbial wisdom. The New Testament portrays Christ as the Wisdom of God (1 Cor. 1:24, 30). Therefore the invitations of Lady Wisdom (Prov. 8:32–36) should be proclaimed in tandem with that of Christ (cf. Matt. 11:27–30).[91] Furthermore one must carefully note any quotations, allusions, or New Testament parallels

---

85. As Hubbard rightly notes, Israel's wise men did not have a different religion from the psalmists and the prophets (*Proverbs*, 29).

86. See Long, *Preaching and the Literary Forms of the Bible*, 58–59.

87. This is Kaiser's term to describe the "informing theology" of chronologically previous scriptural teachings available to the recipients of a particular book of the Bible (Walter C. Kaiser, Jr., *Toward an Exegetical Theology: Biblical Exegesis for Preaching and Teaching* [Grand Rapids: Baker, 1981], 161).

88. Alden, *Proverbs*, 91.

89. Kaiser argues that those promises of material blessings for the covenant keepers involved Israel's corporate calling ("The Old Testament Promise of Material Blessings and the Contemporary Believer," 156–57). Therefore corporate blessing, not individual blessing, may be the ultimate intent of these passages. However, this thesis should be tested with the specific evidence. Proverbs 3:7–10 seems to offer material blessing to the individual (Hebrew singular pronouns are used).

90. Hubbard, *Proverbs*, 30.

91. Cf. Kidner, *The Proverbs*, 16, and Achtemeier, *Preaching from the Old Testament*, 175–76.

to the Proverbs.[92] Also the practical wisdom of the Book of James and other portions of the New Testament, written under wisdom influence, must be explored.[93]

Guideline Two: Utilize the Characteristics and Nature of Proverbial Wisdom as a Foundation for Graphic Communication of Timeless Principles.

Certain essential characteristics of the proverbs, namely, brevity, intelligibility, and "flavor,"[94] make them ripe for proclamation. Josh Billings stated that "genuine proverbs are like good kambrick needles—short, sharp, and shiny."[95] They are thought-provoking to the interpreter. On one hand they prick the mind through their "teasing refusal to explain themselves." On the other hand they prick one into thought by the sharpness of brevity and by vivid pictures and analogies.[96] Recapturing this flavor of being simple and clear yet profound[97] helps produce a good sermon. These characteristics make proverbs memorable, an excellent "handle" on which to attach a timeless principle.

Proverbs are stimulating, not boring. Although not entertaining in the strictest sense, they are sometimes humorous (e.g., 11:22; 26:13–14; 27:14). Through this type of "honest humor," instruction is more likely to be received and retained than through a sermonic tone.[98]

Another important characteristic of proverbs is that they are universal and timeless, not restricted to ancient Israel. Because they have been germinated in the soil of time and experience,[99] the expositor can transplant them into modern society.

> The experiential richness of proverbs means that the environment where they really come to life is the everyday situation where they apply. . . . The best way

92. For a convenient listing of New Testament quotations (or paraphrases) of Proverbs with a comparative analysis in English of the possible source of the quotation (whether Septuagint or Masoretic Text), see Robert G. Bratcher, *Old Testament Quotations in the New Testament,* 3d rev. ed. (London: United Bible Societies, 1987), 85–86 and various other pages. Readers who know Hebrew and Greek may consult Gleason L. Archer and Gregory Chirichigno, *Old Testament Quotations in the New Testament* (Chicago: Moody, 1983), 90–93.
93. According to Osborne, other key passages which have imbibed wisdom influence are aspects of the Sermon on the Mount (especially the antitheses of Matt. 5:21–48 and the emphasis on ethical conduct), the practical exhortations of Romans 12 and portions of the Book of Hebrews (3:12–19; 4:11–13; 6:1–12), social codes (Eph. 5:22–6:9; 1 Pet. 2:11–3:7) and "vice or virtue lists" (Gal. 5:19–23; Col. 3:5–17) (*The Hermeneutical Spiral,* 198).
94. R. C. Trench, cited in LaSor, Hubbard, and Bush, *Old Testament Survey,* 538.
95. Cited in John H. Scammon, *The Book of Proverbs: Good Advice for Good Living* (Valley Forge, Penn.: Judson, 1979), 16.
96. Kidner, *The Wisdom of Proverbs, Job and Ecclesiastes,* 19.
97. See Leland Ryken, *Words of Delight: A Literary Introduction to the Bible* (Grand Rapids: Baker, 1987), 315.
98. Bullock, *Introduction to Old Testament Poetic Books,* 149–51. Also see Kidner, *The Wisdom of Proverbs, Job and Ecclesiastes,* 31.
99. Bullock, *Introduction to Old Testament Poetic Books,* 19, 147.

to teach or study biblical proverbs is to supply a context for each one from someone's actual experiences or from observations of what is going on in society and the world.[100]

Also the expositor should consider the literary and rhetorical effect of proverbs as a factor in making valid and relevant applications. Long suggests that the rhetorical effect of a proverb is to propel the reader in two directions— both backwards and forward. The proverb makes a reference backward by summoning the reader to imagine the kind of experiences that caused its development. It also sends the readers on a memory search for suitable examples. It pushes the reader forward by implying yet future incidents in which it will apply. It provokes the imagination to ponder "other situations in which the wisdom of the proverb may apply and thereby provides an ethical guide for wise response."[101] A sermon from Proverbs should seek to "do the same work and create the same effect as the proverb out of which it grows."[102]

Designed as a manual for successful living, Proverbs provides both negative and positive guidelines. The instruction genre (or admonition form) provides a good foundation for application with its dual emphasis: a prohibition or a negative example to avoid, and/or a positive command or example to be emulated.[103] Proverbs demonstrates that there are only two paths to follow—the way of the righteous (or wise) and the way of the wicked (or fools). This anticipates the New Testament teaching that there is no middle ground.[104]

Though Proverbs is fertile ground for modern application, some cautions are urged. First, one must remember that the proverbs do not necessarily fit all situations and are not promises. A particular proverb can properly apply only when it corresponds with those situations "that are similar in key ways to the ones that called it forth."[105] Second, one must recognize that some proverbs are problematic because of cultural considerations. One must determine whether they are still applicable (as worded) or whether modern equivalents should be substituted in the transfer to today's society. The problem of Proverbs 23:13–14 has already been cited. The context of verse 14 in conjunction with the similar proverb in 13:24 helps clarify the intent of the text. Proverbs 23:14 and 13:24 clearly give love as the motivation for discipline. The latter

100. Ryken, *Words of Delight: A Literary Introduction to the Bible,* 316–17. One reason for the applicability of proverbs is the practical orientation inherent in the design to instruct the young person in his proper place in society. See Osborne, *The Hermeneutical Spiral,* 192.
101. Long, *Preaching and the Literary Forms,* 56–57, 59.
102. Ibid., 59. In discussing Proverbs 15:17, Long illustrates the concept of calling forth memories that illustrate a proverb (ibid., 62–65).
103. Cf. LaSor, Hubbard, and Bush, *Old Testament Survey,* 547, 552, and Mouser, *Walking in Wisdom,* 137–38.
104. See especially John's writings; cf. LaSor, Hubbard, and Bush, *Old Testament Survey,* 552, and Crenshaw, *Old Testament Wisdom: An Introduction,* 80.
105. Long, *Preaching and the Literary Forms,* 57.

verse shows that diligent (and perhaps "careful," as in the NIV)[106] discipline is in view rather than an angry and unrestrained beating.[107]

Several proverbs express their wisdom according to practices and institutions that are foreign to modern audiences. Unless the expositor understands this and is able to translate them properly, the meaning will seem irrelevant or become completely lost.[108] Two examples are Proverbs 25:24 (repeated in 21:9) and 27:15. In the former case, one must realize that flat-roofed houses of Bible times enabled people to sleep there especially in hot weather.[109] A paraphrase for "corner of the roof" might be attic[110] or patio or porch. The other verse (27:15) illustrates the need to comprehend cultural aspects to understand the figures of speech in Proverbs. The meaning is enhanced when one realizes that the dripping of rain did not lull a person to sleep. Rather the dripping referred to the common but obnoxious sound caused by a leaky roof or by bad drainage. Thus a modern equivalent to the irritating noise might be "a leaky faucet."[111] Collins believes that some of these sayings are a "trifle chauvinistic."[112] Whether one agrees with this assessment, the expositor should be aware that the Proverbs were written in a culture in which women were not prominent.[113] In transferring these sayings to modern culture, the teachings of the New Testament should be carefully studied and applied with discernment in light of the concerns of women today.[114]

Thus to understand the cultural background is not all that is needed to make the right transfer to today. For instance it does not guarantee the correct understanding of the figures of speech. The interpretation of 26:8 is complicated since the cultural reference ("tying [or binding] a stone in a sling") is combined with a figure of speech comparing it to the honor to a fool. Osborne rightly suggests that since the sling was used as a weapon, the substitution of the word "gun" would be a modern equivalent.[115] However, he probably misses the point of the comparison by isolating it from the context of

106. The Hebrew word שׁחַר is probably best translated "treat early with discipline" (see Francis Brown, S. R. Driver, and Charles A. Briggs, *A Hebrew and English Lexicon of the Old Testament,* 1007, and Ross, "Proverbs," 982).

107. Cf. similarly Osborne, *The Hermeneutical Spiral,* 199.

108. Fee and Stuart, *How to Read the Bible for All Its Worth,* 202.

109. Alden, *Proverbs,* 155.

110. Hubbard, *Proverbs,* 427–28, and Osborne, *The Hermeneutical Spiral,* 201.

111. Mouser, *Walking in Wisdom,* 59–60, 63.

112. He asserts that they must not be taken as assigning blame to the woman any more than the man (Collins, *Proverbs Ecclesiastes,* 50).

113. Hubbard concludes that the masculine orientation of Proverbs is consistent with the initial purpose to provide leaders for a society in which women did not have the opportunities present-day society gives (*Proverbs,* 27–28).

114. Hubbard, *Proverbs,* 28. Cf. Kathleen A. Farmer, *Who Knows What Is Good? A Commentary on the Books of Proverbs and Ecclesiastes* (Grand Rapids: Eerdmans, 1991), 8–11. The present author does not necessarily agree with the conclusions of either of these writers in this matter.

115. He paraphrases, "Honoring a fool is like putting a bullet in a gun; it will soon go off and disappear" (*The Hermeneutical Spiral,* 201). But as noted above, this is probably not the point of the comparison (in view of the context of 26:1).

Proverbs. As McKane argues, the context of 26:1 is an important key in understanding the point of the figure, namely, the incongruity of giving honor to a fool. Therefore to bind a stone in a sling is "nonsense and an absurdity" since it was designed to be hurled as a projectile.[116]

Guideline Three: Explore the Creative Use of Proverbial Characters.

Imagination and sense of humor may be used in imitation of the proverbial characters. Proverbs 26:14 was not intended as a serious portrait of the sluggard but as a caricature.[117] Kidner states that lessons are better learned from these characters "by a flash of wit than by a roll of sermonic thunder."[118] The tragic comedy of the sluggard and other fools[119] is a seedbed for one's own imagination to illustrate in today's society.[120]

Proverbs 4 could be used by the expositor to warn young people of the dangers of not deciding for the Lord and to motivate them to commitment. Life is a series of forks in the road where decisions must be made.[121] Youth must pay attention to the road (4:21, 25–27) in order not to miss the correct turns. Ultimately there are only two routes to take: "Wisdom Lane" (vv. 10–13), which could be illustrated as a small ordinary-looking lane going up a big hill, and "Folly Freeway" (vv. 14, 17), an eight-lane expressway leading downward with apparently no obstacles or red lights.[122] Verse 19 shows that the ultimate destiny of the fool who fails to heed the warning signs is darkness, symbolizing destruction.[123]

Whybray wisely remarks that the use of creative imagination to visualize the circumstances behind Proverbs 26:14 and other sayings will "reveal a vivid picture of a real human society in all its variety." Much like the great novels of Charles Dickens, "a host of characters pass through its pages: the farmer,

116. McKane, *Proverbs*, 598.
117. R. N. Whybray, *The Book of Proverbs* (Cambridge: Cambridge University Press, 1972), 13.
118. Kidner, *The Wisdom of Proverbs, Job and Ecclesiastes*, 31.
119. Cf. Kidner, *The Proverbs*, 39–43.
120. For instance the present writer has compared the "simpleton" to the caricature of the "mugwump," the proverbial "fence-straddler" in American political history who was portrayed with his "mug" leaning over one side of the fence and with his "wump" (backside) on the other. The tragedy is that while the "simpleton" thinks he is "walking the fence" of a noncommittal lifestyle he is gradually becoming more and more the fool as he follows the stronger pull of folly. See the New Testament verdict for those who fail to make a decision on the highway of life (John 3:18).
121. Alden observes, "The precepts of Proverbs are like signposts" at the critical crossroads of life where the believer might miss the right road (*Proverbs*, 48).
122. Compare Jesus' teaching in Matthew 7:13–14.
123. In light of the New Testament this ultimate destination could be compared to a great canyon (the pits of hell). The wise person will listen to the advice of godly parents and wise teachers concerning the proper route to choose (4:1–2, 10). He must reject the counsel of the wicked man or woman (context of 2:10–20) in order to avoid the treacherous road leading to destruction.

the courtier, the drop-out, the dishonest trader, the adulterous woman, the husband absent on business, the street gang, the schoolboy and the teacher, the rather simple young man, the prostitute, the thief, the gossip, the royal messenger, and many more."[124]

These various characters are good object lessons for young people concerning the foolishness that leads to death, the tragic comedy of the sluggard, the ridiculous naiveté of the simple, and the irreverence and doom of the scoffer. The strong warnings against adultery in Proverbs 5–7 and 9 are very relevant for today's society.[125]

Also drama may be used to communicate the message of the proverbial characters.[126] The possibilities are almost unlimited for depicting the vivid characters in the Proverbs through drama.

The characters in Proverbs may also be correlated with other biblical personalities (whether named or unnamed) who illustrate wisdom themes. For example, Joseph is a classic example of a wise man who feared God.[127] The wise woman of Tekoa (2 Sam. 14) illustrates shrewdness in dealing with others.

Conclusion

Five guidelines for interpreting the Book of Proverbs have been suggested, and three suggestions were made to assist the expositor in proclaiming proverbial wisdom. It is the prayer of the present writer that readers have been challenged to utilize Proverbs more in their teaching or preaching ministry.[128]

---

124. Whybray, *The Book of Proverbs*, 13.

125. For instance the expositor must alert young and old alike to the bitter results of adultery (5:1–14) and the beauty of intimacy in marriage (5:15–23).

126. For instance when the writer's friend A. Dale Travis was preaching on the sluggard, his sons came into the church dressed like "hobos" or "bums." A "conversation" ensued in which the message was illustrated and reinforced.

127. See Kidner, *The Proverbs*, 15–16.

128. Not only is there a need for more preaching from the wisdom books, but the writer agrees with Osborne's recommendation that the wisdom material be used more often "as secondary texts to anchor the application of other Scriptural texts" (*The Hermeneutical Spiral*, 192–93).

Part 2

EXPOSITION
OF SPECIFIC PASSAGES
IN THE
BOOK OF PROVERBS

11

PROVERBS 1:1–19

Allen P. Ross

Introduction to the Book of Proverbs (1:1–7)

Title: The Proverbs of Solomon (1:1)

The proverbs of Solomon son of David, king of Israel:

This verse provides the general heading for the entire book, even though the proverbs of Solomon probably do not begin until chapter 10.

What is a proverb? The usage of *māšāl* (here *mišlê šᵉlōmōh*, "proverbs of Solomon") suggests the idea of likeness. Toy, referring to the Niphal, suggests the meaning "to become like, be comparable with" (p. 3). For example, Psalm 49:12 [13 MT] says that the one who lives only for this life is "like [*nimšal*] the beasts that perish"; and verse 4[5 MT] of the psalm identifies the poem as a wisdom psalm (*lᵉmāšāl*; "to a proverb"). The word appears also in 1 Samuel 10:12, to report how a proverb (*māšāl*, "a saying") came into being: "Is Saul also among the prophets?" His prophesying invited comparison with the prophets. This idea for *māšāl* is also supported by the Akkadian *mišlu* ("of like portions") and the Arabic *miṯlu* ("likeness").

A proverb may then be described as an object lesson based on or using some comparison or analogy. It may be a short saying that provides a general truth (Ezek. 16:44), a lesson drawn from experience (Ps. 78:2–6), a common example (Deut. 28:37), or a pattern of future blessing or cursing (Ezek. 21:1–5). The purpose of a proverb is to help one choose the best course of action among those available—the foolish way is to be avoided and the wise way followed (A. R. Johnson, *Wisdom in Israel and in the Ancient Near East,* ed. Martin Noth and D. Winton Thomas [Leiden: Brill, 1955], 162–69).

Purposes: To Develop Moral Skill and Mental Acumen (1:2–6)

> ²for attaining wisdom and discipline;
>   for understanding words of insight;
> ³for acquiring a disciplined and prudent life,
>   doing what is right and just and fair;
> ⁴for giving prudence to the simple,
>   knowledge and discretion to the young—
> ⁵let the wise listen and add to their learning
>   and let the discerning get guidance—
> ⁶for understanding proverbs and parables,
>   the sayings and riddles of the wise.

The Book of Proverbs has two purposes: to give moral skillfulness and to give mental discernment. The first purpose is developed in verses 3–4; then, after a parenthetical exhortation in verse 5, the second purpose is developed in verse 6.

The first purpose is that the disciple will develop skillfulness and discipline in holy living (v. 2a). "Attaining," from the infinitive *daʿaṯ* (lit., "to know"), encompasses an intellectual and experiential acquisition of wisdom and discipline.

"Wisdom" (*ḥokmāh*) basically means "skill." This word describes the "skill" of the craftsmen who worked in the tabernacle (Exod. 31:6), the "wits" of seasoned mariners (Ps. 107:27), administrative abilities (1 Kings 3:28), and the "wise advice" of a counselor (2 Sam. 20:22). In the Book of Proverbs "wisdom" signifies skillful living—the ability to make wise choices and live successfully according to the moral standards of the covenant community. The one who lives skillfully produces things of lasting value to God and the community.

The other object to be acquired is "discipline" (*mûsār*, cf. 3:5), the necessary companion of wisdom. *Mûsār* denotes the training of the moral nature, involving the correcting of waywardness toward folly and the development of reference to the Lord and personal integrity.

The second major purpose of the Book of Proverbs is for the disciple to acquire discernment (v. 2b). The meaning of the Hiphil infinitive *hābîn* ("to understand, discern") can be illustrated by the cognate preposition *bên* ("between"—"to discern" means to distinguish *between* things, to compare concepts, form evaluations, or make analogies).

The object of this infinitive is cognate to it: "words of insight" (*ʾimrê bînāh*). Proverbs will train people to discern lessons about life, such as distinguishing permanent values from immediate gratifications.

The first purpose statement is now developed. Once again an infinitive is used—the disciple will receive (*lāqaḥ,* "acquire") something worth having. In Proverbs 2:1 the verb *lāqaḥ* ("to accept") is parallel with *ṣāpan* ("to treasure, store up"). What the student receives is discipline (*mûsār*) and prudence (*haśkēl*). The Hiphil infinitive *haśkēl* indicates the (genitive of) result: discipline produces prudent living. To act prudently means "to act circumspectly." The concept may be illustrated by the actions of Abigail, the wife of the foolish Nabal (1 Sam. 25).

The three terms that follow—*ṣedeq, mišpāṭ,* and *mêšārîm*—are adverbial accusatives of manner, expressing how the prudent acts manifest themselves. The first term, "rightness" or "righteousness," means basically conformity to a standard, as in Deuteronomy 25:15, where weights and measures were required to be right. The religious use of the term signifies what is right according to the standard of God's law (see Deut. 16:18–20); namely, conduct that conforms to the moral standards of the covenant community (see Jer. 22:13; Hos. 10:12).

Prudent acts will also exhibit justice. *Mišpāṭ* (NIV, "just") essentially signifies a "decision" like that of an arbiter (see Deut. 16:18). It is applied to litigation (2 Sam. 15:2) and the precedent established by such (Exod. 21:9; used of a custom in 1 Kings 18:18). The term also connotes that which is fitting or proper (Judg. 13:12). Proverbs will develop a life that has a sense of propriety in making decisions.

The third quality is "equity" (NIV, "fair"). *Mêšārîm,* related to *yāšār* ("upright," "straight"), can describe that which is pleasing (Judg. 14:3 ["right one"], 7 ["liked"; lit., "she was right"]). The book will instruct a life style that is equitable, one that incorporates the most pleasing aspects (see Ps. 9:8 [9 MT]).

So the disciple of the Book of Proverbs will acquire discipline that will produce a prudent life, and that prudent life will be demonstrated by "doing what is right and just and fair."

The first purpose statement is now developed from the teacher's point of view—he will give shrewdness to the naive or "simple." (For a discussion of the simple person, see Kidner, *Proverbs,* 39.) This naive person (*peîî*) is one who is gullible (14:15), easily enticed (9:4, 16), and falls into traps (22:3). The instructor wants to give such a one a sense of shrewdness (*ʿormāh;* NIV, "prudence"), the ability to foresee evil and prepare for it (13:16; 22:3). With *ͨormāh* the naive will be able to avoid the traps in life (see Matt. 10:16).

The second half of the verse parallels "simple" or "naive" with "[immature] youth" (*naͨar*) and "shrewdness" or "prudence" with "knowledge" (*daͨaṯ*) and "discretion" (*mᵉzimmāh*, from *zāmam*, "to devise"). This latter expression refers to devising plans or perceiving the best course of action for gaining a goal (Toy, 7). *Daͨaṯ* and *mᵉzimmāh* may form a hendiadys, to be translated "purposive knowledge"; namely, the perceptive ability to make workable plans. Such ability is crucial for the immature youth in this world.

Before elaborating on the second purpose statement for the book, the writer digresses to make an exhortation. The first verb advises the wise to hear and the second gives the purpose—"[to] add to [*wᵉyōsep̱*] their learning."

Parallel to this advice is the counsel for the "discerning" (*nāḇôn*, part. of *bîn*) to get guidance. This person has the capacity of *bînāh*—he is one who is discerning. The "guidance" to be obtained is *taḥbulôt*, from *ḥāḇal*, meaning "to bind" (see *ḥeḇel*, "rope," "cord"). The term may be illustrated with the cognate *ḥōḇēl*, the rope-pulling done by sailors to steer or guide a ship. Cohen says *taḥbulôt* is the discernment to steer a right course through life (*Proverbs*, 2). Proverbs is not simply for the naive and the gullible; everyone can grow by its teachings. Discerning people can obtain guidance from this book so that they might continue in the right way.

The second major purpose of the book is to give mental acumen to the student (see under v. 2). The repetition of *lᵉhāḇîn* from verse 2b shows that this line expands that one. The point is that one needs to develop the ability to understand the language of the sages.

The teachings will develop one's ability in discerning "proverbs" (*māšāl*) and "parables" (*mᵉlîṣāh*). This latter term can refer to a satire, a mocking-poem, or an alluding saying. The verb *lîṣ*, related to the Arabic *lâṣa* ("to turn aside"), may have the idea of speaking indirectly. It may have included the idea of a spokesman, for *mēlîṣ* is an interpreter (Gen 42:23). *Mᵉlîṣāh* may then refer to a saying that has another sense to it that needs uncovering (see H. Neil Richardson, "Some Notes on ליץ and Its Derivatives," *VT* 5 [1955]: 163–79).

The disciple must understand also the "sayings" of the wise. *Diḇrê* is a general term, but with the genitive *ḥăḵāmîm* ("the wise") it becomes specific—the words come from the sages. Their teachings at times take the form of "riddles" (*ḥîḏôt*). This word, if related to the Arabic *ḥâda* ("to turn aside, avoid"), may refer to what is obscure or indirect, such as the riddles of Samson (Judg. 14:13–14) or of the queen of Sheba (1 Kings 10:1).

Motto: The Fear of the Lord (1:7)

The fear of the LORD is the beginning of knowledge,
  but fools despise wisdom and discipline.

Reverential fear of the Lord is the prerequisite of knowledge. The term *yirʾāh* can describe dread (Deut. 1:29), being terrified (Jon. 1:10), standing in awe (1 Kings 3:28), or having reverence (Lev. 19:3). With the Lord as the object, *yirʾāh* captures both aspects of shrinking back in fear and of drawing close in awe. It is not a trembling dread that paralyzes action, but neither is it a polite reverence (Plaut, 32). "The fear of the Lord" ultimately expresses reverential submission to the Lord's will and thus characterizes a true worshiper. In this context it is the first and controlling principle of knowledge. Elsewhere in Proverbs the fear of the Lord is the foundation for wisdom (9:10) or the discipline leading to wisdom (15:33); it is expressed in hatred of evil (8:13), and it results in a prolonged life (10:27).

On the other hand, fools disdain wisdom and discipline. Verse 7b is the antithesis of verse 7a. The term *ʾĕwîlîm* ("fools") describes those who are thick-brained or stubborn (Greenstone, 6). They lack understanding (10:21), do not store up knowledge (10:14), fail to attain wisdom (24:7), talk loosely (14:3), are filled with pride (26:5), and are contentious (20:3). They are morally unskilled and refuse any correction (15:5; 27:22).

Fools are people who "despise" (*bāzû*) wisdom, and discipline; they treat these virtues as worthless and contemptible. This attitude is illustrated in Genesis 25:34, where Esau despised the birthright, and in Nehemiah 4:4, where Sanballat and Tobiah belittled the Jews.

A Father's Admonition to Acquire Wisdom (1:8–9:18)

Introductory Exhortation (1:8–9)

> 8Listen, my son, to your father's instruction
>   and do not forsake your mother's teaching.
> 9They will be a garland to grace your head
>   and a chain to adorn your neck.

The disciple is exhorted to heed parental guidance. "My son," the customary form of address for a disciple, derives from the idea that parents are primarily responsible for moral instruction (Prov. 4:3–4; Deut. 6:7). Here the disciple is to respond to (*šĕmaʿ*; NIV, "listen," with the attitude of "taking heed to") "discipline" (*mûsār*; NIV, "instruction") that is normally the father's responsibility (except in 31:1, where it is the warning of the mother).

The son is also to follow his mother's teaching. *Tôrāh* ("teaching") may be cognate to a verb meaning "to point or direct" (cf. BDB, 434–35), so that the idea of teaching might be illustrated as pointing in the right direction (see Gen. 46:28). At any rate, in Proverbs this instruction is for ordering the life (see also 6:20; 31:26).

For heeding the instruction of the law, the disciple is promised an attractiveness of life. "Grace," the charm that teaching brings to the disciple, refers to those qualities that make him agreeable. The metaphor compares these qualities to an attractive wreath worn round the head.

Obedience will also improve the disciple, the metaphor of the neck pendant speaking of adorning the life. The one who loses the rough edges through disciplined training will present a pleasing presence to the world (McKane, p. 268).

Admonition to Avoid Easy but Unjust Riches (1:10–19)

> [10]My son, if sinners entice you,
>> do not give in to them.
> [11]If they say, "Come along with us;
>> let's lie in wait for someone's blood,
>> let's waylay some harmless soul;
> [12]let's swallow them alive, like the grave,
>> and whole, like those who go down to the pit;
> [13]we will get all sorts of valuable things
>> and fill our houses with plunder;
> [14]throw in your lot with us,
>> and we will share a common purse"—
> [15]my son, do not go along with them,
>> do not set foot on their paths;
> [16]for their feet rush into sin,
>> they are swift to shed blood.
> [17]How useless to spread a net
>> in full view of all the birds!
> [18]These men lie in wait for their own blood;
>> they waylay only themselves!
> [19]Such is the end of all who go after ill-gotten gain;
>> it takes away the lives of those who get it.

The summary statement warns the son not to consent to the enticement of moral misfits.[1] The term for "entice," related to the root of "simple" or "naive" (*pᵉtî*, from *pātāh*) mentioned in verse 4, means "to allure, persuade, entice, or seduce." Here the enticement is to do evil because it comes from "sinners" (*ḥaṭṭāʾîm* in this context describes professional criminals, a gang of robbers).

The nature of the enticement is that the young man is offered a part with professional criminals in a life of crime. The text explains how they waylay the unwary (vv. 11–12). The ambush he is asked to join is vicious; the verb *ʾārab* ("to lie in wait") is used elsewhere of hostile purposes such as murder (Deut.

---

1. For the conditional clause in the MT ("if sinners entice you"), the LXX has rendered a volitive: "Let not impious men lead you astray."

19:11), kidnapping (Judg. 21:20), or seduction (Prov. 23:28). Here the aim is bloodshed.

The attack is also evil. The wicked lie in wait for the innocent (*nāqî*; NIV, "harmless soul"), and their attack is without a cause (*ḥinnām* [untr. in NIV] is often used this way; see 1 Sam. 25:31; Ps. 35:7).

The criminals assure the novice of swift success: they will swallow up victims who are in the vitality of life (*tāmîm*, meaning "full of health," "whole") as surely and swiftly as death opens and swallows its victims (v. 12; cf. Num. 16:32–33); they determine to remove them from the living.[2] They are confident that by sharing the wealth (v. 13), they will fill their houses with "plunder" (*šālāl*). The use of *šālāl* elsewhere for spoils from war suggests that theirs was a life of crime (Cohen, *Proverbs,* 4). So the offer made to the youth is to pursue with the roustabouts a life of easy but ill-gotten gain (v. 14).

The young man's parents strongly advise him to avoid such evil companions because their life style, though it may appear prosperous, leads to destruction. The advice "do not go" (v. 15) counters the allurement of the wicked—"Come along with us" (v. 11). The primary reason for not going is that the sinners' purpose is bloodthirsty (v. 16); therefore their retribution is sure (cf. v. 18). In the final analysis, then, the trap the wicked lay for others in reality will catch them.

There are two ways to interpret verse 17 within the context. One is to see a comparison with the folly of birds who fall into a snare even though forewarned—likewise the wicked fall into the snare God lays because they are driven by lust. The other is to see a contrast between the natural behavior of birds when forewarned and the irrational greed of robbers. In other words, it is futile to spread out a net for birds that are watching, but these men are so blinded by evil that they fail to recognize the trap (v. 18). The blind folly of greed leads to their doom—retribution is the law that will take away their lives (v. 19; see also G. R. Driver, "Problems in the Hebrew Text of Proverbs," *Biblica* 32 [1951]: 173–74).

---

2. The LXX has an editorial variation for verse 12b patterned after Ps. 34:16 (17 MT) and 109:15—"Let us take away the remembrance of him from the earth."

12

WISDOM BUILDS A POEM: THE ARCHITECTURE OF PROVERBS 1:20–33

Phyllis Trible

Wisdom is a woman of many talents. In the Book of Proverbs she appears first as a poet who preaches, counsels, teaches, and prophesies (1:20–33). Her podium is the public arena; there she speaks to all sorts and conditions of people.

Since homiletic, advisory, didactic, and prophetic dimensions of the figure have their being in a poetic mode,[1] the poem itself is primary for understand-

---

From *Journal of Biblical Literature* 94 (December 1975): 509–18. Used by permission.

1. With variations and overlappings of views, scholars examine these dimensions. One group stresses the homiletic character of wisdom as a preacher of repentance: e.g., B. Gemser, *Sprüche Salomos,* HAT 16 (Tübingen: Mohr, 1937), 16–17; H. Ringgren, *Word and Wisdom in the Old Testament* (Lund: H. Ohlsson, 1947), 95–96; W. Frankenberg, *Die Sprüche,* HKAT (Göttingen: Vandenhoeck und Ruprecht, 1898), 22–23. A second group emphasizes the didactic dimension of wisdom as a teacher: e.g., W. McKane, *Proverbs* (London: SCM, 1970), 273–77; cf. C. H. Toy, *Proverbs,* ICC (New York: Scribner, 1904), 20–29. A third position focuses on wisdom as a prophet: e.g., A. Robert, "Les attaches littéraires bibliques de Prov. I–IX," *RB* 43 (1934): 172–81; C. Kayatz, *Studien zu Proverbien 1–9,* WMANT 22 (Neukirchen-Vluyn: Neukirchener Verlag, 1966), 119–29; cf. J. L. Crenshaw, "Wisdom," *Old Testament Form Criticism,* ed. J. H.

ing. Thus we propose to study its literary and rhetorical features in order to make explicit its pattern and posture.[2]

I

Our study contrasts with historical criticism,[3] which focuses on detecting and correcting irregularities in meter, rhythm, and content.[4] That approach does guard against interpretation on a flat surface. The pericope has a history, even though lack of adequate data prevents recovery of that past. In addition, historical criticism provides a negative value: the recognition that this work of art does not necessarily conform to our sensitivities about structure and content. Thereby we learn to let the poem reveal inner integrity. If we cannot recover past character, we may discover present mode.

Form criticism aids this discovery. Christa Kayatz has identified the genre of Proverbs 1:20–33 as a wisdom-sermon (*Weisheitspredigt*).[5] She stresses its impressive affinities with prophetic speech-forms and concludes that, unlike

---

Hayes (San Antonio: Trinity University, 1974), 248. The fourth view of wisdom as a counsellor is studied by P. A. H. de Boer, "The Counsellor," *Wisdom in Israel and in the Ancient Near East: Presented to Professor Harold Henry Rowley,* ed. M. Noth and D. Winton Thomas (VTSup 3; Leiden: Brill, 1955), 42–71, esp. 52. These views assume human models for the figure of wisdom in Prov. 1:20–33. For suggestions that the figure has a mythological background, see R. B. Y. Scott, *Proverbs, Ecclesiastes,* AB 18 (New York: Doubleday, 1965) 39; R. N. Whybray, *Wisdom in Proverbs,* SBT 45 (London: SCM, 1965), 76–104; B. L. Mack, "Wisdom Myth and Mythology," *Int* 24 (1970): 46–60. Cf. R. E. Murphy, "Assumptions and Problems in Old Testament Wisdom Research," *CBQ* 24 (1967): 109–12.

2. For this approach, see J. Muilenburg, "Form Criticism and Beyond," *JBL* 88 (1969): 1–18; R. E. Murphy, "Form Criticism and Wisdom Literature," *CBQ* 31 (1969): 476; D. Greenwood, "Rhetorical Criticism and Formgeschichte: Some Methodological Considerations," *JBL* 89 (1970): 418–26; J. L. Crenshaw, "Wisdom," 262–64. Cf. N. Frye, *Anatomy of Criticism* (Princeton: Princeton University Press, 1957), 82–94; E. D. Hirsch, Jr., *Validity in Interpretation* (New Haven, Conn.: Yale University Press, 1967), 68–69; R. Scholes, *Structuralism in Literature* (New Haven, Conn.: Yale University Press, 1974), 143–47.

3. The phrase "historical criticism" is not altogether adequate or accurate. Other phrases include literary-historical criticism, source criticism, and literary criticism. Though they all have problems, I resist specifically "literary criticism" for this approach. That phrase, along with "rhetorical criticism," as Muilenburg uses it, describes best the contrasting study which we present here. On this issue of terminology, see the relevant comments in the review by E. M. Good (*JBL* 92 [1973]: 287–89) of *Literary Criticism of the Old Testament,* by N. Habel (Philadelphia: Fortress, 1971). Cf. H. Gardner, *The Business of Criticism* (London: Oxford, 1959), 86–87, 97–98.

4. Among others, C. H. Toy represents this approach. To turn the entire poem into couplets, Toy drops vv. 22b, 23a, and 27c. In v. 21 he deletes as glosses "in the city" and "her words" (*Proverbs,* 20–22, 25). B. Gemser deletes "in the city" also, and he thinks that vv. 22c and 23c are perhaps additions, although comparable to v. 27c (*Sprüche,* 16). J. A. Emerton regards v. 22bc as a separate proverb displaced from its original position. *Contra* Toy, Emerton retains v. 23a but "corrects" its short meter by adding a word ("A Note on the Hebrew Text of Proverbs 1:22–23," *JTS* ns 19 [1968]: 609–14). For Whybray, the entire poem is a theological addition to the first discourse of Prov. 1:8–19. Further, verse 29 is a later insertion to link wisdom with the fear of Yahweh (*Wisdom in Proverbs,* 72–75).

5. *Proverbien,* 119. Cf. J. L. Crenshaw, who classifies it as an "imagined speech," a variant of the dialogue or *Streitgespräch* ("Wisdom," 255–56).

Proverbs 8, this poem rests in distinctive Israelite presuppositions without Egyptian influence.[6] Its formal components are words of reproach (*Scheltrede; Anklage*) and of threat (*Drohrede; Mahnung*), interspersed with promise (*Verheissung*).[7] Kayatz outlines the structure as follows:[8]

vv. 20–21:   Introduction of wisdom as a public preacher

v. 22:   Address to the simple, to scoffers, and to fools in the form of a question which reprimands; introduced by *ʿad-mātay*

v. 23:   A warning strengthened by a promise

v. 24:[9]   Reproach-speech, introduced by *yaʿan*

vv. 26–28:   Threatening speech, introduced by *gam-ʾānî* and by *ʾāz*

vv. 29–30:   Reproach-speech, introduced by *taḥat kî*

v. 31:   Threatening speech, introduced by *wᵉ*

v. 32:   Motivation, introduced by *kî*

v. 33:   Closing appeal in the form of a promise

On the whole, these divisions correspond to shifts in content, and they utilize clues to form which introductory words provide. But the divisions neglect repetitions of words, phrases, and motifs for the shaping of structure.[10] When these iterative features interact with content and with other rhetorical devices, a pattern emerges which the analysis of Kayatz does not demonstrate. That pattern is a chiasmus of four concentric circles converging on the center of the poem.

II

This diagram shows the overall architecture:

A   Introduction: an appeal for listeners (vv. 20–21)
   B   Address to the untutored, scoffers, and fools (v. 22)
      C   Declaration of disclosure (v. 23)
         D   Reason for the announcement (vv. 24–25)
         ▷E   Announcement of derisive judgment (vv. 26–27)
         D′   Result of the Announcement, with interruption (vv. 28–30)
      C′   Declaration of retribution (v. 31)
   B′   Address about the untutored and fools (v. 32)
A′   Conclusion: an appeal for a hearer (v. 33)

---

6. Kayatz, *Proverbien*, 122–29, 133–34.
7. Standard terminology for form-critical study is needed; see J. L. Crenshaw, "Wisdom," 262–63.
8. *Proverbien*, 120.
9. Kayatz does not mention verse 25.
10. See J. Muilenburg, "A Study in Hebrew Rhetoric: Repetition and Style," *Congress Volume*, VTSup 1 (Leiden: Brill, 1953), 97–111.

A (vv. 20–21): The poem introduces wisdom crying out for listeners. Four different verbs signify her appeal, and four different prepositional phrases designate her locale:[11]

> Wisdom cries aloud in the street;
>   in the markets she raises her voice;
> on the top of the walls she calls;
>   at the entrance of the city gates she speaks.

Double parallelism makes bold the point: the call of wisdom is inclusive. All people, wherever they are, may listen to her words.[12]

B (v. 22): Having presented wisdom, the poem becomes her voice. Her first word is interrogative: "How long" (ʿad-mātay)? By it wisdom implores and pleads; by it she implies judgment.[13] She addresses her question to the untutored (pᵉtāyîm), to scoffers (lēṣîm), and to fools (kᵉsîlîm).[14] These terms derive meaning from the inclusive call of the introduction. Hence, they describe all people, not just individuals or groups. All are unwise when wisdom begins to speak. Moreover, wisdom fluctuates in her relationship to people. First, she speaks to them directly: "How long, untutored ones, will you love immaturity?"[15] Then she switches to the third person: "How long will scoffers delight in their scoffing and fools hate knowledge?" Ambivalent about the public, wisdom exchanges proximity for distance.[16]

C (v. 23): Proximity returns in the direct address of the imperative: "Give heed (tāšûbû) to my reproof." Here wisdom uses language and style reminiscent of prophetic speech.[17] The imperative summons listeners to conversion, even as it specifies reproach for the unenlightened. To fools who hate knowledge (daʿat, v. 22), wisdom offers knowledge: "I will make known (ʾôdîʿāh)," she says. With this promise of disclosure, she threatens and warns:

---

11. The translation is the RSV, with changes made when necessary or desirable. Here in vv. 20–21, e.g., the RSV obscures the variety of vocabulary by translating two different verbs (*rnh* and *qrʾ*) as "cry."

12. G. von Rad, *Wisdom in Israel* (London: SCM, 1972), 157–66.

13. This interrogative functions similarly in the oracles of Jeremiah: 4:14, 21; 12:4; 31:22; 47:5; cf. also Exod. 10:3; 1 Sam. 1:14; 2 Sam. 2:26.

14. On the nuances of these words, see C. H. Toy, *Proverbs*, 23–24; also W. McKane, who argues persuasively that pᵉtāyîm ought to be translated "the untutored" (*Proverbs*, 273). As for lēṣîm, H. Neil Richardson suggests "babblers" ("Some Notes on לִיץ and Its Derivatives," *VT* 5 [1955]: 163–79, esp. 172), a translation accepted in W. Baumgartner, *Hebräisches und aramäisches Lexikon zum Alten Testament*, 3d ed. (Leiden: Brill, 1967–), 507a.

15. Cf. the translation by W. McKane (*Proverbs*, 212).

16. Thus I treat these shifts in person as a literary phenomenon within the poem and not as a compositional problem (contra, e.g., J. A. Emerton, "A Note," 610–11).

17. C. Kayatz, *Proverbien*, 120–21; H. Ringgren, *Word and Wisdom*, 96.

Now (*hinnēh*)[18] I will pour out to you my thoughts;[19]
I will make known my words to you.[20]

D-E-D (vv. 24–30): The disclosure itself forms the core of the poem. It begins with Reason; it centers on Announcement; it ends with Result. Signal words mark each of the three sections.[21] Reason and Result are inverse parallels of vocabulary and motifs.

Functioning to signify motive, the particle *yaʿan* introduces the Reason for the Announcement (vv. 24–25).[22] The Reason covers two lines. In the first wisdom alternates between her acts and the response of the people, between direct address and indirect speech:

> Because (*yaʿan*) I have called
>   and you refused to listen,[23]
> I have stretched out my hand
>   and no one has heeded.

In the second line wisdom expands upon the negative response of the people. Using solely the second person, she charges:

a   b
you have ignored all my counsel
b′   a′
and my reproof you would not have.

18. On proper translations of *hinnēh*, see T. O. Lambdin, *Introduction to Biblical Hebrew* (New York: Scribner, 1971) 168–70; on its rhetorical usages, see L. Alonso-Schökel, "Nota estilistica sobre la particula הִנֵּה," *Bib* 37 (1956): 74–80.

19. *Rúaḥ* is translated, "thought," possibly as parallel to "word" (*dābār*); cf. C. H. Toy, *Proverbs*, 24; R. B. Y. Scott, *Proverbs*, 40.

20. For "make known" as language of disclosure in prophetic speech, cf. Isa. 5:5; Jer. 16:21; Ezek. 20:5.

21. On the importance of signal-words, see J. Muilenburg, "The Linguistic and Rhetorical Usages of the Particle כִּי in the Old Testament," *HUCA* 32 (1961): 135–60.

22. The use of this particle to designate motive is extensive, especially in prophetic literature. In addition to the parallels which C. Kayatz lists (*Proverbien*, 120), see Amos 5:11; Hos. 8:1; Isa. 3:16; 7:5; 8:6; 29:13; 30:12; 37:29; Jer. 5:14; Ezek. 5:7, 9, 11; 16:36, 43. See J. Pedersen, *Israel* (London: Oxford, 1926), 117; H. W. Wolff, "Die Begründungen der prophetischen Heils- und Unheilssprüche," *ZAW* 52 (1934): 5–6, 8.

23. Although W. McKane allows for a prophetic model behind these words, he plays down this possibility by claiming that the vocabulary and stance of verses 24–25 are those of a wisdom-teacher (*Proverbs*, 274). B. Mack moves in an opposite direction: The words are definitely prophetic style, but they do not signify merely a prophetic role. Wisdom is not quoting Yahweh, as did the prophets (e.g., Isa. 50:2; 65:12; 66:4; Jer. 7:13–15; 11:10–11; Zech. 7:13–14); her speech is itself a word of Yahweh ("Wisdom Myth," 56–57). So while McKane tends to make wisdom less than a prophet (a wisdom teacher without divine authority), Mack views her as more than a prophet (a figure closely identified with Yahweh).

The word reproof (*tōkaḥat*) links this section literally to the command which prefaces it (v. 23). But the link is ironic, for the imperative to heed reproof meets the indicative which spurns reproof. The ring-structure of verse 25 leads directly to the middle of the poem, which itself builds on chiasmi.

In the middle is the Announcement that wisdom intends to mock at the calamity of those who refuse to listen (vv. 26–27). The adverb *gam* commences this section:[24]

a
So (*gam*) at your calamity I will laugh;
b
I will mock when your panic comes;
b′
when your panic comes like a storm,
a′
and your calamity like a whirlwind arrives,
when there comes upon you distress and anguish.

Within this structure chiasm occurs also in the first line itself by the order of object-verb-verb-object (a reversal of the order of v. 25):

c   d
So at (*bᵉ*) your calamity I will laugh;
d′   c′
I will mock when comes (*bᵉbōʾ*) your panic.

The second line, including its third colon, follows a similar pattern, *mutatis mutandis:*

e   f   g
when there comes (*bᵉbōʾ*) like (*kᵉ*) a storm your panic
g′   f   e′
and your calamity like (*kᵉ*) a whirlwind arrives;
e   f   g
when there comes (*bᵉbōʾ*) upon (*ʿal*) you distress and anguish.[25]

---

24. Like *yaʿan*, the occurrences of *gam* are too numerous to cite. A close parallel to its use in Prov. 1:26 is Isa 66:4, where *gam-ʾānî* signals an Announcement which is based on a Reason introduced by *yaʿan*.

25. This third colon occasions the observation that Hebrew literature is not a slave to perfection. Variations occur within patterns, and "yet form is clearly present and registers its effect upon the mind" (J. Muilenburg, "Hebrew Rhetoric," 98–99). In discussions of skewed chiasm, W. L. Holladay points also to this phenomenon of variation ("The Recovery of Poetic Passages of Jeremiah," *JBL* 85 [1966]: 432–35; "Form and Word-Play in David's Lament over Saul and Jonathan," *VT* 20 [1970]: 187–89). Cf. the comments of G. A. Smith on "symmetrophobia" in *The Early Poetry of Israel in Its Physical and Social Origins* (London: Oxford, 1927), 17–20.

As the center, this carefully arranged unit centers thought. Wisdom puts her accent here; she underlines by numerous interlockings of form and content. In using the words *calamity* and *panic*, she proclaims inevitable suffering for the unenlightened. Then she strengthens her threat by repeating these words along with additional images for disaster: panic like a storm; calamity like a whirlwind. As if the point were not yet sufficiently emphatic, wisdom joins two more words: *distress* and *anguish*.[26] Her primary message is patently clear.

A subordinate theme is wisdom's own participation in the troubles of the unwise. She responds derisively to calamity, but she does not initiate it. Trouble comes because the unwise spurn wisdom, but wisdom herself does not send it. In the Announcement she does not specify its origin or agent. Besides, wisdom speaks of herself only twice in this central section: she will laugh and she will mock when disaster mounts sixfold.[27]

The Result of this climactic Announcement returns to the vocabulary and motifs of the Reason which led to it (vv. 28–30).[28] But it is an inverse return, with a strong restatement of the Reason:

D (Reason)	*D' (Result)*
Because (*ya'an*) I have called	Then (*'āz*) they will call me,
and you refused to listen,	but I will not answer;
I have stretched out my hand	they will seek me diligently
and no one has heeded,	but will not find me—Inasmuch as (*taḥat kî*) they hated knowledge and the fear of the LORD they did not choose—
and you have ignored	they would not have
all my counsel	my counsel;
and my reproof	they despised
you would not have	all my reproof.

26. Thus, a rhetorical analysis shows the place and function of v. 27c within the present poem (contra, C. H. Toy; see note 4 above).

27. Toy compares the tone of this Announcement to the prophets exulting "in like manner over the downfall of the enemies of Israel" (*Proverbs,* 27). By contrast, W. McKane finds the Announcement unlike prophetic threats in which Yahweh "declares he will execute judgment." Wisdom laughs and does not intervene personally to effect judgment (*Proverbs,* 275). See likewise W. Zimmerli, "Zur Struktur der alttestamentlichen Weisheit," *ZAW* 51 (1933): 187 n. 1.

28. This division departs significantly from Kayatz's outline above. She understands verses 26–28 as a threatening speech containing two introductory particles, while I see the second particle (*'āz*) as indicative of a new section giving the Result of the Announcement (vv. 28–30). The many parallels of content and theme between verses 28 and 30, on the one hand, and verses 24–25, on the other, argue for the inseparability of the former. On verse 29, see below.

Just as *ya͑an* signals motive, so the particle *ʾāz* marks consequences.[29] Whereas in verse 24a wisdom called (*qārāʾ*) and the people refused to listen, in verse 28a the people call (*qārāʾ*) wisdom and she refuses to answer (cf. Zech. 7:13). Once wisdom stretched out her hand in a gesture of seeking the people (v. 24b). No one responded. Now the people seek wisdom, and they do not find her (v. 28b). She does not respond.

Verse 29 interrupts the Result. Interruption does not mean insertion; it means attention. This verse belongs to the poem, and the poem assigns a special status to it.[30] While proclaiming the dire consequences of her disastrous Announcement, wisdom breaks off to recall that there is, indeed, motivation for the Announcement and its Result. Having given the Reason once, in proper sequence and with particular words (vv. 24–25), now she underscores it in an improper sequence and with a conventional formula of sapiential thought.[31] By employing this formula wisdom ties her motivation directly to divine authority. The people's rejection of wisdom (vv. 24–25) is their rejection of Yahweh (v. 29).[32] Moreover, the phrase "hate knowledge" here in verse 29 reflects wisdom's use of that same phrase in verse 22. Fools who hate knowledge do not choose the fear of Yahweh—even when wisdom offers them her special knowledge (v. 23). So verse 29 belongs to one compelling motif in the poem.

In addition, this theological statement elicits attention by its double particle *taḥat kî*, which is a forceful way of presenting the basis for punishment.[33] The sentence itself is chiastic. As elsewhere in the Result, the third-person form identifies the people:

Inasmuch as (*taḥat kî*)
      a   b
   they hated knowledge
         b′   a′
   and the fear of the Lord they did not choose.

29. As a signal-word for a result, cf. its use in constructions of protasis and apodosis: e.g., Isa. 58:13–14; Prov. 2:4; Job 9:30–31. See also Isa. 35:5–6; 58:8–9; Jer. 22:15–16; 31:13. Cf. Muilenburg, "The Particle כִּי," 135 n. 1.

30. Here I follow the general principle of letting the present poem disclose its inner integrity. This principle neither affirms nor denies a history behind the text. R. N. Whybray holds that verse 29 is an insertion; it can be removed without "any loss of grammatical coherence or metrical balance." Then he avers that its removal tends to improve both the form and meaning of the poem (*Wisdom in Proverbs*, 73–75). That judgment is subject to the judgment of the poem itself as an organic unit with "an ambiguous structure of interlocking motifs" (cf. N. Frye, *Anatomy*, 82, 315–16).

31. *Mutatis mutandis*, the formula appears in Prov. 1:7; 2:5; 8:13; 9:10; 10:27; 14:26–27; 15:16, 33; 19:23; 22:4.

32. McKane does see wisdom emerge "almost as a prophet" with the use of this formula (*Proverbs*, 275).

33. The combination *taḥat kî* is virtually a *hapex legomenon* in the OT; Deut. 4:37 has a textual problem. Cf. *taḥat ʾᵃšer* in 2 Kings 22:17 and Deut. 28:47.

Like its content and meaning, the structure of this interruption conforms to the general design of the poem. Specifically, chiasm occurs in each of the three sections which constitute the core (vv. 25, 26–27, 29).

Verse 30 functions in overlapping ways. It provides a transition from interruption back to Result. While continuing the style of indictment (v. 29), it resumes the thought of consequences (v. 28). Wisdom has declared withdrawal from the people: they will seek but not find her. In verse 30 she describes her withdrawal as their activity: they would not have her counsel and they despised her reproof. What they have rejected she offers no longer. Their negative response is her negative reply. Lastly, verse 30 answers verse 25 with parallels of vocabulary and themes. Juxtaposed, these two verses demonstrate the coalescence of Reason and Result. Having ignored the counsel of wisdom (v. 25), the people would not have it (v. 30). Rejecting her reproof (v. 25), they have despised it (v. 30). This motif of reproof began as an imperative to pay attention (v. 23). It became a motivation for judgment (v. 25) and now it concludes as a declaration of consequences (v. 30).

There are still other links between Reason and Result. First offering herself to the people, wisdom receives four negative responses (vv. 24-25). Three of these carry a negative meaning in the verbal forms themselves: you refused; no one heeded;[34] you have ignored. The fourth employs the adverb not (*lōʾ*) before the verb: you would not have. In the Result this pattern is reversed. The people seek wisdom, and she gives four negative replies (vv. 28, 30). The adverb *lōʾ* shapes three of them: I will not answer; they will not find me; they would not have my counsel. For the fourth, the negative meaning comes in the verb itself: they despised.

Wisdom's ambivalence about the people surfaces again in these verbs. The change from the second to the third person in the Reason is a waver between proximity and distance. Full involvement returns with the Announcement, which is completely in the second person. Proclaiming calamity, wisdom speaks directly. After this climactic utterance, however, she uses only the third person in reporting the Result. Thereby she re-establishes distance from the people, and this distance she keeps.

These many interlocking relationships among Reason, Announcement, and Result secure internal structure as well as external design. The poem continues by completing the circles begun in verses 20–23. Since completion is progress, however, wisdom returns to her beginnings with differences.[35]

C' (v. 31): A summary of natural retribution, this verse corresponds to verse 23, which is a preface to the central section. Yet these two lines have no verbal similarities; they differ in length; and neither one commences with a

---

34. Although this construction (*ʾên maqšîb*) is not parallel to the surrounding forms, my point is that the adverb *lōʾ* is not used in any of these three statements.

35. Cf. W. L. Holladay, "The Recovery of Poetic Passages," 433.

signal word.[36] Together they are perhaps the rhetorical equivalent of synthetic parallelism, aiding the movement of thought.[37] Whereas the imperative (*C*) introduced the center, the declarative (*C'*) comments succinctly upon it:

> They shall eat the fruit of their way
> and with their own devices be satisfied.

This summary leads wisdom to elaborate.

B' (v. 32): Parallels within circles resume as verse 32 answers verse 22. But no longer does direct address alternate with third person forms. Ambivalence ceases. Distance replaces intimacy; separation displaces involvement. Accordingly, the untutored who originally were addressed now join the fools to be spoken about. Further, verse 32 compresses the address of verse 22 by omitting reference to scoffers:

B	*B'*
How long, untutored ones, will you love immaturity? How long will scoffers delight in their scoffing	For (*kî*) the untutored are killed by their turning away
and fools hate knowledge?	and the complacence of fools destroys them.

Instead of turning (*šûb*, v. 23a) to wisdom for life, the untutored and the fools have turned away (*šûb*, v. 32a) for death. Since they have reversed the meaning of repentance, they themselves are responsible for their destruction.

A' (v. 33): With the compression of verse 32, the poem begins to wind down. Its final line completes the diminishing process:[38] "The one who hears me will dwell secure and will be at ease from dread of evil." Beginning with wisdom crying out for listeners, the pericope concludes with wisdom speaking about the one who hears. The contrast is between expansion and retrenchment. The two full lines of the introduction and the one final line of the conclusion move from plural invitation to singular acceptance. In other words, wisdom's meaning is the number of her lines and the number in her verb-form. At first all listen; at last one hears. The poem ends much closer to a

---

36. I do not see *wᵉ* at the beginning of verse 31 having the force of "therefore" (so RSV) or of any other introductory signal-word (cf. C. Kayatz, *Proverbien*, 121).

37. The dotted line connecting *C* and *C'* in the diagram above indicates both parallelism of position and lack of additional parallels.

38. For another instance of "shortening given units of the poem as the poem progresses," see W. L. Holladay, "Form and Word-Play," 188.

whimper than to a bang. Remnant is the manner, matter, and meaning of this ending.

III

In Proverbs 1:20–33 a chiastic architecture is the mode in which wisdom speaks. Her homiletic, advisory, didactic, and prophetic dimensions have their being in this poetic form. Thus, by exploring its literary and rhetorical features, we have perceived pattern and posture:

A Beginning with a public appeal (vv. 20–21)
    B   to all who are unwise (v. 22)
       C that they heed reproof as disclosure (v. 23),
          D wisdom supplies ample Reason in the negative responses of the people to her (vv. 24–25)
             E for her climactic Announcement of derisive judgment when inevitable calamity strikes severely (vv. 26–27)
          D' As the Result, wisdom refuses to respond to the people because they "hated knowledge and the fear of the Lord they did not choose" (vv. 28-30).
       C' She declares continuing trouble (v. 31)
    B' for the unwise who cause their own destruction (v. 32).
A' Alas, the remnant of her hearers is singular (v. 33).

Yet that one who does hear "will dwell secure and will be at ease from dread of evil." To these words of faint hope the woman of wisdom leads all sorts and conditions of people. There she leaves us to make our choice.[39]

---

39. This study was completed during a year of research in Jerusalem, made possible by a fellowship from the National Endowment for the Humanities.

13

LADY WISDOM AS MEDIATRIX: AN EXPOSITION OF PROVERBS 1:20–33

Bruce K. Waltke

Introduction

Biblical scholars who base themselves on historical criticism cannot accept the prophetic claim of Moses and his successors to speak in the name of the Lord. James L. Crenshaw writes:

> Ours is an ethos in which it is no longer possible for many of us to accept the prophetic claim, *ko᾿ ᾿amar ᾿adonay*, as anything more than human intuition crouching itself in revelatory categories. To a generation for whom the transcendental world is sealed off from the one in which we are born, suffer and die, to use Antolé France's summary of human history, the arrogant boast, "Thus hath the Lord spoken," appeals far less than the ancient sage's "Listen, my son, to your father's advice."[1]

From *Presbyterion: Covenant Seminary Review* 14 (Spring 1988): 1–15. Used by permission.

1. James L. Crenshaw, *Prophetic Conflict, Beihefte zur Zeitschrift für die alttestamentliche Wissenschaft* 124 (1971): 116.

Many of these scholars think they find a kindred spirit in the sage who, they claim, derived his moral teachings not by revelation but by a secular, scientific method, and who delivered his teachings in a non-authoritarian way and codified his observations and reflections as traditions. . . . [T]he position of these scholars finds support in such texts as Proverbs 24:30–34 and 4:1–9. Their view finds additional validation in Egyptian sayings and Mesopotamian proverbs, but we lack the time to investigate those provocative and productive areas of research.

It is my primary aim . . . to undermine this scholarly understanding of wisdom literature by showing that the sages received their moral teaching by revelation and delivered them authoritatively. . . . I sought to do this by studying the word "wisdom." "Wisdom" in Proverbs, I argued, designates a fixed, eternal, religio-social order, an order that God created, established, and upheld. Its synonyms are "law," "commandment," "fear of God," and not "counsel" in the sense that it ask its audience to judge its validity. I also argued that Israel's anointed, charismatic king coined his expressions of God's immutable will in proverbs that bore the authority of divine speech. . . . I want to further my case by exegeting Lady Wisdom's sermon in Proverbs 1:20–33. The passage informs us that the sage spoke as Yahweh's mediator and with divine authority.

Lady Wisdom as a Mediatrix (1:20–33)

Lady Wisdom's Personae in Proverbs 1–9

The sage personifies wisdom, the abstract sum of his teachings, under several personae: as a hostess (9:1–6), as a child playing in primordial time (8:22–31), as a "sister" (that is, as a bride) (7:4), and as a guide (6:22). The lecturer aims to demonstrate that she spoke as a mediatrix close to Yahweh in 1:20–33.

Views of Lady Wisdom in Persona in Proverbs 1:20–33

Scholars are not agreed upon Wisdom's persona in this text. Some stress the homiletic character of the address and describe Lady Wisdom as a preacher of repentance (so H. Ringgren[2] and W. Frankenberger[3]). A second group, emphasizing the didactic character of her address, think of Lady Wisdom as a teacher (so McKane[4] and Toy[5]). A third group, noting the word "advice" in verse 25, regard her as a Counsellor (so P. A. H. de Boer[6]). Others see Lady

---

2. H. Ringgren, *Word and Wisdom* (1947): 95–96.
3. W. Frankenberger, *Die Spruche, Handbuch zum Alten Testament* (1898): 22–23.
4. W. McKane, *Proverbs: A New Approach* (1970), 272–77. To be sure, McKane entitles the pericope, "Wisdom as Preacher," but he does not mean by this a preacher of repentance. "The representation is probably that of a charismatic wisdom teacher and no more" (277).
5. C. H. Toy, *A Critical and Exegetical Commentary on the Book of Proverbs*, ICC (1899), 20–29.
6. P. A. H. de Boer, "The Counsellor," *VTS* 3 (1955): 52.

Wisdom as a goddess, a hypostatis of God (so R. B. Y. Scott,[7] R. N. Why-bray,[8] B. L. Mack,[9] and R. Murphy[10]). Still others, noting similarities with prophetic literature, identify her persona as a prophetess.

R. Bultmann, looking to older mythological materials, contended that Lady Wisdom appears as a goddess in Proverbs 1:20–33,[11] and his view gained in popularity when he was followed by W. F. Albright.[12] According to Bultmann, the personification of Wisdom as a goddess is grounded in an "old myth of wisdom," which is mentioned in Proverbs 1:20–33; Job 28; Sirach 24:1–11; Baruch 3:9–4:4; Ethiopic Enoch 42:13; 4 Esdras 5:9; Wisdom of Solomon 7:21–22, and the Prologue of the Gospel of John. Of these, Bultmann said, "the most important passage"[13] is Proverbs 1:20–33. He reconstructs the myth as follows:

> Pre-existent Wisdom, the companion of God at the creation, seeks a dwelling on earth among mankind, but she seeks in vain. Her preaching is rejected. She came to her own, but her own did not accept her. So she returned into the heavenly world and waits hidden there. Mankind truly seeks her now, but none succeeds in finding her. God alone knows the way to her.[14]

His thesis, as Kayatz argued, is flawed.[15] First, as the following exegesis will show, Proverbs 1:20–33 does not present such a myth without radical revision of the text. Second, the story Bultmann reconstructed is found only in Ethiopic Enoch. Finally, no documentation for such a myth exists in extra-Israelite literature.

The other identifications of her persona in Proverbs 1:20–33 are only partially correct. A careful exegesis of Lady Wisdom's discourse and a comparison of its forms and motifs with sapiential literature, both biblical and extra-biblical, and with prophetic oracles will demonstrate that it contains a unique juxtaposition and integration of wisdom and of prophetic speech forms along with unique elements that penetrate one another and thereby undergo deviations to present a new, unique form of address that expresses itself with the

---

7. R. B. Y. Scott, *Proverbs/Ecclesiastes,* The Anchor Bible (1965), 39.

8. R. N. Whybray, *Wisdom in Proverbs,* Studies in Biblical Theology 45 (1956): 76–104.

9. B. L. Mack, "Wisdom Myth and Mythology: An Essay in Understanding a Theological Tradition," *Interpretation* 24 (1970): 46–60.

10. R. Murphy, "Assumptions and Problems in Old Testament Research," *Catholic Biblical Quarterly* 29 (1967): 109–12.

11. R. Bultmann, *Der religionsgeschichtliche Hintergrüng des Prologs zum Johannes-Evangelium* (1923).

12. W. F. Albright, "The Goddess of Life and Wisdom," *AJSL* 36 (1919–20): 258–94.

13. Bultmann, 9.

14. C. Kayatz, *Studien zu Proverbien 1–9: eine formund motivgeschichtliche Untersuchung unter Einbeziehung aegyptischen Vergleichsmaterials, Wissenschaftliche monographien zum Alten und Neuen Testament* 22 (1966): 128f.

15. Kayatz, 128, footnote 2.

highest authority. She is more than a teacher, and a prophetess, she is a divine mediatrix closely related to Yahweh who reveals his fixed order. Let the text decide the issue.

An Exegesis of 1:20–33

Lady Wisdom's speech is organized in two parts: a sermon addressed to fools (vv. 20–27; cf. v. 22) and a statement in third person addressed to the children of the covenant (vv. 28–33). These are not two distinct poems but a unified discourse because they are held together by the consistency of style, namely, Lady Wisdom is the speaker throughout, and by substance, namely, the threat that at the time of judgment there will be no second chance. It is interesting that the Lord Jesus also spoke to the masses with a view to instructing his disciples in the Sermon on the Mount (Matt. 5:1) and in his parables about the kingdom of heaven (Matt. 13:2).

The sermon to fools in 1:20–27 has a twiceness in its structure. It consists of an introduction to Lady Wisdom as a preacher (vv. 20–21) and then her sermon itself (vv. 22–27). The sermon also has two sections: an invitation to fools (vv. 22–23) and denunciation of them (vv. 24–27). Her invitation to them also falls into two parts: an accusatory question ("how long") addressed to older simpletons, with an aside about mockers and fools, indicting the simple ones for loving folly (v. 22), and an admonition to them to repent, strengthened by the extremely majestic promise that they forfeit further revelation when they spurn her (v. 23). The denunciation also falls into two parts: a scolding accusation for not listening to her, introduced by *ya‘an*, ("but since," vv. 24–25), giving the grounds for the judicial sentence that she will mock them at the time of their distress (vv. 26–27). The judicial sentence is twofold: she will not listen to them (v. 26), and they will fall into calamity (v. 27).

Her statement to the covenantal children, re-emphasizing the nature of the judgment—there will be no respite when the inevitable judgment overtakes fools—is organized into three parts: the withdrawal of Lady Wisdom herself from the fool's cries at the time of judgment (v. 28), the inevitability of judgment for those that reject her (vv. 29–31), and a generalizing substantiation condemning fools and commending the wise (vv. 32–36).[16]

---

16. Phyllis Trible, "Wisdom Builds a Poem: The Architecture of Proverbs 1:20–33," *Journal of Biblical Literature* (1975): 509–18. Trible partially succeeds in demonstrating the chiastic structure of this discourse. Presenting and modifying her argument here, however, would take the [writer] too far afield from his stated purpose.

Lady Wisdom's Sermon to Simpletons (vv. 20–27)

THE SETTING (VV. 20–21)

"Wisdom" is a feminine plural noun. Why does the sage present his teaching as a lady rather than a man? "Ultimately," observed Murphy, "the historical reason for the feminine personification eludes us."[17] Instead of looking to history to explain the feminine personification, one should look to linguistics. About a century ago K. Brugmann showed that the grammatical gender of a noun guided the poet's imagination in his personification of lifeless objects: "The imagination used this gender and allowed itself to be led by it. . . ."[18] His study receives confirmation in R. Jacobson's work in Russian gender and personification. The Russians, for example, personify the days of the week as male or female on the basis of the day's grammatical gender.[19] Since *ḥokmâ* is a feminine noun, the poet personifies it as a Lady. Moreover, the form is plural because abstract nouns of quality often occur as feminine plurals.[20]

Lady Wisdom's podium is the most prominent place in the city. "The street," "the public square," "the top of the walls," and "the gateways" designate not diverse localities within the city but aspects of the gate at the entrance into the city. "Street" (Heb. *ḥûṣ* basically means "outside"[21]) may function as a metonym for bazaars (cf. 1 Kings 20:34). In this text and others it parallels "plaza" [Heb. *rᵉḥōbôt*]. The plural forms of "plaza" and "opening of gates" are best taken as plurals of mass.[22] The excavations at Tel el-Qadi, ancient Dan, exposed a large, enclosed plaza between the outer and inner gates. The outer gate functioned as the setting for court sessions and council meetings; the plaza was used for commercial trade and public meetings.[23] Other cities also exhibit a principal square just within the gate. At the gate, not at the temple that embodied the religious life of the city, there existed a play of life involving commerce, the court, and administration that could not be mastered without wisdom. At this central location, where the throngs mulled, Lady Wisdom takes her stand. More particularly she sets her podium on the highest wall. The Hebrew expression rendered "at the head of the noisy streets" (NIV text)[24] is better rendered "on top of the walls" (cf. NIV note). The expression "top of the walls" is a superlative genitive signifying "highest wall."[25]

17. R. E. Murphy, "The Kerygma of the Book of Proverbs," *Interpretation* 20 (1966): 13.

18. K. Brugmann, *The Nature and Origin of the Noun Genders in the Indo-European Languages* (1894), 30.

19. Roman Jakobson, "On Linguistic Aspects of Translation," *On Translation*, edited by R. A. Bower (1959), 237.

20. Cf. B. Waltke and M. O'Connor, *Introduction to Biblical Hebrew Syntax* (1988), para. 7.4.2.

21. C. P. Weber, *Theological Word Book of the Old Testament*, I (1980), 273.

22. Waltke and O'Connor, para 7.4.1.

23. A. Biran, "Tel Dan," *Biblical Archaeologist* 37 (1974): 25–71.

24. M. J. Dahood, *Proverbs and Northwest Semitic Philology* (1963), 4f.

25. Waltke and O'Connor, para. 9.5.3.

Lady Wisdom, having chosen the most advantageous point of the city in order to be heard far and wide, "with full lungs and clear voice,"[26] delivers her speech with emotion and fervor to capture the attention of fools.

Does this setting for personified wisdom reflect a historical situation? Delitzsch rightly said, "To the public appearance of wisdom, as it is here represented, there must be present objective reality, without which the power of conviction departs from the figure."[27] What is the objective reality? How do the masses at the gate hear wise-teaching? Von Rad thinks that the divine religio-social order addresses them in the creation. He said: "Creation not only exists, it also discharges truth."[28] Although this statement is partially true (cf. Job 12:8–9; Pss. 19:2; 97:6; 145:10; Rom. 1:18), creation cannot make the claim Lady Wisdom makes in verse 23, namely, that if responded to she will pour out further knowledge, a knowledge that includes the fear of the Lord (cf. v. 29). As other Scriptures make clear, general revelation is insufficient to make a man wise unto salvation. If it were, why would we need the sage and his special revelation?

H. Ringgren[29] thinks of a wandering wisdom preacher who encounters the people as a ready-made audience at the city gate and calls them to repentance. I prefer to think of the sage as a parent-teacher at home with his own children and other offspring, and as an elder at the gate.[30] As an elder, he would have had the right to give at the gate his opinions both officially and unofficially. Armed with the spirit of wisdom the sage sought to convince fools of their need to repent. Wise men listened to him (1:5), grown-up simpletons and fools spurned him.

SERMON TO SIMPLETONS (VV. 22–27)

The invitation (an admonition with accusation and promise; vv. 22–23). Lady Wisdom directs her sermon to "simpletons" (i.e., undisciplined, raw youth). Donald Trevor characterizes the simpleton as follows:

> His basic need is *ormah* [i.e., craftiness]; he is credulous and weak-willed, easily seduced, possesses *ʾiwweleth* (i.e., folly), is destroyed by intransigent instability (whereas the *kesil* is destroyed by prosperity) yet capable of improvement. He has a youthful lack of discipline and of mature moral integrity.[31]

Kidner says of the simpleton:

26. B. Lange, *Frau Weisheit* (1975), 51.
27. Franz Delitzsch, *Biblical Commentary on the Proverbs of Solomon,* I (reprinted 1970), 67.
28. G. von Rad, *Wisdom in Israel* (1972), 165.
29. Ringgren, 96.
30. R. N. Whybray, *The Intellectual Tradition in Israel* (1974), 31–43; J. L. Crenshaw, "Education in Ancient Israel," *Journal of Biblical Literature* 104 (1985): 601–15.
31. Donald Trevor, "The Semantic Field of 'Folly' in Proverbs, Job, Psalms, and Ecclesiastes," *Vetus Testamentum* 13 (1963): 287.

> Mentally, he is naive . . . ; morally, he is wilfull and irresponsible . . . , a man
> who is empty-headed. . . .[32]

In an aside Lady Wisdom refers to "fools" and "mockers."

"How long" is an accusatory rhetorical question. It does not focus the audience's attention on a future terminus but compels it to realize the acute crisis that menaces the present situation and demands a change of direction. Phyllis Trible writes: "By it wisdom implores and pleads; by it she implies judgment."[33]

Simpletons love not committing themselves to wisdom but remaining in an open state of seduction. Their moral posture becomes ever more in tension and conflict with the inevitable disaster approaching them. The inexorable cause and effect come ever closer together to kiss each other. The simpleton's plight is urgent and acute. Death is at hand. The rhetorical question implicitly contains an admonition: respond quickly, or you will soon perish in the way.

Lady Wisdom admonishes her audience to repent and strengthens her admonition with promise in verse 23. The non-perfective *tăšûbû* followed by the cohortative *ʾabbîʿâ* would be better rendered as an injunctive non-perfective so that verse 23 should read: "Respond to my rebuke and I will pour out my heart to you. . . ." Holladay defined *šub* as follows: "[It] has as its central meaning, having moved in a particular direction, to move thereupon in the opposite direction. . . ."[34]

Its original physical notion gives way metaphorically to the psychic-spiritual turning of the heart away from evil and death toward goodness and life. With this meaning the verb becomes the most important term in the Bible for repentance, especially in the prophets, with Jeremiah leading the way. Lady Wisdom demands more than contrition and sorrow. She demands a conscious and willing turning toward her reproach, a turning that entails nothing less of fools than a radical reorientation of their affections toward her teaching and a total repudiation of self-satisfaction with their folly and love of it.

Once fools make a conscious decision to move toward wisdom and renounce their folly, wisdom promises to equip them for a life in wisdom (v. 23b). "Pour out" connotes "an uncontrollable or uncontrolled gushing forth as, for example, the swollen waters of a wadi" (18:4).[35] The meaning of the pouring out of the Spirit is well illustrated by the phenomena that accompanied Pentecost.

"My heart" would be better rendered "my spirit" or "my words" to you. Emerton correctly noted that the preposition with "you" is *l*, "to" not *ʾal*

---

32. Derek Kidner, *The Proverbs* (1964), 39.
33. Trible, 511.
34. W. Holladay, *The Root SHUBH in the Old Testament* (1953), 53.
35. I. I. Coppes, *Theological Wordbook of the Old Testament*, II (1980), 548.

"upon," suggesting that *nbʿ* as its usual sense in Hiphil, "giving utterance in speech," that is, "the free pouring forth of thoughts and words" (Delitzsch), giving an excellent parallel to "I will make you know my thoughts" [Heb. *debaray*, literally, "words"] (v. 23b). According to Emerton, "spirit" (Heb. *ruaḥ* means "breath") is a metonymy for "words" in Psalm 33:6, Isaiah 11:4, and here. He also noted it is translated "my words" in the Peshitta of Ecclesiastes 16:25. No vizier or prophet ever made promises like this. Lady Wisdom speaks with highest authority, showing that the sage conceives of wisdom as having the high rank in Yahweh's ordered realm. Elsewhere she informs us that kings reign through her (chap. 8). What majestic grace to offer such riches to repentant fools.

The denunciation (vv. 24–27). The denunciation has two parts: the scolding accusation, introduced by "since" or "because" (Heb. *yaʿan*), giving grounds for the judicial sentence (vv. 24–25), and the judicial sentence threatening disaster (Heb. *ʾed*) introduced by "and I" (vv. 26–27).

Consider the accusation (vv. 24–25). Lady Wisdom left a door of hope open to fools in verses 22–23. Now she shuts the door, as indicated by the shift to the perfective tense. Like Isaiah in 41:23–24, Lady Wisdom bases her judicial sentence against the simpletons on their deafening silence.

She uses four predicates to describe the simpleton's rejection of her sermon: two without a negative in 24a and 25a and two with a negative in 24b and 25b. "Rejected me" is better rendered with NEB "refused to listen" because *māʾan* is never used with personal objects but often used with an infinitive in connection with man's refusal to obey God's commands. "Give heed" (Heb. *qāšab* in Hiphil) means "a conscious, willing and attentive use of the ears." "Ignored" (Heb. *pāraʾ* more accurately means "to let loose" and can be paraphrased "to let slip through the fingers." "Accept" is the same word rendered "give in" in 1:10. As to the objects of their rejection the accent falls in verse 24 on the *style* of her appeal and in verse 25 on its *substance*. The verb "called" in verse 24 is the same one rendered "cries out" in verse 21. Wisdom accompanied her invitation with the gesture of stretching out her hand, probably to get the fool's attention. She summarizes the substance of her appeal in verse 25 by the abstract nouns "rebuke" and "advice." Advice, as we noted earlier, refers to God's eternal will. It connotes a strategy for success and the strength to carry it out. P. A. H. de Boer said: "Counsel and action are identical."[36] The gift of the Spirit upon Messiah binds together "counsel and power." Proverbs says little about self-discipline. Repentance and acceptance of wisdom entails the ability to live wisely.

Consider now the judicial sentence (vv. 26–27). The threatening sentence has two accents: (1) "wisdom laughs at the time of calamity" (v. 26), and (2)

---

36. P. A. E. de Boer, *Theologisches Handwörterbuch zum Alten Testament*, I (1975), 752.

calamity will come like a storm (v. 27). The two parts are linked by the chiastic repetition of the two expressions "your disaster" and "your calamity."

Verse 26a should not be translated, "I in turn will laugh at your disaster," but "I in turn will laugh when your disaster comes." Note the preposition with ʾedkem is not *l* or ʾel, or ʿal but *b*. Note also the parallel in verse 27 reads, "when your calamity comes like a storm."

"Laugh" and "mock" express the inward joy and disdain a mighty conqueror feels toward the defeat of his abject enemies (cf. Pss. 2:4; 37:13; 59:8). The victory of wisdom over folly in Proverbs, of the righteous over the wicked in Psalms, is so lopsided that there is a comic aspect to the reversal of fortunes, provoking mockery over the enemy. Lady Wisdom celebrates the working out of the religio-social orders wherein the righteous are rewarded and the wicked are requited. Kayatz[37] noted that this motif of scoffing is not at home in sapiential literature but is encountered in the pre-exilic psalms with reference to Yahweh laughing at the wicked who intend malice toward his saints. Apparently this trait of Yahweh has been applied to Wisdom. Her laughter differs from Yahweh's, however, in that He laughs because He sees the day of calamity approaching, whereas she laughs in the day of calamity. These cross-references to the Lord's laughter show how closely the sage associated Wisdom with God.

Verse 27 picks up and adds meaning to verse 26. Verse 27 focuses on the degree of the coming disaster. The similes "like a storm" and "like a whirlwind" are best melded together into "a storm packing the punch of a whirlwind." The combined simile aims to picture the calamity befalling fools as coming suddenly and as so catastrophic that nothing survives it. "Distress and anguish" express the strong negative emotions produced in the fools by the ruinous disaster. The psyche of fools will change from complacency, stubbornness, and pride to extreme terror when their destruction comes. In Egyptian literature the moral order is worked out in the next life. The Israelite sage leaves the time of fulfillment open.

EXPLICATING ADDRESS TO COVENANT CHILDREN (vv. 28–33)

Wisdom withdraws herself from the fools' cries (v. 28). Whereas verse 26 and verses 29–31 underscore the certainty of judgment, verse 28 emphasizes its finality. The adverb "then" [Heb. ʾāz] takes the audience beyond the judgment itself to Lady Wisdom's deriding laughter (v. 27) and decisive withdrawal (v. 28) after disaster strikes. Fools will cry out to her and earnestly seek her, but she will not respond and will not be found. Bridges comments: "Prayer, once omnipotent, will then be powerless,"[38] and von Rad observes: "This

---

37. Kayatz, 124f.
38. Bridges, *An Exposition of the Book of Proverbs* (1854), 42.

saving voice is not at man's disposal whenever he wishes; he can forfeit it through disobedience, and then it will deny itself to him. . . ."[39]

Judgment is inevitable for those that despise wisdom (vv. 29–31). Lady Wisdom's explanation that judgment is inevitable for unbelieving fools is organized into two parts: the accusation giving the basis for the judicial sentence (vv. 29–30) and the death sentence itself (v. 31). An alert listener will recognize that the structure matches verses 24–27.

Consider the scolding accusation (vv. 29–30). These verses in the explanation of the sermon match the sermon itself in verses 24–25. Both accuse the fools of rejecting wisdom's reproof. The two substantives, "advice" and "rebuke," and the verb "not accept" of verse 25 are repeated in verse 30. Once again, as in verses 24–25, Lady Wisdom uses four verbs to describe the fool's rejection of her preaching: two without the negative, "hate" and "spurned" (vv. 29a–30b), and two negatives, "did not choose" and "have none of" (vv. 29b–30a). The negated verb "choose" means more specifically "a careful choice occasioned by actual needs, and thus a very conscious choice and one that can be examined in light of certain criteria."[40] A careful, well-thought-out choice is apparent when David chooses stones suitable for his sling (1 Sam. 17:40), or when the carpenter selects the wood for his image (Isa. 40:20). Fools, seeing no need for the "fear of the Lord," do not carefully select it as their way of life. In fact, they "decide" against it and sanction other viewpoints.

Now the judicial sentence comes (v. 31). The inevitable and logical outcome of their choice is accented both by the conjunction, *waw*, here meaning "and so" with the non-perfective tense, "will eat," representing a contingent future, and also by the freighted metaphor *way*, which as noted in the preceding lecture involves the course of their life, its specific conduct, and the inevitable outcome. The judicial sentence is expressed by the metaphor of "eating" and of "being filled." The former, "eating," puts the accent on the beginning of their judgment, the latter, "being filled," on its full measure. The significance of "fruit" is clear from the parallels in the sermon itself, "a devastating storm," and "distress and anxiety" (vv. 26–27). The metaphor of fruit evokes the notions of lapsed time and inevitable outcome. As a tree, true to its nature, in the order of creation produces a certain fruit in its season, so also the way of fools after a time inevitably produces in the order of history disaster and distress. Perhaps Lady Wisdom tints the sentence with sarcasm for one normally cultivates the ground in order to eat and live. Fools, however, worked for the fruit that kills them. The time of fruition is known only to God.

Finally, comes generalizing substantiation (vv. 32–33). "For" logically introduces the substantiation for the discourse. Whereas "simpletons" consti-

---

39. von Rad, 163.
40. H. Seebass, *Theological Dictionary of the Old Testament*, II (1975), 74.

tuted the specific addressees of her fictitious sermon, "simpletons" and "fools" refer in a general way for all such folk, including those beyond the scope of the sermon. In this generalization both scolding accusation ("waywardness" and "complacency") and judicial sentence ("kill" and "destroy") are brought together. The condemnation of fools (v. 32) is matched by the commendation of the wise in this generalization, opening the way once again to hope (v. 33).

Concerning the condemnation of fools (v. 32), Lady Wisdom earlier accused morally simple ones of loving their openness to sin (v. 22). Now she accuses them of "waywardness" (Heb. *měšûbâ*) or, more literally, "turning away" (AV, ASV, RSV) (v. 32a). *Měšûbâ* in its other eleven uses occurs in either Hosea or Jeremiah, always with reference to Israel's apostasy, faithlessness, backsliding. It functions as a pun on the admonition "respond"/"repent"/ "turn" (Heb. *šûb*) [in v. 23]. The same pun occurs in Jeremiah 3:12: "Repent, O faithless Israel [Heb. *šûbâ měšûbâ yisrael*] and I will not turn my face against you." Instead of turning toward Wisdom's rebuke, the simpletons turn away from it and implicitly toward sin. Had they turned toward her rebuke they would have found life; by turning away from it they found death. The high rank of Wisdom in God's administration can be inferred when one learns that in the prophets the turning away always has God and His covenant as its objects; here Wisdom and her words take their place. The judicial sentence against simpletons is summed up in one word, "kill," here used as elsewhere with reference to punishment for a crime, including apostasy from Yahweh (Exod. 32:27; Num. 24:5; Deut. 13:10).

Fools are accused of "complacency" [Heb. *šalvâ*] (v. 32b). Although the Hebrew word can signify "peace and quiet" in Proverbs 17:1 and "security" in Psalm 122:7, it signifies perjoratively "feelings of false security" in its other five uses. Feelings of security prompted Jehoiakim to disobey God's prophetic word (Jer. 22:21). For the same reason, the enemies of Antiochus Epiphanes did not arm themselves against him (Dan. 8:25; 11:21, 24), and Sodom was led to do detestable things (Ezek. 16:49). So also fools, deceived by their failure to fear the Lord, feel secure and fail to take precaution against the inevitable destruction. Thus their complacency "destroys" (Heb. *ʾabad*), or better, "annihilates" them.

The discourse concludes with commendation of the wise (v. 33). The opposite of turning away from Lady Wisdom's rebuke is listening to her (that is, obeying her), and the opposite of feeling falsely secure and so perishing is to "live in safety." The verb rendered "live" (Heb. *šākan*) means "to stay, remain, dwell." Hulst rightly said: "Concerning the manner and length of staying nothing can be said from the verb itself."[41] The adverbial phrases, "in safe-

41. A. R. Hulst, *Theologisches Handwörterbuch zum Alten Testament*, II (1976), 906.

ty" and "without fear of harm," express the manner of living and imply its unending duration. *Beṭaḥ*, "in safety," when used positively as here, is normally connected with God. This rather consistent usage elsewhere again points toward a connection between the Lord and Lady Wisdom. Both grant true security to the faithful. The idea of dwelling securely is underscored by the synonym, "at ease," that is, to be so free from misfortune that one holds it in contempt (cf. Job 12:5; Ps. 123:4). Lady Wisdom piles on yet a third adverbial expression to underline the faithful's abiding sense of ease based on objective security—"without fear of harm." The three adverbial expressions strongly contrast the external fate and inner psyches of the foolish and the wise. The word rendered "fear" is the same word rendered "calamity" in verses 26–27.

Conclusion

A conclusion can now be drawn about the persona of Lady Wisdom.

She Is a Teacher

In the first place, Lady Wisdom's address shares similarities in form and in motifs with Egyptian sapiential literature. For example, the admonition in verse 23 to listen to her call, strengthened with promises, are found in Egyptian *sboyets*. Also the accusation of not listening in verse 22 and the implicit threatening statement based on the cause-consequence relationship in verses 24–27 are similar to Egyptian wisdom literature. These forms depict Lady Wisdom as a wisdom teacher.

She Is a Prophetess

On the other hand, some forms and motifs in her speech are not found in Egyptian parallels but only in Israel's prophetic literature. Examples of this phenomenon include, first, the accusatory question "how long" (v. 22). It is unknown in other sapiential literature but is at home in prophetic preaching (cf. Jer. 4:14; 31:22; Hos. 8:5). Second, the call for repentance (v. 23) and the use of *šûb* with this meaning (113 times), is found exclusively among the prophets (cf. Jer. 15:19; 18:11; 25:5). Third, the scolding accusation of not listening, formally introduced with *yaʿan* (vv. 24–25) is prophetic (cf. Isa. 65:12; 66:4; Jer. 7:24ff; 11:8; 17:23; 25:7; 32:33; 34:17; 35:14, 17). Fourth, the rigidly coined sequence of a substantiating accusation with either *yaʿan* "since/because" (vv. 24–25; cf. Isa. 8:3; 30:12) or *taḥat kî* (vv. 29–30; cf. Jude 2:3) or *waw* (cf. Isa. 37:29), followed by the judicial sentence "so . . . then," is not encountered in the sapiential *Gattung* but is met with in prophetic threats. Fifth, the motif of a judicial sentence to destruction introduced by "I" (v. 26) is also prophetic (cf. Jer. 4:18; 21:14; 35:17; 48:16; 49:8). Sixth, the motif of calling in vain at the time of judgment (v. 28), though not found elsewhere in sapiential literature, is met with in the prophets (Mic. 3:4; Isa. 1:15; Jer. 11:11, 14; Hos. 5:6; Ezek. 8:18; Zech. 7:13). And seventh, the condemnation of faithlessness (v. 32) occurs also in the prophets (Jer. 2:19; 3:6, 11f.; 8:12; 14:7; Hos. 11:7; 14:5).

Scholars therefore properly speak of Lady Wisdom's sermon as an intrusion or as an assimilation of the prophetic genre.[42] Kayatz writes:

> It can be determined once and for all that verses 24–31 taken in themselves are a parallel to the prophetic forms of speech.[43]

She Is a Divine Mediatrix

Finally, some forms and motifs are not found in either sapiential or prophetic speeches, and these elements show a very close connection between Yahweh and Lady Wisdom. For example, her laughter at the time of judgment corresponds with Yahweh's laughter in His anticipation of a lopsided judgment wherein right is vindicated and wrong is punished (cf. the pre-exilic psalms, Pss. 2:5; 37:13; 59:9). This striking and unique correspondence shows the close relationship between Yahweh and the mediatrix of his revelation. Second, Kayatz argued that Lady Wisdom's proclamation of judgment after her admonition has been rejected, has more unconditionality and irrevocability than the threats of judgment in the prophets.[44] Third, the motifs of calling and not hearing and of seeking and not being found (v. 28), which are found in prophetic literature, in fact refer in those texts to Yahweh as an expression of His reaction to punish mankind's disobedience and self-will (cf. Mic. 3:4; Isa. 1:15; Jer. 11:11; Hos. 5:6). Both Yahweh and Lady Wisdom withdraw themselves from sinners in the time of judgment. These motifs, which consciously express the speaker's awesome authority, move Lady Wisdom into the closest association with Yahweh. As Yahweh's word demands obedience and as disobedience to Him provokes His judgment, the same is correspondingly valid for Lady Wisdom. Her withdrawal as a savior in the time of judgment has decisive weight. Her refusal to respond signifies judgment in the same way as Yahweh's withdrawal. When she laughs, mocks, and no longer listens, the person is helplessly given over to his self-afflicted, hopeless situation. Fourth, her statement, "I will cause my spirit to bubble over to you," resembles the relationship of Yahweh to His Messiah through the Spirit. No vizier and no prophet ever spoke like that. Finally, both promise security to those that obey them.

---

42. W. Baumgartner, *Israelitische und altorientalische Weisheit* (1933), 15f.; Kayatz, 120–29.

43. Kayatz, 122.

44. Kayatz, 123.

In sum, Lady Wisdom's speech contains forms and motifs that did not originally belong together. She brings together into a new speech form elements that were originally diverse and thus creates a form that expresses divine revelation with the highest authority.

God spoke to the church's fathers through varying psychologies. To Moses he spoke face to face, to the prophets he spoke in auditions, and to the sages he spoke through observation and reflection as seen through the glasses of the covenantal community. Each gave the *logos* of God, a word that bore the authority of the Author himself, and a word that the elect embrace by faith and that the Spirit confirms in their hearts.

14

ADVICE TO YOUNG MEN: PROVERBS 3

Robert L. Alden

The two themes central to chapters 1–7 are advice to young men and the rewards of wisdom. Although chapter 3 is titled with one of those themes, the other is present too (cf. vv. 13–18). "My son" occurs three times (vv. 1, 11, 21) in this chapter as well as in chapters 1, 4, and 6. Absent from this chapter, however, are any specific sins linked to murderers, thieves (chap. 1), or prostitutes (chap. 2). The advice is rather in general terms with much overlapping and repetition.

3:1. Verse 1 is a simple synonymous couplet introduced by "my son." The verbs in this pair are positive and negative; "don't forget" and "remember." The two words for a father's instruction are traditional "law" and "commands," although the Hebrew *torah* usually understood as "law," is really much broader in meaning than what the word implies. Apparently *torah* is from a verb meaning "throw" which came to mean "distribute," and eventu-

From Robert L. Alden, *Proverbs: A Commentary on an Ancient Book of Timeless Advice* (Grand Rapids: Baker, 1983), 35–44. Used by permission.

ally "teach." Since teaching in the Pentateuch is mostly legal the noun has
come to mean law, but if we remember that law is only one facet of the word
torah, we should appreciate its fuller meaning whenever we read "the law of
the LORD" in the Bible.

We cannot imagine that the only thing the father gave his son was rules;
much of his communication must have been in the form of illustration, anec-
dote, advice, and history. For such a range of techniques "teaching," not
"law," is perhaps the better term.

3:2. Obedience to a father's advice will have two desirable benefits, says
verse 2, long life and prosperity. Here again we find a common Hebrew word
limited by its translation into English. The Hebrew word *shalom* in English is
"peace," yet peace is just one dimension of *shalom*.[1] The word includes harmonious relationships within the family, payment of all debts, and the collection of all loans. It means rewards or wages, ultimately even a right relationship with God which comes through Jesus Christ, our peace. Prosperity is but
one, though central meaning of *shalom*.

3:3. Verse 3 has two terms which also deserve more discussion. "Love" or
"loyalty" (Hebrew *ḥesed*) and "faithfulness" (Hebrew *ᵉmet*) overlap somewhat, but *ḥesed* has been the subject of at least two complete books.[2] It is also
the word repeated in all 26 verses of Psalm 136. If we gave the word a long
definition it would be "faithfulness to covenant promise," but if we choose
one word for it it could be one of these: faithfulness, loyalty, love, lovingkind-
ness, mercy, or fidelity. The other term *ᵉmet*, is like our word "amen," implying such attributes as reliability, accuracy, dependability, truth, and faithfulness, its most common translation.

These noble attributes should grace the neck of the young man and be in-
scribed on his heart,[3] but because of the nonlegal nature of Proverbs these
laws are probably not a reference to phylacteries (little leather boxes containing copies of Deut. 6:4 and the Ten Commandments which pious Jews tied
to their arms and foreheads in literal obedience to Deut. 6:8).

3:4. Obedience in these matters will bring acceptance from both God and
men, says verse 4. There is so much we can do to prompt the praise of men,
but how hard it is to win approval from both God and man. True piety must
express itself both horizontally to those we live and work with, and vertically
to the God we serve. Neither way is optional; it is God who requires us to love
both him and our neighbors.

---

1. See Douglas J. Harris, *Shalom! The Biblical Concept of Peace* (Grand Rapids: Baker, 1970).
2. *Die Entwicklung des Begriffes Hasid im Alten Testament* (Lazar Gulkowitsch, Tartu,
1934), and *Das Wort Hesed,* Nelson Glueck (Topelmann: Berlin, 1961).
3. The LXX omits the last phrase of this verse which some say was possibly borrowed from
7:3.

3:5. Verses 5 and 6 are well known, unmarred by grammatical or linguistic subtleties which might alter its straightforward advice. The only thing to note here is that in this verse is a chiasmus where verbs in Hebrew are on the outside while prepositions are inside. Hence in Hebrew order the verse reads:

> Trust
> > in the LORD with all your heart
> > on your own understanding
> Do not lean.

The meaning of the twofold command is obvious, warning against self-deception or the exaltation of one's own learning. It also might be seen as a warning against "trusting your heart," a common abuse among Christians. Trusting the Lord means becoming well acquainted with him through his Word, spending time in his presence in prayer, and seeking the counsel of others in the faith.

3:6. Two synonyms for "way" appear in verse 6, the same ones used in 2:8–20. Most chapters except for 18, 24, 25, and 27 make extensive use of these words. A modern application of this advice might be to consult a road map constantly while driving through a foreign city. The more you study the map the less likely you are to lose your way. Thus the more you study the Bible, the less chance you will find yourself going astray.

Included in the expression "right way" is the idea of the straight, level, or easy way. Doing things God's way is not difficult or burdensome because it is really the easiest, least complicated, and most direct path to happiness.

3:7. The few words of verse 7 include three commands which, if obeyed, would effect a mighty transformation in anyone: (1) Don't think you are wise, (2) revere God, and (3) refuse to do wrong. Most times our God is too small while our heads are too big. That perspective must be corrected if we are to succeed in the business of living. Paul also repeated this advice in Romans 12:16.

3:8. Fortunately most modern translators paraphrase the Hebrew idioms in verse 8. "Healed navels" and "moist bones" which are the literal translation of the Hebrew don't make much sense to us; the expressions are not only foreign but distasteful.

Yet more and more physicians today are realizing how important one's mental and spiritual health are to one's physical health. That relationship was well understood thousands of years ago. If you have a true assessment of yourself and if you really trust God, then you will be healthy and wise.

3:9–10. Verse 10 begins with a conjunction in Hebrew, "then," like almost every verse in the historical portion of the Old Testament. It ties both verse 9 and 10 together in a cause and effect relationship. If we give to God he will bless us. Again the context of this proverb is rural with words like "firstfruits," "barns," and "vats of new wine."

Some commentators say these verses are levitical and therefore out of place in a book like Proverbs. Yet note the other imperatives in this paragraph such as "trust," "remember," "obey," and "turn." Certainly "honor" is not out of context here, and is also not a very detailed cultic command. Nothing is said about what kind of an animal should be sacrificed, how many bushels of grain should be given, where they should be brought, or how they should be burned. The command is "honor the LORD"; the bringing of gifts is ancillary.

Grain and grape juice were basic ingredients of the ancient diet in bread and wine.

The structure of verse 10 is noteworthy because it is a perfect Hebraic chiasmus. In outline form it would look like this:

> They will be full
>   your barns
>   with grain
>   and with wine
>   your vats
> will overflow.

3:11. Another "my son" opens verse 11 beginning a new paragraph. The verse is a simple couplet with each half saying the same thing in different words. In Hebrew the verbs are negative, "do not resist" and "do not resent the LORD's correction and warning." The pianist, artist, or athlete who accepts and acts in response to criticism is the one who excels; it is never easy to be corrected, but to be mature enough to take it and do something about it is a mark of wisdom.

3:12. It is as difficult for the believer to accept discipline from the Lord as it is for a child to receive discipline from his father, says verse 12. A child who is being spanked usually doesn't believe the parent who says he is doing it because he loves him, but likewise it is hard to believe that God who loves us will also send hardship, testing, sickness, or grief. But he does—because he loves us and wants us to grow in faith. Both verse 11 and 12 are quoted in Hebrews 12:5–6 (cf. Rev. 3:19).

3:13. The opening word, "happy" or "blessed," is typical of the poetic parts of the Bible. It appears in Psalm 1:1 and in twenty-five other places in the psalter. Here it serves to add one more reward to those who seek wisdom. Already in this chapter we have seen that such a person is accepted (v. 4), healthy (v. 8), prosperous (vv. 2, 10), and long-lived (v. 2). To these blessings verse 13 adds the promise of happiness.

3:14–15. The rewards of wisdom are silver, gold, and jewels, completing the little saying, "healthy, wealthy, and wise." Yet it is questionable as to what extent this saying should be taken literally. Undoubtedly Solomon thought wisdom and wealth went together, yet a lot of wise people don't strike it rich. That leads us to think these rewards may be figures of speech for other desirable things in life such as job security, satisfaction, or happy homes. Surely these things, like wisdom, cannot be bought with money.

3:16. The picture verse 16 presents is of a gracious lady offering gifts in both hands. She is wisdom who holds long life in one hand, and wealth and honor in the other. Her gifts are offered to anyone who will take them, but taking them involves marrying her or, in less graphic words, embracing or laying hold of wisdom. Who wouldn't wish that a spouse like this would provide one also with wealth and health?

An intricate connection between key words is the one between the noun "honor" in verse 16 and the imperative verb "honor" in verse 9. The connection is as simple as this: Honor the Lord and he will give you honor. The word "honor" is another word worthy of more extended treatment, but essentially here it means to be heavy, weighty, or worthy.

3:17. Verse 17 in the KJV is a beautiful truth:

> Her ways are ways of pleasantness,
> and all her paths are peace.

Once more "way" is used as a term for "life" (see verse 2 for a brief discussion of *shalom*). It's a pity our language has no term as rich as the Hebrew to describe a happy state of being.

3:18. The paragraph closes with verse 18 which sums up the preceding verses. The reward of wisdom is longevity and happiness; to live long and to be happy are basic human goals. The trouble is most people almost kill themselves trying to live long, and push themselves so hard in an effort to have fun that they make themselves miserable. The problem is that man usually defines happiness in materialistic terms which are quite different from the biblical definition. The unregenerate world's way of achieving it is poles apart from the prescription these ancient maxims offer.

3:19–20. Verses 19 and 20 differ from others in this chapter yet also develop the theme of wisdom. They are somewhat reminiscent of the theophany in Job 38–41 and the praise-of-wisdom chapter (chap. 8) in this book. Considerable scholarly discussion surrounds the question of the relationship between God and wisdom. Is wisdom here a part of the divine personality or a vestige of some female deity? Is it another member of the godhead? I think wisdom is either a part of God's personality or else a kind of surrogate for himself. You might read verses 19 and 20 by simply eliminating "wisdom" and substituting "God." The point is that God is the creator of heaven and earth and under his sovereign direction all things endure. The water cycle is but one area he controls.

The lesson here is that if God used wisdom to make and run the world, how vital it is for us to have in order to occupy and subdue the earth.

3:21. Another "my son" begins verse 21 and introduces a new bit of advice. It is not enough to acquire wisdom; it must be retained and at all costs. It is very possible that even if you have found wisdom you might also lose it. Just as marriage must be worked at in order to be good, so the use and application of wisdom also requires constant effort.

3:22. Verse 22 adds little that is new. Wisdom's reward is long life (vv. 2 and 18), "an ornament to grace your neck." The long life theme also appears later in 4:10, 22; 8:35; 9:11; 10:11, 16, 17; 11:19, 30; 12:28; 13:14; 14:27; 15:4, 24; 16:22; 19:23; 21:21; and 22:4.

3:23. Wisdom is not like a good luck charm, talisman, or St. Christopher medal, but is more practical like a flashlight or climber's rope; wisdom will keep you from stumbling or falling. We feel much safer driving on a well-lit street or paved highway than on a dark, gravel road. Wisdom is like that safer road; it prepares you for the eventualities of the unknown journey that lies ahead.

3:24. Verses 24–26 expand on verse 23, speaking of the full-time vigil wisdom keeps over those who have it. A good night's sleep can be a desperate wish especially for those robbed of it by sickness, anxiety, fear, or noisy neighbors. How wonderful for them is the promise of wisdom's fearless "sweet sleep."

3:25. Two Psalms come to mind in connection with verse 25: 91:5–6 and 121:3–6. Because we have espoused wisdom, which means putting our faith in God (in New Testament terms received Christ as our personal Savior) we need not be afraid of the future. All the phobias and fears of people today have no effect on us because we trust God and his power.

3:26. The linking of God with wisdom is even clearer in verse 26, the conclusion of this paragraph. The paragraph started with wisdom and insight and their benefits, but somewhere in the middle the author made a switch from wisdom to God. Exegetically we must not try to distinguish too carefully between God and his wisdom. Notice 1 Corinthians 1:30; God has made Christ to be our wisdom.

3:27. Verses 27–31 begin with "don't" in Hebrew. Verse 27 is difficult to interpret; the words are familiar enough but their usage is so unusual. A wooden rendering would go like this: "Don't withhold good from 'lords' when it is in the 'god' of your hand to do." This may be a play on the words *baʿal*—"lord" and *ʾel*—"god," but both are paraphrased even in the most traditional versions to something like "to those it is due" and "power."

The second idiom has parallels elsewhere (Gen. 31:29; Deut. 28:32; Neh. 5:5; and Mic. 2:1), but the one about "lords" is unique here. Most scholars agree that this verse teaches either punctuality in paying bills or generosity to the poor. This may have been Paul's idea too when he wrote in Galatians 6:10: "As we have opportunity, let us do good to all people" (NIV). That is the force the verse has in most translations but we can't be positive it is accurate. In principle however, this interpretation is supported elsewhere.

3:28. Verse 28 is much less problematic and reinforces the interpretation that verse 27 is concerned with almsgiving and neighborly generosity rather than prompt bill paying. "Tomorrow" might have meant to ancient Israelites what *mañana* means to South Americans; we must not put off deeds of kindness but do them while we still have the chance. One of my favorite sayings goes, "If not now, when? If not here, where? If not I, who?" The answer to who is my neighbor is the same here as it is in Luke 10:29–37 where Jesus gives the parable of the good Samaritan.

3:29. Verse 29 continues the theme of doing good to our neighbor, illustrating another way we are obligated to him. An enemy might not trust us, but a neighbor should. To plot harm against him would be a double crime involving both the crime itself plus a breach of trust.

3:30. The fourth of five "don'ts" in this series is against unnecessary arguing. Certain people just love to argue. They either champion an unpopular cause or, for the sake of argument, take an opposite position. Such discussion may serve to clarify the sides of an issue, but rarely does it build friendships or strengthen community spirit. In Romans 12:18 Paul tells us to do everything possible to live at peace with each other. The Hebrew verb in 3:30 even includes a word which suggests something stronger than argument; this "accusing a man" has legal overtones. How much more must unjustified lawsuits displease the Lord!

3:31. The last warning in this series is against jealousy, immediately bringing to mind the extended treatment of that subject in Psalm 37:1–8. It is too bad that so many children's toys today encourage violence. The mass media is partly to blame for that, but so is our sinful nature which turns to violence rather than love. Only the power of new life in Christ can overcome the spirit of vengeance which seeks to solve all problems through the use of force.

3:32. In verses 27–31 we learned the rules. Now in verses 32–35 we learn reasons for those rules. Don't do any of these bad things because God will surely reward people with what they deserve. Curses for the wicked and blessings for the righteous are mentioned several times in this paragraph, many times in the book, and countless times in the whole Bible.

3:33. Typical of contrasts in this passage is "hatred" toward perverse men versus "confidence" in good ones. We would expect "love" or "blessing" toward the upright man, but "confidence" is an interesting term pointing to the intimacy God enjoys with those who serve him.

The typical contrast of "curse" and "blessing" is presented in verse 33. Each half of this verse includes a word for "house," but probably not too

much significance should be read into that. The sage is not necessarily referring to buildings, but neither is he speaking of families or dynasties.

3:34. Epithets for good and bad men are in verse 34: "conceited mockers"
and "humble men." Arrogance was as distasteful in ancient Israel as it is in our
society, and God hates it just as much as anyone else. In fact he may hate it
more because he can see through people to their hearts. Both James (4:6) and
Peter (1 Pet. 5:5) cite this verse when they urge Christians to be humble.

3:35. The list is complete: verse 32 with "evil" and "righteous"; verse 33
with "wicked" and "righteous" (a different Hebrew word from verse 32);
verse 34 with "conceited" and "humble"; and verse 35 with "wise" and "foolish." A similar list might be made for the contrasting attitudes and actions of
God:

verse 32; hates-confides
verse 33; curses-blesses
verse 34; mocks-favors
verse 35; honor-disgrace

15

BEWARE THE SEDUCTRESS: PROVERBS 5

Kenneth T. Aitken

Proverbs 5:1–14

My son, be attentive to my wisdom,
    incline your ear to my understanding;
that you may keep discretion,
    and your lips may guard knowledge.
For the lips of a loose woman drip honey,
    and her speech is smoother than oil;
but in the end she is bitter as wormwood,
    sharp as a two-edged sword.
Her feet go down to death;
    her steps follow the path to Sheol;
she does not take heed to the path of life;
    her ways wander, and she does not know it.

From *Proverbs* (Daily Study Bible Series) by Kenneth T. Aitken. © 1986 Kenneth T. Aitken.
Used by permission of Westminster/John Knox Press and The Saint Andrew Press.

213

And now O sons, listen to me,
> and do not depart from the words of my mouth.
Keep your way far from her,
> and do not go near the door of her house;
lest you give your honor to others
> and your years to the merciless;
lest strangers take their fill of your strength,
> and your labors go to the house of an alien;
and at the end of your life you groan,
> when your flesh and body are consumed,
and you say, "How I hated discipline,
> and my heart despised reproof!
I did not listen to the voice of my teachers
> or incline my ear to my instructors.
I was at the point of utter ruin
> in the assembled congregation."

This chapter enlarges on the theme of the seductress introduced in 2:16–19. The theme is also developed at length in 6:24–35 and 7:1–27. The space given to it and the vigor with which the destructive powers of the seductress are portrayed leave us in no doubt that the sage saw in her the greatest hazard lying in the path of young men. The Egyptian sages also warned their students against her. But since they were training young men for successful careers, their ethic of sexual morality was primarily an ethic for men in public life. They were anxious to point out that nothing can ruin a promising career so quickly as an illicit affair. That has still a modern ring to it, even in our more tolerant times. The sage of Proverbs, however, takes a deeper and more serious view of the matter. He is teaching his pupils wisdom for living, and in these passages he is anxious to warn that to meddle around with this woman is the height of folly, for her kiss is the kiss of death.

Though the situation is not always clear and seems to vary slightly from passage to passage, the seductress appears to be a married woman who behaves like a common prostitute, either for a fee or to gratify her own desires. She is regularly described as a "loose woman" and an "adventuress" (vv. 3, 20; see also 2:16; 6:24; 7:5). These words actually mean "strange woman" and "foreign woman," neither of which are the normal terms for an adulteress or prostitute. Does this mean that she is a non-Israelite? Away from home, a foreign woman would not be subject to the restraints of her own community nor to those imposed by Israelite society. She would therefore be free to indulge in this kind of behavior if she so wished. The Egyptian sage is thinking of this kind of woman when he warns his pupils:

> Be on thy guard against a woman from abroad, who is not known in her [own] town. . . . Do not know her carnally: a deep water, whose windings one knows not, a woman who is far away from her husband. . . . She has no witnesses when she waits to ensnare thee.

But while something of the sort may lie behind the use of these terms, and most prostitutes in Israel may have been foreign women, they probably intend that the woman belongs to another man rather than that she necessarily comes from another country. The New International Version translates the terms, "adulteress" and "wayward wife."

At all events, she is a very persuasive lady, well practiced in the art of seduction. That is what makes her so dangerous. Although she knows how to make good use of her natural sex appeal to entice her victim (6:25), it is upon her honeyed words and seductive speech that she relies most. We have an example of the kinds of things she says in 7:14–20. Her words have the sweetness of honey and the smoothness of oil (v. 3; see also 2:16; 6:24; 7:5, 21).

She is a sweet talker. Honey was used by housewives to make food more palatable and was proverbial for its sweetness (16:24; 24:13–14; Judg. 14:18; Rev. 10:9–10). Delicious words, full of delectable promise, flow easily from her lips to titillate the taste buds and whet the appetite of her victim until he is completely entranced and captivated by her. In the Song of Solomon 4:11 the same figure is used of the bride's kisses.

She is a smooth talker. The half-hearted resistance of her victim's better judgment is no bar against this woman's wiles. A little coaxing, a little flattery, a little deceit, above all the assurance that it is all completely harmless, and her prey is well and truly caught.

So the seductress holds out promise of pleasure and enjoyment more than enough to entice and captivate hot blooded young men. The reality, however, is something quite different. There is an old saying, "Honey is sweet, but the bee stings"; and this lady has a sting in her tail.

The sting in the tail ("in the end," v. 4) comes in verses 4–6. Notice the stark contrast in verses 3 and 4 between "honey" and "wormwood," and "smoother" and "sharp." Wormwood, a type of plant, was as proverbial for bitterness as honey was for sweetness (see Jer. 9:15; Lam. 3:15; Amos 5:7; Rev. 8:10–11). Here is the lady in her true colors: (1) her honeyed words leave a bitter taste, and (2) her smooth words prove to be the thrusts of a razor-sharp sword (cf. Ps. 55:21). She is a merciless, implacable foe. There is bitter disillusionment here. The experience was not as pleasurable as she had promised. "Never again!" says he; but he will be back, expecting this time it will be. There is also the bitter and sharp pangs of remorse given voice to by the victim in verses 12–14. But this lady's sword has more than one edge; and as verses 5–6 make clear, becoming entangled in her ways leads to more than a bad taste in the mouth and a bad conscience. The seductress is traveling on the road to death, the path to Sheol (see 2:18–19; 7:27, and . . . 1:12), reeling with the unsteady step of a drunkard, from lover to lover, obstinately blind to (or not giving a fig for: "What does she care?" NEB, v. 6) the wrong she does and the harm she brings upon herself and her lovers (cf. 30:20). She is plunging recklessly to her ruin, and she is taking her victims with her. The Authorized Version renders Sheol by "hell," but in Old Testament times Sheol was not thought of as a place of torment and punishment, but as a place of inactivity and death. The seductress's path of death is the opposite of wisdom's path of life. Just as wisdom's path makes life rich and full and really worth living, and leads to ripeness of age . . . so the seductress's path impoverishes life and robs it of meaning, and leads in the end to an untimely death.

The impoverished life of the man who becomes entangled with her is spelled out in frank and sober terms in verses 10–14. It is the antithesis of wisdom's benediction in 3:13–18. In short, he is a destroyed man—personally and socially. He loses every shred of dignity and the respect of his neighbors (v. 9); wastes all his resources—material, physical, and mental (vv. 10–11); is filled with remorse when he learns too late how foolish he has been (vv. 12–13), and is exposed to public disgrace (v. 14). Perhaps behind the scenes is the woman's husband (cf. 6:34–35), denouncing the offender in a public assembly (v. 14) and pressing for as much compensation as he can get (v. 10). The irony of it all is that his energy and hard-won resources serve only to benefit a cruel-hearted woman and her family and associates, while he and his family lose out in every possible way.

More than the figurative language of verses 4–6, what the sage says in verses 10–14 carries a powerful appeal to young men living, as his pupils did, in a close-knit community, and would encourage them to weigh the transient pleasure against its terrible consequences, and ask: "Is it worth it?" This may not be the most searching question to ask, but wisdom dwells in prudence (8:12) as well as being founded on the fear of the Lord (1:7). Wisdom will always weigh up the consequences of an action before acting. Although nowadays this kind of behavior is very often condoned and the greater sin is being caught out, adultery still exacts a high price in damaged relationships, broken homes, and hurt, lonely people.

The seductress, then is a very persuasive and very dangerous woman. The only safe course of action is to keep well away from her (v. 8; cf. 1:10, 15). This advice is well illustrated by the story of Joseph's escapade in Genesis 39, when he has to run away from the seductress as fast as he can, leaving his shirt-tail behind him. But better still, if you can help it, don't get near enough to let her grab your shirt-tail! And this is as much a matter of what we look at (see 4:25; Job 31:1; Matt. 5:28) and what we read, as where we go.

Rejoice in the Wife of Your Youth

Proverbs 5:15–23

> Drink water from your own cistern,
>   flowing water from your own well.
> Should your springs be scattered abroad,
>   streams of water in the streets?
> Let them be for yourself alone,
>   and not for strangers with you.
> Let your fountain be blessed,
>   and rejoice in the wife of your youth,
>   a lovely hind, a graceful doe.
> Let her affection fill you at all times with delight,
>   be infatuated always with her love.
> Why should you be infatuated, my son, with a loose woman
>   and embrace the bosom of an adventuress?
> For a man's ways are before the eyes of the LORD,
>   and he watches all his paths.
> The iniquities of the wicked ensnare him,
>   and he is caught in the toils of his sin.
> He dies for lack of discipline,
>   and because of his great folly he is lost.

While the previous section had most in mind young unmarried men, this one is addressed to the married man, and advises him that the best antidote against the destructive wiles of the seductress is to remain in love with his wife and to keep alight the flame of romance in his marriage.

The Bible is often thought to take a rather dim view of sexual relations and to tolerate them as the means of procreation and no more. But that is a distortion which tells us more about the sexual hang-ups of some of its past interpreters than about what the Bible actually says on the subject. Here we have a passage which speaks enthusiastically about the joys and delights of the sexual relation between husband and wife. Enjoyment, not procreation, is its theme. This theme is taken up in the Song of Solomon, that lovely celebration of human love and fidelity between bride and bridegroom. As in that best of love songs, the language in this passage is frank and earthy, yet sensitive in its eroticism. Imagery connected with water is delicately used to express the pleasure and satisfaction a man ought to obtain through sexual intercourse with his wife (vv. 15, 18; cf. Song of Sol. 4:12, 15) in contrast to the waste which results when he is unfaithful to her (vv. 16–17). Compared to a love affair with a warm and loving wife, consorting with a cold and calculating woman is a poor counterfeit (vv. 19–20); for instead of being a physical *relation* between two people which expresses and deepens love, commitment, and companionship, as God intended it to be and provided for (Gen. 2:18–24), sex is corrupted into a *thing* she gives and he gets, and so it is robbed of true meaning and fulfillment. This debased view of sex as a thing in itself, to be indulged in, played around with, and enjoyed quite separately from a faithful relationship of love and responsibility, is being insidiously promoted today as never before, and we cannot be too much on our guard against it.

So far in this chapter the sage has appealed for a prudent weighing up of the consequences as a deterrent against becoming involved with loose women: it is simply not worth it, for there is everything to lose and nothing to gain. In verse 21, however, he shifts into a higher gear. While the foolish man may take steps to hide his sordid affair from the eyes of others (7:9; cf. Job 24:15) and may put all thought of God out of his mind, God's all-seeing eye is upon him, watching and observing, weighing and judging (see 15:3; Job 31:4; 34:21; Heb. 4:13).

But there is no thunderbolt from heaven to strike him down. Rather, by threading his path to folly's door he is threading a noose around his own neck, like a senseless bird weaving the net which will ensnare it (vv. 22–23; see 1:17–19, which are similar in thought). If we follow the New English Bible in verse 23, this foolish man weaves more than the tangled web which traps him; he also weaves his funeral shroud: "he will perish for want of discipline, wrapped in the shroud of his boundless folly." The word "wrapped in the shroud" (RSV "lost") is the same word the Revised Standard Version translates "infatuated" in verses 19 and 20, but which the New English Bible renders "wrapped." So it appears that the sage makes a play on this word as the key word to underline and drive home the lesson to be learned: wrap up well in the love of your wife (v. 19), and don't become wrapped up with loose women (v. 20), for that is as good as wrapping yourself in a funeral shroud (v. 23).

16

AVOID THE IMMORAL WOMAN: PROVERBS 7

William McKane

G emser's division of the chapter into six strophes is arbitrary (cf.
Ringgren, who supposes that 6:20–7:27 is one piece), and does
not really throw any light on its structure. This is one of the chapters on
which Whybray is most severe, and his "original discourse" consists of vv. 1–
3, 5, 25–27 (pp. 49f.). The rest is rejected for a variety of reasons, verse 4
because in it Wisdom is personified; verses 6–24 because the woman whom
they describe is alleged to be other than the woman of verse 5, and because
verse 25 resumes verse 5; verse 24 because it has been inserted to ease the
transition from the long interpolation to the "original discourse."

From the point of view of form, the chapter has three significant divisions,
verses 1–5, 6–23 and 24–27. The first and the last have recognizably the form
of the Instruction (cf. "My son," v. 1, and "sons," v. 24), and it is only the

From *Proverbs: A New Approach* by William McKane. Published in the U.S.A. by The Westminster Press, 1970. ©1970 SCM Press Ltd. Used by permission of Westminster/John Knox
Press.

long middle section which constitutes a clear departure from the formal elements of the genre. In the opening section, the imperatives lead on to a final clause, "to keep you from the strange woman, from the smooth words of the foreigner" (v. 5), and in the closing section to motive clauses (vv. 26f.). Into the assessment of the central part there enter some textual considerations, and my remarks assume that it is the wisdom teacher and not the woman who looks out of the window in verse 6 (see below), and that this long descriptive passage is a variation on the theme of "instruction," "admonition," or a development of it.

The significance of this development would seem to me to be that it affords greater imaginative and descriptive scope than is allowed by the precise didactic formulation of the Instruction. Here the teacher does not assert his authority prosaically in imperatives, nor does he argue in motive clauses that his demands are reasonable and should be obeyed. Rather, he relies on his descriptive powers and his ability to reconstruct imaginatively the woman's stratagems and seductive conversation, so that the warning is conveyed not by schematized instruction, but by introducing the young man into the ways of the world and bringing him to the woman's house, in order to show him that it is a death trap and that only a fool will satisfy his desire at such a price.

1–5 Instruction and the Woman

[1, 3] In these verses it is the wisdom teacher who asserts his authority and . . . *miṣwā* defines the mandatory form of this instruction (it is communicated in imperatives), while *tōrā* indicates that it has the character of "directive" or "guidance." The strongly conservative nature of this educational discipline is underlined by such verbs as "keep," "store," "bind," "write," in which tenacity of memory and unbroken concentration and attentiveness are desiderated. On the other hand, "write them on the tablet of your heart" (v. 3) represents more than a demand to learn precepts by rote, and points to an inward assimilation of the tradition. Consequently, when this educational ideal of old wisdom is described as authoritative, this does not preclude an important aspect of inwardness. The tradition is not just received as so many arbitrary external demands, but is assimilated as a way of life, and it is through this assimilation that it has the character and unity of wisdom. It shapes fundamental attitudes to life, and especially intellectual attitudes, and so it makes a man what he is.

[2] In verse 2, vitality is consequential on keeping the *miṣwōt* of the wisdom teacher, a reminder which is particularly apposite in view of the connection established elsewhere between the strange woman and death (2:16f.; . . . 7:27). It may be that such a reference to "life" in Proverbs always has some distant connection with the mythological concepts of "the tree of life" (see on 3:18) or "the fountain of life" (see on 10:11), just as "death" is related, however remotely, to the Canaanite god Mot with his gaping throat . . . . At

any rate, it is evident that life is more than breath and that death is not just when the heart stops and the pulse ceases to beat. There is a living death, and so "life" in the fuller sense has qualitative aspects, and it is this more abounding vitality which is said to be consequential on keeping the commandments. In saying that his *tōrā* is to be kept as "the little man of the eye," i.e. the pupil of the eye, the wisdom teacher defines it as illumination or guidance. The pupil, because it is the light of the eye, is precious beyond reckoning, and if a man does not "keep" it, he is consigned to a world of darkness. Likewise, the *tōrā* of the teacher is the light of the mind and without it men have no sure guidance for the conduct of their lives. This recalls the metaphor in 6:23a, "For the *miṣwā* is a lamp and the *tōrā* a light," . . . Certainly 7:3, which differs only in one word from 3:3, is phrased in a way closely resembling passages which deal with law and covenant, and may be a deliberate literary conflation of these passages. . . . Gemser suggests that verse 3a may envisage the signet ring which is a valuable personal possession, or the red thread which has magical virtue. Wisdom is a more effective apotropaic than any amulet, and it is assimilated as a vital principle, not just encountered as external demand.

[4–5] It is worth asking whether there is not some connection between this emphasis on the inwardness of wisdom and the personifications of verse 4. Both Gemser and Ringgren urge that "sister" is a form of address equivalent to "bride" or "wife" (also Boström, pp. 161f.), and that Wisdom is to be seen in this verse as the rival of the strange woman, countering her fatal seductiveness by emerging with the wholesome attractiveness of a bride or wife. A love for Wisdom is like love for a wife, in that it is conducive to stability, honour and welfare. The connection of this verse may, however, be with the thought of the inwardness of wisdom in verse 3, rather than with the strange woman. The relationship which has to be established with wisdom is almost personal in character, and one knows wisdom in the same way as a sister or a relative is known. A deep community with wisdom has to be experienced, and in appropriating it there is an awareness of solidarity and kinship. "Say to Wisdom, You are my sister, and call Discernment a relative." The description of the woman is almost identical to that of 2:16 and has features in common with 5:3, 20 and 6:24.

6–23 The Woman and Her Prey

[6–8] Since it is with this passage that Boström leads in developing his cultic theory of the *ʾiššā zārā*, it is convenient to begin with a consideration of his argument. I have already indicated that I agree with Boström against Snijders that the *ʾiššā zārā* or *nokrīyā* means a foreign woman rather than one whose *mores* make her a social outcast from her own community and who is an "outsider." According to MT of verse 6, it is Wisdom personified or the wisdom teacher who looks out of the window and observes the tactics of the strange woman. Gemser has contrasted the wisdom teacher with the prophet, the one with his attention directed towards the world and its traffic, formulating his worldly wisdom by an inductive method, and the other receiving his word from beyond the world as "revelation" or "disclosure." In order to make room for his theory, Boström has to assume that the original text of verse 6 is preserved in LXX (v. 6b is missing from LXX[B]), and that it is the woman, not the wisdom teacher, who looks out of the window. In this he is followed by Albright (*VTS* iii, p. 10), and both connect παρακύπτο νσα with Aphrodite παρακύπτουσα, a cult attested in Cyprus and Phoenicia, in which Aphrodite or Astarte is the goddess in the window. This goddess is to be equated with the Babylonian Ishtar, named Kililu, who is designated as "she who leans out of the window," "she who sets herself in the window of the house," and the twin characteristics of creativeness and destructiveness (the reverse side of fertility) are reflected in her devotees who also look out of the window as part of the ritual of her cult (p. 104f.).

In order to sustain this interpretation of verse 6 ("For at the window of her house through the lattice she gazes"), the MT of verse 7 has also to be altered to agree with LXX, and so Boström translates: "And she sees a youth among the untutored, she perceives among the young men one who is lacking in wit" (transposing *na'ar* to verse 7a and reading third person instead of first in the verbs). To this Snijders objects (p. 98, n. 72) that even when it is so emended, verse 7 depicts a woman who looks out of the window to observe and not to be observed. The latter is required by Boström's theory. His woman should stand in the window to attract attention to herself, but the woman described by the emended text looks out of the window to catch sight of young men. This is not a decisive objection, since it is arguable that she has to do this in the first place in order to judge the moment when she can display herself to most advantage. The spying-out of possible victims is a necessary reconnaissance. There are other respects in which Boström has overstated his case, for whatever virtue it may have it ought not to be supported by the claim that MT makes no sense. MT makes very good sense, and the transition from it to verse 8 is much easier than Boström allows. One cannot say that verse 8 presupposes LXX in verses 6–7, for "her" in verse 8 can be referred naturally to the woman of verse 5 with the MT of verses 6f. retained. It is then the observant wisdom teacher who seeks the senseless youth crossing into the street beside her corner, and walking in the direction of her house. "Corner" perhaps refers to the harlot's "pitch" located in convenient proximity to her house (v. 8), an interpretation which is reinforced by verse 12: "Now in the streets, now in the squares and beside every corner she skulks." On *'ešnabbī*, "lattice" (v. 6), E. F. F. B. remarks: "The lattice is familiar from old Palestinian houses with a window sill jutting out into the street and a framework of open holes through which one might look out." The lattice affords protection from the light and heat of the sun, and contributes to privacy.

Y. Aharoni (*Archaeology and Old Testament Study*, ed. D. Winton Thomas, 1967, pp. 180f.) notes that the queen looking through the window is a narrative motif in the Old Testament (Judg. 5:28; 2 Sam. 6:16; 2 Kings 9:30), and he has supplied archaeological evidence from Beth-Hakkerem that a window with a lattice arrangement (*>eǔnāb*, Judg. 5:28; Prov. 7:6), supported by a balustrade, was an architectural feature of a royal palace. This he has correlated with the "woman in the window" motif on Phoenician ivory plaques from Samaria, Arslan Tash, Nimrud and Khorsabad, where a window of similar design is shown. Is it, then, Wisdom portrayed as a queen who looks out of the window in Proverbs 7:6? If so, it would appear that a motif associated with Astarte (as queen of fertility) and her devotees has been transferred to Wisdom. . . .

[9] The action takes place at twilight in the evening of the day, a time reference which the rather obscure phrase in verse 9b may be assumed to reinforce. If so, "at the eye (*>īǔōn*, cf. v. 2b) of night and darkness" will be a picturesque synonym of verse 9a (or perhaps we should point *>eǔun* "approach," Accadian *isinnu* "fixed time," cf. 20.20). Boström notes that in Ethiopic Enoch 78.2, one of the four names of the moon, corresponding to its first phase, is *Asonja* ("eye of Yahweh"), and he points to Zech. 9:9, where the planets, sun and moon are designated as "eyes of Yahweh." He suggests that "eye of night" is a profane or secular formulation of "eye of Yahweh" and is to be equated with it, in which case verse 9b establishes that these proceedings took place at the time of the new moon ("the eye of night and darkness"). There is no virtue in Dahood's suggestion (pp. 14f.) that *>īǔōn* is to be derived from *yǔn*, since the translation "sleep" does not suit the verse and Dahood's rendering "quietness" can hardly be derived from *yǔn*.

[10–12] In verse 10, the woman would seem to be depicted as a prostitute with the clothes and the disposition of her class. The meaning of *neṣūrat lēb* has been well elucidated by G. R. Driver (*VT* i, 1950, p. 250) in terms of the parallel semantic development of *ṣnᶜ* and *nṣr* from "guarded," "reserved" to "crafty," "sly" (Syriac, *ṣnī*, "sly"). She has an easy and assured mastery over all the devices of seduction. She has a house, but not a home; she is a woman without roots in her family and community who can only live at fever temperature and whose wanderlust is the index of her homelessness and her alienation from authentic social experience. She is flighty, a rover and wanderer whose feet do not stay in her house (on *sōreret*, which is to be explained with reference to Accadian *sarāru*, "to be unstable," as well as "to be rebellious," see G. R. Driver, *ZAW* 50, 1932, pp. 141f.). It is interesting that in rejecting verses 6–24 as an interpolation, Whybray argues that the woman described in this passage, and especially in verse 10, is not the *>iǔǔā zārā* of verse 5. This he founds on an argument from silence, that the *ʾiššā zārā* is nowhere called or likened to a *zōnā*—a professional prostitute (pp. 49f.). This is no more conclusive than the attempt of Boström to show that the woman of 6:27–35 is not the *ʾiššā zārā,* and both illustrate the unwisdom of trying to make her conform to an exact pattern.

[13] Once the *petī* is in her clutches, she employs all her expertise on him, and she does it with an efficiency and thoroughness which is unhampered by scruple. With a practised immodesty she gets down at once to the business of seduction.

[14] Boström's interpretation of verse 14 can be sustained only if *šillamtī* is translated as a present, "Today I am to fulfil my vows." In this case we may follow him in supposing that the communion meal (*zibᵉḥē šᵉlāmīm*) does not exhaust her cultic obligations, and that her vows are fulfilled in sexual intercourse. If verse 14b is translated, "To-day I have fulfilled my vows" (Gemser, Ringgren), the meaning must be that the communion meal is the outstanding cultic obligation and that she invites the young man to share this with her. This leads naturally to the supposition (cf. Gemser) criticized by Boström that the communion meal is more or less a pretext to lure the young man to her house and that her protestations of cultic devotion are a ruse for winning a customer. This would be a more credible interpretation if in fact the invitation had been to share a communion meal and no more, but in view of the frankness of the woman in disclosing her intentions (vv. 16–20), there is weight in Boström's objections.

[15–18] The "therefore" of verse 15 is directed exclusively towards sexual intercourse and suggests, as Boström's translation of verse 14 allows, that it is this which constitutes the consummation of her cultic devotions. It is as a devotee that she has decked the couch for the communion meal with fine coverlets and prepared the bed for the sacred marriage (so also Ringgren), sprinkling it with myrrh, aloes and cinnamon (on *nwp*, a by-form of *npp*, "to sprinkle," see G. R. Driver, *ZAW* 50, 1932, p. 142).

[19f.] Yet this rather rarified cultic interpretation of the passage is not entirely adequate. While she may do this out of a devotion to Aphrodite παρακύπτουσα, she knows that it has an illicit aspect and that it is an indulgence which her husband would not tolerate. By implication she is aware that it conflicts with accepted notions of domestic and social morality. Hence it has to be supposed that her natural sensuality and eroticism make this kind of religious devotion agreeable to her. This is an aspect of the matter which should not be neglected in assessing the kind of woman who emerges in these verses.

Her husband is far from home on a business trip, and Gemser suggests that enough information is given to justify the conclusion that he is a rich merchant who is engaged in extensive business transactions. He has a purse full of money, and he has a house which reflects his affluence, whose exotic furnishings have been brought from foreign parts. I am unsure how much Gemser is trying to establish. Is he calling in question the actual "foreignness" of the woman and her husband? If so, she and her husband are both Israelites, but she creates an exotic atmosphere in her house by means of foreign furnishings and perfumes which her husband has brought home from his commercial travels. In this matter, some weight should be attached to a passage in the Instruction of *Ani* in which the young man is warned against "a woman from abroad . . . who is far away from her husband" . . . and it is on this analogy that I would understand the foreignness of the woman in the book of Proverbs. She is a *nokrīyā* in the full sense, as Boström says, and she has about her an air of allurement and mystery which excites the desire of young men. She is a foreigner and the wife of a foreigner, settled in a community where she is a stranger and is careless of her reputation, with a husband who is a merchant and is away from home for lengthy periods. So the situation is made for her and, if she wills it, she can be promiscuous with impunity.

Boström's equation of *ʾīšon laylā* with "new moon" (v. 9) would seem to reinforce this interpretation. If it is the new moon and her husband is not to return until the full moon, there is no danger in spending the night with her (v. 18). This is what the woman says in verses 19–20. Her husband is not at home; he has gone on a distant journey and will not return until the day of the full moon. Gemser supposes that her husband returns when the moon is full because travel is safer and swifter at this period of the month. Boström draws verse 9 into his cultic theory by observing that the new moon has everywhere a special connection with sexual intercourse. The conjunction of the sun and moon at the new moon signified for primitive thought the coitus of sun and moon which was celebrated with sexual rites (pp. 123f.). In this he finds a confirmation that it is the ἱερὸς γάμος which the woman wishes to consummate.

This is a convenient place for me to indicate how far I am prepared to go with Boström and in what respects he has overstretched his cultic interpretation. The woman who is the wife of a merchant and whose home has an air of luxury about it is clearly not a common prostitute soliciting for a fee. She is probably, as he contends, a devotee of Aphrodite, in which case *zōnā* (v. 10) will have this specialized sense, and her clothes will also identify her in her cultic role. This does not necessarily imply, however, that it is precisely because she is a devotee that the wisdom teacher warns young men against her. So far as they are concerned she is just a special kind of prostitute, and a particularly dangerous kind, because she gives so much and asks nothing. It is here that I part company with Boström. Boström says that the wisdom teacher issues a warning against participation in a foreign cult and heathen rites. My view is that the wisdom teacher is warning young men against an affair with a married woman who is a prostitute, and that her being a devotee of Aphrodite is not the nub of the matter. Boström attributes to the wisdom teacher a Deuteronomic abhorrence of alien cultic practices, and ignores the circumstance that similar warnings are issued in the Egyptian Instruction in a context of worldly wisdom. For the wisdom teacher, the woman is as fatal to young men as any other *zōnā*, and he is not directly concerned with the special religious reasons for her promiscuity, except in so far as these make her a particularly dangerous prostitute.

The warning in the Babylonian *Counsels of Wisdom* . . . against the temple prostitute should be similarly assessed, and it does not necessarily, as Ringgren supposes (*Word and Wisdom*, pp. 135f.), lend support to Boström's interpretation of the *ʾiššā zārā* in Prov. 1–9. The advice is as follows:

> Do not marry a prostitute whose husbands are legion,
> A temple harlot who is dedicated to a god,
> A courtesan whose favors are many.
> In your trouble she will not support you,
> In your dispute she will be a mocker;
> There is no reverence or submissiveness with her.
> Even if she dominate your house, get her out,
> For she has directed her attention elsewhere. [*ll.* 72–79, *BWL*, pp. 102f.]

Now it is probable that all three words used for prostitute (*ḫarimtu, ištaritu, kulmašitu*) refer to a cult prostitute (see W. von Soden, *Akkadisches Handwörterbush*), but this does not mean that the point of the warning is that one should not get involved in the ritual of a fertility cult. It is clear from *ll.* 75–79 that the advice is differently weighted, and that it is the unsuitability of such a woman as a domestic partner and help-meet which is its gist. It is not so surprising that cult prostitutes are specifically mentioned, since they must have been a common type of prostitute and, moreover, the wisdom teacher may have believed that the effects of this type of prostitution on a woman were particularly demoralizing. Yet it is unlikely that he would have considered any kind of prostitute as a promising homemaker, and it is this canny, earthy concern rather than any abhorrence of cultic connections which informs his remarks. Prostitution leaves its indelible effects on a woman and she cannot be reformed so as to become a biddable, reliable and helpful wife. The old life will erupt into the new, and she will be a vamp with a relationship to her husband like that which she used to have with her clients.

[21] Winton Thomas (*VTS* iii, p. 284) has suggested that *liqḥā* (v. 21) means "her taking ways" (her charm) rather than "her persuasiveness." [22] LXX κεπφωθείς, "simpletons," would seem to indicate that *ptʾm* was vocalized *petāʾīm* by the Greek translator. "He follows her as would untutored youths" makes poor sense. Nor is the singular *petī* much improvement, and in any case the point of the emendation is lost if sense cannot be had from

$p^e t\bar{a}^\jmath \bar{\imath} m$. $pit^\jmath \bar{o}m$ and $p^e t\bar{a}^\jmath \bar{\imath} m$ can be referred to the same consonantal text, but not $pit^\jmath \bar{o}m$ and $pet\bar{\imath}$. She distracts him ($hittatt\bar{u}$) with her ample resources of coquetry, and he is putty in her hands. She routs him ($tadd\bar{\imath}hennū$; "routs" rather than "seduces") with her smooth words. He follows her on an impulse ($pit^\jmath \bar{o}m$ "suddenly," here "impulsively") and the ease with which she manipulates him and the danger in which he stands are conveyed by two figures of speech. He goes, or is brought (LXX), like an ox to the slaughter (22b). The second simile is unintelligible in MT: "Like a bangle to the discipline of a fool." $m\bar{o}s\bar{e}r$, "noose," should be read for $m\bar{u}s\bar{a}r$, and $^\jmath ayy\bar{a}l$, "hart," for $^{\jmath e}w\bar{\imath}l$, with the support of the versions. There are two elucidations of the simile by G. R. Driver, the second superseding the first.

In the first, which is followed by BH, $^c ks$ is associated with Arabic $^c akasa$, "to tie (a camel) with a rope," and is pointed as an infinitive construct qal ($ka^{^c \alpha}k\bar{o}s$), "as a hart is tied to a cord." The youth is likened to an animal which is caught and tied by a cord to a stake ready for killing (*ZAW* 50, 1932, p. 143). Driver's later explanation supposes that $^c ks$ refers to a jerky mode of walking, as in Arabic, and he points $k^{^{ec}}akk\bar{e}s$, "as a hart skips into a noose" (*VT* i, 1951, p. 241).

[23] Driver's second suggestion accords well with "as a bird speeds towards a trap." The sequence would be more logical if the order of 23a and 23b were reversed. The arrow kills the trapped animal or bird and so it is with the youth. He is likened to an unsuspecting animal bounding into a trap, to a bird that is in a hurry to be snared. It is an ambush from which there is no escape, or an arrow will pierce his vitals. All the while, he is sadly oblivious to the fact that his life ($nepe\check{s}$) is at stake (b^e of price; he pays with his life, verse 23).

24–27 Avoid the Gate of Death

[24] . . . In these closing verses the teacher renews his demands on his pupils ("sons"), and urges them to give him their unbroken attentiveness and concentration and to defer to the authority of his words.

[25–27] The remaining verses are constructed in terms of the metaphor of the "road" in such a way as to elucidate the destructive potential of the woman and the lethal effects of associating with her. Commenting on 2:16f. . . . , I have suggested that the mythology of the Canaanite god Mot exercises some influence on the construction of this figure of the woman as a way of death. To be led away by desire for her is to take the road to Sheol and to arrive at the point of no return. This is a deviation from the way of life which does not admit of subsequent correction; it is a commitment to death and there is no way back to a safe road (v. 25). This woman deals instant death to her victims, however powerful, and a great company have been "toppled" by her in many lethal encounters (v. 26). The thought of the gaping throat of Mot is not entirely absent from verse 27 . . . although there is an element of reinterpretation in the verse. The mythology is subject to "transference" and the process of transfer involves some demythologizing. The ways leading to Sheol and the chambers of death converge on the woman's house and it becomes the open throat of the god who swallows up life in death. The house, like the throat of Mot, is a gate of death—the beginning of a descent into the underworld. Mythology is thus made the servant of instruction and edification, and is no longer serious mythology.

17

AN ANALYSIS OF PROVERBS 8:22–31 ACCORDING TO STYLE AND STRUCTURE

Gale A. Yee

This chapter will examine the internal development of the poem found in Proverbs 8:22–31; its structure and how its rhetorical and stylistic features convey meaning and purpose. The third section of a tripartite poem,[1] Proverbs 8:22–31 can be detached for separate study from the rest of the poem on the basis of its distinct content and language.[2] For the most part, scholarly exegesis has concentrated on a historical study of this passage, appealing in particular to Egyptian, Canaanite, and Babylonian my-

From *Zeitschrift für alttestamentliche Wissenschraft* 94 (1982): 58–66. Used by permission.
1. Part 1: vv. 1–11; Part 2: vv. 12–21; Part 3: vv. 22–31; Epilogue: vv. 32–36.
2. On this R. Stecher, "Die persönliche Weisheit in den Proverbien Kap 8," *ZkTh* 75 (1953): 415, remarks: "Dieser hohe Gehalt." verlangt eine entsprechende künstlerische Form." Cf. also W. Vischer, "Der Hymnus der Weisheit in den Sprüchen Salomos 8," *EvTh* 6 (1962): 309; C. H. Toy, *The Book of Proverbs,* 1899, 171; McKane, *Proverbs: A New Approach,* 1970, 343, 351–52; J.-N. Aletti, "Proverbes 8, 22–31. Etude de Structure," *Bibl* 57 (1976): 26.

thologies to illuminate its numerous textual ambiguities and hapax legomena.[3] The poem's meaning, however, may well lie within the poem itself, which is historically bound to Hebrew rhetorical conventions.[4] The rhetorical traits of this Wisdom hymn have been rather neglected. For example, Toy,[5] Oesterley,[6] and more recently, Loretz[7] disregard the structurally significant chiasmus in verses 30b–31, maintaining that the repetition is most likely a gloss by a later scribe. In Skehan's latest examination of the whole structure of Proverbs 8, the chiasmus in verses 30b–31 is also overlooked.[8]

The only attempt to consider in detail the structure of Proverbs 8:22–31 is a recently published article by Jean-Noël Aletti.[9] Contrary to those scholars who find a tripartite structure for the poem (vv. 22–26; 27–29; 30–31), Aletti sees only a bipartite division: verses 22–26 and verses 27–31. He delimits this second strophe in verses 27–31 by pointing out that, from a stylistic point of view, verse 27, "when he established the heavens I was there," is only made explicit in verse 30: "Present, but where? The text answers only in verse 30— next to God."[10] Furthermore, from a grammatical standpoint, the *waw* in וָאֶהְיֶה beginning verse 30 continues the second strophe rather than begins a third strophe.

The second strophe, which deals with Wisdom and her relationship to God and humankind is juxtaposed to the first strophe found in verses 22–26 where God is the active subject. There are three main actors in the hymn: YHWH, Wisdom, and humankind. Noting that the first word of the poem is YHWH, the last is humankind, while the middle is devoted to Wisdom, Aletti then proceeds with his predominant thesis, namely, the syntagmatic and semantic relationships among the characters.

Aletti's method is basically a structural analysis of the poem according to the norms of modern linguistic theory.[11] He arranges the text syntagmatically,

---

3. Cf. C. Kayatz, *Studien zu Proverbien 1–9*, 1966; O. Keel, *Die Weisheit spielt vor Gott: Ein ikonographischer Beitrag zur Deutung des mᵉsaḥäqät in Spr 8, 30f.*, 1974; B. Gemser, *Sprüche Salomos*, 1937, 38–39; M. Dahood, "Proverbs 8, 22–31: Translation and Commentary," *CBQ* 30 (1968): 512–21; G. von Rad, *Wisdom in Israel*, 1972, 151–55; McKane, op. cit., 352–58.

4. Cf. J. Muilenburg, "Form Criticism and Beyond," *JBL* 88 (1969): 1–18; idem, "A Study of Hebrew Rhetoric: Repetition and Style," *VTSup* 1 (1953): 97–111; D. Greenwood, "Rhetorical Criticism and Formgeschichte: Some Methodological Considerations," *JBL* 89 (1970): 418–26; W. Bühlmann and K. Scherer, *Stilfiguren der Bibel*, 1973. For applications of this method, see P. Trible, "Wisdom Builds a Poem: The Architecture of Proverbs 1:20–33," *JBL* 94 (1975): 509–18, and the articles in J. J. Jackson and M. Kessler, eds., *Rhetorical Criticism: Essays in Honor of James Muilenburg*, 1974.

5. Toy, op. cit., 179.

6. W. O. E. Oesterley, *The Book of Proverbs*, 1929, 65.

7. O. Loretz, "Text und Neudeutung in Spr 8, 22–31," *UF* 7 (1975): 578–79.

8. P. Skehan, "Structures in Poems on Wisdom: Proverbs 8 and Sirach 24," *CBQ* 41 (1979): 367. According to his schema v. 30ab becomes a bicolon line and vv. 30c–31a tricolon line.

9. Aletti, op. cit., 25–37.

10. Ibid. 26.

11. He cites especially S. R. Levin, *Linguistic Structures in Poetry*, 1964.

that is, according to the position of various elements in the poem and their consequent relationship with one another. Through this syntagmatic arrangement, Aletti then derives Wisdom's semantic relationship with God and humanity: her passivity, presence, or activity with respect to the other characters. He discovers that there is a dynamic progression in the hymn whereby Wisdom moves from passivity (verses 22–26) to presence (v. 27), to a qualification and situation of this presence (v. 30ab), and finally to activity itself (v. 30c–31). The activity of Wisdom begins *only* with the participle מְשַׂחֶקֶת, "playing," since שַׁעֲשֻׁעָיו, "his delight," functions syntagmatically to qualify and situate Wisdom as next to God and as his continual delight.

The object of Wisdom's activity, מְשַׂחֶקֶת, is humanity. The whole movement of the poem—from Wisdom's begetting by God to her presence at God's side when he organized the world[12]—throws into relief the mediative role of Wisdom between humankind and God, even though the character of this mediation is not specified.[13]

The value of Aletti's analysis is its capacity to pinpoint the characters of the poem and to determine the structural relationships among them. That Aletti is able to demonstrate the authoritative and mediative role of Wisdom as the overriding motif of the hymn through his method is admirable. Moreover, his acute observation that שָׁם אָנִי, "I was there," is in intimate semantic connection with וָאֶהְיֶה אֶצְלוֹ אָמוֹן, "I was beside him, a darling child," sheds more light on a difficult passage.

However, Aletti overlooks a known convention of Hebrew poetry. In maintaining that verse 30b, "I was his delight daily," serves merely to qualify and situate Wisdom in God's presence, Aletti should be faulted with other scholars for dismissing the chiasmus of verses 30b–31. Furthermore, by concentrating on syntagmatic and semantic affiliations among the characters, Aletti's structural analysis does not do full justice to the intricate parallelisms, the important repetitions of particles, and verb forms in the passage. There is little textual or philological examinations of the disputed words to aid in his study of structure. Finally, Aletti himself admits that his two part structure does not fully account for the fact the poem deals with three characters: God, Wisdom, and humankind.[14] The mediative function of Wisdom, which Aletti sees as Wisdom's progression from passivity, to presence, and ultimately to activity, is not adequately conveyed through such a bipartite division.

Anticipating our final results, we find in Proverbs 8:22–31 a threepart structure which highlights Wisdom's preexistence, her role during God's cre-

---

12. According to Aletti, the structure reveals not a cosmology but an organization of the world. This organization delimits Wisdom's activity to the habitable world and thus humanity itself.
13. Aletti, op. cit., 28–37.
14. Ibid., 27–28.

ative activity to insure the safety of the world for humankind, and her inter-action with that humanity. Beginning our analysis, we offer then in Table A an outline of the poem's structure according to Hebrew rhetorical conventions. Textual and lexical problems will be treated in the notes.

Table A

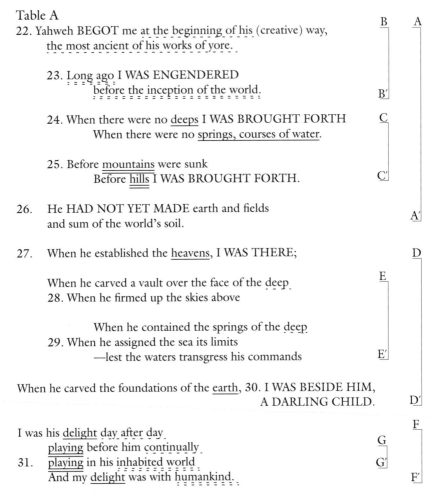

22. Yahweh BEGOT me at the beginning of his (creative) way,
    the most ancient of his works of yore.   B   A

23. Long ago I WAS ENGENDERED
    before the inception of the world.   B′

24. When there were no deeps I WAS BROUGHT FORTH   C
    When there were no springs, courses of water.

25. Before mountains were sunk
    Before hills I WAS BROUGHT FORTH.   C′

26. He HAD NOT YET MADE earth and fields
    and sum of the world's soil.   A′

27. When he established the heavens, I WAS THERE;   D

    When he carved a vault over the face of the deep   E
28. When he firmed up the skies above

    When he contained the springs of the deep
29. When he assigned the sea its limits
    —lest the waters transgress his commands   E′

When he carved the foundations of the earth, 30. I WAS BESIDE HIM,
                   A DARLING CHILD.   D′

                                     F
I was his delight day after day
    playing before him continually   G
31. playing in his inhabited world   G′
    And my delight was with humankind.   F′

As one can see from this table, the poem is divided into three strophes, delineated by stichs A/A′, D/D′, and F/F′ at the far right. The stichs of each strophe are indicated in the column left of the strophe column. The basic poetic technique in the hymn is *parallelismus membrorum*. Not only does our author use simple parallelism of two cola within a particular stich but also distant antithetical parallel pairs which form *inclusiones,* so to speak, framing two of the three strophes. The final third strophe climaxes the poem through a chiasmus punctuated by alliteration. We shall now discuss each strophe, giving reasons for our division and demonstrating the rhetorical characteristics in each which contribute in building the poem.

Strophe A/A′

Verse 22 begins with a subject, YHWH, a finite verb, קָנָה in the perfect, a direct object, "me"—Wisdom, and an adverb of time. The only other occurrence of a finite verb in the perfect with God as its subject is verse 26. The other verbs in verses 23–25 describe God's activity indirectly. The literary relationship between A and A′ is indicated not only by the fact that God is the active subject in both, but by other elements which we give in the following:

	A	A′
Subject	YHWH	He (YHWH)
Verb	begot	made
Object	me (Wisdom)	earth, fields, and sum of the world's soil
Adverb of time	at the beginning	not yet

Note that A and A′ are comprised of antithetical components. Whereas God had not yet made the totality of the created world, indicated by the merismus of verse 26,[15] God begot Wisdom at the beginning. This contrast between Wisdom and the created world thus delineates the first strophe.

Furthermore, each stich of strophe A/A′ and every colon of each stich are connected by means of parallelism. In the first colon of stich B ראשית דרכו "at the beginning of his (creative) way," forms a synonymous parallel with מאז קדם מפעליו, "the most ancient of his works of yore," of the second colon.[16] The whole of B is juxtaposed with B′ in the parallelism of קנני, "(he) begot me," and נסכתי, "I was engendered," as well as in the temporal elements.[17]

15. It seems that the poet is conveying a merismus in v. 26 in his repetition of the synonymous words, ארץ, חוצות, and עפרות תבל all joined by the conjunction *waw*. All four words occur in parallel with each other in several OT passages: ארץ // חוצות in Job 5:10 (cf. Prov. 24:27); ארץ // עפר in Isa. 26:5; 29:4; 47:1; Ps. 44:26; Job 14:8; etc.; ארץ // תבל in Isa. 14:21; 18:3; 26:9, 18 etc.

16. Note especially Isa. 46:10 where ראשית and קדם form a temporal chiastic parallel.

17. We accept the BH emendation for נסכתי from the root סכך, which appears to be a form of נסך. The root סכך occurs in two striking instances. In Ps. 139:13 the psalmist states that he was woven in the womb of his mother. In Job 10:11 Job remarks to God that he was knit together with bones and sinews. The process of gestation in both cases is described metaphorically in terms of a craft. Furthermore, significant for our structural study is the fact that in Ps. 139:13 קנה parallels סכך, which is the same situation here in Prov. 8:22–23. While the usual meaning of the root קנה is "to buy or acquire," the verb is used in Gen. 4:1 and Deut. 32:6 as well as in Ps.

In the cola of stich C/C' "deeps" and "springs" and "mountains" and "hills" are fixed parallel pairs. In the second colon of C the symmetry is preserved by the ballast variant, "courses of water."[18] Moreover, C and C' are interlinked by the repetition of חיל לתי, "I was brought forth," in the first and last cola of the respective stichs.

Strophe D/D'

At first glance the most noteworthy feature of strophe D/D' is the anaphoric series of ב plus the infinitive construct with masculine singular suffix beginning six cola. This constant repetition stylistically forms a unified strophe,[19] and as such many scholars have based their own division of the poem upon this fact. We would proceed even farther in justifying this unity. We have already mentioned Aletti's keen perception of the interrelationship between verse 27 and verse 30a. The adverb שם qualifying אני in verse 27 is made more precise in verse 30a by ואהיה אצלו אמון. Moreover, as we have witnessed similarly in the first strophe, the antithetical fixed pair of שמים in D and ארץ in D' form distant parallel stichs framing the second strophe.

> When he established the heavens, I was there. . . .
> When he carved the foundations of the earth, I was beside him, a darling child.[20]

As in the first strophe, the stichs which are bordered by D and D' are also artistically interrelated. The cola of E are thematically connected: the picture described is God molding the firmament above.[21] Likewise, the cola of E' pro-

---

139:13 where the parenting aspect is unmistakable. The third parallel verb in Prov. 8:24, חוללתי, "I was brought forth (in labor)," also supports the birth imagery found in קנה and סכך.

18. נכבד is a hapax legomenon. The niphal masculine participle would mean "heavy-laden," or with a more nuanced interpretation, "abounding" as in the RSV. This nuance is not found in the LXX. Thus the BH would emend the text to read נבכי, supporting this reading on the basis of Job 38:16, נבכי ים, "springs of the sea," which parallels "recesses of the deep (תהום)." Again in conjunction with תהים, nbk, a derivative of mbk is found in UT 51, IV 21: "At the mbk of the two rivers/At the midst of the streams of the two deeps." We accept the BH emendation. The parallelism of a verse need not always be complete, since a "broken" parallelism can be explained by a phenomenon known as a ballast variant. Here the symmetry of a verse is preserved by the use of extended synonyms or ballast variant. In our case, the lack of a corresponding element for חוללתי would be compensated by the synonym of "springs," namely "courses of water." Both "springs" and "courses of water" would parallel תהמות in v. 24.

19. Muilenburg, *Hebrew Rhetoric*, 99.

20. Job 38 can provide a backdrop for our text. In answer to the questions demanded by God of the mortal Job—"Where were you when I laid the foundation of the earth?"—Wisdom can claim "I was beside him a darling child."

21. There are two possible interpretations of חוג in v. 27: the horizon, the line between the dome of heaven and the disc of earth, or the dome affixed over the surface of the horizon. We opt for the latter interpretation. In Isa. 40:22 and Job 22:14 the חוג is situated above the earth. It is conceived in solid terms since God is able to walk upon it. (Cf. also Job 26:10.) The evidence suggests that the creative God is being cast in the role of architect, carving the vault that separates the waters above it from the earth below it.

duce a thematic unit: God contains the springs of the deep and assigns the sea its limits.[22] Just as in the repetition of חוללתי in C/C′, the rapport between stichs E/E′ can be detected in the repetition of תהום, "deep."

The clause ומים לא יעברו־פיו, "lest the waters transgress his commands," seemingly interrupts the rhetorical succession of ב plus infinitive. However, this clause gives additional evidence of the poet's literary skill. The reason for the poet's selection of certain facets of God's creativity over and above all others is intimated here. It is significant that this clause precedes the peripheral stich D′ which closes the strophe. There is a definable progression of thought from the beginning of the strophe to the end. Stich E corresponds to D in the creation of the upper cosmos; E′ relates to D′ in its concern with that below the earth. The purpose of the vault over the earth (E) according to Genesis 1:7 is to separate the waters which are under the firmament from the waters which are above it. Moreover, a number of OT passages refer to God placing limits upon the sea (E′), articulating the same concern of our poet: that the waters would not violate God's commands.[23] The preoccupation with the waters of the deep reflects the beliefs found in ancient Semitic myths that the primeval oceans continually menace the created world from above and from below.[24] The whole thrust of this strophe is to demonstrate the labors of God in insuring the safety of the created world against the hostile primeval oceans, the sovereignty of God in keeping these waters at bay, and above all else, that during these achievements, Wisdom was at his side, a darling child.

Strophe F/F′

The progression of the poem is climaxed in strophe F/F′. A chiasmus is formed in the interplay between the synonymous words משחקת and שעשעים, which is accented by the alliteration of the two words. Stichs F and G form parallel cola in the temporal expressions יום יום, "day after day," and בכל־עת, "continually." Likewise, in G′ and F′ בתבל ארצו, "inhabited world,"[25] parallel את־בני אדם "humankind." Furthermore, stichs F/F′ contrast each other: in F Wisdom is YHWH's delight, in F′ her delight is with humankind. Thus the chiasmus structurally highlights Wisdom's mediative role.

By means of chiastic structure and parallelism our poet is able to draw themes anticipated by the first two strophes into an interrelated whole. Stich

22. We agree with McKane, op. cit., 355, who translates v. 28b, "when he *contained* the springs of the deep." He detects in vv. 28–29 an allusion to the waters of the deep which continually threaten to engulf the world.

23. Jer. 5:22; Ps. 104:6–9; 148:6; Job 38:10.

24. Cf. L. F. Stadelmann, *The Hebrew Conception of the World*, 1970, 17–27.

25. Several passages, such as Ps. 9:9; 38:8; 89:12; 90:2; 1 Sam. 2:8; Isa. 14:17, 21; 18:3; 26:9, 18, reveal that חבל can be a technical term for the inhabitable part of the world. Aside from our passage חבל is used only in conjunction with ארץ in Job 37:12 which the RSV has translated, "the inhabitable world."

F picks up the motif which terminates the second strophe: as a darling child at God's side, Wisdom is his daily delight. Wisdom's privileged position began when she was engendered by God before he made the world (strophe A/A'). Moreover, Wisdom is not only God's delight who plays before him continually. Wisdom plays also in the created world, a world guaranteed of its security by God's efforts and supremacy (strophe D/D'). The final effect of the poem is produced by the chiasmus of strophe F/F' where Wisdom is not only God's delight; her delight was also with humankind. Wisdom, begotten by God before creation and at his side when he achieved the safety of the created world, now intermingles with humanity. Aletti is certainly correct in asserting that, except through the mediation of Wisdom in the world, the passage is silent on the relationship between God and humanity. The creation of humankind is not described. However, whereas Aletti's bipartite framework does not demonstrate this mediation convincingly, the tripartite division, emphasizing Wisdom's preexistence in A/A' and her honorable position next to God when he accomplished the security of the world in D/D', underscores humankind's indispensable relationship to her in F/F'.

Conclusion

Without dismissing traditional historical analysis, we have tried to show how a rhetorical analysis of Proverbs 8:22–31 conveys the meaning of the poem. For the most part, textual difficulties are resolved structurally according to the conventions of Hebrew style. This climactic poem of Proverbs 8 is a highly intricate poetic piece. It is divided into three strophes: two framed by means of distant antithetical parallelism, while the third is fashioned in a chiasmus. Each stich within the strophes is interlinked by synonymous and antithetical parallelism and repetitions. The whole poem builds structurally to portray Wisdom as the ultimate mediator between God and humanity.[26]

Our article analyses the Wisdom hymn in Proverbs 8:22–31 according to Hebrew rhetorical conventions. As a highly artistic poetic piece, the poem is divided into three strophes: two framed by means of distant antithetical parallelism, while the third is fashioned in a chiasmus. Each stich within the strophes is interlinked by synonymous and antithetical parallelism and repetitions. The whole poem builds structurally to portray Wisdom as the ultimate mediator between God and humanity.

26. While a detailed study of the relationship between Prov. 8:22–31 and the rest of Prov. 8 is beyond the scope of this study, we agree with Von Rad, op. cit., 151, that our poem, although "comparatively self contained," plays a subsidiary role in the chapter. Wisdom who addresses herself to humanity (8:1–9) makes seemingly fantastic claims for that humanity (cf. 8:15–16). It is in such a context that the hymn is placed. Through it Wisdom justifies her claims and the veracity of her words by her antiquity, by her station next to God when he ordered the world for humankind, and by her indispensable mediation between God and that humanity.

18

WISDOM LISTS HER CREDENTIALS: PROVERBS 8:22–31

Kathleen A. Farmer

T he second part of Wisdom's monologue answers an unspoken
question: "Why should we believe wisdom's claims?" What
makes Wisdom's promises more reliable than those made by the seductive
personage described in the previous Instruction? Like the classical prophets
who tell their skeptical listeners how they were called to the prophetic task,
Wisdom tells her audience about her origins. In effect she says, "I trace my
beginnings and my authority back to the LORD."

How Are Wisdom and the Lord Related?

The poetic device of personification creates some problems for the interpreter of this material. The poet has Wisdom speak as if she were a self-con-
scious entity. As a rhetorical device such personification has the effect of en-

From Kathleen A. Farmer, *Who Knows What Is Good? A Commentary on the Books of Proverbs and Ecclesiastes,* ITC Series (Grand Rapids: Eerdmans, 1991). Reprinted by permission.

gaging the reader's emotions to a much higher degree than the mere discussion of an abstract concept could ever do. But the figure of speech leaves us unclear as to what it is that Wisdom represents in this passage. Should Wisdom be understood here as a *characteristic* of the LORD's creative activity or as a *companion* with a distinct identity? Is Wisdom represented as an originally independent divine being, or is she merely a figure of speech, standing for the collective traditions of the wise? Does Wisdom claim to have been created, begotten, or acquired by the Lord? Is her counsel helpful to humankind because she was *instrumental* in the creative process, or is she merely claiming to have been *present* at the world's inception? Arguments for one position or the other revolve around the correct way to understand several obscure and ambiguous phrases in verses 22 and 30.

Ambiguities in 8:22

The word *qanani*, which the RSV translates "created me" in verse 22, could equally well mean "possessed me" (as an attribute or faculty) or "acquired me" (as one acquires a commodity). A number of biblical parallels can be found to support either translation. The biblical evidence for translating *qanani* as "begot me" is dubious (it would make sense only in Gen. 4:1). But there is a similar word in Ugaritic which means "procreate," and the use of birth-related language in Proverbs 8:24–25 makes "begot me" a logically tempting alternative.

The phrase *re'shit darko*, which the RSV translates as "the beginning of his work," is a second stumbling block for the interpreter of verse 22. In Hebrew *re'shit* can mean either "first" (in time) or "first" (in importance). And while *darko* might be construed as "his work," it more commonly means "his way" or "his manner" of acting. The NAB, which renders *qanani* as "begot," translates *re'shit* with "firstborn."

The translations "created," "begotten," and "acquired" give readers the impression that Wisdom is presented here as an independent entity, apart from God. "Created" is favored by many, though the warrants for understanding the term in this way are relatively few. "Created" can imply that wisdom was simply the first of the LORD's creatures (e.g., R. N. Whybray, *Wisdom in Proverbs*, 100–101), whereas "acquired" implies that wisdom "pre-existed" and originated outside the created order (as Bruce Vawter argues in "Prov. 8:22: Wisdom and Creation," 205–16).

However, understanding *qanani* in the sense of "possessed me" leaves open the possibility that Wisdom should be understood here as a personification of an attribute of God. Wisdom existed within God, prior to creation. Wisdom was a quality which the Lord demonstrated in the creation of the universe rather than an entity in its own right. As R. B. Y. Scott argues (*Proverbs–Ecclesiastes*, 71) "possess" is clearly the meaning intended in the twelve other passages in Proverbs where the word is used" (e.g., Prov. 4:5–7). Reading *qanani* as "possessed me" would also bring the picture of Wisdom in 8:22ff. into line with the statement in 3:19: "The LORD by wisdom founded the earth; by understanding he established the heavens."

Begotten or Made?

Proverbs 8:22–31 played an important part in early Christian debates about the nature of Christ. In the fourth century C.E. this passage was used both to support and to refute the Arians' claims. Assuming first that Christ could be equated with "the wisdom of God" (1 Cor. 1:24), the Arians argued that the Son, like Wisdom, was created. And to be a creature, whether the first or the most prominent of creatures, is to be subordinate to the Creator. But those who formulated the Nicean declaration that the Son was "begotten, not made" were inclined to translate *qanani* in Proverbs 8:22 as "begot me" in order to argue that God and Christ were "consubstantial" (of the same essence and status).

Ambiguities in 8:30

Whether or not Wisdom seems to act as a co-equal, as a subordinate agent, or merely as an observer in the process of creation also depends on how one understands an obscure Hebrew word which the RSV translates "master workman" in verse 30. The meaning of *amon*, as it is presently vocalized in the MT, has been a subject of debate since ancient times. The word does not occur elsewhere in the Hebrew Scriptures in this form. Traditionally, interpreters have gone in one of two different directions for their translations, either (1) towards the image of "architect" or "artist" or (2) towards the idea of "infant" or "darling child." Either understanding involves a change in the vowels presently found in the MT, to *omman*, "artisan" (as in Cant. 7:2), or to *amun*, "nursling" (by analogy from the plural in Lam. 4:5).

The "artisan" advocates draw support from the deuterocanonical book known as the Wisdom of Solomon, which calls wisdom a "fashioner" or "craftsman" (Wis. 7:22; 8:6; 14:2 RSV). However, the proponents of the meaning "child" can point to the birth metaphors in Proverbs 8:24–25 and to the reference to "delight" in the second part of verse 30 for corroboration. Those who prefer the reading "begot me" in verse 22 will of course argue for "child" in verse 30.

R. B. Y. Scott suggests that the original speaker intended the phrase to be read as *omen*, which would be an active participle, meaning one who unites or binds together. Thus, Scott translates verse 30a, "Then I was beside him binding [all] together" (*Proverbs–Ecclesiastes,* 68, 72). Scott's suggestion makes the word in question describe Wisdom's function in creation rather than her nature. However, if the participle refers to Wisdom's actions, one would expect it to have feminine form, which cannot be supported by the text. Other suggestions for understanding the term include "confidant" and "counselor," based on similar sounding words in languages closely related to Hebrew (see William McKane, *Proverbs,* 357–58). Of course, the underlying question with which the interpreters are concerned is whether Wisdom is here presented as an active agent participating in creation or whether she is pictured as merely an observer of the Lord's work. Roland E. Murphy sums up the interpreter's dilemma in a nutshell: "Lady Wisdom has received great press by reason of her association with creation, but her precise role remains unclear" ("Wisdom and Creation," 5).

Whether or not Wisdom claims to have been instrumental in the creative process, she clearly does say that she was *present* as the work was done. Thus, in spite of the ambiguities, her speech still functions to legitimate her teachings. In effect she says to those who question her credentials," "You can trust what I say about the structures and the intricacies of life, because I was there to see how it was all put together in the first place."

19

"CATCHWORDS" IN PROVERBS 10:1–22:13

Roland E. Murphy

Chapter 10

V. 1. To the first saying is prefixed a title by the editor that serves for 10:1–22:16. It is not insignificant that the first saying of the collection deals with a "wise son," in view of the frequent repetition of "my son" in chaps. 1–9.

Vv. 2–3. These sayings are bound together by common features: (1) righteous/wicked contrast; (2) chiasmus; (3) both begin with the negative particle (*lōʾ*) and verb.

Vv. 4–5. Both sayings have to do with diligence; v. 4 is characterized by chiasmus, v. 5 by alliteration and nominal juxtaposition.

Vv. 6–7. Both are contrasts between righteous and wicked; "blessing" serves as a catchword.

V. 9. Striking alliteration in v. 9a (*hôlēk battōm yēlek beṭaḥ*).

Vv. 11–12. The verb *ksh* ("conceal, cover") is the catchword for these chiastic sayings.

From Roland E. Murphy, *Wisdom Literature: Job, Proverbs, Ruth, Canticles, Ecclesiastes, and Esther* (Grand Rapids: Eerdmans, 1981). Reprinted by permission.

Vv. 13–15. "Wisdom" and "wise men" bind vv. 13–14 together, and "ruin" ties v. 14 with v. 15, a striking example of juxtaposition of nouns.

Vv. 16–17. "Life" is the catchword which binds these sayings together.

Vv. 18–21. These sayings deal with "lips" (v. 20, "tongue"); the catchwords for vv. 20–21 are *ṣaddîq* ("righteous") and *lēb* ("mind, sense").

Vv. 24–25. The catchwords are "wicked/righteous."

Vv. 27–32. These are bound together by the catchwords, "wicked/righteous" (but v. 29: "upright/evildoers"); in vv. 31–32, two specific catchwords appear: "mouth" and "perverse."

Chapter 11

V. 1. The saying is formed by a simple juxtaposition of subjects and predicates. *Rāṣôn* ("delight," "acceptable") is the catchword for 10:32 and 11:1.

V. 2. There is striking alliteration in v. 2a: *bāʾ zādôn wayyābôʾ qālôn*.

Vv. 3–11. The themes of integrity and righteousness are treated in these verses, as the upright are contrasted with the wicked. Most of the verses begin with either *bĕ* (vv. 7, 9–11) or a form of *ṣdq* (vv. 5–6, 8).

V 4. On v. 4b see 10:2b and also 11:6a. "Righteousness" is the catchword in vv. 4–6, and also "deliver."

Vv. 5–6. The root *yšr* ("straight," "upright")is the catchword for vv. 5–6; cf. v. 3.

Vv. 8–11. Tying two or more of these verses are several catchwords: "righteous, wicked, city, deliver"; vv. 9–12 all begin with the letter *beth*.

V. 15. The onomatopoeia in v. 15a is noteworthy: *resh* (four times) and *ʿayin* (three times); v. 15b is formed by juxtaposition of participles.

Vv. 18–19. The catchword is "justice," and the theme of the good and the evil is continued in vv. 20–21.

Vv. 23–24. These two sayings, which concern quite different things, find a catchword in "only" (*ʾak*).

Vv. 25–26. The verses are tied together by *bĕrākâ* ("blessing," "liberal").

Vv. 29–30. As the MT stands, "wise" is the catchword. However, in v. 30 most modern translations read "lawlessness" (RSV), or something similar, with the LXX. "Righteous" is the catchword for vv. 30–31.

Chapter 12

Vv. 1–3. The catchword is *rš* ("condemn," "wickedness").

Vv. 5–7. The catchwords are "righteous" and "wicked."

Vv. 9–11. These verses deal with the laboring class. "Bread" is a catchword for vv. 9 and 11.

Vv. 12–13. "Righteous" is the catchword; cf. v. 10 also.

Vv. 13–23. The general theme of speech ("lips, "mouth," "truth," etc.) is treated in these verses.

Vv. 15–16. The catchword is "fool."

Vv. 18–19. The catchword is "tongue."

Vv. 20–21. There is the usual contrast between the righteous and the wicked; the catchword is *rāᶜ* ("evil," "trouble").

V. 22. One of several "abomination" sayings (there is a very close parallel to this verse in Amenemope, X, 13:15–16; ANET, 423).

Vv. 26, 28. The catchwords are *derek* ("way") and the root *sdq* ("righteous," "righteousness").

Chapter 13

Vv. 2–4. These lines are tied together by the catchword *nepeš* ("desire," "life," "soul"), which occurs four times. There is a pithy juxtaposition in v. 3: "he who guards his mouth, he who preserves his life" (alliteration: *nōṣēr pîw šōmēr napšô*); "he who opens wide his lips—ruin to him."

Vv. 5–6. The roots *sdq* ("righteous") and *rš* ("wicked") are the catchwords.

Vv. 7–8. The catchwords are the roots *rwš* ("poor") and *ᶜšr* ("rich"). The *yēš*-saying in v. 7 is a paradox, with no moral implication.

V. 12. The saying is formed by the juxtaposition of four terms. "Desire fulfilled" is taken up again in v. 19.

Vv. 13–14. A common motif unites these verses: adherence to the word/instruction is beneficial.

Vv. 15–19. Boström has pointed out modest paronomasia in these verses, e.g., v. 15 begins with *śēkel* ("sense") and v. 16 with *kol* ("everything"); v. 18 speaks of *mûsār* and v. 19 has the phrase *sûr mērāᶜ*.

V. 20. There is a play on the roots *rᶜ* (the catchword in vv. 19–21: "evil," "harm," "misfortune") and *rᶜh* ("companion").

Vv. 21–22. The catchwords are *ṭôb* ("prosperity," "good man"), and *ṣaddîq* ("righteous").

Vv. 23–25. These sayings seem quite disparate, but *ᵓōkel* ("food") may be a catchword reflecting back to v. 23.

Chapter 14

Vv. 1–3. These verses are united by the motifs of wisdom and fear of the Lord (emended text in v. 1, reading "wisdom" with most modern translations, except the NEB). The style in v. 2 is juxtaposition of four participles.

V. 5. The repetition in v. 5b and 6:9a illustrates how certain lines were reused in the formation of new sayings; see also 12:17; 14:25; 19:5.

Vv. 6–8. The root *yd^c* ("knowledge") is the catchword for vv. 6–7, and *kĕsîl* ("fool") for vv. 7–8.

Vv. 11–14. The catchwords are *yšr* ("[up]right") for vv. 11–12, *ʾaḥărît* ("end") for vv. 12–13, and *lēb* ("heart," "perverse" [*sûg lēb*]) for vv. 13–14.

Vv. 15–18. These verses lay down characterizations of the simple and the prudent (vv. 15, 18) the wise and the foolish (vv. 16–17).

Vv. 19–22. Both vv. 19 and 22 have the root *r^{cc}* ("evil"), which is similar to the root *r^ch* ("neighbor") occurring in vv. 20–21, which deal with the poor (*rāš/^căniyîm* [*Kĕtîb; Qĕrê*, *^cănāwîm*]).

Vv. 26–27. "Fear of the Lord" is the catchword for these verses. Synonymous parallelism appears in v. 26, and from this point on to 15:33 it becomes relatively frequent (Skehan, 18).

Vv. 28–29. The root *rbb* ("great," "multitude") is the catchword for these verses. Juxtaposition characterizes vv. 29–30, both of which deal with similar attitudes ("slow to anger," "tranquil mind").

Chapter 15

Vv. 1–4. With the exception of v. 3, these sayings all deal with speech, but the root *ṭôb/yṭb* ("good") is the catchword for vv. 2–3.

Vv. 5–9. Sayings about wise/fools and just/unjust alternate in vv. 5–8, while "abomination" and "wicked" are catchwords uniting vv. 8–9.

Vv. 13–15. *Lēb* ("heart, "mind") is the catchword. In the consonantal text of vv. 13–14, the words *pānîm* and *pĕnê* serve as catchwords, although the *Qĕrê* reading is to be preferred in v. 14b ("mouths"). *Ṭôb* ("cheerful") in v. 15 is a catchword for the "better" (*ṭôb*) sayings that follow in vv. 16–17.

Vv. 16–17. These are "better" sayings, which find a striking parallel in Amenemope VI, 9:5–8; ANET, 422.

Vv. 20–21. The root *śmḥ* ("glad," "joy") is the catchword binding these verses; cf. also v. 23 ("joy").

V. 22. The thought is similar to 11:14, and both have chiastic structure.

Vv. 25–26. These are two "Yahweh" sayings; cf. vv. 29, 33.

Vv. 28–32. A series of catchwords lock these sayings together: "righteous" in vv. 28–29; *šm^c* ("hear, "heed") in vv. 29, 31–32; "admonition" in vv. 31–32; "instruction" in vv. 32–33.

Chapter 16

Vv. 1–7. These are all "Yahweh" sayings, and give evidence of editorial arrangement at this point (see above).

V. 1. Cf. v. 9.

V. 2. See the variant in 21:2; "the ways of a man" appears also in v. 9.

V. 3. This is a rare appearance of a command in the midst of the sayings.

V. 4. Skehan (p. 18) counts this as the middle saying of the 375 proverbs in the Solomonic collection.

V. 5. A variant for v. 5b appears in 11:21.

V. 8. Cf. 15:16.

Vv. 10–11. The catchword is *mišpāṭ* ("judgment," "just").

Vv. 12–13. The root *ṣdq* ("righteousness," "right") is the catchword.

Vv. 13–15. A group of "king" sayings; cf. v. 10.

V. 17. The alliteration and juxtaposition in v. 17b (*šōmēr napšô nōṣēr darkô*) is reminiscent of 13:3.

Vv. 18–19. Catchwords ("spirit," and "pride/proud") and content unite these sayings. The "better" saying in v. 19 introduces *ṭôb* ("prosper" of v. 20), which ties vv. 19 and 20 together.

Vv. 21–24. These sayings deal with a common wisdom theme: speech. There are several catchwords: *mtq* ("pleasant," in vv. 21 and 24); *śkl* ("wisdom," "judicious" in vv. 22–23).

V. 25. This repeats 14:12.

Vv. 27–29. "Man" is the catchword for these verses, which have a common wisdom theme: evil speech. This is perhaps in contrast to vv. 21–24. "Perverse" (v. 28) is repeated in v. 30.

Chapter 17

V. 1. A "better" saying.

V. 3. The first line is repeated in 27:21; the pithiness of the expression is secured by the use of *lě* ("for").

V. 4. The style is juxtaposition; synonymous parallelism increases in chaps. 16ff.

V. 9. In each line two participles are placed in juxtaposition.

V. 11. There is striking alliteration: *ʾak mĕrî/ʾakzārî*.

V. 12. The style is unusual; v. 12a gives an example of danger, only to be surpassed by the example in v. 12b; the total effect is one of comparison.

V. 13. Again the style is unusual; v. 13a is an absolute nominative, or *casus pendens*.

V. 14. In fact, the command in v. 13b is a commentary upon v. 13a.

V. 15. Participles are juxtaposed in v. 15a; an "abomination" saying.

V. 16. The unusual style is best seen in a literal translation of this rhetorical question: Why money in the hand of a fool/to buy wisdom, and (he has) no mind?

Vv. 17–18. The catchword is *rēaʿ* ("brother," "neighbor").

V. 19. In each line two participles are in juxtaposition.

Vv. 21–22. The catchword is *śmḥ* ("joy," "cheerful").

Chapter 18

Vv. 4–8. These verses (if v. 5 refers to judgment) have to do with speech; vv. 6–7 are virtually identical.

Vv. 10–11. The catchwords for these lines are *ʿōz* ("strong") and the root *śgb* ("safe," "high"); v. 11a = 10:15a. The back-to-back positioning of these two sayings is another example of antinomies (cf. 17:27–28); God and wealth are compared with regard to the security they offer.

V. 12. The first line compares with 16:18; v. 12b is exactly the same as 15:33.

V. 13. Another example of nominative absolute, or *casus pendens* (cf. 17:13).

Vv. 18–19. *Midyān* ("disputes," "quarreling") is the catchword for these lines; the text of v. 19 is uncertain. For content, v. 18 is related to v. 17; both deal with disputes.

Vv. 20–21. Both these verses are concerned with speech, and the catchword is *pĕrî* ("fruit").

V. 23. Chiasmus is used effectively here.

Chapter 19

Vv. 1–2. The catchword is *ṭôb* ("better," "good"); the "better" saying in v. 1 resembles 28:6, in the light of which many emend the text.

V. 5. Cf. v. 9, and 6:19; 14:5, 25.

Vv. 6–7. "All" and "friend" serve as catchwords in sayings that continue the theme of v. 4. The third line in v. 7 cannot be translated meaningfully, and is probably corrupt; but v. 7ab makes good sense as an a fortiori saying.

Vv. 11–12. Both sayings deal with anger.

Vv. 13–14. "Father" and "wife" are the catchwords for these verses, which deal with the family; cf. 10:1; 27:15.

Vv. 15–16. The catchword is *nepeš* ("person," "life").

V. 18. This saying is unusual in form here: an imperative followed by a prohibition. The verb *nāśāʾ* ("pay," "set") serves as a catchword for vv. 18–19.

Vv. 20–21. Again, there is unusual form in that v. 20 contains two imperatives; *ʿēṣâ* ("advice," "purpose") is the catchword.

V. 24. The saying is really a description of the conduct of a lazy man, who is pointed out as a bad and hopeless example.

V. 25. Although the saying is in the imperative form, the emphasis is not on following the advice ("strike," "reprove"), but on the way in which one learns prudence and knowledge.

Vv. 26–27. "Son" is the catchword.

V. 27. As with v. 25, the imperative is practically equivalent to an if-clause.

Vv. 28–29. The roots *lys* ("mocks," "scoffers") and *špt* ("justice," "condemnation") are the catchwords for these lines, although some emend "condemnation" to "rods" (*šĕbāṭîm*).

Chapter 20

V. 1. The catchword of 19:28–29 appears again ("mocker").

Vv. 5–6. The catchword is *ʾîš* ("man"), repeated four times.

Vv. 7–9. Each verse begins with the letter *mem* (cf. 11:9–12).

V. 10. Cf. v. 23, and also 11:1; another "abomination" saying, and the style is juxtaposition.

V. 11. Note the onomatopoeia in v. 11a (*yitnakker/nāʿar*); *gam* ("also") is the catchword for vv. 10–12, and *gam šĕnêhem* ("them both," "both alike") ends vv. 10, 12.

Vv. 12–13. The catchword is "eye," and the form in v. 13 is made up of prohibition and command.

V. 14. The saying is rather a description of human activity that contains its own lesson; cf. 19:24.

V. 16. Repeated in 27:13; this is an instruction about giving surety, a common topos in Proverbs. There is a play on words between *ʿrb* ("surety") and *ʿrb* ("sweet") in v. 17.

Vv. 18–19. The form is instructional: a command in v. 18b, a prohibition in v. 19b. Compare v. 19a with 11:13.

V. 22. The form is instructional: a prohibition, followed by a command. *Yhwh* is the catchword for vv. 22–24.

V. 24. This verse, and also vv. 25–26, begin with the letter *mem* (cf. vv. 7–9). "Man" (*ʾādām*) is the catchword for vv. 24–25.

V. 29. Each line presents terms in juxtaposition.

V. 30. "Innermost parts" may be a catchword with v. 27; note also the "king" sayings in vv. 26, 28.

Chapter 21

Vv. 1–3. These are "Yahweh" sayings; the catchwords in vv. 1–2 are "every" and "heart."

Vv. 5–6. Both sayings deal with acquisition of possessions.

Vv. 7–8. Both sayings are characterizations of the unjust; note the onomatopoeia in *hăpakpak derek ʾîš wāzār wĕzak* in v. 8.

V. 9. A repetition of 25:4.

Vv. 11–12. These verses are united by the catchword *śkl* ("instructed," "observes").

V. 17. The repetition of a word within the saying is characteristic also of vv. 21, 23.

V. 23. There is a play on the word "keep" (*šmr*).

Vv. 25–26. The root *ʾwh* ("desire," "covet") is the catchword for these verses.

Vv. 28–29. "Man" is the catchword.

Vv. 30–31. These verses are related in meaning, as well as by the catchword "Yahweh."

Chapter 22

Vv. 1–2. "Rich" is the catchword for these verses, the first a "better" saying, and the second a "Yahweh" saying in which the juxtaposition of the half-lines is striking.

V. 3. This is repeated in 27:12; the onomatopoeia is striking: *ʿārûm rāʾâ rāʾâ wĕyistār*. The letter *ʿayin* begins vv. 2–4.

Vv. 5–6. "Way" is the catchword.

V. 7. The saying is an observation without moral evaluation; note the onomatopoeia in v. 7b: *lōweh lĕʾîš malweh*.

V. 10. As in v. 6, the imperative is equivalent to a conditional clause.

V. 13. Compare 26:13, and also 19:24; the saying is a description of the conduct of the lazy person.

20

ON ORDER AND DISORDER IN PROVERBS 10:1–24:23

Duane A. Garrett

Perhaps the most arresting feature of Proverbs 10:1–24:23 is what seems a complete lack of structure of arrangement in the collection of proverbs. They appear to have been assembled altogether at random. This feature seems odd in light of the Hebrew passion for parallel, chiasmus, merismus, and other such modes of structuring the written word. Thus Whybray has commented that to claim the proverbs have no context but occur in random order "amounts to no more than an admission that modern scholars have so far not been able satisfactorily to discover what such a 'context,' whether literary or theological, might be."[1] In unraveling this problem, several factors must be taken into account.

_____

    1. Whybray, *Wealth and Poverty,* 65.

First, each proverb is an independent unit that can stand alone and still have meaning. Textual context is not essential for interpretation.[2] Also the very disorder of a collection of proverbs can serve a didactic purpose; it demonstrates that while reality and truth are not irrational, neither are they fully subject to human attempts at systemization.[3] The proverbs are presented in the seemingly haphazard way we encounter the issues with which they deal.[4]

Context, however, sometimes qualifies or gives a more precise meaning to a given proverb. Perhaps the best known example of this is Proverbs 26:4–5, where the reader is advised both against and in favor of answering a fool according to his folly. The two proverbs qualify each other, and the whole indicates that there are times when responding to a fool is appropriate and other times when it is not.

On close examination, in fact, many proverbs are found to have been grouped into small collections that provide context for the individual maxims. Proverbs 10–24, therefore, are characterized by both order and disorder. Each proverb has its own meaning, but it may also have a more specific meaning in the context of a small collection of proverbs. Individual proverbs, collections of proverbs, and the random repetition of proverbial themes all serve to reinforce the lessons of the book. Identifying the small collections of proverbs is essential for the use of Proverbs in the church. By observing the context of individual proverbs in small collections and noting how the message of each collection coheres, the preacher or Bible teacher can actually take a congregation through a series of chapters of Proverbs without resorting to rearranging verses topically.[5]

Other examples of proverbs being grouped into related collections may be found in the ancient Near East. Collections one and two of the Sumerian proverbs link sayings into groups either by the initial sign of the saying or by a common topic.[6] The sayings of the Babylonian "Counsels of Wisdom" are also grouped by subject matter.[7]

Many Egyptian texts also have some kind of order. In Ptahhotep (Old Kingdom) the main body of teaching is divided into thirty-seven strophes, each of which begins with a condition (frequently but not always introduced

---

2. Studies include H.-J. Hermission, *Studien zur israelitischen Spruchsweisheit*, WMANT 28 (Neukirchen-Vluyn, 1968), 171–83, and O. Ploger, "Zur Auslegung der Sentenzensammlungen des Proverbienbuches," in *Probleme biblischer Theologie* (Munich, 1971), 402–16.

3. For a good study of the meaning of aphoristic thinking, see J. G. Williams, *Those Who Ponder Proverbs* (Sheffield: Almond, 1981).

4. R. L. Alden, *Proverbs: A Commentary on an Ancient Book of Timeless Advice* (Grand Rapids: Baker, 1983), 10.

5. See D. A. Garrett, "Preaching Wisdom," in *Reclaiming the Prophetic Mantle: Preaching the Old Testament Faithfully*, ed. G. Klein (Nashville: Broadman, 1992).

6. Gordon, *Sumerian Proverbs*, 26, 154–55.

7. Lambert, *Babylonian Wisdom*, 96.

by "if") and then gives instructions appropriate to that condition.[8] The strophes of Aniy are distinguished by an opening imperative followed by explanation and exposition.[9] In Ankhsheshonqy sayings are linked in a chainlike structure by verbal association.[10]

Several types of collections (with many variations and combinations of types) may be observed in the biblical Proverbs:

1. *Parallel collection:* proverbs grouped in an *A-B-A-B* pattern. The elements of the pattern may be individual cola (two-proverb collection; 11:16–17) or whole proverbs (four-proverb collection; 10:27–30).

2. *Chiastic collection:* proverbs grouped in an *A-B-B-A* pattern. Again, the elements of the pattern may be individual cola (two-proverb collection; 18:6–7) or whole proverbs (four-proverb collection; 12:19–22).

3. *Catchword collection:* a group of proverbs that contain a common catchword (15:15–17). Some specific word or phrase is repeated that signals that the verses are related to one another.

4. *Thematic collection:* a group of proverbs that maintain a common theme (10:31–32). That is, they deal with the same subject matter.

5. *Inclusio collection:* a group of proverbs between an inclusio, in which the first and last proverbs are similar or contain common catchwords. For example, 11:23–27 is set off by the catchword "good" as an inclusio in verses 23, 27, and verses 24–26 within that inclusio deal with the theme of generosity and its rewards. A variation on the inclusio is the *A-B* envelope series, which consists of two juxtaposed collections with similar proverbs at the beginnings and ends (as in 15:1–16:8).

In addition, certain sections of Proverbs employ what may be called "random repetition" for didactic purposes. Proverbs 17, for example, randomly returns to the theme of avoiding quarrelsome behavior in verses 1, 9, 14, 19, 27–28. For the reader the unexpected way in which teachings on a particular theme repeatedly appear more emphatically drives home the intended lesson. If related proverbs always stood together in a single cluster, much of the effect would be lost.

8. E.g., strophe 10: "If you are poor, serve a man of worth" (*AEL* 1:66).
9. E.g., "Double the food your mother gave you,/support her as she supported you" (*AEL* 2:141). Sometimes there is slight variation in this pattern.
10. Lichtheim, *Late Egyptian Wisdom,* 64.

21

MOTIVATION
AND ANTITHETIC PARALLELISM
IN PROVERBS 10–15

Ted Hildebrandt

M otivation is a critical issue for employers, administrators, teachers, and parents. It is also a key topic in the Book of Proverbs. This paper will attempt to make contributions to proverbial motivation studies in several areas. A methodology will be developed for digging out the deep semantic motivational structures buried in the sentence literature (Prov. 10–15). By applying this method of analysis to the sentence literature, a rich diversity of motivational forces will be exposed even though there is a dearth of explicit motive clauses. Eight deep-structure categories will provide an initial framework for categorizing and understanding the underlying thought structure of the proverbial sentences. It will be suggested that "approach/avoidance" motivation theory may provide a psycholinguistic reason for the sages' frequent selection of antithetic parallelism as a medium to express their instruction. A dialogue will be initiated between

From *Journal of the Evangelical Theological Society* 35, 4 (December 1992): 433–44. Used by permission.

proverbial motivation study and the vast literature on the psychology of motivation that lies untapped by biblical scholars. Such an integration may yield
fresh insights into a biblical theory of motivation that may be of use to edu-
cators, employers, and parents. Hopefully such a theory will allow us to expose the motivating forces that should and do drive us as we pursue God and
others (Prov. 16:2).

Background: OT Motive Clause Study

Gemser in 1953 first isolated the motive clause as a grammatically subordinate clause usually introduced by a particle (*kî*; *lĕ-* plus infinitive; *lĕmaʿan*;
pen-) that provides motivation for a command (Law: Exod. 20:7; Deut.
22:19; Prophets: Amos 5:4–5; Isa. 34:5–8; Jer. 4:6–8; Writings: Pss. 2:11;
3:7; 95:3–7; Prov. 3:1–2). After surveying the ancient Near Eastern law
codes, Gemser concludes that motive clauses were unique to Israel.[1] While
the absoluteness of his original conclusion has been tempered by the disserta-
tions of Sonsino and Utti, they confirm a wide frequency gap between the
motives of biblical law (30 percent are motivated; 375 of 1,238 commands)
and the ancient law codes (only 5–6 percent are motivated).[2]

The motive clause is usually viewed as a later addition to the admonition
(cf. Prov. 22:28; 23:10–11).[3] Sonsino, following Kitchen's advice, rejects the
idea of unilinear evolution from smaller, literary units to those larger and
more complex.[4] He does affirm, however, that motive clauses are used more
frequently in the later biblical law codes than in earlier codes (Book of the
Covenant = 17 percent; Deuteronomy = 50 percent; Holiness Code = 51 percent).[5] Postel harnesses this developmental pattern in Proverbs and concludes
that the substantially higher percentage of motive clauses in Proverbs 1–9
dates the collection later than Proverbs 10–22.[6] But Sonsino wisely notes that
content may also have a marked effect on the frequency of motivation (78
percent of the law is cultic [27 percent motivated]; 12 percent treats civil matters [29 percent motivated]; 8 percent is ethical/humanitarian [53 percent

1. B. Gemser, "The Importance of the Motive Clause in Old Testament Law," *VTSup* 1
(Leiden: Brill, 1953), 52, 62.
2. R. Sonsino, *Motive Clauses in Hebrew Law: Biblical Forms and Near Eastern Parallels*
(Chico: Scholars, 1980), 153, 172–73, 221; R. Utti, *The Motive Clause in Old Testament Law*
(dissertation; Chicago: Lutheran School of Theology, 1973).
3. W. Zimmerli, "Concerning the Structure of Old Testament Wisdom," *Studies in Ancient
Israelite Wisdom*, ed. J. Crenshaw (New York: KTAV, 1976), 182–83; H. J. Postel, *The Form
and Function of the Motive Clause in Proverbs 10–29* (dissertation; University of Iowa, 1976),
107, 140, 142.
4. Sonsino, *Motive*, 98–99, 193; P. Nel, "Authority in the Wisdom Admonitions," *ZAW* 93
(1981): 419.
5. Sonsino, *Motive*, 98–99.
6. Postel, *Form*, 138; contra C. Kayatz, *Studien zu Proverbien 1–9*, WMANT 22 (Neukirchen-Vluyn: Neukirchener, 1966), 135.

motivated]).[7] Since wisdom is largely of an ethical/humanitarian nature the frequent use of motive clauses is not surprising, especially given wisdom's didactic *Sitz im Leben*. The differences in form and content between the instructions (Prov. 1–9) and brief, pungent sentences (Prov. 10–22) may better account for the difference in the frequency of motive clauses than the date.

Contrary to the absence of motive clauses in ancient Near Eastern legal materials, the use of motivational support is characteristic of the wisdom literature throughout the ancient Near East (Sumerian [*Instruction of Šuruppak*], Akkadian [*Counsels of Wisdom*], Ugaritic [*Instructions of Šube-Awilum*], Egyptian [*Ptahhotep, Ani,* etc.]).[8] Gemser suggests that there is an intrinsic connection between the law and wisdom based on motive clauses (Exod. 23:7 [cf. Prov. 17:15]; Lev. 19:35 [cf. Prov. 11:1]). The legal/wisdom nexus is also found in the Bantu tribes of Africa that utilize proverbial wisdom to clinch arguments in legal courtroom settings.[9] Sonsino highlights several distinctions in the form of legal, as opposed to wisdom, motive clauses (wisdom uses ʾal + second person, legal uses *lōʾ*; wisdom uses nonrepetitive format [contrast Lev. 19:20]; wisdom uses particles to connect motives).[10]

Motive Classification

Gemser classifies the motive clauses into four categories: (1) explanatory character (Deut. 20:5–8; 22:24, 26; Prov. 19:25, 27; 22:6), (2) ethical content (Deut. 5:14–15; 19:21), (3) cultic/theological (Deut. 17:1; 22:5; Prov. 20:22; 22:24–25), and (4) historical (Lev. 19:33–34; Deut. 5:15).[11] It is interesting that neither the ancient Near Eastern legal codes nor biblical wisdom employs motives using historical events.[12]

Sonsino isolates numerous motivational forces: (1) human dignity (Deut. 25:3), (2) compassion (Exod. 22:26), (3) imitating God (20:11), (4) social value (Lev. 21:9), (5) special status of actor (21:7), (6) short value judgment (20:17), and (7) characterization of prohibition (11:41, "it is loathsome"). These draw from four orientations: (1) God's authority (Lev. 19:3, 30), (2) allusions to historical experiences (Exod. 22:20; Deut. 23:8), (3) fear of punishment (Exod. 30:20–21), and (4) promise of well-being (20:12; Deut. 5:16).[13]

---

7. Sonsino, *Motive,* 99, 222–23.
8. Ibid., 153, 168–70.
9. Gemser, "Importance," 64–65; cf. Sonsino, *Motive,* 28–29, 36; T. Hildebrandt, *Proverbial Poetry: Its Settings and Syntax* (dissertation; Grace Theological Seminary, 1985), 89–91; cf. appropriate cautions by J. Crenshaw, "Method in Determining Wisdom Influence upon 'Historical' Literature," *Studies,* ed. Crenshaw, 481–94.
10. Sonsino, *Motive,* 28, 171.
11. Gemser, "Importance," 55–56; Postel, *Form,* 144, 151–57.
12. Sonsino, *Motive,* 172; Postel, *Form,* 146.
13. Sonsino, *Motive,* 105–8; cf. Utti, *Motive,* 92.

Postel sets up a typology of motive content more fitting for wisdom (T= Theological; E = Explanatory; C= Consequential) with motive valences (P = Promissory; D = Dissuasive).[14] The presence of promissory motives in Proverbs warns that the often-cited statement "a proverb is not a promise" is rather simplistic and an inadequate explanation of the consequentially directed proverbial statements (Prov. 3:1–2, 5–6, 9–10; cf. Deut. 8:1). Postel connects his "consequential" category with von Rad's "act-consequence" (order) relationship, supporting it as the center of wisdom literature.[15]

In Proverbs the distribution of motive clauses is concentrated largely in the instructions (Prov. 1–9; 22:17–24:22; 31:1–9) as opposed to the sentences (10:1–22:16; chaps. 25–29). Admonitions are much more frequent in the instructions (Prov. 1–9 = 39) than in the sayings (Prov. 10–22 = 13 [e.g., 14:7; 16:3; 19:18; 20:18–19; 22:6]).[16] Postel notes that 13 of the 17 motive clauses in Proverbs 10–22 are in admonitions and only 4 are in nonadmonitional sentences (13:14; 14:27; 15:24; 16:12).[17] He further differentiates between the instructions and proverbial sentences by noting differences in the content of the motive clauses. A clear contrast emerges in the frequency of motive clauses in the instructions (77.5 percent in 22:17–24:22) as opposed to the sentences (5.3 percent in Prov. 10–22; 12 percent in Prov. 25–29). Postel observes that the motive clauses in the instructions (22:17–24:22) are heavily theological and those in Proverbs 25–29 are heavily consequential while those in Proverbs 10–22 are evenly distributed.[18]

Need for Deep-Structure Motive Analysis

Several lines of evidence caution against concluding that because the sentences contain few motive clauses they are merely empirical observations with little attempt to motivate (energize and direct choices). (1) There seems to be a clear relationship between admonitions and sentences in some of the "duplicate" proverbs in which the same content is formatted as an admonition (22:22–23; 27:11 with explicit motive clause) and as a sentence (14:31; 10:1 without explicit motive clause but clearly motivational in intent).[19] Zimmerli recognizes the sentential deep-structure motivation when he writes concerning the admonition/saying connection that the admonition makes "explicit the implication, already lying

---

14. Postel, *Form*, 58; P. Nel, *The Structure and Ethos of the Wisdom Admonitions in Proverbs* (Berlin: Walter de Gruyter, 1982), 28, 46–48.

15. Cf. the *maʾat* concept; Postel, *Form*, 72–73; G. von Rad, *Wisdom in Israel* (Nashville: Abingdon, 1972), 196; cf. F. Wicker, F. Lambert, F. Richardson and J. Kahler, "Categorical Goal Hierarchies and Classification of Human Motives," *Journal of Personality* 52/3 (1984): 285–305.

16. Nel, *Structure*, 65–66, has a handy listing of all admonitions in Proverbs.

17. Postel, *Form*, 58, 90–93.

18. Ibid., 137, 170.

19. Ibid., 28; Nel, *Structure*, 29.

hidden within the saying."[20] (2) A naive reading of the sentences in Proverbs 10–15 (e.g., 10:1, 4, 5) reveals that many of the sentences go beyond mere empirical observation to being motivationally directive. Thus one must be careful to dissociate the broad deep-structure category of motivation from Gemser's grammatical motive clause. This distinction is critical. When looking at motivation in the sentences it is imperative to penetrate below the surface motive clauses in order to isolate how the sages actually motivated. A deep-structure analysis may provide a link between the sentence (*Aussage*) and admonition (*Mahnwort*) genres. (3) Postel notes that "the *tō'ēbâ* [abomination] clause, so frequent in Old Testament legislation, does not occur in the motive clauses of Proverbs."[21] Yet such "abomination sayings" are found in the sentences but not in explicit motive clauses (11:1, 20; 12:22; 15:8, 9; 17:15; 20:10).[22] A deep-structure analysis would uncover the motivational intent of these abomination sayings, while Postel's surface motive clause analysis has missed the connection. (4) After a deep-structure analysis was performed on the sentences, many of the same motivational themes arose that occurred in the explicit motive clauses of Proverbs 1–9. This provides some verification for the proposed methodology.

Methodology

Raymond Van Leeuwen has insightfully harnessed the deep-structure binary analysis of Dundes by breaking the proverbial sentence into a topic and comment (e.g., topic: "A wise son"; comment: "brings his father joy" [Prov. 10:1a]).[23] The semantic relationship between the topic and comment is specified below. A couple of examples will illustrate the method. First, the line is broken up into topic/comment and then the semantic deep-structure relationship and valences (+/-) between the topic and comment are identified:

Topic		Comment	Proverbs 10:1
A wise son	(+ character)	brings joy to his father	(+ consequence);
a foolish son	(– character)	is a grief to his mother	(– consequence).
	+ Character → + ConSequence (10:1a)	(CS)++	
	– Character → – ConSequence (10:1b)	(CS)––	

20. Zimmerli, "Structure," 183. Nel also mentions the need for a meaning-based analysis of the motive clauses rather than merely a grammatical approach.
21. Postel, *Form*, 146.
22. von Rad, *Wisdom*, 115; R. Murphy, *Wisdom Literature* (Grand Rapids: Eerdmans, 1981), 69.
23. R. Van Leeuwen, *Context and Meaning in Proverbs 25–27* (Atlanta: Scholars, 1988), 48–52; C. Fontaine, *Traditional Sayings in the Old Testament: A Contextual Study* (Sheffield: Almond, 1982), 34–38; A. Dundes, "On the Structure of the Proverb," *Analytic Essays in Folklore*, ed. Dundes (The Hague/Paris: Mouton, 1975), 103–18.

It should be clear from Postel's categories listed above that the consequence, while not in a Gemserian motive clause, acts as a motivation drawing the son to be wise and driving him from becoming foolish. Its motivational force is unleashed by exposing the son to the emotive consequences, whether joy or sorrow, that his character will have on his parents (expectational aspect of motivation).

Topic	Proverbs 11:15	Comment
He who puts up security for another (– act)		will surely suffer (– consequence);
whoever refuses to strike hands in pledge (+ act)		is safe (+ consequence)
– Act →	– ConSequence (11:15a)	(AS)––
+ Act →	+ ConSequence (11:15b)	(AS)++

In Proverbs 11:15 there is no motive clause, and yet its clear motivational intent is to avoid suffering harm (11:15a) and to maintain one's safety (11:15b). In the appendix there is a semantic classification of the types of deep-structure motives used in the sentence literature. Many of the motives used in the explicit motive clauses of Proverbs 1–9 are reiterated, confirming our hypothesis that the sentences are motivational in character even though an explicit motive clause has not been employed.

Deep-Structure Classification Results

In specifying the relationship between the topic and comment, most of the sentences fit into one of the following eight categories:[24]

			Frequency	Examples
Character ⟶	→ConSequence	(CS)	(152)	10:2b, 3a, 6a
	→Act	(CA)	(70)	10:12a, 14a
	→Evaluation	(CE)	(16)	10:20a, 11:1a
Character ⟶	→ConSequence	(CS)	(152)	*supra*
Act ⟶		(AS)	(62)	10:17a, 19a

24. R. B. Y. Scott, *Proverbs* (Garden City: Doubleday, 1965), 5–7; J. Berezov, *Single-Line Proverbs: A Study of the Sayings Collected in Proverbs 10–22:16 and 25–29* (dissertation; Hebrew Union College, 1987), 4–6 (see 53–55 for categories on basis of topic and syntax); Fontaine, *Traditional,* 66–68.

Item ⟶		(IS)	(12)	13:2a, 82
Item ⟶	→Evaluation	(IE)	(7)	10:15a; 13:19a
Act ⟶		(AE)	(13)	11:30b; 12:1a
Character ⟶		(CE)	(16)	*supra*
Appearance ⟶	→Reality	(PR)	(4)	13:7; 14:13

While von Rad and others have emphasized the Act → Consequence connection (62 found in Prov. 10–15) as wisdom's core, the statistics reveal that other frameworks may be more central (e.g., Character → Consequence [152] or Character → Act [70]). Thus the first major hypothesis of this chapter is that Character → Consequence is closer than Act → Consequence to the central core of the proverbial sentences.[25]

The Motivation for Antithetic Parallelism

Looking at the list of motives, we may suggest another hypothesis. The binary valencing of the motivational items that Postel has labeled "promissory" and "dissuasive" might better be coordinated with modern motivation literature (promissory → approach motivation; dissuasive → avoidance motivation).[26] This binary valencing, as Van Leeuwen and pareimologists Dundes and Milner have noted, is descriptive of proverbial literature cross-culturally.[27] Many of the proverbial sentences are beautifully balanced with an approach motivation drawing ("brings joy to a father," 10:1a) and an avoidance motivation driving away ("is a grief to his mother," 10:1b).

It is interesting that Kersovec's monograph on antithesis failed to treat antithesis in the proverbial sentences. Although he acknowledges that Proverbs contains "the greatest number of antithetic parallelisms," he demurs that they are "neither stimulating nor rewarding."[28] Why should the sages in producing wisdom literature show such a preference for antithetic structures (90 percent of Proverbs 10–15; cf. also Psalms 1, 73)?[29] Several hypotheses may be suggested. Atkinson and the massive literature on the psychology of motivation conclude that there is an additive relationship

---

25. Cf. Berezov, *Single-Line*, 84; J. Gladson, *Retributive Paradoxes in Proverbs 10–29* (dissertation; Vanderbilt University, 1978).

26. J. Atkinson and D. Birch, *An Introduction to Motivation* (New York: D. Van Nostrand, 1978), 239, 288–89.

27. Van Leeuwen, *Context*, 48; Fontaine, *Traditional*, 34–36; G. Milner, "Quadripartite Structures," *Proverbium* 14 (1969): 379–83.

28. J. Kersovec, *Antithetic Structure in Biblical Hebrew Poetry* (Leiden: Brill, 1984), 17.

29. U. Skladny, *Die ältesten Spruchsammlungen in Israel* (Göttingen: Vandenhoeck und Ruprecht, 1962), 68; Berezov, *Single-Line*, 84.

between approach and avoidance motivation.[30] This chapter contends that antithesis provides a perfect psycholinguistic structure for doubling the motivational potency of the sentences by combining in an additive sense approach and avoidance motivations (10:1, 3, 5; 142/184 = 77 percent of Proverbs 10–15 are approach/avoidance type). Rather than being nonmotivationally oriented because the sentences lack surface motive clauses, the deep-structure analysis suggests that the sage's use of antithetic structure is extremely potent motivationally.

Proverbs and the Psychology of Motivation

The final area of discussion involves the nature of motivation in Proverbs in light of the vast literature on the psychology of motivation.[31] A brief browsing of the Appendix reveals the wide range of ways in which the sage/father motivates his student/son. It is interesting, for example, how well Bandura's social learning theory of modeling fits the sage's approach: attention processes ("Listen, my son") → retention processes ("do not forget") → motor reproduction processes (Proverbs 5 and 7 walk the son through the situation with the admonition "do this") and motivational processes (abundance of motive clauses in Prov. 1–9).[32]

Approaches to Motivation

Motivational studies treat the initiation, intensity, direction, and persistence of behavior.[33] Motivational theory has gone far beyond naive hedonism (pleasure/pain as motivators) through Hullian drive reduction theory (drive x habit) to the more cognitive value x expectancy (incentive) theories, including achievement, attribution, and intrinsic motivational theories.[34] Proverbs does not ignore the basic motivational drives (hunger, 10:3b; 13:25; 15:15b, 17a; harm, 10:7b, 15b, 16b, 29b, 31b; death, 10:21b, 27b; 11:3b, 19b; 13:9b). Indeed Maslow's hierarchy of needs and motivation in Proverbs in-

---

30. Atkinson and Birch, *Introduction,* 50–52.
31. D. McClelland, *Human Motivation* (Glenview: Scott, Foresman, 1985); B. Weiner, *Human Motivation* (New York: Holt, 1980); J. Houston, *Motivation* (New York: Macmillan, 1985); Atkinson and Birch, *Introduction.*
32. Cf. Houston, *Motivation,* 334; A. Bandura, *Social Learning Theory* (Englewood Cliffs: Prentice-Hall, 1977), 23.
33. Houston, *Motivation,* 6–7; Atkinson and Birch, *Introduction.*
34. For Hullian theory cf. Atkinson and Birch, *Introduction,* 47, 15–16; Houston, *Motivation,* 192–209; for value expectancy theory cf. Houston, *Motivation,* 238; Atkinson and Birch, *Introduction,* 75; for achievement motivation cf. McClelland, *Human;* for attribution theory cf. Weiner, *Human;* for intrinsic motivation cf. E. Deci and R. Ryan, *Intrinsic Motivation and Self-Determination in Human Behavior* (New York: Plenum, 1985); M. Lepper and D. Greene, *The Hidden Costs of Reward: New Perspectives on the Psychology of Human Motivation* (Hillsdale: Erlbaum, 1978).

tersects at many points.[35] Heider noted that man has two basic needs: to understand his world, and to control it.[36] Both of these are employed motivationally in Proverbs.

Proverbs, however, goes beyond drives to tap the student's cognitive evaluations. Proverbs affirms man's ability to choose and unleashes a whole cluster of motivational incentives—not only rousing personal drives but also social concerns (friendships, 14:20; honor/disgrace, 12:8; 14:18; 15:33; status, 12:24; blessing/curse, 11:26; 14:17b, 21b, 22b), altruistic concern for others (10:21a; 12:18; 15:4) and theological motivations (14:2, 31; cf. appendix).[37] Gordon is correct that the ultimate motive is life (8:32–36).[38] Self-preservation, the desire for well-being and the avoidance of harm underlie much proverbial motivation. Rather than demeaning such motivational forces by labeling them as adolescent or crassly egocentric, such "worldly" motivations need to be embraced as having been utilized in Proverbs, the law (Deut. 28; Lev. 26), and even the NT (cf. Austgen's demonstration of such "worldly" motivation in the Pauline epistles: 1 Tim. 5:23; Titus 2:5; cf. Matt. 6:33; Acts 16:3).[39]

Cognitive Motivational Factors

Atkinson's value x expectancy theory may be summarized by the formula Ms x Ps x Ins ([individual's motive for success = Ms] x [probability of success (task difficulty) = Ps] x [incentive = Ins]).[40] When the Mf > Ms (motive to avoid failure > motive to achieve success) a person will attempt to avoid failure. On the other hand when the Ms > Mf a person will strive for success. Motivational theorists have discovered an inverted U-shaped curve relating optimal arousal level, task difficulty, and risk levels.[41] If tasks are too easy (Ps high) or impossible (Ps too low) motivation will be minimal, but if the task is midrange the motivational challenge will be maximized. Wisdom is both challenging and costly (Prov. 4:7–8). She is not, however, unattainable but graciously offers herself to those who will pursue her (1:20–33; 9:1–5). In order to shape character, wisdom digitizes reality into discreet, well-defined choices. This helps the son to recognize more easily characterological patterns of behavior, making choices more accessible although by no means easily attained.

---

35. Houston, *Motivation*, 215–16.
36. Ibid., 255.
37. R. N. Gordon, "Motivation in Proverbs," *Biblical Theology* 25 (1975): 55–56.
38. Ibid., 54.
39. R. Austgen, *Natural Motivation in the Pauline Epistles* (South Bend: University of Notre Dame, 1966).
40. Atkinson and Birch, *Introduction*, 94–96; Houston, *Motivation*, 242.
41. Atkinson and Birch, *Introduction*, 65, 106; Houston, *Motivation*, 83.

The proverbial sentences use approach/approach incentives (better-than proverbs: Prov. 22:1, 4), avoidance/approach (most antithetic sentences: 10:1, 3, 5), and avoidance/avoidance (22:16; 21:27; cf. Atkinson's concept of "negaction" or inhibitory motivation).[42] Through the use of antithetic parallelism the sages maximize the motivational forces by presenting the negative and positive consequences of both wisdom and folly. Thus the approach motivation draws the son to the desired wise choice (10:1a), while the avoidance motivation in the next line drives the son away from the corresponding foolish choice (10:1b).

Attribution Theory Motivation

Weiner and others have stressed the importance of attribution theory in motivational studies.[43] The basic premise of the theory is that man is motivated to seek causes.[44] This aspect of motivational theory is sensitive to the personal attributions made after a task success or failure (why I succeeded/failed = ability, effort, luck, task difficulty).[45] It is noted that success for males leads to effort attributions while they favor ability praise as informational. Females, on the other hand, make ability attributions more naturally but they prefer effort praise, perceiving ability praise as controlling.[46] Thus, some tasks are ego-involving (resulting in attributions about ability, feeling controlled and high personal risk), while others are merely task-involving (attributions made about task difficulty, more informational, less risky).[47]

Though Proverbs relates many tasks to character (10:3, 5) and hence is ego-involving, one must clearly note that the sentences' third-person style is more informationally directive, leaving the choice to the son. These choices result in character attributions and consequences (10:5, 18, 23, 32; 11:12–13; cf. appendix, evaluations section). By teaching these proverbial sentences the sage builds an attributional set into his student. When the student engages in a particular behavior, having internalized the evaluative wisdom grid, he will be able to reward himself by evaluating his choices as wise or foolish.[48]

---

42. Atkinson and Birch, *Introduction*, 50–53.
43. Weiner, *Human*, 275–77.
44. Houston, *Motivation*, 254–55.
45. Ibid., 256.
46. R. Koestner, M. Zuckerman and J. Koestner, "Attributional Focus of Praise and Children's Intrinsic Motivation: The Moderating Role of Gender," *Personality and Social Bulletin* 15/1 (1989): 61–72; C. Dweck, "Motivational Processes Affecting Learning," *American Psychologist* 41/10 (1986): 10–43; C. Sansone, "A Question of Competence: The Effects of Competence and Task Feedback on Intrinsic Interest," *Journal of Personality and Social Psychology* 51/5 (1986): 918–31.
47. S. Harter, "A Model of Mastery Motivation in Children: Individual Differences and Developmental Change," *Aspects of the Development of Competence: The Minnesota Symposia on Child Psychology* 14, ed. W. A. Collins (Hillsdale: Erlbaum, 1981), 252; Koestner, "Attributional," 384.
48. Sansone, "Question," 918.

Proverbs also builds the sons' internal locus of control.[49] He must choose. The outside forces do not determine his character. Thus the father avoids a learned helplessness response where the son gives up because the situation has a locus of control beyond his ability.[50] This internal control builds the son's self-esteem, which is critical to all forms of motivation as the son realizes he must take charge of his world through making responsible choices. The ultimate results/consequences, however, must be released in the fear of the Lord, whose ways are beyond calculation (1:7; 21:31; 20:24).

Extrinsic/Intrinsic Motivation

Deci has championed the notion of the possible undermining effects of extrinsic motivation.[51] It has been found that if a child is paid money (extrinsic reward) to engage in a particular behavior (puzzles) he will make the mental attribution that he is doing the puzzles not because they are enjoyable but because he is being paid (overjustification).[52] Once the payments stop, the behavior will be quickly extinguished. But if the child does a puzzle without pay, he will tell himself that the reason he is doing it is because it is interesting. This intrinsic motivation leads to greater creativity and persistence.[53] At the core of intrinsic motivation is a feeling of self-determination and autonomy. Some of this seems to be developmental since young children are more intrinsically motivated than adolescents.[54]

Superficially, Proverbs appears to be extrinsic in its motivational orientation (10:3). The notions of self-determination are highlighted, however, as each sentence presents the student with a choice whereby he is able to determine his own character and consequences. While Proverbs utilizes the potency of extrinsic rewards (e.g., wealth/poverty), it highlights such intrinsic benefits of character development as that its own reward is more valuable than rubies (4:7; 31:10; cf. evaluation section in the appendix). Indeed, wisdom itself is used as a motivating goal (11:2b; 13:20a; 14:6–7, 18, 23; 15:33). Again the point is to build informational Gestalts for making self-attributions

49. Atkinson and Birch, *Introduction,* 140; B. Earn, "Intrinsic Motivation as a Function of Extrinsic Financial Rewards and Subjects' Locus of Control," *Journal of Personality* 50/3 (1982): 360–63; D. Tzuriel and H. C. Haywood, "Locus of Control and Child Rearing Practices in Intrinsically Motivated and Extrinsically Motivated Children," *Psychological Reports* 57 (1985): 888; J. Condry, "Enemies of Exploration: Self-Initiated Versus Other-Initiated Learning," *Journal of Personality and Social Psychology* 35/7 (1977): 459–77.

50. Houston, *Motivation,* 276.

51. Deci and Ryan, *Intrinsic;* Lepper and Greene, *Hidden;* Condry, "Enemies."

52. M. Lepper, D. Greene and R. Nisbett, "Undermining Children's Intrinsic Interest with Extrinsic Reward," *Journal of Personality and Social Psychology* 28/1 (1973): 129–30.

53. T. Amabile, "Motivation and Creativity: Effects of Motivational Orientation on Creative Writers," *Journal of Personality and Social Psychology* 48/2 (1985): 393–99.

54. Harter, "Model," 237.

rather than to control, which will result in resentment and lack of internalization.[55]

Some have empirically established that the impact of others-oriented motivation leads to more empathic and altruistic behavior.[56] Proverbs clearly employs this type of motivational strategy (10:21; 12:18; 13:22; 14:25; 15:4; cf. appendix).

Motivation and Emotion

Lastly, the bond between emotions and motivation links the affective domain with values motivation at the levels of the individual (10:28a; 12:20b; 15:23a), others (10:1; 11:10; 15:30a) and even for Yahweh (11:1, 20; 12:2, 22; 15:8–9, 26). Emotional anticipation is a key factor in the motivation of behavior. The connection of values motivation and affective responses warns against a cognitive belittling of the emotions. Wisdom also includes such responses as desirable and functional in motivational contexts.[57]

Concluding Summary

This chapter has proposed a methodology for exposing the motivational forces hidden in the sentence literature deep structures that often lack explicit Gemserian motive clauses. It has been suggested that rather than seeing act → consequence as the core of the proverbial sentences, character → consequence may be closer to its center.

A motivationally based explanation was given for the sages' frequent use of antithetic parallelisms. This poetic structure often unleashes a powerful motivation combination: approach (10:1a) + avoidance (10:1b).

While the discussion of the psychology of motivation and proverbial motivation has merely been introduced, it is hoped that it will be found to be a fertile frontier for further exploration. Drive reduction, cognitive expectancies, characterological attributions, and intrinsic/extrinsic motivational strategies, as well as the nexus between emotion and motivation, provide rich areas for further study.

---

55. M. L. Hoffman, "Parent Discipline and the Child's Moral Development," *Journal of Personality and Social Psychology* 5 (1967): 45–57.

56. L. Kuczynski, "Reasoning, Prohibitions, and Motivations for Compliance," *Developmental Psychology* 19/1 (1983): 126–28.

57. Houston, *Motivation*, 272–73; H. A. Simon, "Motivational and Emotional Controls of Cognition," *Psychological Review* 74 (1967): 29–39; I. J. Roseman, "Cognitive Determinants of Emotion: A Structural Theory," *Review of Personality and Social Psychology* 5 (1984); N. L. Stein and L. J. Levine, "Making Sense Out of Emotion: the Representation and Use of Goal-Structured Knowledge," *Psychological and Biological Approaches to Emotion,* ed. Stein, B. Leventhal and T. Trabasso (Hillsdale: Erlbaum, 1990), 45–73.

Much of the motivation literature reveals the need for a value-based motivational theory that can promote moral/faith development.[58] Proverbs presents a value-based motivation that includes a rich variety of intrinsic and extrinsic motivations including personal this-worldly, altruistic/sociological and theological motives. Indeed, both God and the teachers/sages of Israel were concerned about what motivates the heart (Heb. 4:12; Prov. 16:2).

Appendix

Structure of Proverbial Motivation (Proverbs 10–15)

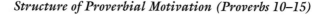

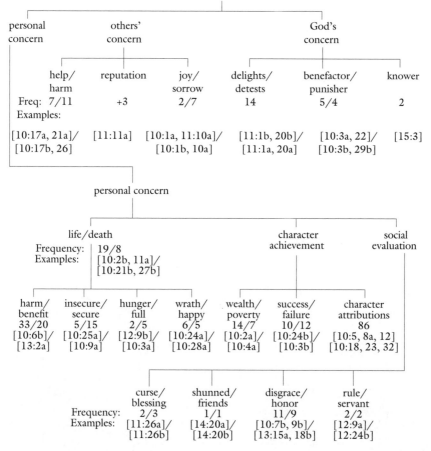

58. L. Kohlberg, *Essays on Moral Development: The Philosophy of Moral Development* (New York: Harper, 1981, 1984); B. Clouse, *Moral Development: Perspective in Psychology and Christian Belief* (Grand Rapids: Baker, 1985); J. Fowler, *Stages of Faith* (San Francisco: Harper, 1981); C. Dykstra and S. Parks, *Faith Development and Fowler* (Birmingham: Religious Education, 1986).

22

RIGHTEOUS AND WICKED LIVING IN PROVERBS 10

Sid S. Buzzell

This long portion of the Book of Proverbs [10:1–22:16] contains 375 sayings. The development of thought is limited to the two (or sometimes more) lines of each verse. Chapters 10–15 continue the subject matter so dominant in chapters 1–9 contrasting the righteous (or wise) with the wicked (or foolish). The remainder of the section (16:1–22:16) is more varied in subject matter.

Most of the verses in chapters 10–15 are contrasts (in antithetic parallelism); the second line in most of the verses begins with "but." Only a few of the verses in 16:1–22:16 are contrasts; most of the verses are either comparisons (in synonymous parallelism) or completions (in synthetic parallelism), with the conjunction "and" introducing the second line in many of the verses.

The frequent change of subject from one verse to another may be intentional, to force readers to grapple with and meditate on the thoughts in one

Reprinted from *The Bible Knowledge Commentary, Old Testament,* edited by John L. Walvoord and Roy B. Zuck, published by Victor Books, 1985, SP International, Wheaton, IL 60187. Used by permission.

verse before moving on to the next. However, occasionally two or more con-
secutive verses are linked by a common subject or word. For example 10:4–5
discusses both laziness and diligence, and 10:11–14, 18–21, 31–32 refer to
talking. "LORD" is mentioned in each verse in 16:1–7, the key word in each
verse in 16:12–15 is "king," 15:16–17 both begin with the word "better,"
each verse in 12:9–11 discusses domestic scenes, and each verse in 11:9–12
begins with the same Hebrew letter.

Proverbs Contrasting Righteous
and Wicked Living (10–15)

10:1. . . . With Solomon having authored chapters 1–9 (see 1:1) and chapters 25–29 (see 25:1), along with 10:1–22:16, he wrote about 84 percent of
the book, all of it of course being inspired by the divine Author, the Holy
Spirit.

A wise son is contrasted here with "a foolish son," in 13:1 with a mocker,
and in 15:20 with a foolish man. A son who has become wise, by heeding his
parents' teachings (5:1–2), brings joy to his father, a fact stated several times
in Proverbs (15:20; 23:15, 24; 27:11; 29:3). A foolish ($k^e s\hat{\imath}l$; see comments
on 1:7) son, on the other hand, grieves his mother. This does not mean that
a foolish son does not grieve his father, as is clearly stated in 17:21, 25; 19:13.
Nor does 10:1 mean that a mother's heart is not gladdened by a son's wisdom. The use of "father" in one line and "mother" in the other is typical of
proverbial literature. Both parents experience either the joy or the grief, just
as both are involved in teaching (1:8; 4:3–4; 6:20).

10:2. To say that treasures are of no value seems like a startling, almost
contradictory statement until one remembers that the treasures are ill-gotten
(cf. 1:19; 28:16; Mic. 6:10), gained unjustly (cf. Prov. 16:8) by theft or deceit. An example of this is addressed in 1:11–14, 18–19. Such treasures are no
good because they dwindle away (13:11; 21:6) and do not forestall death
(11:4). Of course money acquired dishonestly may provide some pleasure and
be valuable for a while but in the long run it does not satisfy.

10:3. Verses 3–5 discuss diligence and sloth. Satisfaction of one's appetite
is related to the LORD (v. 3); poverty and wealth result from laziness and diligence, respectively (v. 4); industry characterizes a wise son and sleep characterizes a shameful son (v. 5). The righteous is literally, "the soul of the righteous." Since "soul" emphasizes the whole person, God has said here that he
meets all one's needs, including the needs of his body for food (cf. Ps. 37:19,
25). The craving of the wicked refers to their evil desires to bring about destruction and disaster. God can keep them from carrying out such plans. Like
many verses in Proverbs, this verse is a generalization. It is usually true that
the godly do not starve and that the wicked do not get all they desire.

10:4–5. If a person refuses to work he will be poor (a word used often in Proverbs), whereas a hard worker eventually is rewarded. (Besides laziness other reasons for poverty are mentioned in Proverbs. . . .) One example of diligence and therefore of wisdom (wise is from the verb *śākal* meaning "to be prudent or to have sound judgment"; cf. 1:3; 16:20) is harvesting in the summer while the crops are ripe. An example of laziness is a son who sleeps rather than works during harvest (in contrast with the ants, 6:6–11). In fact such a person brings shame (the meaning of disgraceful), probably to his parents.

10:6. Whereas a righteous person receives blessings, it is different with the wicked. Violence overwhelms his mouth. The same statement is made in verse 11. Since the word for "overwhelms" can be translated "covers" (as it is in v. 12), the idea is either that his mouth conceals or deceptively hides violence (NIV marg.), or that violence characterizes what a person says. As Jesus stated, "The evil man brings evil things out of the evil stored up in his heart" (Luke 6:45).

10:7. Speaking of blessings and the righteous (v. 6), even *thinking* about righteous people of the past can be a source of spiritual blessing. By contrast most people want to forget the wicked. Like their character, even their names are corrupt, rotting like a corpse.

10:8–9. A wise person is teachable, willing to become wiser (cf. 1:5; 9:9). But a fool (*ʾĕwîl*, a coarse, hardened fool; . . . cf. 10:21) does not quit chattering long enough to learn anything. In Proverbs needless talking is often associated with folly. Such a person comes to ruin, a phrase repeated only two verses later (v. 10; cf. 13:3). "Ruin" is mentioned five times in chapter 10 (vv. 8, 10, 14–15, 29). An honest person (v. 9) is secure (cf. a similar thought in 3:23; 18:10; 28:18) in his walk (his conduct) but a person whose paths are crooked (lit., "twisted"), whose conduct is wicked, in contrast with a person of integrity, eventually will be discovered for what he truly is.

10:10. Verses 10–12 deal with interpersonal relations. Winking maliciously with one's cohorts suggests sinful intentions (cf. 6:13; 16:30; Ps. 35:19). No wonder this leads to grief on the part of the victims of their evil plans, or the victim's loved ones. Yet a talkative fool will himself eventually get into trouble (cf. the same line in Prov. 10:8b).

10:11. The words of a righteous (and wise) person are like a fountain of life (cf. 13:14; 14:27; 16:22; also note 18:4). His words of wisdom are free-flowing and as refreshing as a cool spring to a weary desert traveler. On the second part of 10:11, see comments on verse 6b.

10:12. Hatred results in dissension (cf. 6:14) because people who despise each other can hardly work or live together in peace. Love contributes toward peace because it covers or forgives the faults of others (cf. 17:9). It does not dwell on those faults (cf. 1 Cor. 13:5; James 5:20; 1 Pet. 4:8). "Covers" is *kā-*

sâh, the same word rendered "overwhelms" in Proverbs 10:6, 11. A wicked one's words are covered *over* with violence, but a righteous person covers *up* wrongs by forgiving the wrongdoers.

10:13–14. These statements contrast the wise and the fool. While the discerning person is characterized by his wise statements, one lacking judgment (cf. v. 21; 6:32; 7:7; 9:4, 16; 11:12; 12:11; 15:21; 17:18; 24:30; 28:16) experiences trouble. He may be punished by a rod on the back (cf. 14:3; 26:3). A wise person stores up knowledge; he holds it in for the right occasion without spouting off his knowledge. What a fool says, however, causes him trouble and eventually ruin because he foolishly speaks the wrong things and gets himself in trouble (cf. 10:19).

10:15–16. These verses are together because they both discuss wealth. The first line of verse 15 is repeated in 18:11. Though wealth should not be placed above honor (28:20) and should not be trusted in (11:4; 23:5), it can provide a hedge against some disasters. Poverty is a continually suppressive problem to the poor (cf. 14:20; 18:23; 19:7; 22:7). The Hebrew word here for poor is *dal*, "feeble, weak, helpless," translated "poor" or "helpless" in 19:4, 17; 21:13; 22:16; 28:3, 8, 11, 15; 29:7, 14. Proverbs also uses several other words for "poor" and "poverty."

Wages (10:16) refers not to money but to the natural result or "return" for righteous living. That result is a meaningful life (cf. 3:18, 21–22; 4:4; 7:2a). But the wicked reap trouble (Gal. 6:7).

10:17. The word "life" links verses 16 and 17. A person who learns from discipline is an example to others of the way to a meaningful life, whereas those who refuse to learn from discipline cause others to go astray. One's conduct affects not only himself but others as well, either favorably or unfavorably.

10:18. Each of verses 18–21 refers to some aspects of talking. The subject of hatred was introduced in verse 12, and in verse 18 another thought is added to the subject. When a person hates someone but tries not to show it he is often forced to lie. And hatred often leads to slandering the other who is despised. The second line in verse 18 begins with "and" rather than "but," to show that the two thoughts of hatred and slander are not opposites. Such lying and slandering, born out of hatred, characterize a fool.

10:19. Constant talking will eventually lead to sin and get a person into trouble (cf. "chattering" in vv. 8, 10; also note James 3:2–8). This is obviously folly because the ability to keep silent is wise (cf. Prov. 11:12).

10:20. In contrast with the degrading talk of the wicked (lying, slandering, and gabbing, vv. 18–19) the words (tongue) of the righteous are uplifting and therefore are valued like choice silver. However, with the wicked not even their thoughts (heart) have value, let alone their words!

10:21. The word "tongue" links verses 19 and 20, the word "lips" unites verse 21 with verse 18, and "the righteous" ties verses 20 and 21 together. One of the reasons righteous words are valuable (v. 20) is that they nourish or benefit others spiritually. Death comes to those who are fools (ʾĕwîl; cf. v. 8) . . . because they lack judgment (cf. 6:32; 7:7; 9:4, 16; 10:13; 11:12; 12:11; 15:21; 24:30; 28:16). Since the first part of 10:21 refers to talking, the second part probably implies that fools lack judgment in what they say. Their wrong kind of talking does not even nourish themselves; they are left spiritually undernourished and starved.

10:22. After the word "LORD" the Hebrew adds the word "it" for emphasis. So the first line reads, The blessing of the LORD, it brings wealth. The second line affirms the idea that wealth given by the Lord (to the righteous and diligent) is not accompanied by trouble, the tragedies of ill-gotten gain (cf. v. 2).

10:23. Most of verses 23–32 contrast the righteous and the wicked. A fool (kᵉsîl, a thickheaded person . . .) enjoys sinning, whereas the wise prefer wisdom. This contrast between evil conduct and wisdom shows that wisdom in the biblical sense is moral in nature.

10:24–25. By stressing repeatedly in Proverbs that disaster comes to the wicked and various rewards are for the righteous, Solomon sought to convince the uninitiated and naive that the long-range, not the immediate, fruits of wisdom and folly should be kept in view. Many wicked people dread calamity and they receive it! And the righteous often receive what they want, namely, blessing. God is the ultimate source of both. A storm can come suddenly, bringing disaster to the wicked by destroying their lives and property (c. 1:27; 6:15; 29:1), but the righteous are more secure (cf. 10:9, 30; 12:3).

10:26. Just as vinegar (made from wine) is sour tasting, and as smoke irritates the eyes, so a sluggard . . . aggravates his employers, those who send him to do some work or go on an errand. He is aggravating because he fails to carry out his responsibilities.

10:27–30. These verses mention several blessings that come to the righteous: long life . . . joy, safety, and security. Usually the wicked have none of these, when seen from the perspective of eternity. Longevity for the righteous and the brief lives of the wicked are frequent themes in Proverbs (3:2, 16; 4:10; 9:11; 14:27; 15:24). On the fear of the Lord see . . . also 2:5; 3:7; 8:13; 9:10; 14:26–27; 15:16, 33; 16:6; 19:23; 22:4; 23:17; 24:21. Joy comes to those who love the Lord, but the desires of the wicked for joy are not fulfilled (cf. 10:24; 11:7). By going in the way of the Lord, that is, by following his standards, the righteous have a refuge of safety (mā⁽ôz; cf. Ps. 31:2, 4; Nah. 1:7). They are secure in the land (cf. Prov. 10:9, 25) but the wicked are not (cf. 2:21–22).

10:31–32. These two verses also address the subject of talking (cf. vv. 11–14, 18–21). The righteous speak wise words (cf. v. 11). "Brings forth" is literally, "bears fruit." As a tree naturally brings forth fruit so wise words are a natural result of uprightness (cf. Luke 6:43–45). Thus they are fitting or appropriate. . . . "Perverse," used in both verses 31 and 32, means to be turned away from what is normal (cf. 2:12).

23

PROVERBS 22:6
AND THE TRAINING
OF CHILDREN

Gleason L. Archer, Jr.

Proverbs 22:6 says, "Train up a child in the way he should go, even when he is old he will not depart form it" (NASB). NIV renders the second line thus: "And when he is old he will not turn from it." Before discussing the practical application of this verse, we should examine quite carefully what it actually says. The literal rendering of the Hebrew *ḥᵃnōk lan-naʿar* is "Initiate, train the boy" (*naʿar* refers to a young male from childhood until he reaches majority); the verb *ḥānak* does not occur elsewhere in the Old Testament with the meaning "train up." Normally the verb means "dedicate" (a house or a temple [Deut. 20:5; 1 Kings 8:63; 2 Chron. 7:5], or else a dedication offering [Num. 7:10]). This seems to be cognate with the Egyptian *ḥ-n-k* ("give to the gods," "set up something for divine service"). This gives us the following range of possible meanings: "Dedicate the child to God," "Prepare the child for his future responsibilities," "Exercise or train the child for adulthood."

Next we come to what is translated "in the way he should go." Literally, it is "according to his way" (ʿal-pî darkô); ʾal-pî (lit., "according to the mouth of") generally means "after the measure of," "conformably to," or "according to." As for darkô, it comes from derek ("way"); and this may refer to "the general custom of, the nature of, the way of acting, the behavior pattern of" a person. This seems to imply that the manner of instruction is to be governed by the child's own state of life, according to his personal bent, or else, as the standard translations render it, according to the way that is proper for him—in the light of God's revealed will, according to the standards of his community or his cultural heritage. In this highly theological, God-centered context ("Yahweh is the maker" of both the rich and the poor [v. 2]; "The reward of humility and the fear of Yahweh is riches, honor, and life" [v. 4]), there can be little doubt that "his way" here implies "his proper way" in the light of the goals and standards set forth in verse 4 and tragically neglected by the "perverse" in verse 5. Yet there may also be a connotation that each child is to be reared and trained for God's service according to the child's own personal and peculiar needs and traits.

The second line reads gam kî ("even when") yazqîn ("he gets old"—zāqēn is the word for "old" or "an elder"), lōʾ yāsûr ("he will not turn away") mimmennāh ("from it," i.e., from his derek), which seems to strengthen the interpretation "his proper way," "behavior pattern," or "lifestyle" as a well-trained man of God or good citizen in his community.

What this all adds up to, then, is the general principle (and all the general maxims in Proverbs concerning human conduct are of this character, rather than laying down absolute guarantees to which there may never be an exception) that when a godly parent gives proper attention to the training of his child for adult responsibility and for a well-ordered life lived for God, then he may confidently expect that that child—even though he may stray during his young adulthood—will never be able to get away completely from his parental training and from the example of a God-fearing home. Even when he becomes old, he will not depart from it. Or else, this gam kî may imply that he will remain true to this training throughout his life, even when he gets old.

Does this verse furnish us with an iron-clad guarantee that all the children of conscientious, God-fearing, nobly living parents will turn out to be true servants of God? Will there never be any rebellious children, who will turn their backs on their upbringing and fall into the guilt and shame of a Satan-dominated life? One might construe the verse that way, perhaps; but it is more than doubtful that the inspired Hebrew author meant it as an absolute promise that would apply in every case. These maxims are meant to be good, sound, helpful advice; they are not presented as surefire promises of infallible success.

The same sort of generality is found in Proverbs 22:15: "Foolishness is bound up in the heart of a child; the rod of discipline will remove it far from him" (NASB). This surely does not mean that all children are equally willful and rebellious and that all of them stand in need of the same amount and type of discipline. Nor does it guarantee that a person brought up in a well-disciplined home will never stray off into the folly of sin. There may be exceptions who turn out to be worldly minded egotists or even lawbreakers who end up in prison. But the rate of success in childrearing is extremely high when the parents follow the guidelines in Proverbs.

What are those guidelines? Children are to be accepted as sacred trusts from God; they are to be trained, cherished, and disciplined with love; and they are to be guided by a consistent pattern of godliness followed by the parents themselves. This is what is meant by bringing them up "in the discipline and instruction of the Lord" (Eph. 6:4). This type of training implies a policy of treating children as even more important than one's own personal convenience or social life away from home. It means impressing on them that they are very important persons in their own right because they are loved by God, and because he has a wonderful and perfect plan for their lives. Parents who have faithfully followed these principles and practices in rearing their children may safely entrust them as adults to the keeping and guidance of God and feel no sense of personal guilt if a child later veers off course. They have done their best before God. The rest is up to each child himself.

24

PROVERBS 22:6A: TRAIN UP A CHILD?

Ted Hildebrandt

Careful consideration of lexical and contextual factors suggests that "train up a child in the way he should go" needs to be reexamined. The verb "to train" really refers to a bestowal of status and responsibility. The noun translated "child" denotes the status of a late adolescent rather than a child. "In the way he should go" is best understood as "according to what is expected." The original intent then of this verse addresses a late adolescent's entrance into his place in adult society. This should be done with celebration and encouragement—giving him respect, status and responsibilities commensurate with his position as a young adult. This reinterpretation necessitates fresh application of the proverb beyond the concerns of child-rearing.

T rain up a child in he way he should go and when he is old, he will not depart from it" (Prov. 22:6). This proverb has brought encouragement, hope, anxiety, and guilt to countless parents who have

From *Grace Theological Journal* 9, 1 (1988): 3–19. Used by permission.

faced the uncertainty and confusion of child-rearing. It has provided encouragement to those responsible parents who, after working to balance family, relationships, and careers, find reassurance that all of their labors ultimately will not be in vain. This verse has also provided rays of hope to those who, having reared their child in the best way they knew, have had their hearts broken as their child rebels and goes astray. They agonize under the pain that God recognized to be one of the deepest sorrows of human existence (Matt. 23:37; Hos. 11:1–2; Prov. 10:1). To those parents this verse gives hope that when he is old the prodigal will return. Another group of young parents, sensitive to daily feelings of inadequacy, experiences intense anxiety over the possible long-term damage they see themselves doing to their child. If the child does go astray, this verse seems to point the finger of guilt at them.

Assuming that Proverbs 22:6 is a proverb, and not a promise,[1] the first question of interpretation must be: "What did this verse originally mean when it was recorded in the book of Proverbs?"[2]

חֲנֹךְ: Train Up or Initiate?

"Train up" is an initial verbal imperative, found only five times in the Old Testament. The tension between how this word is used elsewhere in Scripture and the alleged pedagogical, semantic component found in the translation "train up" (KJV, NASB, RSV, NIV, TEV [teach]) has been passed over by many commentators.

To Stimulate Desire

Since there are so few uses of חֲנֹךְ in the Old Testament, many have overemphasized etymology and ignored the cautions that Barr has so clearly articulated.[3] With the recent psychological concentration on needs,[4] there has been a renewed emphasis on the alleged etymological root of חֵךְ חָנַךְ (pal-

---

1. W. Mouser, *Walking in Wisdom* (Downers Grove, Ill.: InterVarsity, 1983), 13–14; J. Williams, *Those Who Ponder Proverbs: Aphoristic Thinking and Biblical Literature* (Sheffield: Almond, 1981); N. Barley, "A Structural Approach to the Proverb and Maxim with Special Reference to the Anglo-Saxon Corpus," *Proverbium* 20 (1972): 737–50; "The 'Proverb' and Related Problems of Genre-Definition," *Proverbium* 23 (1974): 880–84; and the classic work on the proverbial form and nature of the proverb, A. Taylor, *The Proverb* (Cambridge: Harvard University Press, 1931).

2. A good example of the errors of putting application before interpretation is Proverbs 29:18, "Where there is no vision the people perish" (KJV). How this verse has been misused for "good causes"! Fortunately, most modern versions (NIV, TEV, LB, RSV) have changed this incorrect understanding.

3. James Barr, *Comparative Philology and the Text of the Old Testament* (Oxford: Clarendon, 1968), 266–67.

4. David Keller, "Child Discipline: A Scriptural View," *The King's Business,* December 1970, 49, and J. A. Walter, *Need: The New Religion* (Downers Grove, Ill.: InterVarsity, 1986).

ate),[5] and on an Arabic cognate (*ḥanakun:* desire). The Arabic image is of a mother preparing date jam which is gently rubbed on the gums of a newborn baby, thereby enhancing the infant's appetite for and ability to digest succulent condiments.[6] Yet to suggest that the assumed etymological root determines or shades the meaning of the word in Proverbs 22:6 is like saying that when one uses the word "cute" it is shaded by its early Elizabethan root meaning of "bow legged." Thus, it cannot be assumed that etymology determines current meaning/usage. One should be doubly leery about reading in a *suggested* etymology [חֵךְ (palate) or *ḥanakun* (desire)] when none of the biblical usages has anything to do with such sensual, cuisinal nuances.

Another way of establishing this oral-appetitive meaning for חָנַךְ is on the basis of the use of פִּי (mouth) in the idiom "mouth of his way" (דַרְכּוֹ). This was possibly used for literary effect in Proverbs 22:6.[7] Such an oral meaning fixation seems unlikely, however, in light of the apparent absence of such inferences elsewhere (Exod. 34:27; Deut. 17:10–11; etc.).

To Train

Most commentators accept, without discussion, the translation of "train up" as the meaning of the word חָנַךְ in Proverbs 22:6.[8] By "train up" is meant the careful nurturing, instructing, and disciplining of the child in an attempt to in-

---

5. BDB (335) and KB (320) take חָנַךְ as denominative from the noun חֵךְ (palate, gums, roof of the mouth). Cf. Gleason Archer, R. L. Harris, B. K. Waltke, eds., *Theological Wordbook of the Old Testament,* vol. 1 (Chicago: Moody, 1980), 301.

6. Both BDB (335) and KB (315) link it to an Arabic cognate *ḥanaka* referring to the rubbing of the palate (gums = *ḥanakun*) of a child with oil and dates before he begins to suck, thus making the material more digestible and palatable (cf. also *TDOT,* v[ol]. 19f.; Delitzsch, *Commentary on the Old Testament,* vol. 6 [Grand Rapids: Eerdmans, 1973], 87). The nexus with Egyptian Execration text (2000 b.c.), *ḥnk.t,* "tribute, offering," or the Neo-Punic, *ḥnkt*(?), "memorial tombstone," is doubtful, as Dommershausen observes (cf. Albright, "The Predeuteronomic Primeval," *JBL* [1939]: 58).

7. James Collins, "A Hermeneutical and Exegetical Examination of Proverbs 22:6" (M.Div. thesis, Grace Theological Seminary, 1983), 29.

8. Toy, *Proverbs* in ICC, 415; McKane, *Proverbs: A New Approach* (Philadelphia: Westminster, 1970), 564; Whybray, *The Book of Proverbs,* in the Cambridge Bible Commentary (Cambridge: Cambridge University Press, 1972), 124; Bridges, *A Commentary on Proverbs* (Carlisle, Penn.: The Banner of Truth Trust, 1846), 402–4; Charles Fritsch, *Proverbs* in *The Interpreter's Bible* (New York: Abingdon, 1955), 907; W. G. Plaut, *Book of Proverbs* (New York: Union of American Hebrew Congregations, 1961), 227–28; Edgar Jones, *Proverbs and Ecclesiastes,* in the Torch Bible Commentaries (London: SCM, 1961), 183–84; Julius Greenstone, *Proverbs with Commentary* (Philadelphia: The Jewish Publication Society of America, 1950), 234–35; T. T. Perowne, *The Proverbs* (Cambridge: Cambridge University Press, 1916), 142; and Otto Zöckler, *The Proverbs of Solomon* in Lange's Commentary (New York: Charles Scribner and Son, 1904), 192. Zöckler illustrates the point with several proverbs ("What little Johnnie does not learn, John learns never" and "Just as the twig is bent the tree's inclined"). Similarly, modern experiments of Piaget ("The Mental Development of the Child" in *Six Psychological Studies by Piaget,* ed. O. Elkind [New York: Random, 1967]), categories of [E. H.] Erikson (*Childhood and Society* [New York: Norton, 1963], 247–74), and the work of others highlight the importance of early childhood training. Many affirm that 85 percent of the child's personality is formed by the time he is 6 years of age. Such findings, chaining early childhood to later life, are held to be supported

culcate a wise and moral character. Such training is frequently mentioned in Proverbs (Prov. 13:24; 19:18; 22:15; 23:13–14; 29:15, 17; cf. Heb. 12:5f.). Consequently, this proverb is cited in support of a plethora of educational and developmental child-rearing philosophies, paradigms, and programs.

The importance of early child training cannot be overemphasized, particularly given the destructiveness of the absent/preoccupied-parent syndrome that plagues American home life. However, until the original meaning of Proverbs 22:6 is explicated, we dare not jump to dynamic, family-focused, modern applications of the verse.

It may be suggested that the discipline/instruction view of חָנַךְ is confirmed by a lone use in Aramaic concerning training for fasting on the Day of Atonement.[9] Modern Hebrew uses synonyms like לָמַד or English glosses like "education" and "apprentice/pupil."[10] In modern Hebrew, חִינּוּךְ means "education."[11] One wonders, however, if such later developments are based on an assumed interpretation of this verse, which has therefore affected the consequent use of this verb in modern times.[12] This verb and its noun forms do not occur elsewhere in Scripture with this discipline/instruction meaning. If instruction was the point, why were the more instructional and frequently-used wisdom verbs not employed (לָמַד, מָסַר, שָׁמַע, יָדַע [Hi])? Or why were there not more generic verbs used (לְקַח, נָתַן) with the usual wisdom nouns attached (e.g., righteousness, wisdom, knowledge, discernment)?

One further tendency should be resisted in developing the semantic components of this word. Every nuance of the word should not be imported into its use in a particular context. Reich, for example, collects several divergent meanings of חָנַךְ (dedication, discipline [train up], desire) and develops each of them in light of early childhood training. Such a technique is to be avoided as a violation of valid semantic theory.[13]

To Dedicate/Initiate

The four other occurrences of "train" (חָנַךְ) in the Old Testament are in contexts of dedicating or initiating the use of buildings. This dedication/ini-

---

by this biblical proverb (see, e.g., Paul Meier, *Christian Child-rearing and Personality Development* [Grand Rapids: Baker, 1977]).

9. Marcus Jastrow, *A Dictionary of the Tarqumim* (New York: Pardis House, 1950), 483.

10. Even-Shoshan, Abraham. המילין העברי (Jerusalem: Qiriyat Sepher), 800; R. Sivan and E. A. Levenston, *The New Bantam-Megiddo Hebrew and English Dictionary* (New York: Schoken, 1977), 91.

11. S. C. Reif, "Dedicated to חנך," *VT* 22 (October 1972): 501. Cf. Sivan and Levenston, *Megiddo Dictionary*, 118.

12. This is not ignoring the fact that modern meanings may be helpful in understanding ancient words (vid. James Barr, *Comparative Philology*, 38–75, 223–37; W. Chomsky, *Hebrew: The Eternal Language* [Philadelphia: 1957], 206–30). Yet, it does make this writer a little reticent—fearing an anachronistic, semantic projection back into the text.

13. William Reich, "Responsibility of Child Training: Proverbs 22:6" (M.Div. thesis, Grace Theological Seminary, 1971), 27, 35–41.

tiation is usually accompanied by great celebration. Deuteronomy 20:5 talks about the initiation of a new house as the reason for a man's not going off to war. The parallel references in 1 Kings 8:63 and 2 Chronicles 7:5 are both in the context of the celebrations surrounding the dedication of the Solomonic temple. Reif follows Rankin when he observes that in Deuteronomy 20:5 the word should be understood as the "initial use of" rather than a formal dedication. Dedication is the moving of an object from the realm of the profane to the realm of the sacred.[14] In ritual contexts, however, both dedication and initial use aspects are closely linked. Since the practice of dedicating houses is not found in the Old Testament or in the later Jewish religious traditions, the dedication interpretation seems less likely in Deuteronomy 20:5. The idea of "initiating the use of" is more consistent with the context.[15]

Reif carefully discerns the cultic use of חָנַךְ in 1 Kings 8:63 (2 Chron. 7:5).[16] Here the cultic setting causes a coalescing of the idea of dedicating the sacred building with the idea of its initial use. While "make holy" (קָדַשׁ) and "anoint" (מָשַׁח) may be more frequently and exclusively used in dedication contexts, they may be sequentially related to the meaning of חָנַךְ (cf. 1 Kings 8:63 and 8:64 where the inner court must be קָרַשׁ before it can be חָנַךְ). The LXX translation ἐγκαινίζω—while etymologically stressing the idea of newness and initial use—has lexical glosses that favor the idea of dedication.[17]

This cultic initiation/dedication use is affirmed through the eight uses of the noun form חֲנֻכָּה which occur exclusively in cult object dedication celebrations (Num. 7:10, 11, 84, 88; 2 Chron. 7:9; Neh. 12:27; Ps. 30:1 [title]). Again in Numbers 7, Reif carefully distinguishes that the "anointing" (מָשַׁח) and "consecrating/dedicating" (קָרַשׁ) come before the "initial use" (חָנַךְ) of the Mosaic altar (cf. Num. 7:1, 10–11, 84, 88).[18] Similarly, Psalm 30:1 is a song that celebrates the initial use of the temple rather than focusing on the dedication of the structure itself. It is interesting that the word for the feast of Hanukkah is derived from the same root and focuses on the Maccabean celebration of the initial use/rededication of the second temple after its being profaned by Antiochus Epiphanes.

The same basic noun form is used four times in biblical Aramaic to describe the initial use/dedication of the second temple (Ezra 6:16–17) and of Nebuchadnezzar's 90-foot image of gold (Dan. 3:2–3). Jastrow also provides ex-

---

14. Reif, "Dedicated to חנך," 495–501; O. S. Rankin, *The Origins of the Festival of Hanukkah: The Jewish New-Age Festival* (Edinburgh, 1930), 27–45; and Reif, "The Festival of Hanukkah," in *The Labyrinth*, ed. S. H. Hooke (London, 1935), 159–209. Also Rashi (M. Rosenbaum and A. M. Silbermann, *Pentateuch . . . with Rashi's Commentary translated into English and Annotated* [London, 1929]; *Genesis*, 57; *Sefer HaShorashim* [Berlin, 1847], 111).

15. *TDOT*, vol. 5, 20.

16. Reif, "Dedicated to חנך," 497.

17. BAGD, 214; LSJ, 469. Cf. Latin *dedicare*.

18. Reif, "Dedicated to חנך," 497ff.

amples of the use of this word by later Jewish sources to describe the dedication of an altar.[19]

In summary, the root חָנַךְ is used as a verb four times other than in Proverbs 22:6. All four are in the context of the celebration of the initiation or dedication of a building (temple). The eight noun uses all have reference to the cultic initiation of material objects (altar/temple/wall). The four uses in biblical Aramaic parallel this usage exactly (idol/second temple). What is to be made of this data, which clearly does not favor the normal pedagogical reading of Proverbs 22:6 as "train up"?

חָנַךְ Analysis

The relationship between wisdom and the cult has been shown not to be mutually exclusive.[20] Nevertheless, importing cultic meaning ("to dedicate") into a proverbial setting is problematic to those who are sensitive to wisdom as a literary genre. Several commentators have realized this problem yet have attempted to include the idea of dedication in their definition of training.[21] The vast majority of writers, however, virtually ignore the above data and simply attach the meaning "train up" to the Hebrew term חָנַךְ with no further comment about the semantic bifurcation.

Barr[22] and others[23] have indicated the hazards of carelessly carrying over components of meaning from one context into another. All of the above usages of חָנַךְ have inanimate objects (altars, houses, temples, walls) as their object. When the word has an animate object, it should not be assumed that the meaning will necessarily be homogeneous. For example, the meaning of the word "runs" will have a different set of semantic components depending on whether it is used for something animate or inanimate: "the boy runs" or "the faucet runs." The question becomes: what does חָנַךְ mean when applied to people? Jastrow provides several examples in postbiblical Aramaic where the term is used of the high priest, who is inaugurated, and Isaac, who was initiated (חָנַךְ) into the covenant on the eighth day.[24] In Genesis 14:14 there is a very important use of חָנַךְ where Abraham rescues Lot by sending out his 318

---

19. Jastrow, *Dictionary,* 483f.

20. For an excellent study on the relationship of wisdom and the cult, vid. Leo Perdue, *Wisdom and the Cult* (Missoula, Mont.: Scholars, 1977), 225–26.

21. Derek Kidner, *Proverbs* (Downers Grove, Ill.: InterVarsity, 1964), 147; Robert Alden, *Proverbs* (Grand Rapids: Baker, 1983), 160; Reich, "Responsibility of Child," 32–35.

22. Barr, *The Semantics of Biblical Language* (London: Oxford University Press, 1961), 144–46.

23. Moisés Silva, *Biblical Words and Their Meaning* (Grand Rapids: Zondervan, 1983); John Lyons, *Semantics* (Cambridge: Cambridge University Press, 1977); Eugene Nida, *Exploring Semantic Structures* (Leiden: Brill, 1975); G. N. Leech, *Semantics* (Harmondsworth, Eng.: Penguin, 1974); F. R. Palmer, *Semantics* (Cambridge: Cambridge University Press, 1981); and John Beekman and John Callow, *Translating the Word of God* (Grand Rapids: Zondervan, 1974), 90–100.

24. Jastrow, *Dictionary,* 483f.

"trained" (חֲנִיכָיו) men. It would be a mistake to think of these men as novices. Rather they seem to be sent out as men who were strong, experienced, and already initiated into military affairs. It is interesting that the Arabic root proposed under "desire" also may be read "make experienced," which fits well the sense here.[25]

Similarly, in the Taanach letters (Akkadian documents dating from just before the Amarna age [fifteenth century B.C.]), Albright has found a complaint from Amenophis of Egypt that Rewassa of Taanach, in the context of mustering troops for war, had not sent his "retainers" (ha-na-ku-u-ka) to greet Amenophis. Thus both in Genesis and in the Akkadian Taanach letters the root חָנַךְ, when applied to people, refers to one who is initiated and experienced, having duties commensurate with his status as a military cadet who has completed his training. What makes this example even more inviting is that later in the Genesis 14 passage these same military cadets (retainers/squires) are called נְעָרִים (14:24).[26] The connection of חָנַךְ with נְעָרִים (young men) is significant because these are the same word roots used in Proverbs 22:6 which are usually translated "train up" and "child."

Thus, while the term later acquired the meaning "to train" in a didactic sense (similar to לָמַד), it is better to see this word as having specific reference to the inauguration process with the bestowal of status and responsibility as a consequence of having completed an initiation process. In short, the word חָנַךְ focuses not so much on the process of training as on the resultant *responsibility* and *status* of the one initiated. This meaning of חָנַךְ in Proverbs 22:6 moves away from a strictly parental admonition for providing the child with good instruction. חָנַךְ will be returned to in order to show how this new initiation interpretation fits into Proverbs 22:6, after discussing the term translated "child" (נַעַר).

נַעַר: Child or Cadet?

The second lexical problem that the interpreter faces in Proverbs 22:6 is how to render the term נַעַר. Who was this נַעַר that was to be initiated with celebration, status, and responsibility? In this verse נַעַר is generally translated "child" (KJV, NIV, NASB, RSV, TEV, NEB, et al.) or "boy" (NAB). MacDonald, in a study based on an analysis of hundreds of Ugaritic and

---

25. *TDOT* [vol. 5], 20; BDB, 335; and Collins, 23.

26. Albright, "A Prince of Taanach in the Fifteenth Century B.C.," *BASOR* 94 (April 1944): 24–25. Cf. *CADH* 6:76. Note also that Montgomery, in working on the name Enoch (*ḥanok*), concludes that if it comes from the same root (Gen. 5:24), it means "initiated" as one who walked with God ("Some Hebrew Etymologies," *JQR* 25 [1934–35]: 261). Similarly, Albright calls him "retainer (of God)" (Albright, "Predeuteronomic," 96).

Hebrew usages, has demonstrated that the age-focused idea of "child" is insufficient for understanding who the נַעַר was.[27]

Status

Looking at the contexts in which the word נַעַר is employed, three things immediately present themselves. First, the age span is so diverse that age cannot be the primary focus of the word. It is used of infancy: for a child yet unborn (Judg. 13:5–12); one just born (1 Sam. 4:21); an infant still unweaned (1 Sam. 1:22); or a three-month-old baby (Exod. 2:6). However, Joseph at 17—already a man in that culture—is also called a נַעַר (Gen. 37:2). When he is 30 years old—surely beyond childhood—he is still called a נַעַר (Gen. 41:12, 46). Thus, MacDonald is correct when he states that the renderings "child, lad, young man, and servant" are "inadequate and produce a totally false impression of the person involved."[28] Second, the נַעַר is frequently active in strictly adult activities (war [1 Sam. 17:33, 42; Judg. 6:12; 8:20]; cultic priestly functions [Judg. 18:3–6, 20]; special spy missions [Josh. 6:22]; personal attendance on a patriarch, prophet, priest, king, or son of a king [Gen. 18:7; 2 Kings 5:1–27; 1 Sam. 1:22, 24–25; 2 Sam. 9:9; 13:17]; or supervision of the whole Solomonic labor force [1 Kings 11:28]). The term נַעַר is often applied to one who is designated as an אִישׁ (man) (2 Sam. 1:5, 10, 13). While he may be a young male, the point is not his age but his societal status and resulting responsibility. Third, there are numerous terms that focus on the age of a young male when age is the point (טַף, יוֹנֵק, עוֹלֵל, עֶלֶם, בֵּן, יֶלֶד).[29] It is not merely with these terms that נַעַר finds its semantic field. Rather, it is equally at home with terms like עֶבֶד (servant) or זָקֵן (elder).

An upper-class role and societal status are consistently ascribed to the נַעַר. MacDonald reports that in the historical books there are no examples of a נַעַר of lowly birth.[30] Thus, whether the נַעַר is just an infant (like Moses [Exod. 2:6], Samuel [1 Sam. 1:22, 24–25], or Samson [Judg. 13:5]) or an adolescent (like Jacob/Esau [Gen. 25:27], Joseph [Gen. 37:2], or Solomon [1 Kings 3:7]), high status is the point—not merely age. Similarly, the feminine נַעֲרָה also means a high-born young female, as can be seen by its usage in reference to Rebekah (Gen. 24:16), Dinah (Gen. 34:3), Pharaoh's daughter (Exod. 2:5), and Queen Esther (Esther 2:4).

27. John McDonald, "The Status and Role of the Na'ar in Israelite Society," *JNES* 35, 3 (1976): 147–70. This article has been summarized briefly also as "The 'Naar' in Israelite Society," *Bible and Spade* (winter 1977): 16–22. The results of this detailed and conclusive study have not yet been utilized for interpretive purposes.
28. MacDonald, "The Status and Role of the Na'ar in Israelite Society," 147.
29. Ibid., 150.
30. Ibid., 149.

Personal Attendant

MacDonald also develops two realms in which the status of the נַעַר may be seen: (1) in the domestic realm; and (2) in military contexts.[31] The נַעַר was frequently a special personal attendant of a person of status. Thus not only was Abraham's נַעַר called on to prepare the special meal for the three heavenly visitors (Gen. 18:7–8), but later Abraham's trusted נְעָרִים accompanied him to mount Moriah for the sacrificing of Isaac (Gen. 22:3). Similarly, Joseph was a נַעַר over Potiphar's household and later came, as a נַעַר, into unique headship over Pharaoh's kingdom (Gen. 41:12). Joshua, as the personal attendant of Moses, was called a נַעַר (Exod. 33:11). When Saul was searching for his father's donkeys he was accompanied by, and listened to the advice of, his נַעַר (1 Sam. 2:17; Ruth 2:5, 21). The point of the above list is to demonstrate that the role of a נַעַר was a personal attendant of a person of status. MacDonald distinguishes between the upwardly mobile status of the נַעַר and the more menial עֶבֶד (servant); the נַעַר could be put in charge over the עֲבָדִים.

Military Cadet

It is significant how frequently the נַעַר is found in military contexts. He is one step above the regular troops, but not yet a mighty warrior such as Joab or Abner. When Joshua had to send out spies—hand-picked men to run reconnaissance on Jericho—he selected two skilled נְעָרִים (Josh. 6:22). Such an important mission would not have been left in the hands of novices. Gideon, the fearful "mighty man of valor" (Judg. 6:12) is told to take his trusted נַעַר and go down to scout out the Midianite camp (Judg. 7:10–11). Thus the seasoned warrior, Gideon, is accompanied by a squire, who, judging from the importance of the mission, is extremely skillful and trustworthy. Jonathan, climbing the cliffs of Wadi Suwenit, took a trusted נַעַר to face the formidable Philistine host. He and his armor-bearer fought and slew 20 men (1 Sam. 14:14). It should be clear that the armor-bearer was himself a warrior, though of inferior status to Jonathan. David, as he faced Goliath, was also designated as a נַעַר—hence the impropriety of his fighting the Philistine champion from Gath (1 Sam. 17:31ff.).

Several points may be derived from the above data. First, it is clear from the military contexts that inexperienced children are not meant. Rather the word designates soldiers with status above the regular troops, yet clearly and sharply distinguished from the heroic warriors like Goliath, Joab, and Abner. The status of the נַעַר is also seen in his personal attendance on a person of status. The word is also used to describe sons of people of status. This usage is particularly important in Proverbs, which is addressed to the royal sons. Status, not age per se, was the focus of נַעַר. While such clear societal structuring

31. Ibid., 151, 156.

is somewhat foreign to the more egalitarian American culture, we dare not ignore it. Class distinctions were clearly marked not only in Israel, but also, as
MacDonald and Rainey have shown, at Ugarit, where the only ancient cognate for the term נַעַר is a term of status used for guild members serving in the
domestic sphere and as superior military figures.[32] Again, the focus is on status, not age. Thus when the messianic king is called a נַעַר, his status and function are being highlighted (Isa. 7:14–16).

נַעַר *in Proverbs*

How does understanding of the role of the נַעַר in Israelite society affect
Proverbs 22:6? Due to various archaeological finds of the last one hundred
years, it is possible to verify the presence of wisdom literature in all of the
major cultures of the ancient Near East (Sumer, Mesopotamia, Ugarit,
Egypt). In each of these cultures, wisdom literature was associated with, written for, and promulgated by the king[33] and his administrators—particularly
the scribes.[34] The situation in Israel was the same, for king Solomon (1 Kings
4:31–32; Prov. 1:1; 10:1) and king Hezekiah (Prov. 25:1) are explicitly associated with the Israelite wisdom tradition. In this royal setting, terms of status,
such as נַעַר, are to be expected. The proverbs helped prepare young squires
for capable service at the head of the Israelite societal structure. Thus the suggestion that נַעַר was a term of status, rather than merely of youthfulness, fits
well with the original setting of proverbial wisdom literature not only in Israel, but also throughout the ancient Near East.

More to the point, however, is how the term נַעַר is actually used in Proverbs and whether its usage there is consistent with how it is used in other literary genres. It is used seven times in Proverbs (1:4; 7:7; 20:11; 22:6, 15;
23:13; 29:15). Proverbs 1:4–5 announces that it is to the נַעַר and to the sim-

32. Ibid., 150. A. F. Rainey, "The Military Personnel of Ugarit," *JNES* 24 (1965): 17–27.
Also vid. the Merneptah Inscription and a fourth century A.D. Samaritan Chronicle that clearly
distinguishes between regular soldiers and the "na'ar" (McDonald, 152).

33. Some helpful treatments of this topic are: Malchow, "The Roots of Israel's Wisdom in
Sacral Kingship"; Leonidas Kalugila, *The Wise King*; Norman W. Porteous, "Royal Wisdom,"
VTSup 3 (1969): 247–61; and Humphreys, "The Motif of the Wise Courtier in the Old Testa-
ment" (Ph.D. dissertation, Union Theological Seminary, 1970). Also vid. Humphrey's article,
"The Motif of the Wise Courtier in the Book of Proverbs," in *Israelite Wisdom: Theological and
Literary Essays in Honor of Samuel Terrien* (Missoula, Mont.: Scholars, 1978), 177–90.

34. A. Leo Oppenheim, "A Note on the Scribes in Mesopotamia," *Assyriological Studies* 16
(1965): 253–56; and R. J. Williams, "Scribal Training in Ancient Egypt," *JAOS* 92 (1972): 214–
21; Benno Landsberger, "Scribal Concepts of Education," in *City Invincible: A Symposium on
Urbanization and Cultural Development in the Ancient Near East*, ed. C. Kraeling and R. M.
Adams (Chicago: University of Chicago Press, 1960), 123–27; A. F. Rainey, "The Scribe at
Ugarit," *Israel Academy of Science and Humanities Proceedings* 3 (1969): 126–46; J. H.
Johnson, "Avoid Hard Work, Taxes, and Bosses: Be a Scribe!" Paper, Oriental Institute, Univer-
sity of Chicago, n.d.; Åke W. Sjoberg, "In Praise of the Scribal Art," *JCS* 14,2 (1972): 126–31;
and Barry Halvorsen, "Scribes and Scribal Schools in the Ancient Near East: A Historical Survey"
(Th.M. thesis, Grace Theological Seminary, 1981).

ple, wise, and discerning that the Book of Proverbs is addressed. Clearly in this context there is no hint that age is the key issue; rather, the נַעַר and simple are grouped together (as are the wise and discerning) *according to their relationship to wisdom*. It is obvious from the message of Proverbs 1–9 (especially chaps. 5 and 7) that the נַעַר was not a child. The very content of the proverbial material (sexual advice [Prov. 5:1–6, 15–21; 31:10–31]; economic counsel [10:5; 11:1]; political instruction [25:6–7; 29:12]; social graces [23:2]; and military advice [24:6]) indicates that the נַעַר was a late adolescent or young adult. In Proverbs 1:4, the issue of the status is not in the foreground, but his need for wisdom. In Proverbs 7:7 the פְּתָאִים (simple) and the נַעַר are again paralleled, with the נַעַר described as one lacking judgment. Proverbs 20:11 tells the נַעַר that his behavior will be noticed and that it will reveal his heart. Proverbs 22:15 speaks of applying the rod of discipline to the נַעַר to drive out folly. The point is that in spite of his naive bent for folly, he can be molded and instructed. Finally, Proverbs 29:15 says that a נַעַר left to himself will disgrace his mother.

Before concluding this analysis of נַעַר, it is worth noting that the נַעַר in 22:6a is paralleled via grammatical transformation (noun/verb) with growing old. Although MacDonald argues that when the נַעַר and זָקֵן (elder) are paralleled they are both terms of societal status, his case is disrupted by his own examples (Ps. 37:25 [cf. also Deut. 28:50]; 148:11–13; Jer. 6:11). While status difference between the נַעַר (squire) and the זָקֵן (elder) may be the point in some cases, it seems that the age component is sometimes more prominent than he is wont to accept. Furthermore, because of the verbal nature of זָקֵן in Proverbs 26:6b, the aging process, rather than rank, seems to be in view.

It should be clear that this verse should not be employed as biblical support for early childhood training, since the proverbial נַעַר was surely an adolescent/young adult. He is a royal squire who is in the process of being apprenticed in wisdom for taking on royal responsibilities consistent with his status as a נַעַר.

"According to His Way"

The Moral View

The third semantic structure (עַל־פִּי דַרְכּוֹ) must be addressed before bringing the assessment of Proverbs 22:6a to a conclusion. There are four views that have been suggested for understanding the meaning of "his way" (דַרְכּוֹ). McKane holds what can be called the narrow "Moral View."[35] He maintains that in wisdom there is one right way, the way of life, and it is to

---

35. McKane, *Proverbs: A New Approach,* 564; cf. also Deane, et al., *Proverbs: The Pulpit Commentary* (Chicago: Wilcox and Follet, n.d.) 422; Collins, "A Hermeneutical and Exegetical Examination of Proverbs 22:6," 30–32; and Alden, *Proverbs,* 160.

this way that the young man is directed. It is this way upon which he should go. The juxtaposing of דֶּרֶךְ with a moral qualifier, whether positive—way of חַיִּים (life) [6:23]; בִּינָה (understanding) [9:6]; טוֹב (good) [2:20]; צְדָקָה (righteousness) [16:31]—or negative—way of רָע (evil) [2:12]; רְשָׁעִים (wicked) [4:19]—is quite common in Proverbs, as McKane observes. However, in these cases דֶּרֶךְ is explicitly accompanied by a character qualifier. A qualifier is given in Proverbs 22:6, but it is not a moralistic one. A similar view, although broader in understanding, is the view held by many that דֶּרֶךְ refers to the broad parental shaping of the child in the דֶּרֶךְ—meaning the general direction of righteousness, wisdom, and life—upon which that child should travel as he grows older.[36] Again the absence of moral or wisdom qualifiers (wise, righteous, upright, foolish, wicked, etc.) leaves this approach without decisive support.

The Vocational View

This view suggests that the training and the דֶּרֶךְ being described are vocationally oriented.[37] However, דֶּרֶךְ is not usually found in a vocational setting. Indeed the modern anxiety over vocational selection and training was not of great concern in the ancient Near East, in that the son often was trained in the same craft as the father.[38] Furthermore, vocational selection is not really an issue in Proverbs. Rather, diligence, righteousness, uprightness, and shrewdness are encouraged regardless of vocation.

The Personal Aptitude View

Many recent commentators have opted for the personal aptitude view.[39] Such an interpretation wisely advises that the parent must be keenly aware of the child's developing capacities, interests, and inclinations and must tailor the training process to enhance his unique abilities. Toy and Oesterley suggest that there is more of an element of fate or destiny. For them, the child should be trained according to the manner of life for which he is destined.[40] Delitzsch is correct in observing that "the way of the Egyptians" is the manner of acting which was characteristic of the Egyptians (Isa. 10:24). The "way of the eagle" (Prov. 30:19) is the manner of movement characteristic to the eagle. But the conclusion drawn from that data is incorrect because נַעַר is read as "child." It is concluded that "his way" means the unique way for *that*

---

36. Zockler, *The Proverbs of Solomon*, 192.
37. Deane, et al., *Proverbs*, 422; and Jones, *Proverbs and Ecclesiastes*, 183f.
38. Collins, "A Hermeneutical and Exegetical Examination of Proverbs 22:6," 31.
39. Kidner, *Proverbs*, 147; Delitzsch, *Commentary*, 86; Oesterly, *The Book of Proverbs* (London: Methuen), 185; and Toy, *Proverbs*, 415–16. McKane also mentions Ringgren as holding this view (*Proverbs: A New Approach*, 564), as well as Perowne (*The Proverbs*, 142). Much earlier it was held by the Jewish writer Saadia (Plaut, *Book of Proverbs*, 228).
40. Oesterley, *The Book of Proverbs with Introduction and Notes*, 185; and Toy, *Proverbs*, 415–16.

child.[41] A suggestion more consistent with the term נַעַר will be offered below. Delitzsch is correct, however, in using נַעַר to specify more clearly what is meant by דֶּרֶךְ.

The Personal Demands View

A small minority of writers have taken "according to his way" in an ironic sense. They suggest that the verse is saying that if you rear a child by acquiescing to his desires and demands, when he is old you will never break him of it. Thus the child, left to himself, will become irretrievably recalcitrant—spoiled, continually demanding his own way.[42] But such a giving up on the נַעַר is opposed to the optimistic outlook that Proverbs has on the teachability of the נַעַר (Prov. 1:4). To the ruggedly individualistic and developmentally sensitive modern mind,[43] the personal aptitude and personal demands views surely are attractive. However, they do not reflect the ancient proverbial *Weltanschauung*.

The Status View

Delitzsch is correct that the meaning of "the way" must be determined by the noun that is the antecedent of the suffix (his). If נַעַר is understood as a high-born squire, then it may be suggested that "according to his way" means according to the office that he will occupy. He is to be "broken-in" (חָנַךְ) as a נַעַר. Thus, "his way" should be the way befitting the dignity of a נַעַר. "His way" should also reflect an awareness of his developmental limitations and need for instruction. This solution fits the Proverbial ethos and is consistent with the above-stated view of who the נַעַר was in the structure of Israelite society.

A Standard of Comparison

The initial part of the prepositional phrase, "according to his way," should be read "according to the measure of his way."[44] It is used quite frequently with reference to the measure or standard of the words of Pharaoh (Gen. 45:21), Yahweh (Exod. 17:1; Num. 3:16, 39), Moses (Exod. 38:21), and Pharaoh Necho (2 Kings 23:35). In a more abstract sense, it is used when one is measured against a standard, whether it be words (Exod. 34:27), what the vower is able to pay (Lev. 27:8), or the Law (Deut. 17:11). Thus it fits very well with initiating a נַעַר in accordance with the standard of who he is and what he is to become as a נַעַר.

41. Delitzsch, *Commentary*, 86f.
42. Ralbag as recorded in Greenstone, *Proverbs with Commentary*, 234.
43. E. H. Erikson, *Childhood and Society* (New York: Norton, 1963), 247–77.
44. BDB, 805; and Collins, "A Hermeneutical and Exegetical Examination of Proverbs 22:6," 33–34.

Conclusion

Options

A graph of the options presented in this chapter provides a three-dimensional perspective on the choices. The more probable choices are given higher positions on the axes.

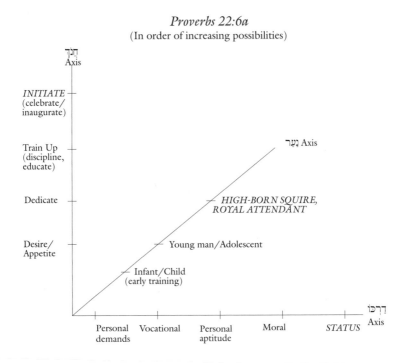

Proverbs 22:6a
(In order of increasing possibilities)

What was the original intent of the verse? Several negative features must set the stage. Proverbs 22:6 is not a promise; it is a proverb and as such it does not describe truth comprehensively. Rather, it gives a single component of truth that must be fit together with other elements of truth in order to approximate the more comprehensive, confused patterns of real life. Second, this verse should not be seen as a paradigm for a comprehensive parental or educational process of instruction into which a particular theory of instruction or child-rearing may be read. Third, this verse should not be employed as direct biblical support for early childhood training since the proverbial נַעַר was not an infant. Fourth, the phrase "according to his way" should not be understood as addressing developmental or personal aptitude issues, although obviously in child-rearing such parental sensitivities are crucial.

Suggested Interpretation

It is apparent that the usual translation of "child" for נַעַר is inadequate. The primary focus of נַעַר was his high-born status as a squire. In Proverbs the נַעַר is a late adolescent/young adult. Furthermore, the word usually translated "train up" (חָנַךְ) was shown to be used almost universally with the dedication/initiation of temples, houses, altars, or walls. Thus to חָנַךְ a young squire would be to recognize his status as a נַעַר and initiate him into his official capacities/responsibilities with the respect and excitement fitting his status. "According to his way" meant according to the standard and status of what would be demanded of the נַעַר in that culture. Thus the squire's status is to be recognized and his experience, training, and subsequent responsibilities are to reflect that high stature. Finally, this interpretation fits well in the context (Prov. 22:1–9) which talks about societal relationships and responsibilities, particularly of the wealthy.[45]

What are the advantages of this interpretation? First, it makes sense of several difficult lexical problems that have formerly been ignored. Second, it fits the ethos of the Proverbial and wisdom materials. Third, it fits the words חָנַךְ, נַעַר, and דֶּרֶךְ into a coherent whole.

Dynamic Modern Potentialities

Does the above interpretation of original intent destroy all modern application? The child-rearing interpretation has been so convenient and potent in addressing a major concern of many parents. Can this verse, with this proposed interpretation, provide for our world the dynamic interpersonal power that it must have originally evoked? First, the נַעַר was the one being initiated and being given the recognition of the status which his title bestowed on him. Does this not teach that in initiating an adolescent into a position, the young person should be given the respect and dignity due the title under which he is being trained? If given that type of recognition, he will willingly continue his services when he gets older because he has gained in that position the dignity, respect, and responsibility which provide him a healthy level of satisfaction.

This idea of initiating someone with an appropriate level of dignity, respect, and responsibility also fits well in a familial setting. The late adolescent (נַעַר) should be treated with dignity and respect in view of creation (Gen. 2) and redemption (Rev. 20, etc.). Thus he should be given experience, training, status, and responsibilities correspondent to his role in the kingdom of God. An adolescent should be initiated into the adult world with celebrations. His status as a redeemed image bearer should demand parental involvement in terms of opening horizons, patient instruction, and loving discipline. It is his do-

---

45. Roland Murphy cogently shows how Prov. 22:1–9 centers around the theme of riches. "Proverbs 22:1–9," *Int* 41,4 (1987): 398–402.

minion, destiny, and status that the parent must keep in mind. The parent must not violate the adolescent's personhood by authoritarian domination, permissive allowance of immaturity, or overprotection from the consequences of his actions.

This verse also teaches that when someone engages in an activity for the first time, a celebration of the event would encourage him in the correct path (e.g., Jewish Bar-Mitzvah celebrations). Thus, a word or deed of encouragement (recognition and celebration) that bestows respect and responsibility commensurate with status is one of the most powerful aspects of parental involvement in the life of an adolescent. It is also effective for employer/employee relationships.[46]

These initial attempts at dynamically understanding this verse in light of modern relational structures suggest that a reinterpretation of a verse in its original setting need not eliminate dynamic applications. Both careful interpretation and application are critical if God's Word is to be unleashed in a world that is in desperate need of a word of wisdom from the Sovereign of the Universe.

46. Rudolf Dreikurs, *Children: The Challenge* (New York: Hawthorn/Dutton, 1964), 36–56. Larry Crabb and Dan Allender, *Encouragement: The Key to Caring* (Grand Rapids: Zondervan, 1984).

25

THE TEACHING OF AMENEMOPE AND ITS CONNECTION WITH THE BOOK OF PROVERBS

John Ruffle

Historical Introduction

It is a curious fact that the announcement of the discovery of the *Teaching of Amenemope* was in connection with an Old Testament *crux*. Renouf[1] cited a passage as a possible clue to the meaning of אברך (Gen. 40:43) in the same year (1888) Budge[2] recorded the purchase of the Papyrus in Egypt and although Renouf's use of it has not been accepted, the *Teaching* has remained of immense interest to Old Testament scholars ever since. After these two brief mentions, the papyrus received no more attention until 1922 when Budge[3] published a description of its contents and considerable portions of the text in transcription and translation. In his publication of the complete manuscript a year later, he briefly noted[4] one or two passages similar in thought to passages from the Book of Prov-

From *Tyndale Bulletin* 28 (1977): 29–68. Used by permission.

1. Renouf, L. (1888) *PSBA* 2, 6.
2. Budge, E. A. W. (1888) *By Nile and Tigris,* I, London, 337.
3. Budge, E. A. W. (1922) *Recueil d'Études Égyptologiques dédiées à la memoire de Jean-Francois Champollion* Paris, 431–46.
4. Budge, E. A. W. (1923) *Facsimiles of Egyptian Hieratic Papyri in the British Museum* 2d series London, 9–18, 41–51, pls. I–XIV.

erbs and a popular account of the *Teaching*, published two years later,[5] contained speculation on how this similarity might be explained.

Another work[6] appeared in 1924, claiming a closer connection than Budge had allowed and suggesting how it had originated. Erman demonstrated that the *Teaching of Amenemope* was closely parallel with the portion of Proverbs sometimes subtitled "Words of the Wise" (22:17–24:22) and claimed that it was possible to use the Egyptian text to elucidate the *crux* in Proverbs 22:20. Budge believed that *Amenemope* contained ideas[7] of Semitic origin but Erman reversed the direction of the connection and claimed that Proverbs 22:17–24:22 were the work of a Jewish scribe translating the Egyptian book with suitable adaptations to make it acceptable to his fellow Hebrews.

Erman's article aroused great interest in the work throughout the world of Old Testament studies. Articles appeared in a multitude of journals, all following Erman's thesis and adding more and more examples of parallels to the seven which he had modestly proposed. Indeed it looked remarkably as though an academic parlour game of "Spot the Parallel" was in progress, with marks awarded for each ingenious parallel suggested and bonus points for emendations of the text. Typical of these articles is the work of Gressmann,[8] based on Erman's[9] and Lange's[10] German translations.[11] He was able not only to find in Proverbs 22:17–24:22 the thirty sections to which Erman's emended text of 2:20 referred but also to link each one of these sections with a chapter in *Amenemope*. The principal English work at this time was a translation by Griffith[12] linked with a study of the parallel passages by Simpson who differed from Erman in suggesting that the evidence pointed to the fact that "the proverbial literature of the Near East knows no national boundaries" and that both Egyptian and Hebrew writers had drawn on this common stock of wisdom material.[13]

These different accounts of the origin of the similarity were developed by Oesterley[14] and Humbert[15] but the difference of opinion did not in-

---

5. Budge, E. A. W. (1924) *The Teaching of Amen-em-Apt, Son of Kanekht* London.

6. Erman, A. (1924a) *Sitzungsberichte der Prussischen Akademie der Wissenschaften* (Sitzung der philosophisch—historischen Klass vom 1 Mai) 15, 86–93.

7. Budge, E. A. W. (1924) 103.

8. Gressman, H. (1923a) *Vossiche Zeitung* Nr 294 (2nd June) 2f and (1924b) *ZAW* n.f. 1, 272–96 (reviewed by Weill. J. (1925) *Rev. des Etudes Juives*, 80. 1, 108–12).

9. Erman, A. (1924b) *OLZ* 27 241–52.

10. Lange, H. O. (1924) *Nordisk Tidskrift udgifret of Letterstedska Foreninger* 94–107 and (1925) *Das Weisheitsbuch des Amenemope aus dem Papyrus 10474 des British Museum* (Series Det kgl Danske Videnskabernes Selskab Historisk-filogisk Meddelelser 11, 2 Copenhagen).

11. See also Sellin, E. (1924) *OLZ* 45 n.f. 1 26 cols. 1873–1884.

12. Griffith, F. Ll. (1926) *JEA* 12, 191–231.

13. Simpson, D.C. (1926) *JEA* 12, 232–39.

14. Oesterley, W. O. E. (1927a) *The Wisdom of Egypt and the Old Testament* London and (1927b) *ZAW*, 45 n.f. 4, 9–24.

15. Humbert, P. (1929) *Récherches sur les Sources Égyptiennes de la Litterature Sapientiale d'Israel* Neuchatel.

volve any doubt about the relationship of the two texts and few hesitated to use the Egyptian text as a basis for emendation of the Hebrew. A note of caution and disbelief was introduced by the articles of Brunet[16] and Herzog[17] but they appear not to have received any serious consideration in academic circles and the situation described by Gardiner in 1942 in the first edition of the *Legacy of Egypt* was of "complete unanimity" on the dependence of Proverbs on *Amenemope*.[18] Gardiner's claim was not entirely true however, for in addition to the work of Brunet and Herzog, Oesterley,[19] writing in the same book as Gardiner, had once again proposed the theory of a common source and yet another point of view had been expressed by Kevin, who claimed that the Egyptian sage had relied on a Semitic original and that his work was limited to making an Egyptian adaptation of the *Words of the Wise*.[20] With the introduction of this theory most of the possible permutations had been covered. Kevin's theory was poorly argued however and the weight of opinion was clearly behind either a hypothetical common source or borrowing from the Egyptian text. In 1951 Baumgartner suggested that the common source had been abandoned as a working hypothesis, claiming that "the theory that Amenemope is original of Proverbs 22:17–23:11 has now been generally accepted."[21] The attempt to dispute this historical connection between the two texts, or to trace both back to an earlier Hebrew collection of proverbs had been given up.

It was, therefore, a bubble of considerable size which Drioton attempted to prick when he suggested that it was the Egyptian text which was borrowed and traced it back to a Semitic original from which it might be assumed that the compiler of Proverbs had also drawn his material.[22] Drioton's argument followed the lines of Kevin's, pointing to difficulties in the Egyptian text which could be resolved if it were assumed that they arose out of attempts by a not over-bright scribe to render a Semitic text into Egyptian. Kevin had been completely ignored but an Egyptologist of Drioton's stature could not be brushed aside so easily. Even so, his theory was at once challenged by several scholars and it is clear that the weight of opinion is solidly against him. His philological arguments were effectively answered by R. J. Williams[23] and

16. Brunet, A. (1949) *Sciences Écclesiastiques* 1, 19–40.

17. Herzog, D. (1929) *Zeitschrift für Semitistik und verwandte Gebiete* 7, 124–60.

18. Gardiner, A. H. (1942) (Ed. S. R. K. Glanville) *Legacy of Egypt* Oxford 62–72.

19. Oesterley, W. O. E. (1942) *ibid* 246–48.

20. Kevin, R. O. (1930) *Journal of the Society of Oriental Research* 14, 115–57.

21. Baumgartner, W. (1951) (Ed. H. H. Rowley) *The Old Testament and Modern Study* Oxford 210–37.

22. Drioton, E. (1959a) *Mélange Bibliques* (Andre Robert Festschrift) Paris 254–80 and (1959b) *Sacra Pagina: Miscellanea Biblica Congressus Internationalis Catholici de re Biblica* 1 Paris, 229–41 (= *Bibliotheca Ephemeridum Theologicarum Lovaniensum* 12–13).

23. Williams, R. J. (1961) *JEA* 47 100–106.

B. Couroyer[24] and his suggestion that the borrowing was made in an Israelite colony in Egypt in the VIIth century B.C.[25] has been ruled out by the discovery of two more manuscripts confirming, if confirmation were needed, the much earlier date of the Egyptian text.

The interest which Drioton's theories aroused rapidly abated once they were refuted and it seemed to be generally assumed that it was reasonable to revert to the *status quo*. In 1964 for instance, Gray[26] in his commentary on 1 and 2 Kings twice referred to "the incorporation of a section of the Wisdom of Amenemope in the Book of Proverbs" and Helck says, "that Proverbs 22:17–23:11 is largely dependent on the Teaching of Amenemope is now generally accepted."[27]

There does now seem to be, however, a more cautious note creeping into the various discussions of the relationship and noticeably less tendency to emend the Hebrew text to conform to the Egyptian. In her recent study, Irene Grumach has restated the earlier idea of a common source on which both Amenemope and Proverbs 22:17–23:11 are based.[28] The wheel seems to have turned full circle but it remains to be asked whether any corresponding progress has been achieved.

Date and Authorship of the Two Works

The full text of the *Teaching of Amenemope* is preserved on a papyrus in the British Museum (B.M. 10474). It has recently been skillfully conserved and there are very few places where the reading is in doubt. The hieratic is neat and regular with only a few strange signs, and can be dated between the XXIInd and XXVIth Dynasties, i.e., between 950 and 650 B.C. The layout of the text is worthy of comment; after a long introduction the text is divided up into chapters which are marked off with headings: First chapter, Second chapter, etc. and these and a few other lines are in rubrics. More importantly, the text is not arranged continuously but in lines that we would describe as verse. The lines are of varying length but the parallelism and poetic form of the content is clear and corresponds almost exactly to the physical lines of the text.

An ostracon in the Cairo Museum, copied by Professor J. Černý but now seemingly untraceable in the Museum storerooms, originally seems to have contained the text of chapter 1 and first part of chapter 2. Professor Černý, whose authority on this subject is unquestionable, told me that he dated this ostracon to the late XXIst or possibly early XXIInd Dynasty.

24. Couroyer, B. (1961a) *RB* 67 208–24, 395–400.
25. Drioton, E. *À la Recontre de Dieu* (A. Gelin Festschrift).
26. Gray, J. (1964) *I & II Kings* London 140, 2d ed. (1970) 146f.
27. Helck, W. (1968/9) *AfO* 22, 26.
28. Grumach, I. (1972) *Untersuchungen zur Lebenslehre des Amenemope* (Münchner Ägyptologische Studien, heft 32) Munich.

A similar date has been suggested by B. J. Peterson for a fragmentary sheet of papyrus in the Medelhausmuseet in Stockholm which carries two columns of text partially covering chapters 7 to 11.[29] Besides these copies there are three writing boards, one in Turin, one in the Louvre and one in the Pushkin Museum in Moscow.[30] The Turin writing board (no. 6237) preserves the bulk of chapters 24–26 and, with only one exception, follows exactly the same line division as the B.M. text. It is interesting that, as well as preserving these divisions, there are marginal signs reading Day 4, Day 8, Day 10, Day 12, and Day 18, irregularly spaced but possibly indicating set portions for a pupil's study. The text is very closely related to the B.M. text but Griffiths' suggestion that the Turin scribe used the B.M. text as an exemplar is stretching credibility.

Very little can be made of the Moscow board beyond identifying the text as parts of chapters 4 and 5, and the Louvre board contains 3 lines from the Introduction. Posener has shown that these boards belong to a class that can be dated to the XXVth Dynasty, c. 750–650 B.C.[31]

Finally, a graffito from Medinet Habu,[32] the temple of Ramesses III at Thebes, and a second writing board in Turin,[33] both preserve the first line or title of our text.

The XXIInd Dynasty date of the Stockholm and B.M. papyri and the Cairo ostracon indicate a date for the composition before 1,000 B.C. Although some of the internal evidence, the vocabulary, orthography, and grammar often suggests a later date, yet there are some examples of these same three points which would seem to follow Middle Kingdom usage of about 1,800 B.C. Most of the personal names were in use by the XVIIIth Dynasty and common in the XXth and, although Horem ma'akheru, the name of the son of Amenemope for whom the Teaching was written, is not otherwise found before the Late Period, the name of the scribe of the B.M. papyrus, Senu, is not otherwise found after the XXth Dynasty. The use of the *Teaching* as a school text in Dynasty XXV suggests that it was established as a classic during the Ramesside period if not earlier and on the basis of the Stockholm and Cairo copies, even an XVIIIth Dynasty date would be acceptable.

Few Egyptologists would dispute that the *Teaching* was cast in its present form by a scribe called Amenemope but Old Testament scholars are less happy about the ascriptions of the authorship of Proverbs to Solomon (Prov. 1:1; 10:1; 25:1) although it is difficult to see why this should be so.

29. Peterson, B. J. (1966) *JEA* 52, 120–28.
30. Posener, G. (1966) *Rev d'Eg*, 18, 45–65.
31. *Ibid.*
32. Edgerton (1937) *Medinet Habu Graffiti Facsimiles* (OIP 36) pl. 10 no. 30.
33. Posener, G. (1973) *Rev d'Eg*, 25, 251–52.

R. B. Y. Scott is unhappy about Solomon's authorship because, apart from the actual ascriptions in the Book of Proverbs, the "tradition" rests on the description of his achievements in 1 Kings which includes passages containing so many superlatives that they "must be recognized as legendary by any sober historian."[34] But must we, by the same token, dismiss the claims of a many-sided genius like Imhotep, a vizier, doctor, compiler of one of the first medical texts, architect and engineer, designer and builder of the Step Pyramid, who also managed to find time to put together a wisdom book which was sufficiently important to be listed among the top 8 works of literature by a New Kingdom scribe? If Imhotep is too remote, perhaps an artist, soldier, historian, and statesman like Sir Winston Churchill might be a better example.

Perhaps part of the problem lies in the use of the word "author." It would, I believe, be quite unreasonable to argue that one man actually composed all the maxims to be found in this book and it is better to talk of a "compiler" than an "author," who assembled together a collection of current folk proverbs such as

A soft tongue can break a bone (Prov. 25:15),
A door turns on its hinges, a sluggard on his bed (Prov. 26:14),

and other epigrams from other sages whose teaching he was willing to incorporate into his own, the men referred to in Proverbs 22:17 and 24:23 as "the wise."

But there is also much linking material, advising the hearer of the value of paying attention to the precepts and longer passages where what might have been a relatively simple proverb such as Proverbs 3:14 "Wisdom is more profitable than silver," has been expanded, the metaphor developed and the whole built up into a short homily. To this extent one can talk of an author and I really do not see why this work could not be undertaken if not by Solomon at least by a scribe working directly under his supervision. The counselors and scribes whom David and Solomon gathered around them and who are frequently mentioned in Samuel and Kings (2 Sam. 8:17; 15:37; 20:25; 1 Kings 4:3; 2 Kings 22:8–10; etc.) are the sort of men who could well be set to such a task.

The Solomonic date for this enterprise is supported by stylistic and linguistic parallels in the Canaanite and Ugaritic literature of the late Bronze Age.[35]

The note at Proverbs 25:1 about the transmission of the following five chapters and the explicit attribution of the final two chapters to other sources suggest an intention to ensure that the book is correctly ascribed. There

---

34. Scott, R. B. Y. (1974) *Proverbs Ecclesiastes* (Anchor Bible) New York, 11.
35. Albright, W. F. (1960) *Wisdom in Israel and in the Ancient Near East* Leiden (*VTSup* 3) 1–15; Storey, C. I. K. (1945) *JBL* 64, 319–37; Kitchen, K. A. (1978) *TB* 28.

seems to be no logical reason to discount this in favor of any substantial editing at a later date.

General Points of Connection

It is plain that Proverbs, along with other biblical wisdom books, has much in common with the wisdom writings of other parts of the ancient Near East. Wisdom literature is one of the most important classes of texts from the ancient civilizations of Egypt and Mesopotamia and sufficient examples survive to illustrate both the different national or cultural preferences and, at the same time, the underlying similarity of thought and expression.

The different preferences can be seen from the fact that various types of wisdom were not apparently universally equally popular. In the various cultures there appear to be differing preferences for certain forms and differing emphases or degrees of interest in certain subjects. Mesopotamian wisdom,[36] for instance, includes several collections of folk proverbs while in the Egyptian and Hebrew corpus there are only isolated examples quoted in stories or letters, and the evident enthusiasm of Mesopotamian writers for contrived debates or literary contests between two entities such as Summer and Winter, Bird and Fish, or Silver and Copper, is not shared by the Hebrew and Egyptian writers.

It is difficult to know to what extent these apparent preferences are simply due to the accident of survival. There are, for instance, no known examples of fables from Egypt before Dynasty XXVI (*c.* 650 B.C.) though they are known from Mesopotamia and the Old Testament (Judg. 9:7–15; 2 Kings 14:9; Isa. 10:15; 24:16; etc.) yet there are papyri of Ramesside date (Dynasty XXI–XXII) which contain pictures of animals playing musical instruments and games like chess, or hunting or driving each other in scenes reminiscent of Aesop's fables. This may well indicate that the fables existed, and may even have been written down, but the texts either have not survived or have not yet been discovered.

In one important aspect, the contents of Hebrew wisdom literature can be distinguished from that of the surrounding nations. Many writers have pointed out that, in contrast to the Mesopotamian and Egyptian sages who usually stress the material advantages of following their advice, Hebrew חכמה is a whole way of life or attitude of mind that is most concisely summed up in the text that appears on the foundation stone of Tyndale Library—The Fear of the Lord is the Beginning of Wisdom. (Prov. 9:10).

---

36. In this article I have used the adjective "Mesopotamian" as a blanket term to cover both Sumerian and Akkadian wisdom literature. The Sumerian texts that we have all date from about 2,500 B.C. onwards and were apparently accepted in the traditional scribal corpus.

If we have to be cautious about differences of form and content we can be more affirmative about the similarities of thought and expression where the subject matter does coincide. The similarities become particularly noticeable in the class of wisdom literature to which Proverbs and *Amenemope* belong. The folk wisdom enshrined in these collections of precepts is the distillation of the accumulated experience of related peoples with cognate languages living in similar circumstances and meeting comparable situations. It is not surprising that they have much in common; it would be noteworthy indeed if their reactions were particularly disparate. In fact, much of this wisdom relates to the community of experience shared not only by the inhabitants of the ancient Near East but by all men everywhere. It is, in short, good sense.

Leaving aside for the time being "the Words of the Wise," the similarities of thought and expression identified by such writers as Erman, Gressmann, and Simpson between the remaining chapters of Proverbs and *Amenemope* can be matched by other passages from Hebrew, Egyptian, and Mesopotamian literature. This becomes clear at all levels from the structural passages which give the works their basic form, through the general and specific content of the books to the details of vocabulary and figurative imagery.

It is not surprising that there should be similarity between the structural passages and that many books should begin with an injunction like Amennakht:

> Pay attention, and listen to my words, Do not pass over what I say
>
> > (*Teaching of Amennakht*, 3–4).[37]

Amenemope's words

> Give your ears, listen to the things which are spoken
> Give your mind to interpret them
>
> > (*Teaching of Amenemope* iii. 9–10)[38]

are typical of this injunction and there are several parallels in Proverbs (e.g., 1:1–7; 3:1; 4:1–2; 10:20; 5:1; 7:1–3; etc.) and in other wisdom texts, for example,

> Give ear, O my people, to my law:
> Incline your ears to the words of my mouth
>
> > (Psalm 78:1).

---

37. Posener, G. (1955) *Rev d'Eg* 10, 61–72; Lichtheim, M. (1976) *Ancient Egyptian Literature* (Berkeley) 2, 176–78.
38. Simpson, W. K. (1973) *The Literature of Ancient Egypt*, New Haven 241–65; Lichtheim, M. (1976) 2, 146–63.

Nor is it surprising that they should stress the value of their advice: Amene-mope's self-recommendation

> If you spend your time with these things in your heart
> You will find it a success
> You will find my words a storehouse of life
> And your body will prosper on earth

> (*Teaching of Amenemope* iii, 17–iv, 2)

has several parallels in Proverbs, for example, Proverbs 2:20–22; 3:1, 2; 4:10 etcetera, but they are not only two books to urge their own worth. One of the first known wisdom writers, the Egyptian Old Kingdom vizier Ptahhotep, claims:

> If you listen to the things which I have told you
> All your plans will be advanced (?)
> Their truth is their value
> Their memory passes from the mouths of men (i.e., they are quoted from memory)
> Because of the value of their precepts

> (*Teaching of Ptahhotep* 507–11).[39]

In fact Ptahhotep and Amenemope both use the same words to describe this process:

> May you join me, your body *(ḥrt)* being prosperous *(wḏz)* on earth

> (*Teaching of Ptahhotep* 637),

> (If you attend to these instructions)
> . . . your body *(ḥrt)* will prosper *(wḏz)* on earth

> (*Teaching of Amenemope* iv, 2).

Still on this question of general form, many of the writers also impart their advice as from a father to his son. This is made very explicit in the *Teaching of Ptahhotep* where he explains how the king allowed him to set up a school in which to teach his own son and those of other courtiers, and W. G. Lambert has shown that in the scribal guilds of Mesopotamia the teacher-pupil rela-

39. Simpson, W. K. (1973) 159–76; Lichtheim, M. (1973) *Ancient Egyptian Literature* (Berkeley) 1, 61–80.

tionship was often expressed as father-son.[40] The pattern lasts from Ptahhotep through to Ahiqar and both Amenemope and Proverbs conform to it.

Nor is it any more surprising that most books give similar advice about subjects of general interest. It is, for instance, wrong to mock the afflicted:

> Whoso mocketh the poor reproacheth his Maker:
> And he that is glad at calamity shall not be unpunished
>
> (Proverbs 18:5)

is often compared with

> Do not laugh at a blind man nor scorn a dwarf
> Nor spoil the plan of a lame man
> Do not scorn a man who is the hand of God
> Nor be fierce of countenance towards him when he has erred
>
> (*Teaching of Amenemope* xxiv, 9–12),

but the thought also occurs in Mesopotamian wisdom

> Do not insult the downtrodden and . . .
> Do not sneer at them autocratically
> With this a man's god is angry
> It is not pleasing to Shamash, who will repay him with evil
>
> (*Counsels of Wisdom* 57–60).[41]

Protection of the poor is also important: the Egyptian writer Khakheper-resonb reminds us that

> There is no champion for the wretched to rescue him from one stronger than himself
>
> (*Lament of Khakheperresonb* Vs. 4),[42]

and Rekhmire claimed on his autobiographical tomb stele as one of his many virtues

> I judged poor and rich (alike), I rescued the weak (lit. the broken of arm) from the strong.
>
> (*Rekhmire, Biographical Inscription,*

40. Lambert, W. G. (1957) *JCS* 11, 1–14 and 112 and (1960) *Babylonian Wisdom Literature* Oxford 13–14.
41. Lambert (1960) 96–107.
42. Simpson, W. K. (1973) 230–33.

line 20).[43]

This helps to put into context the parallel claimed between Proverbs 22:22 and *Teaching of Amenemope* iv, 4–5. . . .
Rather it is right to give alms, and it will meet with divine approval:

Withhold not good from them to whom it is due,
When it is in the power of thine hand to do it.

(Proverbs 3:27)

Do not refuse your hand to one whom you do not know who comes to you in
    mortal poverty.

(*Teaching of Ani* v, 10).[44]

Do not eat bread while another stands (by) and you do not stretch out your
    hand towards the bread for him. He will know it (or perhaps: it will be
    known) for eternity.

(*Teaching of Ani* viii, 3).

The one begging for alms honour, clothe;
Over this his god rejoices.

(*Counsels of Wisdom* 61–65).

Several writers are concerned with a normal family life:

A virtuous woman is a crown to her husband:
But she that maketh ashamed is as rottenness in his bones.

(Proverbs 12:4)

If you are a man of standing, found in a house,
Love your wife as is proper. . .
Keep her from getting control.

(*Teaching of Ptahhotep* 325–26, 332),

and they warn particularly about the dangers of involvement with the strange
woman of Proverbs 2:16

To deliver thee from the strange woman,

43. Davies, N de G. (1943) *The Tomb of Rekhmire at Thebes* New York 81.
44. Lichtheim (1976) 135–46.

Even from the stranger which flattereth with her words;

(Proverbs 2:16)

Beware of the woman from abroad, who is not known in her town.

(*Teaching of Ani* iii, 13)

Family life includes of course proper respect for parents, which seems to include caring for your aged mother:

. . . despise not thy mother when she is old

(Proverbs 23:22b)

Double the food which you give to your mother, and carry her as she carried you.

(*Teaching of Ani* vii, 19)

and helping home your drunken father!

Give your hand to an old man who is sated with beer,
Respect him as his children (would).

(*Teaching of Amenemope* xxv, 8–9)

(A good son is one)
Who takes his hand in drunkenness;
Who carries him when sated with wine.

(*II Aqht* i,31).[45]

Reliability in a messenger is recommended by both Proverbs and Ptahhotep:

As the cold of snow in the time of harvest, so is a faithful messenger to them
    that send him;
For he refresheth the soul of his masters.

(Proverbs 25:13)

If you are a confidant
Whom one noble sends to another,
Be completely reliable when he sends you,
Carry out the message as it was spoken.

(*Teaching of Ptahhotep* 145–48)

45. Gibson, J. C. L. (1978) *Canaanite Myths and Legends* Edinburgh, 104.

If an official sends you on an errand, deliver it as he said it.
Do not take from it or add to it. He who leaves (a message alone) produces joy.

(*Teaching of Kheti, son of Duauf* x,3)[46]

as is also a proper degree of attention from an official towards a petitioner:

Whoso stoppeth his ears at the cry of the poor,
He also shall cry, but shall not be heard.

(Proverbs 21:13)

It is not (necessary) that everything which (a petitioner) asks should come to
pass, but a good hearing is soothing to the heart.

(*Teaching of Ptahhotep* 275–76)

and other Egyptian writers agree that a soft answer turns away wrath:

Do not raise an outcry against the one who has attacked you. . .
The rash man in his hour,
Withdraw before him, leave him alone
God knows how to answer him.

(*Teaching of Amenemope* iv, 10 and v,
15–16)

Do not speak evil to one who attacks you (?). Your voice on the day of a brawl,
let it remain in your heart. You will find it good when the time for bearing
affliction comes to you.

(*Teaching of Ani* vi, 15–vii, 1)

Let him beat you, with your hand in your bosom
Let him curse you, while you keep silence.

(*Teaching of Amenemope* xxvi, 2:3)

The writer of the *Counsels of Wisdom* advises returning good for evil in line
with Proverbs 25:21 and *Amenemope* XXII 3–8:

If thine enemy be hungry, give him bread to eat;
And if he be thirsty, give him water to drink.

(Proverbs 25:21)

---

46. Simpson, W. K. (1973) 329–36; Lichtheim (1973) 184–92.

Do not return evil to the man who disputes with you;
Requite with kindness your evil-doer,
Maintain justice to your enemy,
Smile on your adversary.
If your ill-wisher is . . . nurture him.
Do not set your [mind] on evil.

(*Counsels of Wisdom* 41–46)

and it is better to avoid other people's quarrels:

He that passeth by, and vexeth himself with strife belonging not to him,
Is like one that taketh a dog by the ears.

(Proverbs 26:17)

Do not loiter where there is a dispute
For in the dispute they will have you as a testifier
Then you will be made their witness,
And they will bring you a lawsuit not your own to affirm.
When confronted with a dispute, go your way; pay no attention to it.

(*Counsels of Wisdom* 32–36)

Lying and slander are abhorrent to Hebrew, Egyptian, and Babylonian writers.

He that hideth hatred is of lying lips;
And he that uttereth a slander is a fool.

(Proverbs 10:18)

Do not act as witness to a false statement,
Or remove another man by your tongue.

(*Teaching of Amenemope* 16, 1)

Do not utter libel, speak what is of good report.
Do not say evil things, speak well of people.
One who utters libel and speaks evil.
Men will waylay him with his debit account to Shamash.

(*Counsels of Wisdom* 127–30)

One who utters slander, who is guilty of backbiting,
Who spreads vile rumours about his equal,
Who lays malign charges against his brother, . . .

(Only a portion of the text is preserved; the lines quoted apparently belong to a list of evil-doers.)

(Hymn to Ninurta obverse, 5–9)[47]

Lack of sincerity was frowned upon:

> Do not speak with a man insincerely,
> That is the abomination of God.
> Do not separate your heart from your tongue,
> Then all your plans will be successful.

(Teaching of Amenemope xiii, 15–18)

> With a friend and comrade do not speak . . .
> Do not speak hypocrisy, (utter) what is decent.

(Counsels of Wisdom 148–49)

> Do not converse (with a tale) bearer,
> Do not consult (with a . . .) . . . who is an idler;
> In (your) good grace you will become as a mind for them,
> Then you will reduce your own output, forsake your path,
> And will let your wise, circumspect mind be considered rebellious.

(Counsels of Wisdom 21–25)

for careless talk diminishes respect:

> Do not pour out your heart to everybody,
> So that you diminish respect for yourself
> Do not spread round your words to the multitude
> Or associate to yourself one who is indiscreet.

(Teaching of Amenemope xxii, 11–16)

> Keep your tongue from answering your superior
> And guard yourself from his rebuke
> When he makes a statement to snare you
> And you may be released by your answer,
> Discuss the answer with a man of your own rank
> And beware of blurting it out.
> When heart is hurt, words are swifter
> Than the wind at the Nile mouths.

47. Lambert (1960) 118–20.

(A man) is ruined and built up by his tongue.

(Teaching of Amenemope xi, 15–20)

Do not open your heart to a stranger so that he may reveal your speech to your
    disadvantage.

(Teaching of Ani vii, 7–8)

In the multitude of words there wanteth not transgression:
But he that refraineth his lips doeth wisely.

(Proverbs 10:19)

Beware of careless talk, guard your lips;
Do not utter solemn oaths while alone,
For what you say in a moment will follow you afterwards,
But exert yourself to restrain your speech.

(Counsels of Wisdom 131–34)

Let your mouth be restrained, and your speech guarded.

(Counsels of Wisdom 26)

My son, do not chatter overmuch till thou reveal every word which comes into
    thy mind, for in every place are their eyes and their ears; but keep watch over
    thy mouth, let it not be thy destruction (?)

(Ahiqar 96, 97)[48]

and malicious gossip is rebuked by several Egyptian writers:

If you hear anything, good or bad,
Put it away, unheard.
Put a good report on your tongue,
While the evil remains hidden in your heart.

(Teaching of Amenemope xi, 8–11)

Choose the good and speak good while the evil lies hidden in your body.

(Teaching of Ani vii, 10)

Hide what is said in your house, act as one who is deaf.

(Teaching of Ani ii, 10)

Do not recount a calumny,

48. Cowley, A. E. (1923) *Aramaic Papyri*, Oxford, 223.

You should not even listen to one.

> (*Teaching of Ptahhotep* 350–51)

If you hear a bad report, you should not understand . . .

> (Teaching on Berlin Ostracon P.
> 14371 line 2.)[49]

(The text is broken but the editor compares it with the passage from *Amene-mope.*)
In fact a wise man refrains from all gossip:

> He that goeth about as a tale-bearer revealeth secrets:
> But he that is of a faithful spirit concealeth the matter.

> (Proverbs 11:13)

> . . . and he hears a thing and does not reveal it.
> Behold, this is precious before Shamash.

> (*Ahiqar* 93)

The impartial administration of justice was a matter of common concern to all people of the ancient Near East. At the installation of an Egyptian vizier in the XVIIIth Dynasty (Rekhmire *c.* 1450 B.C.)[50] he was reminded that he should "see to it for yourself that everything is done in conformity with the law . . . and precedent. . . ." Obviously judges and other public officials were potentially subject to corruption. The advice to Rekhmire continues, "As for the official in public view, the winds and waters report all that he does; so his deeds cannot remain unknown. . . . The abomination of god is partially. . . . Look upon a man whom you know like one whom you do not know." Even a judge who was above bribes might be impressed by a person's dress or standing:

> Do not defraud a man in the law court,
> Or remove the just man.
> Do not pay attention to a man in fine clothes
> Or heed him who is shabbily dressed
> Do not receive the gift of a strong man
> And oppress the powerless for him.

> (*Teaching of Amenemope* xx,
> 21–xxi, 4)

49. Hintze (1954) *ZAS* 79, 33–36.
50. Davies (1943) 85–88; Sethe (1909) 1102–17.

Thou shalt not wrest judgment; thou shalt not respect persons: neither shalt
thou take a gift; for a gift doth blind the eyes of the wise, and pervert the
words of the righteous.

(Deuteronomy 16:19)

Justice is a great gift of God
He dispenses as he wishes.

(*Teaching of Amenemope* xxi, 5–6)

As well as the major crimes that were considered in these courts the wisdom writers show themselves thoroughly up to date with an interest in con-
sumer protection and fair trading:

Do not tamper with the balance, or falsify the weights. . .
Do not make yourself deficient weights . . .
Do not make yourself an ephah measure which holds two. . .

(*Teaching of Amenemope* xvii, 18;
xviii, 4; 21)

Thou shalt not have in thy bag divers weights, a great and a small.
Thou shalt not have in thy house divers measures, a great and a small.
A perfect and a just weight shalt thou have; a perfect and a just measure shalt
thou have;

(Deuteronomy 25:13–15a)

The merchant who [practises] trickery as he holds the balances,
Who uses two sets of weights, thus lowering the . . .
The merchant who practises trickery as he holds the corn measure,
Who weighs out loans (or corn) by the minimum standard,
but requires a large quantity in repayment,

(*Hymn to Shamash* 107–8
and 112–13)[51]

(text goes on to describe his fate).

(The whole of *Amenemope,* chapter 16 deals with the subject of true weights
and measures, on which the *Hymn to Shamash* also has much to say.)

A false balance is an abomination of the Lord;
But a just weight is his delight.

(Proverbs 11:1 and cf. 16, 11; 20:10
and 23)

51. Lambert (1960) 121.

The honest merchant who weighs out loans by the
maximum standard thus multiplying kindness,
It is pleasing to Shamash, and he will prolong his life.

(*Hymn to Shamash* 118–19)

As well as these mundane issues there are theological observations that these writers have in common. Man's inability to understand God's plans is a common theme:

The heart of a man plans his way
But God directs his step.

(Proverbs 16:9)

and

There are many plans in a man's heart
But it is the counsel of God that will stand

(Proverbs 19:21)

can be compared with

God is in his success
Man is in his failure
The words which men say are one thing
The things which God does are another.

(*Amenemope* xix, 14–17)

and

Truly you do not know the plan of God.

(*Teaching of Amenemope* xxii, 5)

Both passages can be compared with

The will of a god cannot be understood; the way of a god cannot be known.
Anything of a god (is difficult) to find out.

(Proverb on BM 38486 7–8)[52]

52. Lambert (1960) 264–65.

and

> Who knows the will of the gods in heaven?
> Who understands the plans of the underworld gods?
> Where have mortals learnt the way of a god?
>
> *(Ludlul bel nemeqi* II, 36–38)[53]

Because of this man's plans come to nothing and his position in life is always subject to change:

> Boast not thyself of tomorrow;
> For thou knowest not what a day may bring forth.
>
> (Proverbs 27:1)

> The plans of men never come to pass
> (But) the decrees of God come to pass.
>
> *(Teaching of Ptahhotep* 115–16)

> (Whatever) men do does not last for ever,
> mankind and their achievements alike come to an end.
>
> *(Counsels of a Pessimist* 9–10)[54]

> There is no man who knows (how) this plan (will turn out?)
> when he plans for the morrow.
>
> *(Teaching of Ptahhotep* 345)

> He who was alive yesterday is dead today.
> For a moment he was dejected, suddenly he is exuberant.
>
> *(Ludlul bel nemeqi* II, 39–40)

> As for the rich man of last year, he is a beggar this year.
>
> *(Teaching of Ani* viii, 6)

> Prepare not thyself on this day for tomorrow ere it be come,
> is not (?) yesterday like today upon the hands of god?
> Meditate not plans for the morrow: today is not over until tomorrow comes.
>
> (Teaching on Ostracon Petrie XI rto 1
> and vso 5)[55]

---

53. Lambert (1960) 21.
54. Lambert (1960) 107–9.
55. Černý, J. and Gardiner A. H. (1957) *Hieratic Ostraca* 1 Oxford pl. 1.

Prepare not for the morrow before it arrives;
One knows not what mischance may be in it.

(*Eloquent Peasant* 183–84)[56]

A man's plans are all subject to the will of God and this cannot be changed so there is no point in worrying about the future:

There is no-one whom Fate and Fortune do not know.

(*Teaching of Amenemope* ix, 11)

One cannot escape what has been determined.

(*Teaching of Ptahhotep* 480)

Do not go to bed, fearing the morrow,
When day dawns, what is the morrow like?
Man does not know the morrow is like.

(*Teaching of Amenemope* xix, 11–13)

Lo! I live today; tomorrow is in the hand of God.

(Pap. Leiden I 369 5–6)[57]

Do not arrogate to yourself the power of God,
(As though) there were no Fate or Fortune.

(*Teaching of Amenemope* xxi, 15–16)

Even in the face of disaster, however, Amenemope claims that

Poverty when in the hand of God, is better
Than riches in the storehouse.

(*Teaching of Amenemope* ix, 5–6)

a thought that finds echoes in an Assyrian proverb:

It is not wealth that is your support,
It is your god.

(*Assyrian Proverb Collection* 42–43)[58]

56. Simpson (1973) 31–49.
57. Wente, E. (1967) *Late Ramesside Letters* (SAOC 33) Chicago 18–19.
58. Lambert (1960) 225.

as well as in Proverbs:

> Better is a little with the fear of the Lord
> Than great treasure and unrest with it.
> Better a meal of herbs and love there
> Than an ox (from the) stall and hate with it.

(Proverbs 15:16–17)

In fact the worshiper will be rewarded by his God and will prosper:

> Reverence begets favour,
> Sacrifice prolongs life,
> Prayer atones for guilt
> The god-fearing man is not slighted by [the god?]

(*Counsels of Wisdom* 143–46)

> It is to the Sun when he rises that you should pray,
> Saying, "Grant me prosperity and health."
> He will give you your needs in life,
> And you will be safe from fear.

(*Teaching of Amenemope* x, 12–15)

> Unless you seek the will of the god, what luck have you?
> He that bears his god's yoke never lacks food, though it be sparse.

(*Theodicy* 239–40)[59]

> Every day worship your god;
> Sacrifice and benediction are the proper accompaniment of incense.
> Present your free-will offering to your god.
> For this is proper toward the gods.
> Prayer, supplication, and prostration
> Offer him daily, and you will get your reward.
> Then you will have full communion with your god.

(*Counsels of Wisdom* 135–41)

Righteousness is more important as an act of worship than attention to detail of the ritual sacrifice:

> More acceptable is the character of one upright of heart,

---

59. Lambert (1960) 63.

than the ox of the evil-doer.

(Teaching for Merikare 128–29)[60]

Has the Lord as great delight in burnt offerings and sacrifices as in obeying the
voice of the Lord? Behold to obey is better than sacrifice and to hearken than
the fat of rams.

(1 Samuel 15:22)

A man's moral behavior affects not only his own wellbeing, but all his family,
for good or ill, cf. Exodus 20:5:

A righteous man who walks in his integrity
Blessed are his sons after him.

(Proverbs 20:7)

He that is greedy of gain troubleth his own house;
But he that hateth gifts shall live.

(Proverbs 20:27)

(A wrong-doer's) property is taken out of the ownership of his children,
His possessions are given to another.

(Teaching of Amenemope viii, 7–8)

His heir will not assume control of his property
Nor will his brothers take over his estate.

(Hymn to Shamash 116–17)

Subject matter apart there are numerous instances of linguistic contact between Hebrew and Egyptian, and of course even more between Hebrew and
the other Semitic languages. R. J. Williams has listed many examples, including personal names, individual words, and idiomatic expressions although
some of his examples seem to stretch the point.[61] I find it difficult to imagine,
for instance, any significant connection between the picture of Elijah in
1 Kings 18:42 sitting on Mount Carmel with "his face between his knees"
and Egyptians doing the same thing as a sign of mourning.

Several of the literary images in Proverbs also reappear in other wisdom
books:

Wisdom is compared with a priceless treasure

60. Simpson (1973) 180–92.
61. Williams, R. J. (1971) (Ed. J. R. Harris) The Legacy of Egypt Oxford.

If thou seek her as silver,
And search for her as for hid treasures;

(Proverbs 2:4)

Good speech is hidden more than emerald,
(but) it may be found among the servant girls at the millstones.

(*Teaching of Ptahhotep* 58–59)

There is that speaketh rashly like the piercings of a sword;
But the tongue of the wise is health.

(Proverbs 12:18)

Be a craftsman in speech, (so that) you may be strong, for the tongue is a sword
to (a man) and speech is more powerful than any fighting.

(*Teaching for Merikare* 32)

or with a well

Counsel in the heart of man is like deep water;
But a man of understanding will draw it out.

(Proverbs 20:5)

O Thoth (the god of wisdom) thou sweet well for a man thirsting in the desert!
It is sealed up to him who finds his mouth (useful), it is open to the quiet one.
 The quiet one comes and finds the well,
but (for) the rash man, thou art (blocked).

(Pap. Sallier I viii,5)[62]

A woman is compared with a ditch:

For a whore is a deep ditch:
And a strange woman is a narrow pit.

(Proverbs 23:27)

Do not know her (a strange woman) carnally: a deep water, whose windings one
knows not, is a woman who is far from her husband.

(*Teaching of Ani* iii, 14)

62. Caminos, R. (1954) *Late Egyptian Miscellanies* Oxford 303–29.

Much has been made of a long sustained metaphor in Amenemope's Fourth Chapter (v.20–vi.12) where the sense seems to be the comparison of the hothead and the quiet man with two trees.[63] The first flourishes for a short while but is soon cut down and used to build a ship that is eventually burnt, far away from its home. The second grows steadily in an orchard, producing abundant crops and giving pleasant shade for its owner. This passage is often compared with the simile of the god-fearing man in Psalm 1:

> (A man who fears the Lord) shall be like a tree planted by the streams of water,
>   that bringeth forth its fruit in the season:
> Whose leaf also does not wither; and whatsoever he doeth shall prosper.
> The wicked are not so:
> But are like the chaff which the wind driveth away.

(Psalm 1:3–4)

and with the two men in Jeremiah

> (A man who trusts in his own strength) shall be like the heath (or tamarisk) in the desert, and shall not see when good cometh; but shall inhabit a parched place in the wilderness, a salt land and not inhabited.
> Blessed is the man that trusteth in the Lord, and whose hope the Lord is.
> For he shall be as a tree planted by the waters, and that spreadeth out his roots by the river, and shall not fear when heat cometh, but his leaf shall be green; and shall not be careful in the year of drought, neither shall cease from yielding fruit.

(Jeremiah 17:6–8)

This comparison is entirely fair for there is clearly a basic simile common to all three passages but there is a particular aspect of the Egyptian figure which is not reproduced in the Hebrew passages. I believe it is significant that the first tree "floats far from its place" and is eventually burnt while the second "reaches its end in the grove" where it was first planted. This seems to me to reflect the Egyptians' horror of dying in some foreign country and having their body destroyed by fire and the ultimate fate of each tree which is not touched on in the Old Testament passages is of great importance in the Egyptian book.

I think it is important to give these points of contact at some length since they help us to view the common issues between Proverbs and *Amenemope* against their proper background. There are undoubtedly numerous parallels in other texts as well so it can be no part of the argument that the Words of the Wise is directly borrowed from *Amenemope*.

---

63. Drioton, E. (1962) *Mélanges V.V. Struve* 76–80.

I now turn to a detailed discussion of the first part of the Words of the Wise, Proverbs 22:17–23:11.

The Words of the Wise and the Teaching of Amenemope

Proverbs 22:17–18	Amenemope iii, 9–11, and 16
Incline your ear, and hear the words of the wise;	Give your ears, listen to the things which are spoken;
And put your heart to my knowledge.	Give your mind to interpret them.
For it is pleasant if you keep them within yourself	It is profitable to put them in your heart,
	(12–15) no parallel?
They are established together on your lips.	They will act as a mooring post to your tongue.

A number of emendations have been suggested to this passage in spite of the fact that it makes good sense as it stands. Several writers[64] would like to take דִּבְרֵי חֲכָמִים out of the text and put it as a title and substitute a second דְּבָרַי to correspond with דְעָתִּי although the antithesis of "the words of the wise" on the one hand and "my knowledge" on the other hand make just as good parallelism, and in fact some writers emend[65] לדעתי to לדעתם (following the LXX) to correspond with *Amenemope*.

More interesting is the suggestion[66] that יחדו in verse 18 should be emended to כְּיָתֵד "like a tent peg" on the basis of the Egyptian *nˁyt* "a mooring post," the translator having adapted a riverine metaphor into one drawn from desert life, but again it is possible to read the unemended text with good sense. May we not take יכנו in the well-attested sense of "being prepared or ready" and יחדו as referring to all the proverbs or even specifically to the "words of the wise" and "my knowledge" and translate "so that they are altogether ready on your lips."

This is a structural passage and other passages can be brought forward telling the reader that it will be advantageous to pay attention to the advice he is given. . . . If the Hebrew text is emended unnecessarily in three places, we may read with R. J. Williams:[67]

---

64. Toy, C. H. (1948) *A Critical and Exegetical Commentary on the Book of Proverbs* (International Critical Commentary) Edinburgh 423 followed by Erman (1924) 88, Simpson (1926) 236 *et al.*

65. Erman (1924) 88, Humbert (1929) 18, and Simpson (1926) 236.

66. Gressman (1924b) 274, reads יתד, Sellin (1924) 1236, reads כיתד as do Humbert (1929) 18, Simpson (1926) 236 *et al.*

67. Williams (1971) 279.

> Give ear and hear *my words*
> Set your mind to *know them*
> For it is fine that you keep them within you
> That they be fixed *as a tent peg* on your lips

and we have a passage at first sight closely parallel to the Egyptian text but lacking three lines from the center and still showing small variations such as the unusual singular use of אֹזֶן compared with the Egyptian dual form, and the absence of a possessive pronoun with Egyptian *"words."* It is perhaps also significant that *wḥ* and ידע, *nfr* and נעים, *ns* and שפת are not entirely synonymous and one might have expected a translator to use a more precise translation such as לֵב instead of בֶּטֶן to correspond with Egyptian *ib*. It is legitimate to argue that the Hebrew scribe should be allowed some freedom in his rendering of the Egyptian but then it is surely fair to ask why a satisfactory Hebrew text should be emended to conform if it is a free translation. It seems to be a case of wanting to have one's cake and eat it. It would be easier to see how the Hebrew passage could come to be written by someone acquainted with the Egyptian text but recalling it from memory and making up or omitting what he could not remember.

Proverbs 22:19–20	*Amenemope* i, 7 and xxvii, 7–8
In order that your trust may be in the Lord	
I have instructed you today, even you	i, 7 To direct him on the path of life,
Have I not written for you previously (?)	xxvii, See for yourself these thirty chapters
about counsels and knowledge?	They are pleasant, they educate.

Proverbs 22:19 is sometimes[68] compared with *Amenemope* i, 7 but requires reading אֹרְחֹתֶיךָ instead of אַף־אַתָּה. The emendation is supported by the LXX but the use of a similar metaphor is hardly enough to suggest a link between the two texts. אַף־אַתָּה is moreover an acceptable Hebrew construction similar to the use of גַם־אָנִי in Gen. 27:34,[34] and there is no reason why emendation should be necessary.

In verse 20 comes the crux, שִׁלְשׁוֹם in the *Kethibh* for which the *Qere* suggests שָׁלִשִׁים and for which Erman[69] made his famous suggestion שְׁלֹשִׁים on the basis of *Amenemope* xxvii, 7, but I believe it should be treated with some reserve.

---

68. Gressman (1924b) 274.
69. Erman (1924) 89 E.

Firstly, a numeral in Hebrew can only stand by itself when the noun it qualifies is in close proximity and unambiguously linked.[70] We would therefore have to assume that a word such as דברים had dropped out. Specifications of measure, weight or time may be omitted[71] but דברים hardly qualifies in this category.

A second objection is that שָׁלִשִׁים is not as firmly supported by the context as some commentators suggest. It had been proposed[72] before the *Teaching of Amenemope* was known but without meeting acceptance. Before Erman's suggestion was made scholars had divided this section into different numbers of maxims and Erman himself did not suggest that "30" in its Proverbs setting had any significance. He suggested that the Hebrew compiler had inserted it mechanically from the Aramaic or Hebrew translation which he postulated, and thought that the word had lost its significance in its new context. Gressmann and Sellin however were sure that they could find 30 divisions within this part of Proverbs and most other scholars have been persuaded by their arguments, but it is remarkable that the divisions are not more obviously distinguished, especially since שָׁלִשׁ itself is not explained by a noun. For instance, Scott[73] and Whybray,[74] to quote two recent writers, have to take 23:23 out of order and treat it as one maxim so that 23:22 and 24/25 can be grouped to form another. Does 23:26 belong with verses 27 and 28 or is it a separate maxim?[75] Should 23:12 and 23:19 be counted or not? Where does 22:28 fit? Once we begin looking for 30 sections it becomes easy to find them, but it is arguable whether they are indisputably clear and obvious.

If we accept שָׁלִשִׁים are we obliged to accept the idea that this part of Proverbs is based on Amenemope? Could there have been a preference for 30 chapters as the ideal form of a wisdom book? I do not know of one but there might be a connection with *mᶜbꜣyt*, the Egyptian Court of Thirty which has been suggested as a possible prototype for David's heroic thirty (2 Sam. 23).

If we do not accept שָׁלִשִׁים how do we overcome the problem of שָׁלְשׁוֹם? There are a number of possibilities not the least being a hitherto unknown meaning of שָׁלִשִׁים (one might point to the Arabic *salsu*, "a necklace," or *salsala* "to bind together,"[76] perhaps referring to a collection of wise sayings, or to the Akkadian adverbial use *šalāšī* "three times"[77]), or one might retain שָׁלְשׁוֹם and add אתמול before it. This requires no more emendation than

70. Gesenius W., and Kautzsch E. (1910) *Hebrew Grammar* (Trans. A. E. Cowley) Oxford para. 126, x.

71. *Ibid*. para. 134, n.

72. Vaccari, quoted Brunet (1949) p. 28 fn. 4 and Perles, F. (1906) *Jewish Quarterly Review* 18, 290.

73. Scott (1974) 141.

74. Whybray, R. N. (1972) *The Book of Proverbs* (Cambridge Bible Commentary on NEB) Cambridge 137.

75. Gressman (1924b) and Toy (1948) differed about this although both have 30 sections.

76. See the standard lexica.

77. See von Soden, W. (1974) *Akkadisches Handwörterbuch*, Wiesbaden, 1146.

שְׁלִשִׁים—a word has to be supplied whichever is chosen—and a reading "previously" would form good parallelism with הַיּוֹם in verse 19b. I confess to have spent some fruitless effort trying to see if the present text could have arisen by mistake from the words for 3,000[78] but I do think that emendation of שָׁלִשִׁים to מְשָׁלִים is at any rate no worse than many other suggested alterations.

There is obviously a problem in the Hebrew text at this point. I am not convinced that the reading "Thirty" is the only solution or that it inevitably points to a link with the Egyptian text.

Proverbs 22:21	Amenemope i, 5–6
To teach you the certainty of truth	To know how to rebut an accusation to the one who makes it.
To return words of truth to the one who sent you.	To return a charge to the one who made it.

This is the vaguest of parallels; the two texts do not even deal with the same subject. Amenemope the bureaucrat claims that his teaching will enable a man to refute an accusation while the Proverbs writer is concerned that the reader should be convinced of the importance of truth, particularly in carrying back information. It is closer, in fact, to the sense of Ptahhotep's words.[79]

Earlier suggestions that אֱמֶת should be omitted after אֲמָרִים[80] which would weaken the point of the Proverbs passage and make it slightly nearer Amenemope can be rejected now that Dahood has shown that this is a perfectly acceptable genitival construction using the enclitic.[81]

Proverbs 22:22	Amenemope iv, 4–5
Do not extort from the poor because he is poor:	Guard yourself from robbing the poor
Nor crush the destitute in the gate.	From being violent to the weak. (lit. the broken of arm.)

A good example of a passage of general advice where it would be difficult to think of any new twist. There is no close verbal parallel though it would have been possible to make a literal translation of the Egyptian phrase "broken of arm" into idiomatic Hebrew, and one wonders why anyone translating directly from the Egyptian would not do so. To crush the afflicted *at the gate* could perhaps refer

78. After 1 Kings 4:32.
79. *Teaching of Ptahhotep* 145–48 see p. 305 above.
80. Erman (1924a) 88, D. Humbert (1929) 20 *et al.*
81. Dahood, M. (1963) *Proverbs and North-west Semitic Philology* Rome 47.

to some form of legal oppression through the city court which met traditionally at the gate of the city. In this case of course the connection between the two texts is even more remote.

Proverbs 22:24, 25	Amenemope xi, 13, 14; xi, 17, 18
Do not associate with a bad-tempered man (lit. the owner of a temper)	Do not associate with the rash man (lit. the hot man)
Nor go with a hot-tempered (lit. man of hot tempers)	Nor approach him for conversation. . . .
Lest you learn his ways,	When he makes a statement to snare you
And take a snare to your soul.	And you may be released by your answer.

The basis of this proposed connection is twofold; the metaphor of the snare or lasso although it is a common figure in Hebrew and the phrase חמות איש which Simpson thinks the Hebrew writer has coined to render the Egyptian p3 smn "the hot man,"[82] although the phrase occurs in the singular as it is here in the Egyptian (איש חמה) in Proverbs 15:18 and איש אף and בעל חמה (Prov. 29:22) show the same usage.

It is worth commenting that the reason Proverbs gives for keeping away from the hothead is that one will learn his ways and ensnare oneself while Amenemope does not suggest that his reader will become a hothead. In the gap between lines 14 and 17, he has moved on to a different subject entirely and is talking about how to answer a superior who is trying to set a trap.

Proverbs 22:26–27

Commentators seem generally agreed that this passage does not have a parallel in Amenemope.

Proverbs 22:29	Amenemope xxvii, 16–17
You perceive a man, skilled in his work	As for the scribe who is experienced in his office
He shall stand before kings	He will find himself worthy to be a courtier
He shall not stand before obscure men	

82. Simpson (1926) 237.

Here there is clearly similarity of thought but it is hardly original or confined to these two books. Almost all the Egyptian advice for young scribes is based on the theme that a successful scribe manages to avoid the unpleasant tasks and has an assured and comfortable future.

> As for the scribe, every place in the Residence is his, and he will not be poor therein.
>
> *(Teaching of Kheti, son of Duauf,*
> iv, 3–4)

Proverbs 23:1–3	Amenemope xxiii, 13–18
When you sit to eat with a ruler	Do not eat food in the presence of a noble
Consider carefully what is before you	Or cram your mouth in front of him
And put a knife to your throat	If you are satisfied pretend to chew
If you are a man of appetite	It is pleasant in your saliva
Do not desire his delicacies	Look at the cup in front of you
For it is bread of deceit.	And let it serve your need.

The question of behavior at a noble's table also interested Ptahhotep but all three texts are concerned about different aspects. Ptahhotep advised his reader how to behave generally to create a good impression, Amenemope wants him to avoid appearing greedy. It is left to the writer of Proverbs to suggest moral grounds for abstaining, as well as moderation.

Proverbs 23:4–5	Amenemope ix, 14–x, 5
Do not toil to become rich	Do not strain to seek excess When your possessions are secure
Cease from your own understanding (or perhaps, (in view of your wisdom, stop)	If riches are brought to you by robbery They will not stay the night in your possession
	When the day dawns they are no longer in your house.

You cause your eyes to fly to it and it is not (there)	Their place can be seen but they are no longer there The earth opened its mouth to crush and swallow them And plunged them in Dust. They make themselves a great hole, as large as they are. And sink themselves in the underworld.
For wealth makes for itself wings	They make themselves wings like geese,
And flies to heaven like an eagle.	And fly to heaven.

This is generally considered an undoubted piece of borrowing and is often quoted as an example.[83] It is based almost entirely on the metaphor in verse 5 for obviously considerably more than half the Egyptian passage has been lost in the "translation." Some, but not all, of this omission can be explained by the fact that *Amenemope* ix, 1–3 contain references to the Egyptian underworld which a Hebrew writer might omit as unsuitable or incomprehensible. It should also be pointed out that after the first two lines Amenemope is talking about goods wrongfully acquired whilst the writer of Proverbs is rebuking an unseemly effort to amass unnecessary wealth.

This objection aside, there is clearly a common use of the metaphor likening riches to birds as they seem to grow wings and take flight. There is no difficulty about the change of the bird from Egyptian geese to a Hebrew eagle for it would be natural for a writer to choose a species with which his readers were accustomed.

This metaphor is known however elsewhere in the ancient Near East for a Sumerian proverb makes almost exactly the same point: "Riches are migratory (?) birds which cannot find a place to settle down."[84] and an Egyptian dream book suggests that if a man sees himself in a dream watching the catching of birds, it means that his property will be taken away.[85] That riches are transient and ephemeral is known only too well to most men; Ani comments that "last year's rich man is this year's beggar" (*Ani* viii, 6), and birds are used elsewhere in the Old Testament as figures for such passing entities as the glory of Ephraim in Hosea 9:11 or groundless abuse in Proverbs 26:2.

There does, however, seem to be in this passage more than the simple use of a common metaphor for both are built up in the same way—the stolen riches and the wealth both make themselves wings and both fly up to heaven.

    83. Oesterley, W. O. E. (1929) *The Book of Proverbs with Introduction and Notes* London 199 and Williams (1971) 277/8.
    84. Sumerian Proverb I. 18, 19 according to Gordon E. I. (1959) *Sumerian Proverbs* Philadelphia 51.
    85. Papyrus Chester Beatty III Recto 7, 28: Gardiner, A. H. (1935) *Hieratic Papyri in the British Museum* IIIrd Series, London.

Nevertheless, the substantial differences between the first parts of the two passages and the relative frequency of the metaphor partially undermine the case for a direct link.

Proverbs 23:6–8	*Amenemope* xiv. 5–10, 17 and 18
Do not eat the bread of one evil of eye	Do not covet the property of a poor man
And do not desire his delicacies	Lest you hunger for his bread
For as he thinks within himself, so he is.	As for the property of a poor man it obstructs the throat. And wounds the gullet.
"Eat and drink," he says to you	It is like a false oath that makes something (evil) happen to him
But his heart is not with you.	And his heart is deceitful within him.
Vomit the morsel which you have eaten	xiv, 17 The large mouthful of bread, you have swallowed it and vomited it out (immediately)
And spoil your pleasant words	You are deprived of your advantage

There are two problems with this comparison that we have met before: firstly the two passages are not about the same subject—the Egyptian is about coveting the property of a poor man, the Hebrew about sharing the property of an evil man—and secondly in the six-line gap in the Egyptian there has been a further change of subject to the description of a man vainly trying to cover up a mistake.

Oesterley pointed out that "the Hebrew sage entirely misapprehended the meaning of these (Egyptian) passages."[86]

Proverbs 23:9	*Amenemope* xxii, 11–12
Do not speak in the ear of a fool	Do not pour out your heart to everybody,
For he will despise your prudent discourse.	So that you diminish respect for you (yourself)

These are clearly two quite different subjects.

To say "Don't talk to a fool because he will not appreciate your wisdom" is quite a different matter from saying "Don't lay bare your soul to everybody because you will lose all respect." Even Humbert who saw more parallels than

---

86. Oesterley (1929).

most dismissed this as "Rapprochement assez lointain."[87] Both are specific applications of the common theme of wisdom; "A still tongue makes a wise head."[88]

Proverbs 23:10–11	*Amenemope* vii, 12, 15; viii, 9–10
Do not remove an ancient boundary And do not enter into the field of the orphan.	vii 12 Do not remove the boundary stone on the boundaries of the cultivated land.
For their redeemer is strong He will plead their cause against you.	Nor throw down the boundary of the widow. viii 10 Lest a dread thing carry you off.
And compare Proverbs 22:28	
Do not remove the ancient boundary which your fathers have made.	

Shifting a boundary stone to increase the size of your own field must have been a simple and common crime especially when the victim was a defenseless widow or orphan. There are numerous references which show the importance of boundaries in an agriculturally centered economy in the Old Testament and in Egyptian and Mesopotamian literature. The threat that a "dread thing will carry you off" is hardly comparable with the suggestion that the perpetrator will be disagreeably surprised to find that the defenceless orphan in fact has a powerful ally who will take him to court.

W. G. Lambert has pointed out to me that it is more common to find injunctions against oppressing the poor *man* and suggested that it was possibly significant that these verses referred to property owned by a widow or an orphan.

Conclusions

I think we are at last in a position to draw some conclusions. Those who have paid attention and listened to my words will not be surprised if I confess to some doubt about the existence of a direct connection between Proverbs and Amenemope. The connection so casually assumed is often very superficial, rarely more than similarity of subject matter, often quite differently treated and does not survive detailed examination. I believe it can merit no more definite verdict than "not proven" and that it certainly does not exist to the extent that is often assumed, as for example by Gray whom I quoted earlier.[89]

87. Humbert (1929) 25.
88. See above and below.
89. Gray (1964).

Several of the supposed parallels do not seem to me to be parallel at all, for instance 23:21 and 24 and most of the others are either structural passages, 23:17–20, or of almost universal application, 23:22, 29. Even the apparently incontrovertible link provided by the emendation of שִׁלְשׁוֹם into שָׁלִישִׁים can be shown to have other possible explanations or implications.

Brunet placed great weight on the difference of order in which the two sets of passages appears[90] and this has not been satisfactorily explained. If the passages from Amenemope are numbered in order as they appear in the Egyptian text their appearance in Proverbs is as follows, 2, 10, 1, 3, 6, 4, 11, 9, 5, 7, 8, 4, an order which cannot be explained on grounds of sense or style.

Brunet also found it strange that 22:26–27 had no Egyptian original. Verses 19 and 23 could be explained as positive additions specifically introducing references to Jahweh which could not be expected in the Egyptian text but which a pious Hebrew editor might feel obliged to insert, but verses 26 and 27 consist of a purely practical piece of advice for which one searches Amenemope in vain. Should we perhaps supply the missing portion? But if we assume a chapter has dropped out of Amenemope we shall end up with 31 chapters!

I think that both Brunet's points are valid and have not been properly answered. I believe there are other problems. One looks in vain for some unique point. If only Amenemope could have broken with tradition and advised a little gentle corruption or peculation, a crafty heave at a boundary stone, some subtle hints on unfair trading practices, or some blatant outright thuggery. Then if Proverbs had managed to copy some of that we would have two texts standing out like naughty deeds in a good world and a much surer case for dependence.

Is it significant that those points which seem to receive particular attention from Amenemope do not appear in Proverbs? There is hardly any mention of his contrasting figures, the hothead and the quiet man, and no mention of his philosophical acceptance of the inadequacy of man to which he devotes several lines

> God is in his success
> But man is in his failure
> The words which men say are one thing
> But the things which God does are another.
>
> *Teaching of Amenemope* xix, 10

is suggested as generally parallel with Proverbs 14:21 and would surely have been acceptable to the most upright Hebrew. It is difficult to make out a case for omitting this idea from *The Words of the Wise* on theological grounds.

90. Brunet (1949).

Amenemope's many metaphors from river life are also missing but this is easier to explain for they would be edited out because they would be largely meaningless in a Palestinian context.

Some of the suggested parallels only "work" if the passage from Proverbs is compared with a piece from *Amenemope* in which there is a large gap. Proverbs 22:24, 25 and 23:6–8 are both examples of this and in each case there has been a change of subject in the interval in *Amenemope*. This substantially undermines the similarity.

A case could be argued for dependence on the grounds of the cumulative effect of a number of similar passages. Brunet would accept only 5 of the 11 usually cited, namely Proverbs 22:17–18, 20, 22, 24–25 and 29. I would be rather more generous, accepting all these apart from 24–25, and in addition Proverbs 23:1–5 and 10. That is to say I would agree that these verses in Proverbs can be matched with passages in Amenemope which deal with a similar subject. This gives us a total of 11 verses of Hebrew text out of 24 and it does not seem to me to be wholly conclusive evidence of direct borrowing.

What about the theory of a common source, first proposed by Oesterley[91] and taken up recently by Irene Grumach[92] and Helck?[93] Dr. Grumach postulates a late XVIIIth-Dynasty wisdom book of maxims in the order in which they appear in Proverbs which Amenemope used in his composition freely altering the order, and adding new material. This hypothetical book meanwhile passed into a Canaanite version and thence into Proverbs. As if to make this *Alte Lehre* more convincing Dr. Grumach reconstructs it. It is impossible to rule out such a possibility but it has no basis in fact and until some manuscript evidence for this text is discovered it can only be theoretical. A similar argument applies to Helck's suggestion that Proverbs 22–23 is based on an epitome of Amenemope which served as a *Gedachtnisstutze*. He supplies some rather tenuous evidence to show that such epitomes existed in Egypt but it is a far cry from one text, which preserves the initial lines of the chapters of the *Teaching of Ammenemes* to one that has excerpts from the beginnings, ends, and even the middles of an apparently arbitrary selection of chapters in a completely different order. This epitome is again a purely hypothetical entity.

I would be prepared to accept that about half of the first part of the *Words of the Wise* can be considered to deal with the same subjects as *Amenemope* and that this could be an indication of some sort of relationship closer than coincidence.

I cannot believe that there is sufficient correspondence to justify a claim that Proverbs was borrowed from *Amenemope* in the sense that that term is

91. Oesterley (1927a).
92. Grumach (1972).
93. Helck (1968/9).

normally understood, and there is no justification in my view for any emendation of the Hebrew text to bring it in line with the Egyptian.

The sort of relationship that can be demonstrated can be adequately explained by the suggestion that this passage was contributed by an Egyptian scribe working at the court of Solomon based on his memories of a text that he had heard and, may be, used in his scribal training. I believe this proposal fits all the requirements: a striking metaphor and the thirty chapter framework are remembered clearly, and the subject of much of the *Teaching* is recalled though the details and order are muddled. It seems to me that this conforms with the internal evidence of the Hebrew text and the specific note that this is part of a section based on the teaching of wise men, it conforms with our knowledge that Amenemope was used in Egyptian scribal schools, and it conforms with the known facts of the historical situation in which Proverbs was probably compiled.[94] There is plenty of evidence for cultural contact with the surrounding countries and foreigners are specifically mentioned as holding senior positions at the Israelite court. It has been suggested that some of Solomon's officials, listed in Kings 4, 3 might have been Egyptians or, at least, have Egyptian names[95] and that the title of Secretary of State in David's and Solomon's court may have been expressed by the Egyptian word for a scribe, *šš*.[96]

I think it is not at all unreasonable to suggest that in his search for wisdom Solomon would extend his interest beyond his national boundary. 1 Kings 4 demonstrates a knowledge of the existence of the wisdom of the people of the East and all the wisdom of Egypt and what could be more reasonable than that Solomon should question a cultured Egyptian at his court about this wisdom?

Postscript

At this stage in the argument I would like to introduce for consideration a text that has not previously been discussed in this context: the source will be revealed in due course. It is a collection of precepts, known by their original title as *Precepts of the Elders*—a title which is itself significant—and like the ancient Near Eastern books they describe "all the ways in which a young (man) of the better sort was expected to conduct himself; how he was to behave to his superiors, his equals, and his inferiors; how he was to revere his elders, show compassion for the unfortunate, refrain from light words, and in all circumstances be most scrupulously polite."

Ptahhotep might well have written

---

94. For a recent description see E. W. Heaton (1974) *Solomon's New Men* London.
95. Grollenberg, L. H. (1957) *Atlas of the Bible* London 71; *cf.* Mettinger, T.N.D. (1971) *Solomonic State Officials* Lund 29 *et passim*.
96. Cody, A. (1965) *RB* 72, 381–93.

Take care how you go in (to the Lord's house), for without your noticing it you will be watched. Come respectfully, bow, and make your greeting. Do not make faces when you eat; do not eat noisily and without care like a glutton, do not swallow too quickly or in a careless manner; do not take great mouthfuls of maize cake, nor stuff your mouth, nor swallow like a dog, nor tear the cakes to pieces, nor hurl yourself upon what is in the plate. Eat calmly, or you will be mocked.[97]

and the advice given throughout his *Teaching* by Amenemope is echoed by the *Precepts:*

One must speak calmly, not too fast, nor heatedly, nor loud . . .
Keep to a moderate pitch, neither high nor low, and let your words be mild and serene.
(A true gentleman should be) humble and not overweening, very wise and prudent, peaceable and calm.

Moreover it would avail nothing to feign these virtues for "our Lord God sees what is in the heart and he knows all secret things."

Part of the addresses to the emperors on their election also resembles closely passages in Amenemope's *Teaching*

Take care never to speak lightly, for that would make your person despised.[98]

Another passage

Say nothing, do nothing with too much haste; listen to those who complain to you or bring you news calmly and to the end . . . do not be partial; do not punish anybody without reason.

has much in common with Ptahhotep's advice to officials and the charge to the Vizier recorded in the tomb of Rekhmire.[99]

The cares of kingship weighed heavy in the minds of the writers of the *Precepts* as they did upon the Middle Kingdom rulers of Egypt.

Lord (they said to him), it is you who will now carry the weight and burden of this state. The burden of government will be upon your back. It is upon your shoulders, in your lap and between your arms that our God has set the task of governing the people and they are fickle and prompt to anger. It is you Lord, who for certain years are going to sustain this nation and care for it as if it were a child in a cradle . . . Consider, Lord, that from now on you are to walk upon

97. Translations by J. Soustelle (1964) *The Daily Life of the Aztecs* Harmondsworth 233ff.
98. Cf. *Teaching of Amenemope* XXII, 11 and 12; above.
99. See above.

a very high place along a narrow path that has great precipices to the right and the left. . . Your people are protected by your shade, for you are (like two varieties of trees) which give a great round shadow; and the multitudes are protected by your branches.

Do not suppose, Lord, that the mat and the throne of kings is a place of pleasure and delight, for on the contrary, it is one of great labour, sorrow and penance.

The acceptance of the task of government, the concern to sustain the nation, as well as the cautious use of power remind us strongly of the *Teaching of Merikare*. It is also interesting to notice the literary imagery used in this passage; the comparison of the nation with a child, the dangerous path and the protective tree all have biblical parallels, for example, Hosea 11:1, Psalm 23:4, and Ezekiel 31:6. The references to the place where the emperor carried out his official duties provides a very close verbal link with the Egyptian title *šš ntms* "a scribe of the mat," describing a scribe of the royal administration.[100]

This text is not some papyrus or cuneiform tablet which has been gathering dust unnoticed in the store rooms of Birmingham City Museum, it is in fact the *ueuetlatolli* of the Aztecs, as they were recorded by Bernadion de Sahagun and others in the sixteenth century A.D. The parallels that I have drawn between them and ancient Near Eastern wisdom are in no way exhaustive, but the fact that they can be produced so easily underlines what should be obvious anyway, that such precepts and images are universally acceptable and hence that similar passages may occur in Proverbs and Amenemope simply by coincidence.

100. Gardiner, A. H. (1947) *Ancient Egyptian Onomastica* Oxford I 91.

26

PROVERBS 25–26

Sid S. Buzzell

25:1. Hezekiah's men, perhaps royal scribes, copied (lit., "removed," i.e., from one book or scroll to another) more than 100 of Solomon's proverbs. This was about 250 years after Solomon wrote them. Hezekiah's men grouped many of these proverbs in units of similar thoughts.

25:2. Verses 2–7 are sayings about the king. Though the king probably was Solomon, these proverbs applied to all kings of Israel and Judah. God has chosen not to reveal everything about himself and his plans (cf. Deut. 29:29). This means that kings, to make proper decisions, must investigate matters fully. Whereas God delights in concealing some things, kings delight in being investigative.

25:3. This verse is the first of many verses in chapters 25–26 that make comparisons, using the words "like" or "as"; 12 are in chapter 25 (vv. 3, 11–14, 18–20, 23, 25–26, 28) and 13 in chapter 26 (see comments on 26:1).

God hides some of his knowledge from kings, and kings hide some of their knowledge from their subjects. Rulers, responsible for knowing what is going

Reprinted from *The Bible Knowledge Commentary, Old Testament,* edited by John L. Walvoord and Roy B. Zuck, published by Victor Books, 1985, SP International, Wheaton, IL 60187. Used by permission.

on and for investigating issues fully (25:2), need not reveal everything they know. "Search out" in verse 2 and unsearchable in verse 3 connect these two verses.

25:4–5. Just as undesirable slag is removed from . . . silver (cf. 27:21), so wicked people are to be removed from the king. Getting rid of wicked assistants (cf. 20:8, 26) enables a king to have a righteous reign. The last line of 25:5 is nearly identical to that of 16:12.

25:6–7. It is wrong for a person to try to promote himself to a king, claiming to be great when he is not. It is far better for the king to promote him than for the king to humiliate him in front of a nobleman whose position the status seeker is desiring. Christ illustrated this in a parable (Luke 14:7–10).

25:8. In Hebrew the words "seen with your eyes" are the last words of verse 7 (cf. KJV, NASB). Some versions (e.g., NIV, RSV) put those words with verse 8. The phrase makes verse 7 long for a proverb and also makes far less sense there than with verse 8.

Verse 8 warns against hastily taking another person to court (cf. 24:28). The reason is that the plaintiff may lose the case and be ashamed, for what he thought he saw may not have been what actually took place.

25:9–10. In providing evidence against a neighbor in a court case a plaintiff may be forced to betray a friend's confidence. As a result the friend may shame him and the plaintiff may have an irretrievable loss of reputation. It is risky business to accuse others publicly in court.

25:11–12. An appropriate and properly timed word (cf. 15:23; 24:26)—which sometimes may be a rebuke . . .—can be attractive and valuable, like gold apples set against a silver sculpture or carving, or like a gold earring or other ornament.

25:13. Snow in the mountains (not snow falling on the crops in the dry season) is refreshing during the heat of harvesttime. Similarly a trustworthy messenger is refreshing to one who sends him (cf. 13:17). An unreliable messenger is referred to in 10:26 and 26:6.

25:14. Clouds and wind usually give farmers promise of rain. But if no rain comes, the farmers are keenly disappointed. Similarly people who claim they will give presents but never keep their promises are frustrating to the supposed recipients. A person ought not promise something if he knows he cannot follow through.

25:15. Patience and a gentle (lit., "soft") tongue (cf. 15:1) can be unusually influential, accomplishing far more than loss of temper and harsh words. A soft tongue breaking a hard bone is an unusual figure of speech—how can a tongue break a bone? The idea is that softly spoken words can accomplish difficult things. Also persuading a ruler to follow some difficult course of action takes patience.

25:16–17. Just as eating too much honey can cause a problem (cf. v. 27; 27:7), so visiting a neighbor too often may cause him to hate the frequent visitor. Overdoing anything can be a problem. "Seldom" is literally, "make precious": that is, "make it valuable" by its rarity. A person should refrain from frequently visiting his neighbor, to avoid being a nuisance, but he should visit enough so that his visits are valued.

25:18. Giving false testimony in court against a neighbor . . . can crush, divide, or pierce like a club . . . sword, or . . . arrow. Lying can wound a person's character and even destroy his life as effectively as weapons.

25:19. A bad tooth and a lame foot can be problems, especially because a person relies on them to eat and walk. Also relying on a person who turns out to be untrustworthy can be disappointing and troublesome. Job expressed this concern over his friends (Job 6:14–15). An example of an unreliable person is one who lies in court (Prov. 25:18).

25:20. Trying to perk up by songs a person who is discouraged or depressed (a heavy heart) is as cruel as stealing his garment in cold weather. It is also like pouring vinegar . . . on soda; it is useless and it causes a violent reaction. Being insensitive and unsympathetic does much harm.

25:21–22. Kindness to one's enemy—giving him food and water—is like heaping burning coals on his head (quoted by Paul in Rom. 12:20). Sometimes a person's fire went out and he needed to borrow some live coals to restart his fire. Giving a person coals in a pan to carry home "on his head" was a neighborly, kind act; it made friends, not enemies. Also the kindness shown in giving someone food and water makes him ashamed of being an enemy, and brings God's blessing on the benefactor. Compassion, not revenge, should characterize believers (cf. Prov. 24:29). Alternately, light on this passage may come from an Egyptian expiation ritual, in which a person guilty of some wrongdoing would carry a pan of burning coals on his head as a sign of his repentance. Thus treating one's enemy kindly may cause him to repent.

25:23. As surely as an Israelite could predict the consequences of a north wind, so one can predict the consequences of a sly tongue (lit., "a tongue of secrecy," i.e., a slanderous tongue). One brings rain and the other angry looks. Slander leads to anger. However, in Palestine rain does not normally come from the north. So perhaps this saying originated outside Palestine (Derek Kidner, The Proverbs: An Introduction and Commentary, p. 160).

25:24. Solitude in cramped quarters with peace is better . . . than . . . living in a spacious house with a cantankerous, contentious wife. This verse is identical to 21:9 (also cf. 21:19).

25:25. The impact of receiving good news (cf. 15:30) from a friend or relative who lives far away is like a refreshing drink of water to a tired person. In Bible times news traveled slowly; thus long periods of anxious waiting usually followed the departure of a loved one or friend to a distant land.

25:26. A righteous man who lets his reputation be compromised is like pure water being tainted and ruined by mud or other pollutants. The value of a pure spring or well in an arid country lends force to the statement. Once a spring or well is contaminated it may never be pure again, and disappoints those who come to it for a drink. A righteous person who defects to sin disappoints others who look to him.

25:27. Seeking to exalt oneself (seeking one's own honor; cf. v. 6; 27:2) is as bad as overeating honey (cf. 25:16; 27:7). Both bring problems.

25:28. Without walls a city was vulnerable to enemy attacks. And an undisciplined person, who lacks self-control (cf. 14:17, 29; 16:32; 29:11), is also vulnerable to trouble.

26:1. Thirteen verses in this chapter are comparisons, using the words "like" or "as" (cf. comments on 25:3). Each of verses 1, 3–12 refers to a fool or fools. Snow in summer or rain in harvest is inappropriate, highly unusual, and potentially damaging to crops. Putting a fool in a position of honor (cf. 26:8) is inappropriate (cf. 19:10) and may injure others who follow him as a model.

26:2. The unpredictable, fluttering nature of a bird's flight demonstrates a person's inability to place a curse on another who does not deserve it. Balaam experienced that same inability (Num. 23:8).

26:3. Just as a horse is motivated by a whip and a donkey is controlled by a halter rather than by reason, so a fool needs to be controlled by a rod (physical punishment) because he does not respond to appeals to his intellect (cf. 10:13; 14:3; 19:29).

26:4–5. These two sayings belong together; they complement each other. Their point is that one should not be drawn down to a fool's level (v. 4) but at times he must use the fool's language to refute the fool so he does not become conceited (v. 5; cf. vv. 12, 16). Wisdom is needed to determine when to apply verse 4 and when to apply verse 5. The Jewish Talmud suggests that verse 4 pertains to foolish comments that can be ignored and that verse 5 refers to erroneous ideas that must be corrected. "You" in verse 4 is emphatic and may be translated "you, even you."

26:6. Sending . . . a message by . . . a fool is useless and potentially damaging. It is like cutting off one's feet, that is, the message does not get delivered; it is as if the sender tried to take it himself by walking the distance without feet. Drinking violence is self-damaging, just like relying on an unfaithful messenger.

26:7. A fool cannot be trusted with a message (v. 6); also a proverb in his mouth (cf. v. 9) is as useless as limp legs to a lame man (cf. 25:19). A fool does not know what to do with a proverb; he does not understand it or apply it. Feet (26:6) and legs (v. 7) tie these two verses together.

26:8. It is senseless and possibly harmful to tie a stone into a sling. The stone might slip out and damage the thrower. So bestowing honor on a fool, for whom honor is inappropriate (v. 1), is senseless and may damage the reputation of the one giving the honor. His wisdom will be questioned.

26:9. As seen in verse 7, a proverb spoken by a fool is useless. Here it is compared to a thornbush in the hand of a drunkard. This could mean one of several things: (1) The drunkard may inflict damage on others by waving a thornbush around dangerously. (2) He may be so insensitive to pain that he does not feel a thorn in his hand, much as a fool is insensitive to wisdom. (3) A man who is so drunk that he cannot pull a thorn out of his hand is like a fool who cannot apply a proverb that he can quote (Robert L. Alden, *Proverbs: A Commentary on an Ancient Book of Timeless Advice*, p. 187). Perhaps the first meaning is to be preferred.

26:10. The absurdity of an employer hiring a fool or any passer-by is like a berserk archer (cf. v. 18) indiscriminately shooting without aiming. Hiring "just anybody" will actually harm the hirer.

26:11. As a dog eats its vomit (quoted in 2 Pet. 2:22), so a fool cannot learn from experience. He returns to his habits even though they are disgusting.

26:12. Concluding the series of statements on the fool (vv. 1, 3–12) is this saying that even a fool is better off than one who is wise in his own eyes (cf. vv. 5, 16). Self-conceit or pride blinds a person to his sense of need; at least a fool may sense his need for correction.

The last part of verse 12 is repeated in 29:20b. Pride and being proud are addressed frequently in Proverbs (3:34; 8:13; 11:2; 13:10; 15:25; 16:5, 18–19; 18:12; 21:4, 24; 29:23; cf. 26:5, 12, 16).

26:13. Verses 13–16 speak about the sluggard (cf. 6:6–11). The sluggard goes to bizarre measures to avoid leaving his house, such as saying a lion is roaming loose. . . .

26:14. The sluggard, though tossing in bed, seems anchored to it as a door is joined to the jamb. He will not even exert the energy needed to get up.

26:15. This picture of a lazy person starving because he refuses to feed himself is also found in 19:24. . . .

26:16. In his self-conceit (cf. vv. 5, 12) the sluggard thinks he is smarter than anyone (seven men). Yet his answers lack discretion (lit., "taste").

26:17. Verses 17–28 refer to quarrels (vv. 17, 20–21), deceit (vv. 18–19, 24–26), gossip (vv. 20, 22), and lying (vv. 23, 28). One who grabs a dog by its ears may expect to be bitten. So is a passer-by, someone not directly involved, who meddles in (lit., "excites himself over") another's quarrel. He causes trouble for himself by interfering in a situation he knows little about.

26:18–19. The berserk archer is again referred to (cf. v. 10) to picture a troublemaker. After deceiving his neighbor he tries to avoid being accused by saying he was only joking. But that is humor in bad taste. His deception, like a deadly arrow, has already done its damage.

26:20–21. Fire and strife relate these two verses. A quarrel dies down without gossip (cf. gossiping in 11:13; 16:28; 18:8; 20:19; 26:22) just as a fire goes out when its fuel is removed (v. 20). Conversely quarreling contributes to ("kindling" is lit., "heat up") strife (cf. 17:1; 18:6; 20:3; 22:10; 23:29; 30:33) just as charcoal and wood build up a fire.

26:22. See . . . 18:8, where the same statement is made. Here gossiping fits with 26:20–21.

26:23. A coating of glaze refers to an attractive coating over a piece of pottery. This is likened to fervent (*dālaq*, "to burn or kindle") lips and an evil heart. A person who tries to disguise his evil motives and character by zealous speech is like an attractive glazed-over jar. (Note Jesus' reference in Luke 11:39 to the clean outside of the cup and dish; also note Matt. 23:27).

26:24. Verses 24–26 expand the idea in verse 23 ("lips . . . heart," and "speech" tie verses 23–25 together). A malicious person plans deceit (cf. v. 19) but seeks to disguise it by his smooth talk ("lips").

26:25. This verse warns against being taken in by a malicious person whose words are charming (cf. vv. 23–24) but whose heart (cf. vv. 23–24) is filled with seven (i.e., numerous; cf. "seven men," v. 16) abominations (cf. 6:16–19).

26:26. "Malice" (*śin'āh*) is translated "hate" or "hatred" in 10:12, 18; 15:17 (cf. the verb *śānē'*, "hates," in 26:28). Though a scoundrel can hide his feelings temporarily through deceit, they will eventually be known. The assembly refers to any group called together for some purpose. Perhaps this group is assembled to administer justice.

26:27. Destruction by one's own devices is the subject of this verse and of Psalms 7:15; 9:15; 35:8; 57:6. If Proverbs 26:27 is related to verses 23–26 the point is that attempts to trap or destroy others will eventually turn on the schemer (cf. 1:18–19; 28:10). Many times Proverbs affirms that sin boomerangs.

26:28. People who lie are actually hateful (see comments on malice in v. 26; they desire to harm others by slandering their reputations). And people who flatter to help achieve their selfishly deceptive ends (cf. vv. 23–26) bring ruin either to themselves, their victims, or both.

27

THE FOOL
AND THE WISE
IN DIALOGUE:
PROVERBS 26:4–5

Kenneth G. Hoglund

Don't answer a fool according to his folly,
    lest you yourself become like him.
Do answer a fool according to his folly,
    lest he be wise in his eyes.

Prov. 26:4–5

The apparent contradiction of Proverbs 26:4–5 has been the source of uneasiness for generations of exegetes. In the earliest recorded discussion of Proverbs' suitability for the canon, some pointed to

From *The Listening Heart. Essays in Wisdom and the Psalms in Honor of Roland E. Murphy, O. Carm.*, edited by Kenneth G. Hoglund, Elizabeth F. Huwiler, Jonathan T. Glass, and Roger W. Lee (Sheffield Academic Press, 1987), 161–77. Reproduced by permission of Sheffield Academic Press.

the opposing directions of these two admonitions as reason for excluding the work. The rabbis resolved the matter by positing a conditional variability behind these admonitions. In cases dealing with Torah, one should correct the fool's error, but in most other cases it is better not to answer the fool (Babylonian Talmud Shabbat 30b). This same hermeneutical principle of conditional variability in the application of the admonitions has appealed to many interpreters as a way out of a seemingly irresolvable conflict in teaching (see, for example, Oesterley 1929, 231). However, this approach suffers from several critical weaknesses. To begin with, no argument is offered to demonstrate that this conditional variability is derived from the text itself and not simply a convenient way to explain away the tension between these two admonitions. Rarely is the same conditional variability applied to other admonitions in Proverbs using the same absolutist language. Furthermore, the positing of conditional variability behind the admonitions does not provide any insight into how the juxtaposition of these two commands came about in this portion of the Book of Proverbs.

A variation on the approach of postulating a conditional variability holds that these admonitions reflect a process of maturing understanding. As the observation of life experiences brought additional insights, the absolutism of verse 4 was tempered with the positive command of verse 5, the result being a relativization in applying the admonitions (Zimmerli 1933, 187–88; von Rad 1962, 1:422; Murphy 1969, 293–94; Murphy 1984, 63). While this approach serves to explain the juxtaposition of the admonitions, it still fails to address several critical questions. If such additions to admonitory statements were reflections of "another order which has in the meantime come into the field of vision" (von Rad 1962, 1:422), it seems odd that parallel antinomies are so rare in Proverbs.[1] Also, the use of absolutist language in both of these admonitions would seem to be a weak choice for expressing the kind of relativization that this approach envisions.

One element shared by the vast majority of commentators on these two verses is the assumption that these admonitions functioned as two independent commands at some point prior to their incorporation into their present context (see the discussion in van Leeuwen 1984, 9–27). The difficult nature of these admonitions is thus a function of their proximity to each other, not the individual content of either command. Hence, before attempting to arrive at some interpretive framework for explaining their apparent contradiction, one must first give consideration to the literary context in which these two ad-

---

1. Among others, von Rad (1962, 1:422) offers Prov. 17:27–28 as another example of juxtaposed contradictory sayings that point to an openness to experience. A careful weighing of these two sayings, however, would clearly note the use of 17:28 as building on the theme of 17:27, signaled by the use of *gam* at the beginning of the verse. The point is simply that restraint in speech is part of the expected behavior of the wise—after all, even a fool looks wise by keeping quiet.

monitions have been set and how their juxtaposition functions within that context.

The Literary Context of Proverbs 26:4–5

It has long been noted that 26:4–5 stands in the midst of a group of sayings (vv. 1–12) marked by the repetitive use of "fool" (*ksyl*). The binding force of this repeated term led Toy to call 26:1–12 "a Book of Fools," claiming these verses were "a string of sarcasms on the class most detested by the sages" (Toy 1899, 471; see also Greenstone 1950, 272; Gemser 1963, 93; Scott 1965, 21 for similar expressions). Given that this distinctive pattern of *kysl* differentiates 26:1–12 from both what goes before it and what follows (25:2–27) relates to matters of social relations while 26:13–16 uses the repetition of ʿsl, "slug-gard"), these verses represent a deliberately arranged unit of sayings and ad-monitions. The organizing principle behind this unit consequently becomes a critical concern in approaching the interpretation of the relationships among the parts of this unit, especially the juxtaposition of verses 4 and 5.

On its surface, the repeated use of *ksyl* in 26:1–12 would suggest that these elements have been gathered together on the basis of a common catchword. Several authors have noted the recurrence of this form of arrangement in chapters 25–27 (Skladny's "Collection C") and presume this is a stylistic trait of the editor. Such groupings would have functioned to assist memorization of individual sayings or to keep them in loose thematic blocks (Barucq 1964, 19; McKane 1970, 413–14; Murphy 1984, 63–64, 77). In a clearly reasoned presentation, van Leeuwen has recently argued that these larger units possess a more meaningful character and function as a distinct composition, creating an interpretive context broader than the individual wisdom statements (van Leeuwen 1984, 41–54).[2] The ordering of these individual elements goes beyond casual associations, creating instead a connected discourse through the medium of seemingly discrete teachings. Such is the case for 26:1–12, which evidences clear structural and thematic interrelations, demonstrating that these verses function together as a coherent didactic unit.

One may note first that all of these sayings and admonitions deal with re-lationships of various types, with the possible exception of verse 2. All of these relationships are directed toward the fool. Moreover, as van Leeuwen has shown, the term "fool" always occurs in the second colon of the wisdom say-ings (van Leeuwen 1984, 128). In a thematic sense, the unit as a whole is con-cerned to delineate an understanding of the relationship of the fool with

---

2. Most of the analysis presented here was worked out independently of van Leeuwen's analysis of Prov. 26:1–12. While both efforts concur on seeing the pericope as a coherent teach-ing, the interpretation of the unit set forth in this essay differs considerably from van Leeuwen's conclusions.

something and/or someone (Scott 1972, 158). Using the categories of form criticism, one may also clearly distinguish four sections in 26:1–12. For example, verses 1–3 are wisdom sayings, followed by verses 4 and 5, which are admonitions. In verses 6–11 the composition returns to wisdom sayings, while verse 12 is cast in the form of a "better" proverb (Murphy 1984, 66–67; see also van Leeuwen 1984, 126–27). The form of verse 12 is particularly significant since Ogden, among others, has pointed out the rhetorical function of the "better" proverbs as either introductory or summary statements (1977, 491–92). It seems apparent from this pattern of varying literary forms that the troubling juxtaposition of verses 4 and 5, as well as verse 12, is intended to be emphasized within the unit by being contrasted with the wisdom sayings that surround them.

Moving still deeper into the intertwining nature of the components of this unit, one can find structural and thematic correlations to these sections of homogeneous literary forms. In verses 1–3, for instance, it is immediately apparent that each of these sayings comprises three elements. The compositional technique of using $k \ldots k \ldots kn$, as in verses 1 and 2, has been recognized as common in this section of the Book of Proverbs (Gemser 1963, 95–97; Murphy 1984, 77). However, here in verses 1 and 2 the grammatical and phonetic parallelism is even stronger. Both verses build on the $k \ldots kn$ pattern, but the pattern is supplemented by repeating similar prepositional elements:

1. *ka ... ba ... weka ... ba ... ken*
2. *ka ... la ... ka ... la ... ken*

The chiastic arrangement of the negatives within the third sections of these sayings has been noted by van Leeuwen, as has the chiastic interplay of *kbd* in verse 1 and *qll* in verse 2 (van Leeuwen 1984, 138–39):

1. *ken lo ... kbd*
2. *ken qllt ... lo ...*

Verse 3 is also a part of this patterning. Though the $k \ldots k \ldots kn$ are not written, it is possible that these prepositional elements in verse 2 take on a double role and apply to both verses 2 and 3. This would be a stylistic device similar to that Dahood has argued for in the Psalms (1970, 436). The double role of the $k \ldots k \ldots kn$ pattern here is largely a function of the proximity of verses 2 and 3, strengthening the meaning already present in verse 3 if it was originally an independent saying. However, the relationship between the two verses in their present setting is unmistakable. For example, the use of *le* and the definite article in verse 3 strongly parallels the arrangement in verse 2:

2. *ka . . . la . . . ka . . . la . . . kn . . .*
3. *. . . la . . . la . . . le . . .*

Understood in this way, verse 3 could be translated along the lines of, "As a whip for the horse, as a bridle for the ass, so a rod for the back of fools."

One also notes the shift in the tenor of the elements of verse 3 from verses 1 and 2. While the three parts of verse 1 focused on conditions that did not "fit" (snow in summer, rain in harvest, honor for a fool), and the parts of verse 2 focused on parallel objects that did not "alight" (a bird in flitting, a swallow in flying, a causeless curse), the parts of verse 3 positively state three relationships that are appropriate between an object and an animate being (a whip for the horse, a bridle for the ass, a rod for the back of fools). Indeed, one can take the observed structural alignment into the area of the meaning of verses 1–3. Honor is not appropriate to a fool (v. 1). Since in the saying's viewpoint it is obvious that a "causeless curse" does not rest on someone or something (v. 2), so the fact that a rod is appropriate to the "back of fools" (v. 3) implies that this has been earned or, in the language of this unit, "caused" by the nature of the fool.

Skipping for the moment the elements that bind the admonitions of verses 4–5 together, it is possible to perceive phonetic, structural, and thematic grounds for seeing verses 6–8 as a distinct subsection that relates to verses 1–3. Verse 6 possesses three parts that, while not formally bound together by *k . . . k . . . kn*, certainly mimic this form of relational parallelism. Moreover, just as verse 3 establishes a parallel among relations that carry pain upon use, verse 6 establishes a parallel among relations that are self-destructive, causing pain to the protagonist (for the self-destructive import of this saying, see Toy 1898, 473–74; Perowne 1916, 162; Gemser 1963, 94). Verse 7 focuses on the impossibility of fulfilling the potential of something (Toy 1898, 474; McKane 1970, 598). Though only bipartite in form, the verse may provide a faint echo of verse 2, which also presents a lack of fulfillment, the "causeless curse" that is ineffective. Finally, verse 8 contains a strong suggestion of relationship to verse 1, both in its repetition of *kbd* and in the use of a *k . . . k . . . kn* format (van Leeuwen 1984, 140–41). The repetition of *kbd* serves to form an envelope construction with verse 1, and as such verse 8 can be seen as the summary for this three-verse cluster (vv. 6–8). The theme of the cluster is the futility of interacting with the fool. Relying on the fool is self-destructive (v. 6) and even a proverb can be rendered impotent when uttered by a fool (v. 7). The inevitable conclusion is the vanity of honoring a fool, a vanity aptly expressed by the image of a stone inextricably fastened in a sling, incapable of fulfilling the role for which it was intended.

Verses 9–11 evidence similar elements that point to another cluster of three sayings. Verse 9 contains a compact expression in the first half of the saying, ending with the distinctive *byd škwr* (see Toy 1899, 475). The *byd škwr* is reminiscent of the *byd ksyl* of verse 6 and introduces the parallel between the "drunkard" (*škwr*) and the fool. A number of commentators have noted that the second part of verse 9 repeats the second part of the saying at verse 7, but without catching the fact that an important distinction exists between the two sayings. Where verse 7 merely notes that "a proverb in the mouth of fools" is ineffectual, verse 9 emphasizes the danger of such a condition (see for example, Toy 1899, 475; Scott 1965, 159; McKane 1970, 598–99; for the understanding advanced here see Perowne 1916, 163).

While the translation of verse 10 has plagued interpreters, it seems as well to point to a dangerous condition engendered by the fool. Taking the Masoretic text's *rb* as "archer" (following Gemser 1963, 95; see Dhorme 1984, 236–37 for a discussion of the word), the saying can be translated, "(Like) an archer who wounds all is one who hires a fool or a passing drunkard." The image of an archer indiscriminately shooting into a crowd casts into bold relief the danger which the sage perceives in trying to employ either a fool or a drunkard in some task. The parallel of the fool and the drunkard noted in verse 9 is again reinforced here. Also there is the unmistakable effort to build on the theme of verse 6, though here the result is not simply self-destructive but more pervasive damage extended to a corporate humanity.

A final summary to this cluster is found in verse 11. The employment of the commonly observed tendency of dogs to return to their vomit (see 2 Pet. 2:22) provides a deliberately offensive parallel to the saying's final comment on the fool as one unable to break an established pattern (Delitzsch 1890, 188). As van Leeuwen has argued, this is a clear effort to build on the drunkard-fool parallel since the word *q* ("vomit") as a noun is predominantly associated with drunkenness outside of this passage (van Leeuwen 1984, 140). Further, the saying uses the drunkard-fool parallel of verses 9–10 to create a transition from the damage caused by the fool to the final reflection on the dilemma of the fool found in the following verse.

As noted above, verse 12 is cast in the form of a "better" proverb, often utilized as an introductory or summary statement. The first half of the proverb establishes a condition addressed to the audience of the teaching ("Do you see a man wise in his eyes?"), presupposing that the audience possesses the necessary insight to recognize such an individual. The phrase "a man wise in his eyes" is a stock expression in Proverbs as several commentators have noted (Barucq 1964, 201; McKane 1970, 17–18; see also van Leeuwen 1984, 150 n. 43 for an apt response to some aspects of McKane's views). Here, however, the phrase recalls the second half of the admonition at verse 5, where the same contrast is drawn between the fool and the one "wise in his eyes." The second half of verse 12 brings the point home with finality—"there is more hope for the fool than for him." Before assessing the way in which verse 12 functions as a summary for this ordering of teachings, the admonitions at verses 4–5 need to be analyzed.

At verse 4 one is presented with a simple negative command, followed by an explanation for the command. The "folly" of the fool is a frequent theme in Proverbs, usually connected with the manifestation of the fool's nature (Prov. 13:16; 14:8, 24, 29; 16:22; see also Donald 1963, 287). As such, to refrain from answering "according to his folly" is to hold back from reducing one's response to the level of fool. The reason is that otherwise one runs the risk of becoming "like" the fool.

This explanation raises the question as to exactly how one comes to resemble the fool. While the admonition provides no definitive answer, most commentators have assumed that by thinking on the level of the fool, one may become locked into thinking foolishly. Delitzsch is representative in this regard, arguing that the fool's "folly" consists in asking pointless questions: "He who recognizes such questions as justifiable and thus sanctions them places himself on an equity with the fool" (1890, 175–76). Indeed, this concept fits well with verse 1 in that honor (or respect, sanction) does not fit the fool (Gemser 1963, 93; McKane 1970, 595). To bring one's response to the level of the fool is to give tacit validity to the fool's thought, to give "honor" to the fool. By so doing, one risks giving similar validity to other foolish thoughts, and thus resembling a fool.

The following admonition at verse 5 posits the precise opposite of verse 4, in both structure and theme. One is commanded in this second admonition to answer the fool "according to his folly," that is, to bring one's response to the level of the fool. The reason is that failure to communicate with the fool will leave him open to becoming "wise in his own eyes." The implication to be derived from the form of verse 5 is that being "wise in his own eyes" is a state worse than being a *ksyl*, since one should undertake efforts to prevent the fool from being caught in such self-evaluation.

There is little reason to conclude, as some commentators have, that these admonitions are playing on subtle distinctions in the phrase "according to his folly" (e.g., Delitzsch 1890, 176; Greenstone 1950, 274; Scott 1965, 159). As can be seen in the grammatical structuring of verses 4 and 5, one would be hard-pressed to express a clearer set of antithetical admonitions. In both admonitions answering "according to his folly" has the same meaning, to bring one's answer to the level of the fool.[3] Furthermore, as can be seen in the larger literary context of 26:1–12, the juxtaposition of these antithetical

3. The phrase "according to his folly" (*k*'*wltw*) plays the same grammatical, rhetorical, and structural role in both admonitions. To make the argument that in 26:4–5 there is a play on the sense of "according to," one would have to produce an example of two structurally similar expressions where the same nuancing of *k* is present. No commentator who advocates this understanding of the admonitions has offered such an example.

admonitions is intended to express an ambivalence at the heart of the vocation of the wise.

Moving now to the matter of the interpretation of Proverbs 26:1–12 as a unit, it is possible to see a definite movement of ideas toward the conclusion of verse 12. One must recognize that "honor" is not fitting to a fool (v. 1), and since one knows a causeless curse is ineffective (v. 2), there must be something about the nature of the fool that causes the rod to be effective as a control for the fool (v. 3). One should not give validity to the fool and foolish thought or else one may become "like" the fool (v. 4). However, one really should answer the fool on his foolish level or else the fool will be left to his own self-evaluation (v. 5). It is futile to deal with the fool (v. 6). The fool is incapable of actualizing the potential of wisdom (v. 7). It is totally futile to give validity to the fool (v. 8). Worse than this, the fool will do damage with wisdom (v. 9). Trying to put the fool to some worthwhile task is damaging to all (v. 10). There is no point to it; a fool cannot change his nature (v. 11). But consider those left to their own self-evaluation. Such people are locked in their own selves. There is more hope for even a fool to change than for those trapped in their own self-evaluation (v. 12).

From this understanding of the thematic development in 26:1–12 it is possible to see how verse 12 functions as the summation of the entire pericope. The first part of the saying emphasizes the marked character of the one "wise in his own eyes" and points back to the admonition of verse 5. The second part of verse 12 brings the "bottom line" into clearer focus: a fool has more potential to turn from his behavior than the one "wise in his own eyes." The implication of verse 12 is that one has some hope, slight though it may be, to influence the fool. There is no way to influence the one "wise in his own eyes," locked in his own self-evaluation.

Indeed, the conclusion of verse 12 is that the admonition of verse 5 is ultimately the best option for the wise in interacting with the fool. To leave the fool in his foolishness is to allow a condition that will lead to a further decline from the ideal of openness to wisdom. Despite the frustrations of dealing with the fool and the damage a fool can cause, the wise still has an obligation to attempt to teach the fool. Still, the truth of the second part of verse 4 is not contradicted. By responding to the fool in terms he can understand, one runs the risk of contamination and may find oneself becoming foolish.

The literary unit of 26:1–12 functions as a coherent effort to wrestle with the dilemma of the wise in dialogue with the fool. The juxtaposition of contrasting admonitions at verses 4–5 delineates the crux of the dilemma as the clash between the sage's didactic responsibilities and the potential risk in fulfilling these same responsibilities. To enter into dialogue with the fool is both an obligation and a threat for the wise. The conclusion that the wise must enter into the dialogue with the fool is not without a certain amount of ambivalence. To enter into an exchange with the fool is no guarantee of persuading the fool to be open to wisdom. Indeed, one may be engaging in a futile enterprise or worse, setting the stage for a wider scope of damage. Still, without the dialogue the fool is left to the tyranny of his own standards and becomes that much further removed from appropriating wisdom.

The Dialogue with the Fool Outside of Proverbs

The conclusion that the literary context of Proverbs 26:4–5 consists of a coherent effort to wrestle with the dilemma of the dialogue with the fool would be strengthened if one could find parallel reflections in the larger ancient Near Eastern wisdom tradition. This would be particularly significant if such parallels also reflected the same ambivalence posited for the contradictory admonition at 26:4–5.

In his landmark study of Proverbs 26:1–12 van Leeuwen cites the Mesopotamian composition known as *The Pessimistic Dialogue between Master and Servant* as a parallel to the clashing admonitions of verses 4 and 5. He sees the work's employment of contradictory sayings as an attempt to know the full range of options present in Mesopotamian wisdom tradition, an attempt doomed to a failure that leads to pessimism (1984, 148 n. 38). While one cannot deny that the *Pessimistic Dialogue* uses contradictory sayings as an integral structural technique, in this composition the technique is utilized within a different setting and for a different purpose than those of Proverbs 26:1–12. Rather than being a reflection on a dialogue, the work presents an actual exchange between two parties. The dialogic interplay of the master and servant in the Mesopotamian text takes place as part of a complex social relationship unclear to the modern interpreter. Moreover, it is not at all certain that pessimism is the conclusion of the work since the abundant irony and satire in the interplay suggest a comedic aspect to the author's intention (Speiser 1954, 103–5). As has been argued above, the contradiction expressed in Proverbs 26:4–5 is the crux of a dilemma, which an anonymous sage is seeking to explore. The contradictions of the *Pessimistic Dialogue* are not elucidated or struggled with, but simply put forth in a point/counterpoint structure. Consequently the consideration of the *Pessimistic Dialogue* as a parallel does little to enhance the understanding of the ambivalence expressed at 26:4–5.

Closer parallels to the dilemma of interacting with the fool can be found in Ben Sira. Working within the mainstream of Israelite wisdom tradition, Ben Sira nonetheless reflects a certain development of this tradition. In thematic terms, the subject matter of the composition is basically that of earlier Israelite wisdom (Sanders 1983, 3–12). Regarding Ben Sira's form, Roth (1980) has pointed out the prevalent use of groupings of discrete sayings to form connected thematic units in the work. Beyond their shared thematic concerns, however, these units are frequently bound by poetic devices such as chiasm and *inclusio* to reinforce their relationship (DiLella, 1982).

One potential parallel may be found at Sirach 21:12–26 where a series of sayings focus on the contrast in the value of education for the fool and the wise.[4] The opening saying expresses the dilemma of education: "The one who is not astute (*ʿarum*) cannot be taught, but there is an astuteness which can increase bitterness." In Sirach 21:13–14, the contrast in receptivity to learning between the fool and the wise is emphasized:

> The learning of the wise man is a swelling flood,
>   and his counsel is as a living spring.
> The interior of the fool is like a broken jar,
>   and any learning is not retained.

This contrast finds further elaboration in verse 15 where the wise is described as hearing a proverb, recognizing its value, and adding to it. The insolent person (*zed*), however, does not perceive its value and tosses it away. After comparing the reception accorded the speech of the wise person to that given the speech of the fool (vv. 16–17), the focus turns to the value of learning for both classes:

> Like leg-irons on the feet is learning to fools,
>   and like manacles on the right hand.
> A fool pours forth his voice in laughter,
>   but the astute man smiles in quiet.
> Like a gold ornament is learning to the wise,
>   and like a bracelet on the right arm.

> [Sir. 21:19–21]

After a string of sayings exploring the differences in behavior regarding domestic confidences between the fool and the wise, the author closes with the wry observation, "In the mouth of fools is their mind, but in the mind of the wise is their mouth" (21:26).

This pericope struggles with the inability of the fool to be educated. By a series of observations cast in the form of wisdom sayings, the unit skillfully reveals the essential attitudinal difference between the fool and the wise. As 21:19–21 compactly expresses, for the fool instruction is nothing more than an encumbrance, whereas for the wise this same encumbrance becomes an ornament. The final summation notes the fool's inability to be self-reflective

---

4. While many begin the pericope with 21:11, the phrase "fear of the Lord" in that verse is a repetition of the same phrase in 21:6. Verse 11 then functions as a summary of the preceding pericope, claiming that wisdom is, for Ben Sira, a necessary component to keeping sin at bay. This same understanding of the boundaries of the pericope has been used in Snaith 1974, 107–8.

in speech, again contrasted with the wise who considers speech before vo-
calizing it.

While there are no clashing admonitions within this pericope (there are no
admonitions in the unit as a whole), there is the employment of contrasting
observations structured and juxtaposed in such a manner as to intensify their
oppositional message. Yet there is still a sense of ambivalence over this matter
of one's receptivity to learning (a condition called "astuteness"), as is evident
from the opening statement of the section. Without "astuteness," it is impossible to be open to learning, but "astuteness" can lead to bitterness (21:12).
The work provides no resolution to this issue, merely offering it as a concern
before exploring the reasons why the fool does not learn.

A second possible parallel may be found at Sirach 22:7–15. Here the author resorts to a more direct style utilizing several admonitory sayings as well
as the more common wisdom sayings. The section opens with two related observations on the futility of trying to teach the fool:

> Like mending a pot is teaching a fool,
>   or rousing one in a deep sleep.
> Like relating something to one overcome by sleep,
>   is relating something to a fool;
>   when it is finished he will say, "What was that?"

[Sir. 22:7–8]

The images of mending a pot or trying to rouse the deep sleeper convey
graphically the magnitude of the task of teaching the fool. While not impossible, it is a task fraught with difficulty. Following this sober evaluation is an
extended comparison between the dead and the fool. The thrust of the comparison is that on several levels, the dead person is more fortunate than the
fool.

Next, the author directs the focus toward the appropriate way for the wise
to interact with the fool given the considerations that have been already set
forth:

> Do not talk long with a fool (*ksyl*),
>   and with a fool (*ʾwyl*) do not visit.
> Protect yourself from him lest he trouble you,
>   and do not be defiled by his emptying.
> Turn away from him and you will find rest,
>   and you will not be wearied by his confusion.

[Sir. 22:13]

Here the text states in no uncertain terms that the sage not only faces the ir-
ritation of trying to deal with a fool, but is endangering his own character by

such interaction. To be subjected to the fool's ranting ("his emptying") is only to harm one's self (MacKenzie 1983, 93). The text continues the emphasis on the burdensome nature of fools in verses 14–15, comparing this group with a variety of dense, heavy materials.

The section draws to a conclusion in verses 16–18 with a series of comparisons drawn from contemporary architectural practices. The mind imbued with wisdom can face a crisis without fear, just as a wooden beam securely set in a structure is not torn free in an earthquake (v. 16). Moreover, the mind fixed on informed thinking is like a plaster decoration on a solid wall (v. 17). All this is in contrast to the fool, whose timid heart cannot stand against fear, just as exposed fencing cannot stand against the wind (v. 18). These sayings seem to emphasize the stability of the mind of the wise in the face of adversity, in contrast to the instability of the fool. However, should the wise become like the fool, disaster looms. A structural beam torn loose in an earthquake would bring down the entire building, and stucco applied to a flimsy wall would separate from the face of the wall and collapse. In this sense, verses 16–18 provide an illustration of the protection the sage ensures by following the admonitions of verse 13, in contrast to the disaster one might court by being "defiled" by the fool.

Both parallels cited from Ben Sira deal with the wise in relation to the fool. In these pericopes, one encounters a series of wisdom sayings and admonitions that can easily stand as independent elements but have been brought together and arranged in such a manner as to express a coherent point of view. That point of view emphasizes, first of all, the unteachability of the fool, and secondly, the danger the wise is exposed to by interacting with the fool. In both of these regards, numerous parallels to the sentiments of Proverbs 26:1–12 are evident.

While neither pericope contains as direct an expression of ambivalence over interacting with the fool as Proverbs 26:4–5, there remains a certain tension in the author's position with respect to the wise interacting with the fool. While Sirach 21:12–26 exposes the causes of the fool's ineducability as a defect in attitude, it also cautions against a certain kind of learning. In Sirach 22:7–15 the burdensome nature of dealing with the fool is articulated, along with the risks that are encountered in such dealings. Still, at Sirach 42:8 the same author enjoins the wise to correct the "ignorant and the fool" as an action reflecting one's learning and worthy of receiving community approval. In spite of attitudinal problems, the burdensome nature of the task, and the risks, the sage is still expected to interact with the fool and provide instruction.

The Fool and the Wise in Dialogue

The contrasting admonitions of Proverbs 26:4–5 presuppose a dialogic encounter between the fool and the wise. To "answer a fool according to his folly" suggests a question or comment has been made by the fool to the wise. In the process of providing an answer, the wise enters into an intellectual exchange with the fool on the fool's level of comprehension in the hope of preventing further obstruction of the fool's receptivity to instruction (vv. 5, 12). Nor is this dialogue without sanction within the wisdom tradition. No less a figure than Lady Wisdom dialogues with the simple and the foolish to instruct them (Prov. 8:5–6).

Still, for the wise there are ample grounds for hesitancy in engaging in such a dialogue. One risks becoming like the fool in thought, thus losing the very aspect of one's self that makes a person "wise" (26:4). The bulk of the sayings in 26:1–12 focus on the dangers and futility of dealing with the fool, a theme also present throughout the Israelite wisdom tradition. One should not stay around a fool (Prov. 14:7), since the fool takes no delight in understanding (18:2). It is futile to argue with a fool (29:9), for the fool hates learning (15:5).

It is no wonder then, that the dialogue between the fool and the wise requires some reflection on the part of the very group that has the most to lose in the encounter. The sage is placed in a dilemma in which either option possesses liabilities. One could choose not to answer the fool, thus ending the dialogue and preventing personal and societal damage, as well as avoiding the waste of energy and time in a futile enterprise. This certainly would minimize the short-term liabilities of such a dialogue, but raises the possibility of encouraging the further movement of the fool away from potential illumination. One thus has, in the perspective of 26:1–12, little choice but to take the risks and answer the fool, thus engaging in a dialogue as perilous as it is unrewarding.

The totality of the instruction in 26:1–12 is directed toward a group that both sees itself as removed from the nature of the foolish and still accountable in some way to insure the foolish fall no further from the ideal of wisdom. As such, the pericope and its clashing admonitions represent a class-ethic as opposed to a more general instruction intended for any pious Israelite (see Kovacs 1974, 176, 186–87). It is the wise who are confronted with the responsibility for maintaining or cutting off the dialogue. The parallels noted in Ben Sira emphasize the unrestricted nature of this dilemma; it occurs in all times and in all places where the wise seek to live responsibly.

The juxtaposition of antithetical admonitions at Proverbs 26:4–5 cannot simply be resolved by reference to a concealed situational variability. Nor, for that matter, do these two contradictory commands provide evidence of some form of "relativization" of wisdom teaching. Rather, as shown by their setting in a coherent presentation of the futility and risks in dialoguing with the fool, these two admonitions give a condensed expression to a profound ambivalence. For the wise, the dialogue with the fool may require the ultimate loss of all that marks one as a member of the wise. This tension expresses a strong sense of self-identity on the part of Israel's wise, and a deep appreciation for the ambiguity of life experiences.

28

A Manual
for Future Monarchs:
Proverbs 27:23–29:27

Bruce V. Malchow

Past scholars generally agreed that the Hezekiah collection in the Book of Proverbs consists of two earlier groupings, chapters 25–27 and 28–29. Skladny then demonstrated that chapters 28–29 were gathered as a collection for future monarchs. It was intended to show them how to rule.[1] Skladny's conclusion has been widely accepted. Although Crenshaw generally recognizes little influence on the royal court on Proverbs, even he says of chapters 25–29, "Here as nowhere else the powerful individual (ruler) with whom all subjects had to reckon is acknowledged."[2]

This article intends to go farther in clarifying chapters 28–29. An important model for its methodology was provided by Bryce's study of Proverbs 25:2–27.[3] He showed that that passage was a collection for the training of

From *Catholic Biblical Quarterly* 47 (April 1985): 238–45. Used by permission.

1. U. Skladny, *Die ältesten Spruchsammlungen in Israel* (Göttingen: Vandenhoeck und Ruprecht, 1962), 58–62.
2. J. L. Crenshaw, *Old Testament Wisdom: An Introduction* (Atlanta: John Knox, 1981), 75.
3. G. Bryce, "Another Wisdom-'Book' in Proverbs," *JBL* 91 (1972): 145–57. A slightly altered version of this material occurs in *A Legacy of Wisdom* (Lewisburg: Bucknell University Press, 1979), 135–55.

courtiers and that it was intricately arranged and structured. A similar, careful plan of editing appears to have guided the collector of chapters 28–29, as will be demonstrated below.

First, there is a conspicuous unity in the form employed in these chapters. All of the verses are individual, two-line proverbs. Most of them are antithetic couplets.

Secondly, the editor of chapters 28–29 has organized his material through the use of strategically placed proverbs employing the words *saddîq* ("righteous") and *rāšāᶜ* (wicked"). These chapters begin (28:1) and end (29:27) with couplets using these words. Then there are four proverbs within the collection that contain these terms and occur at intervals (28:12, 28; 29:2, 16). These four are integrally related to each other and form a symmetrical pattern. Thus, the first and third couplets have rather similar first lines.

> When the righteous rejoice, there is great glorying (28:12a).
> When the righteous come to power,[4] the people rejoice (29:2a).

Then the second line of the first proverb and the first line of the second match.

> but when the wicked rise, a man hides himself (*yĕḥuppaś*) (28:12b)
> When the wicked rise, a man hides himself (*yissātēr*) (28:28a).

Next, both the second line of the second couplet and the second line of the fourth treat the destruction of the wicked.

> but when they perish, the righteous come to power (28:28b).
> but the righteous will look upon their overthrow (29:16b).

Also, the second line of the second couplet and the first line of the third mention the rise of the righteous to a position of authority.

> but when they [the wicked] perish, the righteous come to power (28:28b).
> When the righteous come to power, the people rejoice (29:2a).

Finally, the second line of the third couplet is comparable to the first line of the fourth.

> but when a wicked one rules, people groan (29:2b).
> When the wicked come to power, transgression increases (29:16a).

---

4. W. McKane, *Proverbs: A New Approach* (OTL; Philadelphia: Westminster, 1970), 639.

Thus, every one of the eight lines in these four couplets is related to at least one other line outside its own verse, and two lines correlate to two others. The four proverbs as a unity point out the responsibility of a sovereign to reign righteously. Since this whole collection is structured around these four, this seems to be its primary exhortation to its reader, the future ruler. Besides these four proverbs and the first and last ones in chapters 28 and 29, only one other verse contains the contrasting terms *saddîq* and *rāšāʿ*: 29:7. Since this verse does not correlate in content with the others, fit the pattern apparent in them, or have a strategic placement, it does not seem to be part of the editor's scheme of arrangement. 29:7 is also the only verse in chapters 28 and 29 that has both of the terms *saddîq* and *rāšāʿ* in the singular.

When this pattern of structure has been recognized, the remaining proverbs can be divided into the following groups: 28:2–11, 13–27; 29:1, 3–15, 17–26. All of the multi-verse units have a great deal of internal unity in content and manner of expression. Thus, the first group, 28:2–11, centers on the law and justice to the poor. These topics are very apropos for the future sovereign to whom they are addressed. Judging was an important function of monarchy. And rulers had a special responsibility to judge the needy and unprotected fairly (Isa. 11:3–4; Jer. 22:3, 16; Ps. 72:1–4). The beginning of 28:2–11 directs the attention of future sovereigns to this concern. They are warned that rulers do not last long in an evil land but are encouraged that a land's order or justice will long continue under an understanding person. Verse 3 presently speaks against a poor person who oppresses the poor. But *BHS* and McKane are probably correct in emending *rāš*, "poor," to *rōʾš*, "principal."[5] Then this verse criticizes a ruler who oppresses the needy. That same concern for the poor recurs in verses 6, 8, and 11. And verse 5 speaks of those who understand justice.

The theme of the law appears in verses 4, 7, and 9. If this collection comes from a monarchical setting, Toy is probably correct in contending that the *tôrâ* here is the instruction of the wise.[6] Such instruction often dealt with the same concerns as the other proverbs in this group. The demand for social justice was an important topic in the teaching of the wise.[7] Especially verse 4 fits well with this concern. Those who keep the instruction of the wise strive against the wicked, especially in the lawcourt. The only proverb in this group to be still considered is verse 10, which describes the future of those who mislead the upright. Leading and misleading is another appropriate matter for monarch's reflection.

5. Ibid., 629.
6. C. H. Toy, *A Critical and Exegetical Commentary on the Book of Proverbs,* ICC (Edinburgh: Clark, 1899), 496–99.
7. J. C. Rylaarsdam, *The Proverbs. Ecclesiastes: The Song of Solomon,* Layman's Bible Commentary 10 (Richmond: John Knox, 1964), 88; B. V. Malchow, "Social Justice in the Wisdom Literature," *BTB* 12 (1982): 120–24.

In addition to unity of content, all of the couplets in 28:2–11 are connected to adjoining verses by assonance. Thus, *kēn* and *ʾēn* unite verses 2–3. Three
word combinations couple verses 3–4: *geber-yitgārû, rōʾš-rāšāʿ, māṭār-šōmĕrê*.
In addition, the second word in verses 3–7 has the same sound: *rōʾš, tôrâ, rāʿ,
rāš,* and *tôrâ*. Verses 5–6 are also related by *mĕbaqšê* and *mēʿiqqēš. Bēn* and
bĕnēšek link verses 7–8. Verses 8–10 all begin with the letter *mēm* and are connected by *tarbît-tôrâ-rāʿ*. Furthermore, verses 8–9 are joined by *hônô-ʾoznô,*
and verses 9–10 by *tĕpillātô-yippôl*. Finally, *yĕšārîm* and *ʿāsîr* link verses 10–11.

The same kinds of interconnections are found in 28:13–27. First, there is
a unified content. In this case the content corresponds to that of the verses
giving structure to the whole collection, namely, the verses that precede and
follow 28:13–27 (vv. 12, 28). The last line of verse 12 and the first of verse
28 read, "When the wicked rise, a man hides himself." All of the couplets in
verses 13–27 mention types of wicked people. In order, they are the concealer
of transgressions, those who harden their hearts, the wicked ruler, the oppressive ruler, the blood-guilty, the perverse, the follower of worthless pursuits,
one who hurries to be rich, the partial person, the greedy one (vv. 22, 25),
the flatterer, the robber of parents, those who trust in their own minds, and
one who raises the eyes to avoid seeing the poor's need. The reference to each
of these is a caution to the future monarch against becoming such a person or
an instruction on dealing with such people when they are encountered. Two
of the couplets are specifically about rulers (vv. 15–16). Three of them seem
to have a judicial setting: those about blood-guiltiness (v. 17), partiality
(v. 21), and robbery (v. 24). These would be especially applicable to sovereigns, as would those dealing again with the poor (vv. 15, 27). Also, a monarch would be a particular target for the flatterer (v. 23).

Similarly, assonance links most of the couplets in verses 13–27. Verses 13–
18 are all united by the series *mĕkasseh, maqšeh, mōšēl, maʿăšaqqôt, ʿāšuq,* and
nĕʿqaš. Verses 14–15 have *ʾašrê* and *ʾărî*. Besides assonance, verses 15–16 are
connected by two different words for "ruler." Another possible bond is that
the "one" into which a person falls (v. 18) may be the "pit" mentioned in
verse 17. The assonance between verses 18–19 occurs in *yiwwāšēaʿ-yišbaʿ* and
dĕrākayim-rēqîm. The tie between verses 19–20 is *ʾadmātô-ʾĕmûnôt*. The first
words in the second lines of verses 20–22 are *wĕʾāṣ, wĕʾal,* and *wĕlôʾ. Lahôn,
lāšôn,* and *lĕʾîš* link verses 22–24. Verses 24–25 are related by *ḥāber-rĕḥab*.
Verses 25–26 are united because both contain the word *bōṭēaḥ*. There is assonance between verse 27 and the following couplet, which is one of the verses
giving structure to the collection. It occurs in *lārāš ʾēn-rĕšāʿîm* and *rab-yirbû*.

Verse 1 in chapter 29 is an independent verse between 28:28 and 29:2, the
central structural verses in the collection. Verse 29:1 introduces a new topic,
the necessity of heeding discipline. It is an appropriate subject for the royal
student, as it is for any pupil. This topic will recur several times in the follow-

ing material. It is noteworthy that Bryce also found a couplet introducing a new thought at the center of 25:2–27 (v. 16).[8] There also the verse came between groups of proverbs with common content. This seems to be a part of the editing procedure for those collecting proverbs.

Like the two previous groups in chapter 28, 29:3–15 has unity of thought and expression. Also, like 28:13–27, the closest lines of the verses providing structure for the whole collection, namely, the lines that precede and follow 29:3–15 (29:2b and 16a), are related to this unit's content. They both mention the rule of the wicked, and much of verses 3–15 deals with that situation. Verse 3 warns the future monarch of the damage that consorting with harlots can do to his estate. Verse 4 describes a "king" who demands gifts. Verse 5 alerts future rulers that flatterers may trap them. Verse 6 is a general description of the danger of evil. As chapter 28 did frequently, verse 7 warns future sovereigns that if they are wicked, they will not know how to fulfill their obligation of rightly judging the poor. Verse 8 admonishes them that they or their courtiers could kindle discord in the cities of the realm through a scoffing attitude. Verse 9 alerts future monarchs to the chaos that a fool will cause in their lawcourts.[9] In verse 10, they hear of the injustice that will occur if they or those under them are bloodthirsty. Verse 11 warns them that they will be fools if they express all of their anger or ideas. Verse 12 makes clear to them that, if a "ruler" is gullible when officials lie, they will be wicked. Verse 13 again brings up the oppressor of the poor, and verse 14 tells the "king" the happy results of judging them fairly. After verses 3–14 have dealt with the dangers of misrule, verse 15 returns to the discipline theme of verse 1.

As previously, there are word-links between the couplets in verses 3–15, with only a couple of exceptions. In addition, *yiśmaḥ-yĕsammaḥ* connects verse 3 with the adjoining structural verse, verse 2. Within the group, verses 3 and 4 share the word *ʾîš*. There is assonance between *ʾāreṣ* in verse 4 and *rešet* in verse 5. *Pôrēś-pešaʿ* and *rĕʿēhû-rāʿ* unite verses 5–6. Both verses 6 and 7 contain *ṣaddîq*. The first words in verses 8–10 are *ʾanšê, ʾîš*, and *ʾanšê*. In addition, verses 8–9 have *ḥăkāmîm-ḥākām*. Assonance is present in *yĕšabbĕḥennâ-maqśîb* in verses 11–12, and both verses share *kol*. *Rĕšāʿîm-rāš* link verses 12–13. Verses 13–14 are connected because they contain different words for the poor. And there is assonance between verses 14–15 in *ʾĕmet-ʾimmô*.

Finally, the content of 29:17–26 is not unified like that of the previous groups, but all of the topics in 29:17–26 correspond to those discussed in those groups. First, the discipline theme of 29:1 and 15 is stressed by repetition in the alternating verses 17, 19, and 21. Verse 18 is relevant to the future monarch because it warns of a cause of anarchy, i.e., lack of vision. In this setting, "vision" probably refers to the inspired utterances of sages (Job 4:12–

8. G. Bryce, *Legacy*, 142.
9. C. H. Toy, *Proverbs*, 509.

17; 32:8–10; Proverbs 2:6).[10] The second half of verse 18 repeats a frequent concern of 28:2–11, observing the instruction (*tôrâ*) of the wise.[11] Verses 20 and 22 urge reserve in expressing ideas and anger, as 29:11 did. Verse 23 reiterates the call of 28:26 for humility. Verse 24 expresses a truth for the sovereign's lawcourt, as 28:17, 21, and 24 did. Like 28:5, 29:25 notes the wisdom of relying on Yahweh. And verse 26 similarly reminds the monarch that consistent justice comes from Yahweh rather than the ruler.

Although the content of verses 17–26 has looser internal connections than the previous groups, this unit has word-links among all of its verses and with the structural verses on either end, verses 16 and 27. *Pāšaᶜ-napšekā* bind verses 16–17. Verses 17–19 are related by *binkā-bĕʾên-wĕʾên*. In verses 19–21, there is the series *ᶜābed-bidbārāyw-ᶜabdô*. *Bidbārāyw* in verse 20 also connects with *bidbārîm* in verse 19. The last words in verses 19–21 constitute another series between these verses: *maᶜāneh-mimmennû-mānôn*. *Mānôn* in verse 21 also provides a link with *mādôn* in verse 22. Verses 22–23 are united by two different words for "man" and the pair *ûbaᶜal-ûšĕpal*. *Tašpîlennû ûšĕpal* in verse 23 corresponds to *sónē* napšô in verse 24. There is assonance between *yaggîd* in verse 24 and *yĕsuggab* in verse 25, and both verses begin with the letter *ḥet*. *Móqēš* in verse 25 relates to *mĕbaqšîm* and *mōšēl* in verse 26, and both verses contain the name Yahweh. Finally, verses 26–27 share the word *ʾîš*.

Thus, Proverbs 28–29 prove to be a carefully structured collection. It is organized around six strategically placed and interrelated couplets. It has a basic unity in literary form. Its four groups of proverbs have unified contents in the first three cases and couplets related in content to the three previous groups in the last case. Also, in each unit the verses almost always have word-links to those adjoining them. The central proverb, 29:1, introduces a new thought, which is echoed later in the collection. Therefore, chapters 28–29 are an intricately arranged collection serving as a manual for future monarchs.

An additional proposal may yet be made. In dividing the Hezekiah collection, critics usually grouped 27:23–27 with chapters 25–27. However, no one contends that 25:1–27:22 is directed to future rulers. Yet 27:24 seemingly asks a monarch whether a crown lasts for generations without care. And the word used for crown, *nēzer*, was always used for the royal crown during the period of the monarchy.[12] This problem is usually solved by emending *nēzer* to something else. But it seems better to retain the textual reading and see 27:23–27 as an introduction to chapters 28–29, rather than as the end of chapters 25–27. At least two commentators in the past have been dissatisfied

10. R. B. Y. Scott, *Proverbs. Ecclesiastes*, AB 18, 2d ed. (Garden City, N.Y.: Doubleday, 1965), 170.

11. B. Gemser, *Sprüche Salomos*, HAT 16, 2d ed. (Tübingen: Mohr [Siebeck], 1963), 100.

12. R. N. Whybray, *The Book of Proverbs*, Cambridge Bible Commentary (Cambridge: Cambridge University Press, 1972), 159.

with connecting these verses with chapters 25–27 and regarded them as an independent unit.[13] The following will attempt to show that they are even better viewed as the beginning of chapters 28–29.

Some scholars have already noted that 27:23–27 may well have had a royal court setting rather than a rural one, although they have not identified the object of the passage as the ruler. They have shown that there was no sharp division between city and country in Jerusalem and that the farmer theme was used in the capital (Isa. 28:23–29). Some members of the court owned country estates.[14] So the passage would be applicable to the monarch.

But the significance of the text may well go beyond its apparent advice about shepherding. Perhaps that was its only import when it was first coined. But the editor may have had more in mind when placing it at the head of his manual for future rulers. Especially verses 23–24 may now be symbolic advice to the monarchs not to neglect their people. Although a number of previous commentators have not identified this specific meaning, they have suggested that the passage has some broader, symbolic sense.[15]

And verses 23–24 could well be royal advice because the symbol of the shepherd is so often used for Near Eastern and Israelite monarchs. It was a constant feature of Mesopotamian usage. In the oldest period it was frequently employed in Sumer.[16] Then it appears among the Old Babylonians in the Code of Hammurabi.[17] And it is still apparent in Assyrian[18] and Neo-Babylonian writings.[19] The shepherd symbol is also used in various periods of Egyptian history, especially the First Intermediate and Middle Kingdoms, but with less frequency than in Mesopotamia.[20] Finally, "shepherd" is a regular title for rulers in Israel (1 Kings 22:17; Jer. 6:3; Ezek. 34:23; Mic. 5:3–4; and Ps. 78:70–71).

All that is said in Proverbs 27:23–27 remains within the shepherd imagery that could be applied to monarchs. This is true of the reference to goats in

13. C. H. Toy, *Proverbs*, 457; J. C. Rylaarsdam, *Proverbs*, 82.

14. R. N. Whybray, *Proverbs*, 158; H.-J. Hermisson, *Studien zur israelitischen Spruchweisheit*, WMANT 28 (Neukirchen-Vluyn, Neukirchener V., 1968), 65.

15. J. C. Rylaarsdam, *Proverbs*, 87; D. Kidner, *The Proverbs. An Introduction and Commentary*, Tyndale OT Commentaries (London: Tyndale, 1964), 168; W. G. Plaut, *Book of Proverbs: A Commentary*, The Jewish Commentary for Bible Readers (New York: Union of American Hebrew Congregations, 1961), 279.

16. *ANET* 159, 265–66; C. J. Gadd, *Ideas of Divine Rule in the Ancient East* (London: Oxford University Press, 1948), 38; H. Frankfort, *Kingship and the Gods* (Chicago: University of Chicago Press, 1948), 238.

17. *ANET*, 164.

18. Ibid., 281, 289; H. Saggs, *The Greatness That Was Babylon* (New York: New American Library, 1962), 353; H. Frankfort, *Kingship*, 239.

19. *ANET*, 440; W. Eichrodt, *Ezekiel. A Commentary* (OTL; Philadelphia: Westminster, 1970), 469.

20. *ANET*, 443; W. Eichrodt, *Ezekiel*, 469; J. A. Wilson, *The Culture of Ancient Egypt* (Chicago: University of Chicago Press, 1951), 120, 132; J. Jeremias, " *Poimēn, Archipoimēn, Poimainō*," *TDNT* 6 (1968), 486.

verses 26–27 since normal flocks in Israel contained both sheep and goats (Gen. 30:32; Ezek. 34:17).[21] Both of the terms in verse 23, $\bar{so}^{,}n$ and $\bar{e}der$, apply to such a flock consisting of both kinds of animals.

The contents of verses 25–27 can be understood in harmony with this royal application. Apparently the connection between verse 25 and verses 26–27 is that the provision laid up is used to feed the flock, and thus they become profitable.[22] When that meaning is transferred to ruling, the passage says that, if monarchs provide well for their subjects, they will return the favor. Subjects will provide income for their sovereign and add to the riches mentioned in verse 24. The one phrase that still requires some explanation is verse 26b, which connects goats to the price of a field. That can be and has been understood benignly like the rest of the passage. Scott interprets verse 26b to mean that "goats will provide profit from the land,"[23] that is, the use of land to feed goats is a good investment. Another possibility is the NEB's translation, "The he-goats are worth the price of a field." So verses 25–27 as a whole point out the value of the kind of good rule presented in chapters 28–29.

One objection that has been raised to applying verses 23–27 to a future ruler is that verse 24 contradicts the Judahite belief that the dynasty of David is eternal.[24] However, in the first place, it is not clear that the concept of an eternal dynasty was consistently upheld in Judah (Ps. 132:11–12).[25] Verse 24 does not necessarily come from a time or circles that accepted it. Furthermore, verse 24 may not be intended to apply to the whole dynasty. Individual future monarchs may be receiving the warning that their crown will not remain on their heads forever. It will remain for even a shorter time if they neglect their people.

Our conclusion, then, is that Proverbs 27:23–29:27 is a unified collection addressed to future monarchs. Verses 23–27 are the introduction to the carefully organized material in chapters 28–29. This introduction addresses royal readers and admonishes them to pay attention to the situation of their people lest they lose their riches and crown through neglect of their duties.

---

21. W. S. McCullough, "Goat," *IDB* 2:407.
22. C. H. Toy, *Proverbs*, 494.
23. R. B. Y. Scott, *Proverbs*, 163.
24. R. N. Whybray, *Proverbs*, 159.
25. B. Halpern, *The Constitution of the Monarchy in Israel*, HSM 25 (Chico, Calif.: Scholars, 1981), passim; J. Bright, *Covenant and Promise* (Philadelphia: Westminster, 1976), 64.

29

WORDS OF AGUR:
PROVERBS 30:1–33

David A. Hubbard

T he feast of wisdom to be enjoyed in chapter 30 seems to come
from a table other than Solomon's. The change of chef in no
way diminishes the quality, whether of content or artistry. Indeed, this chapter is unmatched in the book in its variety of forms—from dispute, to prayer,
to instruction, to description of social chaos, to playful numerical games
whose wry humor catches our consciences.

Title

30:1 The words of Agur the son of Jakeh, *his* utterance. This man declared to
Ithiel—to Ithiel and Ucal:

Prov. 30:1

The sayings, whether through verse 9 or perhaps verse 14, are credited to one
"Agur," a name otherwise unknown in the Old Testament. And *"Jakeh"* his

father is mentioned only here. If we transliterate rather than translate *maśśā*ʾ ("*his utterance*," a common prophetic word for "oracle," Isa. 13:1; 15:1; Nah. 1:1; Hab. 1:1; Mal. 1:1; but used in Proverbs just twice—here and 31:1), we may gain further information about "Agur, the son of Jakeh," the man of Massa or the Massaite (see Ishmael's son in Gen. 25). This reading would identify Agur as a tribal sage or chief of Massa's tribe in North Arabia, an area whose wisdom was legendary (1 Kings 4:29–34). As confusing as it may seem, if "*utterance*" should be read as the proper name Massa, Ithiel and Ucal, who defy identification, should be translated as phrases. What the phrases mean is more difficult to say. Despair seems to be the mood: "I am weary, O God, I am weary and worn out" (NEB). Or even more desperately: "There is no God, there is no God and I am exhausted" (McKane, p. 258; see Anchor Bible). Thus is set the melancholy tone for the dialogue that follows (vv. 2–9).

In what sounds like skepticism and doubt, Agur's words are closer to those of Job or Ecclesiastes than to the bulk of Proverbs. They demonstrate that dealing with the uncertainties of faith was part of the ministry of the teachers along with the instruction in wise conduct (see Ps. 73 for another example).

Confession/Dispute of Ignorance

> 30:2 Surely I *am* more stupid than *any* man,
>   And do not have the understanding of a man.
>   3 I neither learned wisdom
>   Nor have knowledge of the Holy One.
>
>   4 Who has ascended into heaven, or descended?
>   Who has gathered the wind in His fists?
>   Who has bound the waters in a garment?
>   Who has established all the ends of the earth?
>   What *is* His name, and what *is* His Son's name,
>   If you know?
>
> Prov. 30:2–4

For "*surely*," read "for": it introduces the reason for the despair that borders on agnosticism. Human limitation is the theme. "I am more beast than man" would accurately paraphrase the first line (see Ps. 73:22 for Heb. *baʿar* as "beast"; Prov. 12:1 contains similar wording). The thought is expanded and clarified in verse 3. The "*understanding*" (Heb. *bînâh*; 1:2) that he lacks is "*wisdom*" that stems from the fear of God and "*knowledge*" (see 1:7) of the will and ways "*of the Holy One*" (see 9:10). The Hebrew plural form of "holy" expresses the excellence and majesty of God, as the Being utterly different in power, glory, and purity from anything in the whole creation.

The three synonyms, "understanding," "wisdom," "knowledge," echo the opening verses of Proverbs, but with all the joy and confidence drained away. What the wise teachers held out as the purpose of their training, Agur confesses to have missed.

All the questions in verse 4 call for God as the answer. Their nearest biblical parallel is Job 38, when the Lord's voice blasts from the whirlwind with questions that force Job to acknowledge his ignorance and yield to God's wisdom. It is likely, in light of these similarities to Job, that God is speaking, whether directly or indirectly through the lips of a sage. Agur can hardly be the speaker. The knowledge of God's activities implied in the questions does not fit the stupidity which he confessed.

The point God seems to make in the questions is that no unaided human knowledge can probe these mysteries—a theme sounded in Job 28. Agur should not despair of his ignorance. It is a problem he has in common with all who have not learned to fear and trust God in His revealed word. *"Name"* stands for character. To know the name, especially the covenant name "Yahweh" is to know the person of God as Creator and Redeemer (Exod. 3:13–14). *"Son"* here may have initially stood for a wise teacher, since "son" is regularly used of an apt pupil in Proverbs. But the wording *"what is His Son's name"* opens the passage for a New Testament interpretation: "No one knows the Son except the Father. Nor does anyone know the Father except the Son, and the one to whom the Son wills to reveal Him" (Matt. 11:27).

The mystery of God's ways has more than one meaning. God threw that mystery at Job to shake his complacency and self-confidence. God pressed that same mystery on Agur to relieve him of his depression and assure him that he was not alone in his doubt and ignorance.

My seat mate looked at his watch as we neared Chicago on a flight from Louisville. He had just found out the nature of my occupation. His statement came quickly and bluntly: "You have twenty-two minutes to convince me that I should not be an agnostic." I continued our conversation on a nonreligious topic. He interrupted to repeat his challenge: "Twenty-two minutes." I looked him in the eye and said, "I'm not even going to try."

He took charge immediately. "Well, I'll tell you one thing: no one can convince me that the universe is here by chance. There's too much pattern and design in it. It could not have happened by itself." I answered slowly and quietly. "You have just drummed yourself out of the agnostics' corps. They have ripped the epaulets from your shoulder and stripped the sword from your side. No one can say what you said about creation and remain an agnostic."

Then I paused a minute and smiled. "I'm sure glad you acknowledge God's power in the universe. I was afraid that He might have to let the plane crash before we landed in Chicago so that I could hear you pray."

Admonition on God's Word

> 30:5 Every word of God *is* pure;
>   He *is* a shield to those who put their trust in Him.
>   6 Do not add to His words,
>   Lest He rebuke you, and you be found a liar.

Prov. 30:5–6

These verses contain the teacher's comments on the divine word to Agur. They underscore the reliability of what God has said: It is *"pure,"* unmixed with any dross of error, bright and shiny like refined silver (see Ps. 12:6); it is strong like a military *"shield"* (see 2:7; Song of Sol. 4:4), probably a reference to the small round or rectangular protective devices made of leather, wood, or metal and carried by hand or slung over the shoulder. Paul's "shield of faith" (Eph. 6:16) connects *"shield"* and *"trust"* as does this proverb.

Such reliability cannot be improved on. Therefore, in what is called "an integrity formula" expressing the completeness of God's word (see Rev. 28:18) and based on Ps. 18:30 and Deut. 4:2, the hearer, probably Agur, is warned against adding thoughts of his own, which if contrary to divine teaching would brand him as *"a liar."*

Prayer for Moderate Blessings

> 30:7 Two *things* I request of You
>   (Deprive me not before I die):
>   8 Remove falsehood and lies far from me;
>   Give me neither poverty nor riches—
>   Feed me with the food allotted to me;
>   9 Lest I be full and deny *You,*
>   And say, "Who *is* the LORD?"
>   Or lest I be poor and steal,
>   And profane the name of my God.

Prov. 30:7–9

The conversation between Agur, God, and a teacher closes with the teacher's model prayer which picks up the theme of lying from verse 6 and in the *"of You"* makes clear that the Lord has been party to the whole discussion. The prayer is an example of persistence: *"before I die"* means "as long as I live." This is not a cry for rescue from immediate crisis but for continual help with never-ending problems. The first petition, which uses the imperative mood like an admonition—*"remove falsehood and lies"*—requires no expansion or motivation clause. The damaging results to the person who deals in dishonesty and to his victims are obvious. "Falsehood" (Heb. *shāw'*; here only in Proverbs; frequent in Psalms, see 12:2, and prophets; see Jer. 2:30; 4:30) is literally "emptiness," worthless behavior or speech. Lies are regularly condemned in Proverbs for their disruptive impact on the social and especially judicial welfare of the community (6:19; 19:5, 9, 22).

The second petition (again an imperative)—*"Give me neither poverty nor riches"*—is more subtle and is accompanied by the substantial explanation of verse 9. Both petitions place the nouns—falsehood, lies, poverty, riches—at the head of the Hebrew sentence to thrust them, not the verbs, into prominence. The petitioner knows what help he needs in terms both of protection and supply, and he asks for it in the straightforward manner of the children of God (Matt. 7:7–11). He counts on the Lord to determine his basic needs and to meet them. *"Feed me"* in its Hebrew form portrays the divine hand extending a loaf of bread (*"food"*) and telling him exactly what his portion is to be. The idea of allotted food brings to mind memories of my Depression boyhood, namely, the picture of my watchful mother dispensing equity among five children at the dinner table. "Give us this day our daily bread" (Matt. 6:11) is the New Testament form of this request.

The most fascinating thing about the prayer is the balanced and worldly wise wisdom present in the motivation clauses beginning with *"lest"* (v. 9). Overabundance (*"full"*) may lead to an arrogant self-sufficiency that loses all sense of dependence on God. *"Who is the Lord?"* is a question in form but a statement in intent—"I have no need of the Lord." Poverty, on the other hand, may drive a person to the desperate act of stealing. Theft has profound theological consequences. It profanes—the word means to "seize" or "snatch" in a violent way, as Potiphar's wife clutched at Joseph's garment (Gen. 39:12)—*"the name of my God."* It does so by breaking God's law against stealing (Exod. 20:15; Deut. 5:19) and by declaring that God will not provide for His own as God has promised.

The world-view expressed here is remarkable. The supplicant knows both the frailty of his own human nature and also the sanctity of God's name. Earthly sins have heavenly significance. And the ultimate result of human crime is to insult the name of the Lord who made us, and who made us for better things than lying and stealing.

The brief yet dramatic discussion introduced by Agur's name seems to end here. In verse 10 the subject changes sharply. A word on the flow of the structure may be the best way to sum up the gist of the passage.

vv 1–3 Agur confesses an inability to know God.

v 4 God raises questions that show both the mystery and majesty of God.

vv 5–6 A teacher affirms the trustworthiness of God's words and warns against adding to them.

vv 7–9 A teacher offers a model prayer illustrating dependence on God for life's basic spiritual and physical provisions.

The prayer, then, may be seen as the practical conclusion to a discussion that began with doubt and disbelief. We come to know God not by speculation or meditation but by calling on Him daily for His practical help at our neediest points.

Admonition on Slandering a Servant

> Do not malign a servant to his master,
> Lest he curse you, and you be found guilty.
>
> Prov. 30:10

The close, almost familial, bond between servant and master (see chap. 29) is the background of this warning. *"Malign"* suggests a harsh use of the tongue in words of "slander" or "false condemnation" (see the same verb root *lāshan* in Ps. 101:5 where "neighbor" is the target). Meddling seems to be the crime involved, since the servant is given the right to defend himself by dressing down (*"curse"* is not used here in a technical sense) his accuser. The *"guilty"* verdict (the verb *ʾāshēm* is frequent in the law, see Lev. 4:13, 22, 27, and prophets, see Jer. 2:3; Ezek. 22:4; Hos. 4:15, but used only here in Proverbs) does not place the scene in a courtroom but suggests guilt in the eyes of the servant, the master, any one in the community who overheard the meddling, and the meddler himself. It is the master's role to handle a servant's or a child's misbehavior. To interfere with that responsibility is to ask for guilt and shame. Busybodies win no popularity contests.

Description of Spiteful Behavior

> 30:11 *There* is a generation *that* curses its father,
> And does not bless its mother.
> 12 *There* is a generation *that is* pure in its own eyes,
> *Yet* is not washed from its filthiness.
> 13 *There is* a generation—oh, how lofty are their eyes!
> And their eyelids are lifted up.
> 14 *There is* a generation whose teeth *are like* swords,
> And whose fangs *are like* knives,
> To devour the poor from off the earth,
> And the needy from *among men.*
>
> Prov. 30:11–14

A significant sector of Israel's society seems to have run amok. Life is out of hand in ways that the prophets denounced. *"Generation"* at the head of each verse calls repeated attention to a substantial group within the land that bears wretched characteristics. The passage anticipates Jesus' use of "generation" as reference to a group or circle of His countrymen (Matt. 3:7; 12:34; 23:33). Whereas most of the proverbs focus on the foolish or wicked as individuals, here the suggestion must be that a substantial minority or even a majority of the citizenry are bound together in the four kinds of rebellious conduct described. *Dishonor of parents* heads the list (v. 11), in defiance of the first admonition of the book (1:8) and the commandment given with a promise in the law (Exod. 20:12; Deut. 5:16 . . .). Next (v. 12) is *flagrant self-righteousness,* described in the contrast between claiming to be *"pure,"* newly washed, unsoiled, while being caked with *"filthiness,"* a mild translation of the Hebrew *ṣoʾāh* which is "excrement" as 2 Kings 18:27 shows. Third (v. 13), there is lofty pride symbolized in the snooty looks that pour barrels of haughtiness on the heads of those thought to be beneath them (see 6:17). Finally (v. 14) comes oppressive greed that (note the *"swords"* and *"knives"*; see Abraham's knife in Gen. 22:6, 10 for the same word) consumes (*"devour"*) the *"poor"* and *"needy"* with a savage ferocity, feeding on their meager goods, shrunken land, and well-bent backs with a cannibalism that Micah so graphically described (3:1–3). *"Men"* (v. 14) perhaps should be read as "land" (by adding an *h* in Hebrew) to complete the parallelism with *"earth"* and to acknowledge the rapacity with which the rich robbed the poor of their lands.

Numerical Sayings on Greed

> 30:15 The leech has two daughters,
> "Give *and* Give!"
> There are three *things that* are never satisfied,
> Four never say, "Enough!":
> 16 The grave,
> The barren womb,
> The earth *that* is not satisfied with water—
> And the fire never says, "Enough!"

Prov. 30:15–16

The first saying, though not strictly a numerical proverb since it contains one number not two (on the *x, x + 1* structure of numerical sayings see 6:16), is attached to verse 15 both because it contains the number *"two"* and because its implicit subject is greed. The *"two daughters"* of *"the leech"* are probably the two suckers found at the head and tail. Their endless appetite is voiced in *"Give and Give!"* Whether this is what they cry as many versions suggest or what they are named, the point is the same: they crave inordinate amounts of blood and serve as an object lesson from the creation of the greed that motivates much human behavior. Though very different in form from verses 11–14, these numerical sayings pick up some of the themes and sound them another way. Hence, verses 15–16 play off the note of greed in verse 14.

Four items of insatiable appetite are listed, items that never say *"Enough!"* (Heb. *hôn* means wealth and power and describes what is plentiful or bountiful): The *"grave"* with its bottomless capacity to absorb the dead (on Sheol see 1:12); the *"barren* [lit., "shut up" or "oppressed"] *womb"* which craves conception and birth to sustain the family line and name, as well as to fulfill its basic purpose; the *"earth"* ever and always open to receive the moisture of dew, rain, and melted snow, especially in the dry Middle Eastern climes where these sayings were spawned; *"fire"* which, whether in a friendly setting like an oven or firepit or in a hostile one like the burning of houses or crops, feeds endlessly on fuel. Often, the last item in the numerical series is both the climax and the main point. That does not look to be the case here.

These sayings like most of the numerical family are not mere observations on how the created world works, though they are insightful at that level. At heart they are illustrations drawn from creation to shed light on the behavior of creation's most puzzling creature: the human being, whether individually or in community. No wonder, given the endemic nature of our greed, God capped the Decalogue with commands against coveting (Exod. 20:17; Deut. 5:21)! No wonder Paul concluded an epistle on joy with one of the chief keys to it: "I have learned in whatever state I am, to be content" (Phil. 4:11)!

Saying on Respect for Parents

> 30:17 The eye *that* mocks *his* father,
>   And scorns obedience to *his* mother,
>   The ravens of the valley will pick it out,
>   And the young eagles will eat it.
>
> Prov. 30:17

This proverb harks back to the theme of verse 11, while featuring the haughty *"eye"* of verse 13. Note that mockery and lack of *"obedience"* (for the other Old Testament use of this word see Gen. 49:10; another reading supported by LXX is "seniority") do not have to be voiced or acted out. The set of the eye can convey volumes of disrespect. God so hates such dishonor that He has geared the creation to inflict punishment for it: *"ravens,"* the strong, loud black birds that scouted for Noah (Gen. 8:7) and fed Elijah (1 Kings 17:4), will join with the *"young eagles"* ("vultures" may be a better translation here) to inflict fearsome judgment on the arrogant eye. The parental disrespect may have to do with refusing them proper burial. The fitting judgment then would be the exposure of the ungrateful son's body so that birds of carrion would scavenge from it.

Numerical Saying on Love

> 30:18 There are three *things which* are too wonderful for me,
>   Yes, four *which* I do not understand:
> 19 The way of an eagle in the air,
>   The way of a serpent on a rock,
>   The way of a ship in the midst of the sea,
>   And the way of a man with a virgin.
>
> Prov. 30:18–19

Here the point is made in the final line: the venturesome and mysterious ways of the soaring *"eagle"* (often a symbol of vigor and vitality; Ps. 103:5; Isa. 40:31), the slithering *"serpent"* (not usually poisonous in Palestine, but see Amos 5:19; 9:3), the sailing *"ship"* (a source of wonder to Israelites who, unlike the Phoenicians, were not at home in the sea and on ships)—these all build to a climax in the mystery and adventure of affection and attraction between a young man and an eligible young woman. The Bible provides accurate and detailed documentation of *"the way of a man with a virgin"* and of her way with him in the Song of Solomon. The repetitions of "way" form a sort of pun on a key word of Proverbs which usually stands for a total pattern of life and behavior but here focuses on one important component of it. The positive picture of romance here contrasts with the warnings against illicit relations (2:16–19; 5:1–14; 6:20–29; 7:1–27) and connects with the admonitions to marital fidelity (5:15–23), while preparing for the picture of a competent and virtuous woman in 31:10–31.

Description of a Callous Adulteress

> This *is* the way of an adulterous woman:
> She eats and wipes her mouth,
> And says, "I have done no wickedness."
>
> Prov. 30:20

The contrast between the last line of verse 19 and this saying is patent. *"Way"* connects the two. The virgin entered the wonders of love with wide-eyed expectation and eager openness to its surprises. The *"adulterous woman"* (for the adulterous man, see 6:32) treats the act of intercourse as though it were a casual meal, a snack grabbed on the run. No mystery, no wonder, no commitment, no real pleasure! And to top it off, no admission of guilt or shame! Her covenant with her husband seems meaningless, and her sense of responsibility to God appears to have evaporated. However, her denial of *"wickedness"* (on Heb. *ʾāwen*, see 6:12, 18) may be a left-handed confession of guilt. "Beware of what you deny" was the way a therapist friend of mine put it.

Numerical Saying on Social Chaos

> 30:21 For three *things* the earth is perturbed,
> Yes, for four it cannot bear up:
> 22 For a servant when he reigns,
> A fool when he is filled with food,
> 23 A hateful *woman* when she is married,
> And a maidservant who succeeds her mistress.
>
> Prov. 30:21–23

The stability of a community is the theme. Four instances are listed that upset it. Their impact is described by humorous exaggeration: *"perturbed"* can also describe an earthquake (Amos 8:8), and *"for"* is literally "under," with the implication that the earth itself rattles and loses its poise under the influence of these acts of social upheaval. *"A servant"* is not trained to serve as king (*"reigns"*) and may mishandle the authority either by complacency or by abuse of power. *"A fool"* stuffed with *"food"* (lit., "bread") may become crude, rude, loud, and boorish, thinking he has merited such lavish fare and is welcome in such high-class company. *"A hateful,"* or better "unattractive" and therefore previously rejected as a suitable marriage partner, *"woman"* may react high-handedly in overcompensation for her years of being looked down on. *"A maidservant"* may become puffed up with haughtiness and treat with disdain the rest of the household, including her fellow servants if she *"succeeds"* or usurps the position of *"her mistress."* In the ordered structures of Israelite society changes of station were not the norm and the education and preparation for such changes were usually lacking. Rash promotions can lead to illustrations of the "Peter principle," the assigning of persons to tasks beyond their competence, with substantial hurt to them and to others. On the other hand, the Old Testament celebrates the success of Joseph, Esther, and Daniel, who were gifted with the talents and attitudes to rise from servitude to high places and rendered distinguished service.

Numerical Saying on Wise Behavior

> 30:24 There are four *things which* are little on the earth,
> But they *are* exceedingly wise:
> 25 The ants *are* a people not strong,
> Yet they prepare their food in the summer;
> 26 The rock badgers are a feeble folk,
> Yet they make their homes in the crags;
> 27 The locusts have no king,

> Yet they all advance in ranks;
> 28 The spider skillfully grasps with its hands,
>   And it is in kings' palaces.

Prov. 30:24–28

This lesson seems especially fitting for younger or less gifted students. Its point is that persistent, thoughtful effort will pay off even for those who seem less promising. The form departs from the usual numerical saying in listing only one number—*"four"* (see the leeches' two daughters in v. 15). Furthermore, the verses seem not to build to a climax; each illustration from nature contains an important lesson, to amplify the theme that size does not count nearly as much as wisdom (v. 24).

"Plan ahead" is what we learn from the *"ants"* (v. 25) who overcome their lack of physical strength by starting their *"food"* preparation *"in the summer"* and setting aside enough to carry them through the winter. The *"rock badgers"* (v. 26), animals about the size of rabbits but with smaller ears and shorter legs like guinea pigs, illustrate the maxim, "Make wise choices," by living in rocky crags where they can hole up to escape animals of prey or human hunters (Ps. 104:18). "Hang together or you'll hang separately" is the motto of the *"locusts"* (v. 27) who without an apparent leader (*"king"*) move across the land in ordered *"ranks"* like a well-drilled army (see Joel 2:7). "If at first you don't succeed, try and try again," is the slogan of the "lizard" (a better translation than *"spider"* of the Hebrew word found here only in the Old Testament); probably a type of gecko, harmless and awake at night to feed on insects, who can slip through tiny cracks, lie quietly and blend into stone or wood surroundings to make itself comfortable in royal *"palaces."* I have never slept in a royal palace. But I did enjoy the company of a pet lizard in a room that I occupied in a state guest house in India. Its surefooted tenacity and sneaky persistence testify to the veracity of this proverb. In an age where brilliant thinking and high technology are admired, it is good to hear again the importance of basic virtues like careful planning, wise choosing, community loyalty, and dogged (or "lizarded") persistence. The little engine that said "I think I can, I think I can, I think I can" is no fairy tale but a true symbol of how progress is made and service rendered by those whose determination may be greater than their stature or talent.

Numerical Saying on Stateliness

> 30:29 There are three *things which* are majestic in pace,
>   Yes, four *which* are stately in walk:
>   30 A lion, *which* is mighty among beasts
>   And does not turn away from any;
>   31 A greyhound,

> A male goat also,
> And a king *whose* troops *are* with him.

Prov. 30:29–31

The subject changes from the small (v. 24) to the stately. *"Majestic"* and *"stately"* translate the same Hebrew word, which literally means "those who do things well." The point is the importance and impact of behaving like leaders. The first two verses are clear in Hebrew and show where the saying is headed, even though it is very difficult to translate with precision. The proud courage of the *"lion"* sets the pace; it will not shy away from any foe (v. 30; see Isa. 30:6; Job 4:11). *"Greyhound"* (v. 31) is also translated "cock" or "horse"; the Hebrew word occurs only here and cannot be rendered with certainty. Any of these animals could be cited for its preeminence among others of its kind. The same is true of the *"male goat"* that marks off its territory and fights all other claimants to its ewes. The last line seems to be the climax that makes the point about how a *"king"* should behave and be viewed. Unfortunately the line is not clear: *"troops"* represents a guess at the Hebrew word, though not a wild guess (see "lead his army," NEB; similarly NIV); "at the head of this people" is McKane's reconstruction.

Appropriate words these are for would-be leaders. They frame a how-much-more argument: if animals perform with dignity their roles as prominent members of the pride, flock, or herd how much more should human beings called to be heads of the government or its various branches! "King" (v. 31) may link these verses to the preceding ones, especially verse 27: if the locusts who have no king perform together in such an orderly fashion, how much more should Israel's daughters and sons who have leadership ordained by God!

Admonition on Anger

> 30:32 If you have been foolish in exalting yourself,
>   Or if you have devised evil, *put your* hand on *your* mouth.
>   33 For *as* the churning of milk produces butter,
>   And wringing the nose produces blood,
>   So the forcing of wrath produces strife.

Prov. 30:32–33

This concluding proverb reaches back to the words on pride in verse 12, highlights *"wrath"* (v. 33) as one of its inevitable by-products, and features *"strife"* (Heb. *rib* which covers a range of arguments from personal quarrels to formal lawsuits; 15:18; 17:1, 14) as the bottom line. Only one hope is offered for checking this inevitable process: *"put your hand on your mouth."*

Don't say what you feel about your inflated sense of self-importance (*"exalting yourself"*) or about the scheming way (*"devised evil"*) you are going to get and retain the upper hand on your neighbor.

If you miss that one checkpoint and fail to cool down and think soberly about the impact of your words, the chain reaction sets in and moves step by step from pride to scheme to anger to quarrel. The relentless nature of the process is twice illustrated and once stated. The language is deliberately repetitive. The same Hebrew word (*mîṣ*) which means "pressing" or "pressure" is used three times with appropriate translations: with *"milk,"* *"churning"*; with *"nose,"* *"wringing"*; with *"wrath,"* *"forcing."* And as the English indicates, the same verb is used to point to the results in all three cases: *"produces."* The argument says that unchecked pride will lead to anger and strife with the same predictable effect that tells a farmer that churning milk will always result in butter and that tells a wrestler that twisting and pushing an opponent's nose will regularly draw blood.

So the collection of numerical sayings, admonitions, and descriptions ends at verse 33 where it began in verse 15—with examples of lessons learned from the way God's created order works. The lessons are to be studiously and faithfully applied in everyday life to honor the covenant Lord, to work peace and harmony in society, and to fulfill our potentials as human beings.

30

THE "WORDS" LEMUEL'S MOTHER TAUGHT HIM: PROVERBS 31

Kathleen A. Farmer

About Ruling Wisely (31:1–9)

Again in 31:1 the word *massaʾ* may be understood as an ethnic designation (in which case the text reads, "The words of King Lemuel of Massa . . .") or it may be understood to mean an "oracle" (which would make the heading say, "The words of King Lemuel, an oracle . . ."). In either case the text is clear in its assertion that these are Lemuel's mother's teachings.

The opening words, "What, my son? What, son of my womb?" (v. 2), sound very much like a mother scolding her child. The word used here for "son" is in Aramaic, a language which is closely related to Hebrew. By the end of the sixth century B.C.E. Aramaic was the dominant spoken language in Mesopotamia. It was commonly used in official communications and would thus

From Kathleen A. Farmer, *Who Knows What Is Good? A Commentary on the Books of Proverbs and Ecclesiastes,* ITC Series (Grand Rapids: Eerdmans, 1991). Reprinted by permission.

be familiar to most people in the ruling hierarchies of both Israel and other nations in the Fertile Crescent.

We might imagine a queen mother addressing a very young king or soon-to-be-king, but no actual historical information is available. In verses 3–4 Lemuel's mother seems to be questioning her son's behavior with regard to women and alcoholic beverages. Kings cannot let themselves be lured away from the serious business of ruling, insists the queen mother. The text does not say that women "destroy kings" but that the young king must not give his "strength" either to women or to anything else which might distract him from his responsibilities. Wine and strong drink are specified as the most likely distractions (v. 4). Alcohol could make the king forget what he should be doing and "pervert the rights of all the afflicted" (v. 5). This is not to say that wine does not have an appropriate use. In the queen mother's opinion, wine can be used as a sedative or as a pain-killer. It may be acceptable, she says, for the desperately ill to resort to strong drink (v. 6) or for the poor to drink in order to "forget their poverty" (v. 7), but a king needs to stay sober in order to do his duty!

Lemuel's mother holds up a rather idealistic picture of kingship for her son to follow. Clearly, she expects him to take an active role in upholding the rights of the powerless in his realm (vv. 8–9). This would not have been unusual among both Israelite and non-Israelite peoples in the ancient Near East. . . . Unfortunately, the prophets, the historians, and the wise in Israel testify to the repeated failure of kings to live up to the envisioned ideal.

The Concluding Acrostic (31:10–31)

The last twenty-two verses in Proverbs are in the form of an acrostic poem in which each verse begins with a new letter of the Hebrew alphabet in the traditional order. Interpreters argue over whether this acrostic poem should be considered a part of Lemuel's mother's advice or whether it is an independent (and thereby presumably "Israelite") composition. Some people think that the many sayings which speak so strongly against "foreign women" in other parts of the book indicate an attitude on the part of the wise which would not allow them to conclude the book with the words of a foreign queen. Others apparently fear that attributing the concluding words to a foreign queen mother diminishes the "authority" or the impact the poem might have on the reader. Claudia V. Camp suggests that "a poem about the ideal Israelite housewife—the mainstay of society in the post-exilic period—has been placed in the concluding (and therefore conclusive) position in the book . . . , displacing the instruction of a foreign queen" (*Wisdom and the Feminine in the Book of Proverbs*, 252–53). However, we have seen that the opinions of the collectors of Proverbs were not homogenous. Those who preserved the words of the wise for our edification frequently saw fit to juxtapose

contradictory observations and claims. It is equally clear that those who finalized our whole canon of Scripture saw fit to include both the Book of Ezra
with its strictures against foreigners and the Book of Ruth with its illustration
of the role a foreign woman plays in the lineage of David. The xenophobia of
one part of the postexilic community was balanced by other powerful claims
that "foreigners who join themselves to the LORD" are perfectly acceptable in
the LORD's house, which "shall be called a house of prayer for all peoples"
(Isa. 56:6–7). Thus, it is by no means certain that those who made this poem
into the conclusion for the whole Book of Proverbs intended to divorce it
from its apparent relationship to the words of Lemuel's mother. I suggest simply that our ancestors in the community of faith believed that this poem (regardless of its origins) made a fitting end to the first half of their two-volume
collection of wisdom. They saw it as an integral and perhaps even as an indispensable part of what the "wise" had to say to their contemporaries and to us.
Whether or not the material originated with Lemuel's mother, it is now a part
of the way our ancestors witness to us through the Scriptures. And what they
say to us is that the ideals of a wisdom way of life are the essence of what it
means to "fear the LORD."

In Praise of a Woman Who "Fears the Lord"

As the text now stands the acrostic seems to be the continuation of the
queen mother's advice to her royal offspring. The word (*ḥayil*) which the RSV
translates "good" in Prov. 31:10 (cf. KJV "virtuous," NIV "of noble character,"
NEB "capable") is the same word that is translated "strength" in verse 3 and
"excellently" in verse 29. When this word is used elsewhere in the OT, it is
usually understood as a reference to power (meaning either physical strength,
strength of character, or will power). The best way to determine how the
word should be translated in verse 10 is to pay attention to what else is said
about the woman who is praised in the subsequent lines of the poem.

Whoever it is who speaks in verses 10–31 says that the woman pictured
here will be hard to find, but she will be worth her weight in precious stones
to the man who is clever enough to marry her. He will be able to rely on both
her abilities and her goodwill (vv. 10–12). He will discover that a woman who
"fears the LORD" (v. 30) is worth much more to him than one who has only
the perishable qualities of charm and beauty.

According to the poem, the range of this ideal woman's abilities and the
reservoirs of energy and endurance from which she draws are truly formidable. She is pictured as organizing, overseeing, and tending to all the needs of
a large estate, which includes the buying, selling, and planting of fields (v. 16).
She is not averse to hard physical labor (v. 17). She produces (or at least helps
to produce) both the raw materials (vv. 13–14) and the finished products

(e.g., clothing, food, footwear) needed by the members of her household, which includes servants as well as children (vv. 15, 19, 21).

She is engaged in commerce, making "linen garments" to be sold on the open market (v. 24). Her merchandise is "profitable" (v. 18), and she plans ahead well enough that she can cope with sudden emergencies (v. 21). The phrase, "Her lamp does not go out at night," could mean that she works far into the night (as well as getting up while it is still dark, v. 15). But more probably this refers to her foresight in providing herself with enough oil to burn (as in the parable of the five wise virgins at the marriage feast in Matt. 25:1–12). And best of all, in addition to everything else she does, "She opens her hand to the poor, and reaches out her hands to the needy" (Prov. 31:20).

At this point in the praise of the "ideal wife," the modern reader is probably inclined to ask where the woman's husband is and what he is doing while she is engaged in all these admirable (but undoubtedly exhausting) activities. "Her husband is known in the gates," we are told in verse 23, where "he sits among the elders of the land." If the passage as a whole describes the "ideal wife," then the comment in verse 23 is probably intended to serve as an inducement to the prospective husband. The implication seems to be that the husband is freed by his wife's activities to participate in the legal and judicial activities that take place within the city gates. While he is not precisely a man of leisure, his activities are certainly pictured as being less strenuous than hers. We may also get the impression that he has gained his respected position in the community primarily through his wife's endeavors.

The poem concludes with (1) a description in verse 28 of the rewards such a woman might expect to receive: her children and her husband constantly praise her, (2) a comment in verse 30 on what qualities are most valuable in a woman (the fear of the LORD is more enduring than beauty or charm), and (3) a final piece of advice: a woman like the one described here should be given "the fruit of her hands" as well as praise for what she does (v. 31).

As Camp aptly says, "While her husband nominally controls 'the fruit of her hands,' he is directed in no uncertain terms to give it to her" (91).

Some readers have suggested that this "wife" is nothing more than a figment of some man's imagination (a "dream woman" who frees him from all his responsibilities). She certainly could not be seen as a "typical" wife or as a model for all Israelite women to emulate, since the woman described in the poem clearly is thought of as a member of the affluent, landowning, or even ruling classes. She is not an ordinary woman but rather an extraordinary one. She is also said to speak with wisdom, and "the teaching of *ḥesed* ('faithfulness'; RSV 'kindness') is on her tongue" (v. 26), which would be in accord with the picture verses 1–9 give us of Lemuel's mother. If this were Lemuel's mother picturing the kind of woman she would like for her son to marry, we might discount some of the details as wishful thinking on her part. On the other hand, the mother may be picturing some of the roles she herself has had to play in life.

However, I think the force of logic is on the side of those who see personified Wisdom mirrored in this down-to-earth and yet idealized picture of a skillful, prudent, and diligent woman who effortlessly manages her household and family affairs. References to Wisdom personified as a woman are scattered throughout the framework of the canonical form of Proverbs. We have seen how Wisdom has been poetically portrayed as a human female engaged in a variety of human occupations. Wisdom can act like a prophetess (1:20ff.), a darling child (8:30), a counselor to kings (8:15), a lover (4:6–9; 8:17, 21), a wife (as in 31:10ff.), or a mother (8:32ff.) She is a woman who "builds her house," fills it with treasures, prepares meals, and invites visitors in to participate in the feast she provides (9:1; 14:1; 24:3–4). The word translated "her household" in 31:21, 27 is the same as that translated "her house" in other passages. Wisdom, like the strong woman, is "more precious than jewels" (3:15) and is also capable of providing security for those who trust in her.

Thus, the concluding acrostic does not seem at all "foreign" to the images of wisdom which play a central part in the Instructions and a minor part in the other collections. Wisdom, who is pictured in the first chapter of Proverbs as a prophet of her own power and in the eighth chapter as a part of God's creative plan, is appropriately portrayed in the concluding portions of the book as a tower of strength for those who will trust in her ability to give them what they need (31:11). As Thomas McCreesh says, Wisdom "is not some lofty, remote ideal for those initiated into her mysteries, but a practical, ever-present, faithful guide and lifelong companion for all who choose her way" ("Wisdom as Wife: Proverbs 31:10–31," 46).

The collection which begins with the assertion that "the fear of the LORD is the beginning of knowledge" (1:7) thus ends with a hymn of praise for one who manifests in her life both the ideals of wisdom and the "fear of the LORD" (31:30).

31

CHIASM AND SYMMETRY
IN PROVERBS 31

Murray H. Lichtenstein

The Hebrew text of what is now designated Proverbs 31 combines two distinct poems, the first being instructions introduced by the rubric "The Words of Lemuel" (vv. 1–9), and the second being an alphabetical acrostic celebrating "The Excellent Wife" (vv. 10–31).[1] While in the LXX the two poems do not appear consecutively,[2] as in the Hebrew, one nevertheless observes several features common to both poems which may, in fact, account for their juxtaposition. Thus, for example, the actual instructions ascribed ostensibly to Lemuel or rather to his mother, begin with specific reference to women (v. 3 *nāšîm*), as does the second poem (v. 10 *ʾēšet*). The latter poem, in fact, is devoted entirely to the subject of a certain kind of

From *Catholic Biblical Quarterly* 44 (April 1982): 202–11. Used by permission.

1. A simpler form of this chapter was delivered as a paper at the Hudson-Delaware sectional meeting of the Society of Biblical Literature, held at Princeton Theological Seminary on 5 May 1980.

2. The order of the Hebrew verses observed in LXX is as follows: 31:1–9; 25:1–28; 26:1–28; 27:1–27; 28:1–28; 29:1–27; 31:10–31. For a succinct statement of the problem of the divergent order in the MT and the LXX of poems and parts of poems following chap. 24 in the Book of Proverbs, see H. B. Swete, *An Introduction to the Old Testament in Greek* (1902; reprint, New York: KTAV, 1968) 240–41.

woman, presumably one who would have met the standards of even the rather distrustful mother encountered in the first poem. More specifically, in the first poem it is the *ḥayil* (v. 3) of the king, however one interprets the term,[3] which is to be protected from women, while in the second poem *ḥayil* (vv. 20, 29)[4] constitutes the quintessence of the kind of woman depicted. So, too, the concern voiced for the needy *ʿānî* and *ʾebyôn* in "The Words of Lemuel" (v. 9) is echoed in the characterization of the excellent wife as also being particularly solicitous for their welfare (v. 20). Even as Lemuel is charged to "speak up" (vv. 8, 9; *ptḥ pyk*) on behalf of the wretched, so the woman of the second poem "speaks up" (v. 26: *pyh ptḥh*) with wisdom and graciousness.

Beyond these thematic and verbal links, however, there are striking stylistic and structural analogies to be drawn between the two poems of this chapter. More specifically, both poems feature a chiasm in some of their lines: Each poem presents one example of the pattern: A:B :: B:A, in which the initial order of key terms is reversed in their repetition, thus creating an elegant symmetrical balance of equal but opposite words and phrases. What is more remarkable, however, is that both poems employ chiasm as something more than an isolated literary ornament. Rather, the use of symmetrical chiastic order in lines of both poems is directly related to the larger symmetrical patterns characterizing the overall structure of each poem. In fact, in both poems the chiasm actually articulates the distinctly symmetrical structure of the individual poems.

In the first poem of Proverbs 31 one observes the following structure. In verse 1 there is a rubric identifying the piece, and in verses 2–3 an introductory exhortation from mother to son,[5] followed by an initial prohibition directed specifically to him. The main structural unit of the poem now begins in verse 4 and extends to the end of the poem in verse 9. This coherent unit has its own introductory

---

3. In Prov. 31:3 *ḥylk* would seem best translated by the general and comprehensive "your power." Here *ḥayil* appears in poetic parallelism with the perennially difficult *drkyk*, for which various emendations have been proposed, e.g., *yrkyk*, "your loins" (see now BHS); *ddyk*, "your love," or *lbbk*, "your heart" (see C. H. Toy, *Proverbs*, ICC [Edinburgh: Clark, 1899], 541).

Given the well-attested meaning of *ḥayil* as "strength, vigor" (e.g., Ps. 33:16 *ḥyl // kḥ*; cf. Isa. 43:17 *ḥyl wᶜzwz*), one is prompted to read the term parallel to *ḥylk* in Prov. 31:3 as *hdrk*, "your splendor." To be compared are such combinations as *kḥ* and *hdr* (Ps. 29:4) and *ᶜz whdr* (Prov. 31:25; cf. Ps. 96:6), as well as the actual association of the terms *ḥyl* and *hdr* (Ezek. 27:10). The identical confusion between *hdrk* and *drkk* seems to have taken place in reverse in Ps. 45:5 (*whdrk* being dittography of the last word of the preceding verse). Clearly, the semantically and stylistically apt reading *hdrk* in Prov. 31:3 obviates the need to appeal to the already overworked Ugaritic *drkt* "sovereignty, dominion," the very existence of which in Hebrew remains problematic (contrast M. Dahood, "Ugaritic DRKT and Biblical DEREK," *TS* 15 [1954]: 629).

4. In Prov. 31:10, 29 the term *ḥayil* is used in the derived sense of "excellence, merit, or skill" (see Gen. 47:6; Exod. 18:21; Prov. 12:4; Ruth 3:11; 1 Chron. 9:13).

5. While the sense of the words *bn ndry* in v. 2 is not exceptional, i.e., a son granted as the result of a vow made to God, the expression itself is unattested elsewhere in the Hebrew Bible. One is tempted to read here instead *bn nᶜwry* "son of my youth," as in Ps. 127:4. This suggestion appears all the more plausible in light of the sequence *bnym—pry bṭn—bny hnᶜwrym* in Ps. 127:3–4, which would then correspond to the sequence in Prov. 31:2: *bry—br bṭny—br nᶜwry*.

exhortation, independent of the initial exhortation of verse 2, being part of the "staircase" parallelism of verse 4: ʾal lamĕlākîm lĕmôʾēl, "it is not for kings, O Lemuel. . . ."[6] Further, the unit begins speaking impersonally about the behavior of kings rather than about the specific behavior of Lemuel, as previously. The main body of the unit, verses 4–7, may be schematized as follows:

A. A prohibition against yayin and šēkār, "wine and beer,"[7] followed by the justification that the king's drinking (yišteh) might lead to forgetting (yiškaḥ) his judicial duties to the detriment of the poor.

B. An injunction to provide šēkār and yayin, "beer and wine," to the distraught, followed by the justification that drinking (yišteh) and so forgetting (yiškaḥ) provide merciful relief to the wretched.

The two components of this literary unit are thus contrasting. The first is negative, addressing itself to the dangerous abuse of intoxicants, whereas the second is positive, addressing itself to their beneficial use. This conceptual contrast between abuse and use is highlighted by the structural and verbal symmetry of the two contrasting components, each consisting of an injunction specifying the intoxicants as yayin and šēkār and a justification employing the two verbs šātâ and šākaḥ. Most striking, however, is the actual articulation of the balanced contrast through the use of chiasm.[8] That is, just as the initial order of yayin and šēkār is reversed in the second component to read šēkār and yayin, even so are the two symmetrical components the conceptual reverse of one another. The use of chiasm in "The Words of Lemuel" as a structural means of heightening conceptual contrast may be viewed, for example, alongside a contextually analogous application in Proverbs 9. Thus, in two symmetrically balanced scenes Lady Wisdom and Dame Folly both extend the identical invitation to the foolish and mindless (9:4, 16) from atop the city heights (9:3, 14). However, while Wisdom proffers elaborately prepared *food* and *wine* (9:5), Folly speaks of her "stolen" *water* and "furtive" *food* (9:17).

Returning to the main structural unit of "The Words of Lemuel" (31:4–9), one observes that the two juxtaposed symmetrical components (vv. 4–7)

6. While the LXX treats lmwʾl as a phrase, "from (the mouth of) God," its position here as the final element of the first stich of a "staircase" parallelism may be taken as further confirmation that the word is a personal name in the vocative.

7. For the same sentiment expressed in this verse, compare the Sumerian instruction: "When you are drunk (lit., drink beer—Sumerian kaš = Akkadian šikāru), don't judge!" For the latter, see B. Alster, *The Instructions of Suruppak* (Mesopotamia: Copenhagen Studies in Assyriology 2; Copenhagen: Akademisk Forlag, 1974), 41, 99.

8. See the brief observation of S. Talmon that "literary inversion may be connected with reversal of contents," i.e., from positive to negative and vice versa. The observation is made, however, without reference to either the specific verses considered here or to the specific kind of structural analysis proposed here. See *Qumran and the History of the Biblical Text*, eds. F. M. Cross and S. Talmon (Cambridge/London: Harvard University Press, 1975), 360, 394 n. 159.

are followed by a two-verse coda (vv. 8–9). In this concluding coda, no less than in the two main components, symmetry is achieved through verbal and stylistic repetition. Thus, the coda contains two positive injunctions addressed directly to the king, each employing the imperative phrase *pĕtaḥ pîkā*, "Speak up!" and the juridical term *dîn*.[9]

The second poem in Proverbs 31, the alphabetical acrostic celebrating "The Excellent Wife," exhibits a strikingly analogous structure and style. Like the preceding "Words of Lemuel," it may be viewed as comprised of two symmetrically balanced components, followed by a two-verse coda, which is again characterized by verbal repetition. So, too, chiasm has once again been effectively exploited by the poet to articulate the symmetrical structure of the main body of the poem, albeit in a somewhat different manner.[10]

The main body of the poem (Prov. 31:10–29), i.e., the poem exclusive of the two-verse coda (vv. 30–31), is framed by means of verbal *inclusio*. In fact, two mutually reinforcing verbal frames have been created through the use of *hysteron proteron*.[11] Thus, the word *ḥyl* in verse 10 (the first line of the poem) is matched by its repetition in verse 29 (the last line preceding the coda). So, too, the word *bʿlh*, "her husband," in verse 11 (the second line of the poem) is matched by its repetition in verse 28 (the next to last line preceding the coda). While the main body of the poem is thus set off by means of the two concentric verbal frames *ḥyl—ḥyl* and *bʿlh—bʿlh*, the concluding coda (vv. 30–31) is marked off as a coherent structural unit through the change of person, from second to third, and most especially by the repetition of the root *hll*, "to

9. If one follows the LXX, it would seem stylistically preferable to construe *dîn* in Prov. 31:8b not as a noun but as an imperative, "Champion the cause!" as in v. 9b, which would yield a more perfect symmetry. In this case, the preposition *ʾel*, introducing v. 8b, cannot be retained and may be best viewed as a dittography of the preceding *ʾlm*. For the figurative use of the term *ʾillem*, "mute," see Ps. 38:14–16. Also to be compared is the following passage from an Egyptian prayer of thanksgiving: "Thou art Amon, the lord of the silent man, who comes at the voice of the poor man" (*ANET*, 380 with n. 5, which explains the term "silent man" as "a common expression at this time for the submissive or humble"). Note also the Sumerian proverb: "The poor are the silent ones of the Land (i.e., of Sumer)," in E. I. Gordon, *Sumerian Proverbs: Glimpses of Everyday Life in Ancient Mesopotamia* (1959; reprint, New York: Greenwood, 1968), 196, no. 2.32.

10. Literary appreciation of the structure of "The Excellent Wife" has concentrated almost exclusively on its external structure, i.e., on its use of the alphabetical acrostic form. Consequently, its internal structure has gone largely unnoticed and has been quite often mistaken for an "unnatural" ordering of the poetic lines (see C. H. Toy, *Proverbs*, 542), or a "randomness" and "uneven progress" (see W. McKane, *Proverbs: A New Approach* [The Old Testament Library; Philadelphia: Westminster, 1970] 665–66), which are seen as being dictated solely by the exigencies of the acrostic (cf. e.g., R. B. Y. Scott, *Proverbs and Ecclesiastes*, AB 18 [Garden City, N.Y.: Doubleday, 1965], 186; M. Zer-Kabod, "ʾĒšet Ḥayil," *Beth Mikra* 23–24 [1965]: 26–27).

11. For the structural use of *hysteron proteron* as a framing device in biblical, ancient Near Eastern, and other literature, see the analysis and discussion in M. H. Lichtenstein, *Episodic Structure in the Ugaritic Keret Legend: Comparative Studies in Compositional Technique* (unpublished doctoral dissertation: New York: Columbia University, 1979), 208–56.

praise," in each of its two constituent verses: *tithallāl* in verse 30 and *wiyhalĕlûhā* in verse 31.

The structural symmetry of the main body of the poem is articulated specifically through the use of chiasm. It will be observed that verses 10–18 and verses 21–29 comprise two constituent components, each consisting of nine verses. Separating these two components are verses 19–20, which read as follows:[12]

> Her hands (*yādêhā*) she eagerly[13] applies (*šillĕhá*) with dexterity,[14]
> And her hands (*kappêhā*) work the distaff.
> Her hand *(kappāh)* she holds out to the poor,
> And her hands (*yādêhā*) she eagerly extends (*šillĕhá*) to the wretched.

Here the chiasm of *šillaḥ yād—kap* and *kap—šillaḥ yād*[15] sets off verses 19–20 as a highly symmetrical structural unit, which is concentrically framed and, thus, self-contained. Indeed, the structure of verses 19–20 directly corresponds to that of the larger poetic unit in which it is imbedded, creating external as well as internal symmetry:

$$
\begin{array}{ll}
\text{— } \textit{ḥyl} \text{ (v. 10)} & \text{— } \textit{ydyḥ šlḥḥ} \text{ (v. 19a)} \\
\text{┌ } \textit{b'lḥ} \text{ (v. 11)} & \text{┌ } \textit{kpyḥ} \text{ (v. 19b)} \\
\text{└ } \textit{b'lḥ} \text{ (v. 28)} & \text{└ } \textit{kpḥ} \text{ (v. 20a)} \\
\text{— } \textit{ḥyl} \text{ (v. 29)} & \text{— } \textit{ydyḥ šlḥḥ} \text{ (v. 20b)}
\end{array}
$$

12. The translation offered here aims specifically at reproducing the order and arrangement of the Hebrew terms, necessitating some departure from both English syntax and style. Also to be noted is the difficulty in rendering the Hebrew parallel pair *yd // kp*, where the latter term is employed as a poetic synonym of the former, rather than as "palm," as such. The more literal rendering would, of course, obscure the equivalence of idioms such as *pāraś yād* and *pāraś kap* in the sense of extending a "helping hand" (see Isa. 65:2 alongside this usage in Prov. 31:20).

13. The usual idiom is *šālaḥ yād*, i.e., with the verb in the *qal* conjugation, and the use of the *piel* here and in v. 20 merits some reflection in the English translation. The nuance conveyed by the term "eagerly" is, of course, but one of a number of possible nuances (e.g., "constantly," "energetically") which may lie behind the Hebrew usage.

14. The more traditional rendering of *kyšwr* as "spindle," or the like, is based on the parallelism with *plk*, "distaff," and seems to be without any independent philological basis. For the translation adopted here, see M. H. Lichtenstein, "Psalm 68:7 Revisited," *JANES* 4 (1972): 108–10. For the positive feminine attribute of skill with the distaff, see the above reference; add now J. C. Greenfield, "Early Aramaic Poetry," *JANES* 11 (1970): 50.

15. The presence of chiasm in these verses has already been noted and commented upon by M. Dahood in *Ras Shamra Parallels I*, ed. L. Fisher, AnOr 49 (Rome: Institutum Biblicum, 1972), 237, no. 305, but without reference to its structural role in the poem as a whole. Note also Dahood's apt suggestion to read *kpḥ* (v. 20) as defective for *kpyḥ*, "her hands," making for an even more symmetrical congruence in the poetic unit. A good contextual parallel supporting Dahood's suggestion is afforded by Isa. 65:2, "I constantly held out my hands (*pēraśtí yādáy*) to a disloyal people" (NJV), where the idiom directly corresponding to *pāraś kap* involves the plural "hands."

The chiastic unit comprised of verses 19–20 serves as a central pivot for the two flanking nine-verse components which are included in the same larger framed unit, namely, verses 10–29:

    A. Nine-verse unit (vv. 10–18)
        Chiastic unit (vv. 19–20)
    B. Nine-verse unit (vv. 21–29)

Components A and B are effectively set off from one another, defined as coherent units, and are juxtaposed in symmetrical balance by the intrusion of the likewise symmetrical chiastic unit comprised of verses 19–20.

Significant here is the fact that the symmetry of the two components, as exemplified and expressed by their respective positions on either side of the chiastic unit, is by no means based solely on their identical verse-count. Rather, the two nine-verse components also balance one another in terms of both general theme and specific language. Thus, the subject matter of the first component recurs in the second, each nine-verse unit respectively extolling the excellent wife's incomparability (vv. 10, 29), the explicit or implicit benefit accruing to her husband (vv. 11, 23), her ethical or moral qualities (vv. 12, 26), her expertise in handicrafts (vv. 13, 22, 24), as well as in domestic management (vv. 15, 21, 27) and in commercial enterprise (vv. 16, 24), and her characteristic industriousness (vv. 15, 18, 27).

Here, as in the two symmetrical components of "the Words of Lemuel," verbal repetition is effectively exploited as a means of symmetrically balancing the two components. Thus, in the relatively short space of 18 verses the following 14 terms are shared by both components:[16] *byt* (15, 21, 27); *kl* (11, 23, 28); *ḥgr* (17, 24); *ḥyl* (10, 29); *ywm* (12, 25); *ky* (18, 21); *kl* (12, 21); *l* (18, 21); *lḥm* (14, 27); *mkr* (10, 24); *ntn* (15, 24); *ʿz* (17, 25); *ʿśh* (13, 22); *qwm* (15, 28).

The same kind of correspondence between the two flanking components is also evident with respect to idiomatic usage. The idiom, "to gird the loins with power," in the first component (v. 17) employs the metaphor of donning clothing to express the manifestation of strength, as does its counterpart in the second component (v. 25), "Power and splendor are her raiment." So, too, the conventional combination *ṣmr wpštym*, "wool and flax,"[17] in the first component (v. 13) is balanced, somewhat artificially, by the exceptional combination *šš wʾrgmn*, "lin-

---

16. Obviously some of the terms included in this list are more significant indicators than others. Thus the recurrence of common particles such as *ky*, *kl*, and *l* cannot be viewed in quite the same light as the repeated verbs and nouns; and, even in the latter categories, some terms are more common than others. Most significant, therefore, is the cumulative weight of all the various verbal elements shared by the two nine-verse components: particles, verbs, nouns, phrases (*byth*, vv. 15, 21, 27; *klh*, vv. 11, 23, 28) and, more generally, verbal roots.

17. Note especially the poetic usage of the combined terms *ṣmr wpštym* as hendiadys for "clothing" in Hos. 2:7, 11.

en and purple,"[18] in the second (v. 22). The two sets of paired items are further linked by the shared context of manufacturing (ʿśh) cloth or clothing.

It will be further observed that the pervasive symmetry of the poem "The Excellent Wife" is also evident with respect to the concluding two-verse coda. As in "The Words of Lemuel," the verbal repetition occurring within the coda (hll, verses 30, 31) itself imparts internal symmetry. Yet there also exists an external symmetry between the two-verse coda and the two-verse chiastic unit, directly corresponding to the symmetrical balance of the two nine-verse components:

  A. Nine-verse unit (vv. 10–18)
       Two-verse chiastic unit (vv. 19–20)
  B. Nine-verse unit (vv. 21–29)
       Two-verse coda (vv. 30–31)

As in the latter case, the correspondence between the two two-verse units is not based solely on their identical verse-count. Rather, both two-verse units are linked thematically. Thus, the chiastic unit couples the practical and moral virtues of the excellent wife, namely, her manual dexterity and her extended hand in support of the unfortunate. So, too, the coda juxtaposes, and so combines, the woman's piety[19] and her more concrete or material achievements, both being accounted fit subjects or objects of praise.[20]

18. While śś, "linen," and ʾrgmn, "purple (dyed) cloth," do appear together in extended lists of materials (see especially the provisions for building the tabernacle in Exod. 25–28, 35–39), they are never combined, as such. The closest the two terms come to juxtaposition in poetry is in Ezek. 27:7, but even there, as elsewhere, the term actually combined with ʾrgmn is tklt. Thus, in Jer. 10:9 the expression tklt wʾrgmn lbwšm represents a more traditional usage than our śś wʾrgmn lbwšh (Prov. 31:22b). Another more likely combination would have been śś wmšy "linen and silk" as suggested by Ezek. 16:10, 13. In any event, the attempt to pair-off śś, "linen," with some other fabric seems to have been dictated by the desire to balance the more traditional pairing-off of šmr wpštym, rather than by any conventional usage of its own.

19. The phrase yrʾt yhwh (v. 30), referring to the piety of the excellent wife is often emended according to what is claimed to be the reading of the LXX (see, most recently, BHS). It will be observed, however, that the phrase itself is attested in the LXX (phobon kyriou), together with the favored reading (synetē = ḥkmh/nbwnh) in what appears to be a rather artificial conflation of two different idioms in which the excellent wife is alternately the one praised and the one praising. The same kind of confusion exists as to who is praised and who is praising in the LXX of v. 31 (as contrasted with the MT). In other words, the problem seems to lie not with the MT so much as with the LXX itself, and, in this case, emendation of the former on the basis of the latter does not inspire confidence.

20. Strikingly, the combination of moral and practical virtues in the coda (as in the chiastic unit) integrates the two kinds of attributes as represented in the two nine-verse components. It will be observed that each of the latter includes one example of moral virtue (A: v. 12; B: v. 26), incorporated into their more practically oriented catalogues of praiseworthy achievement. Note also that the integrative function of the coda in "The Excellent Wife" corresponds to that of the coda in "The Words of Lemuel," where the combined mention of judicial responsibility and concern for the needy (Prov. 31:8–9) likewise integrates the respective concerns of the two constituent components (A: vv. 4–5; B: vv. 6–7).

A suggestive, but by no means problem-free parallel both to the symmetrical structure of "The Excellent Wife," and to the specifically structural role of chiasm in that poem may be sought in the poetic unit in Jeremiah 10:2–10.[21] Here again one observes two thematically and verbally symmetrical components (although not of equal length or verse-count) flanking a chiastic unit, all of which is followed by a concluding (one-verse) coda. While the two flanking components (vv. 2–5 and vv. 8–9) describe the nature of idolatry, both the chiastic unit (vv. 6–7) and the coda (v. 10) describe the God of Israel. The two flanking components not only share the same theme, but some of the same language as well:

A. verses 2–5	B. verses 8–9
hbl hw³	*hblym*
ʿs	*ʿs hw³*
mʿsh yd	*ksp*
hrš	*zhb*
ksp	*mʿsah hrš*
zhb	*yd (y.swrp)*

As for the pivotal chiastic unit, the text is as follows:

> There is none like you (*m³yn kmwk*), O Lord,
>> You are great, and great is your name in might.
>>> Who does not hold you in awe, King (*mlk*) of
>>> Nations (*gwym*), for it is your due.
>>> For among all the wise of the nations (*gwym*)
>>>> and among all their kings (MT *mlkwtm*)[22]
> There is none like you (*m³yn kmwk*), O Lord.

The unit may be viewed either as a framed chiasm (*mlk-gwym* and *gwym-mlk*), or as a case of *hysteron proteron:*

---

21. The unit has been defined as such and then discussed from the standpoint of rhetorical criticism in J. R. Lundbom, *Jeremiah: A Study in Ancient Hebrew Rhetoric,* SBLDS 18 (Missoula, Mont.: Scholars, 1975), 43–44. While the present discussion follows, in large part, Lundbom's overall structural analysis, there are significant differences in approach. Thus, for example, Lundbom's chief emphasis is on vv. 6–7 and is concerned with the presence of *inclusio,* making no mention of the presence or role of chiasm. Further, whereas Lundbom, indeed, recognizes the thematic and structural symmetry of vv. 2–5 and 8–9 (as well as vv. 6–7 and v. 10), no mention is made of their *verbal* symmetry, as detailed below. While the structural analysis advanced by Lundbom, and modified here, seems certain enough, it must be readily admitted that the poetic unit itself (mostly absent from the LXX) is replete with numerous textual and exegetical problems.

22. Parallelism (cf. Isa. 19:11), as well as chiasm, suggests the reading *mlkyhm,* "their kings," for which see the variant in Theodotion (cited in *BHS*) *tois basileusin autōn.*

mʾyn kmwk A		
mlk	B	
gwym		C
gwym		C
mlk	B	
mʾyn kmwk A		

However analyzed, it is clear that verses 6–7 constitute a self-contained symmetrical unit, featuring chiasm, and that this unit is flanked by two thematically and verbally symmetrical components, a structural pattern analogous to that observed in "The Excellent Wife." Further, the coda which seems to conclude this poetic unit in Jeremiah 10, namely, verse 10, symmetrically balances the chiastic unit not only thematically, as already indicated, but verbally as well, repeating the significant terms *mlk* and *gwym*.

While parallels may indeed be adduced for the structural patterns of both "The Words of Lemuel" and "The Excellent Wife,"[23] the most intriguing correspondence remains that between the two poems themselves. As initially observed, the two poems which are now joined together to form the final chapter of the Book of Proverbs share certain key words, themes, and subjects which may have prompted some "editorial decision"[24] to juxtapose the two originally independent pieces. The subsequent discussion has sought to highlight a further point of correspondence existing between the two poems on specific stylistic and structural grounds. Thus, both "The Words of Lemuel" and "The Excellent Wife" exhibit pervasive symmetry on a variety of levels: verbal, thematic, and structural. In the main body of the first poem (Prov. 31:4–7) the most striking symmetry is one of "equal and opposite," in the sense of juxtaposing two identically phrased and identically structured components of equal length, which manifest opposite approaches to the same subject, namely, intoxication. In the main body of the second poem (Prov.

23. Note, for example, the partial structural parallel afforded by Ps. 25, which exhibits verbal symmetry between its first and last three alphabetical verses (*npš, ʾl ʾbwš, ʾwyby, qwh*; cf. *bṭḥ b* and *ḥsh b*), serving to frame the acrostic, following which is a hyper-alphabetical coda which concludes the piece (Ps. 25:22; cf. Ps. 34:23). Here, as opposed to the case of Jer. 10:2–10, the acrostic format leaves little doubt as to defining the poetic unit. However, just as in the case of the Jeremiah passage, textual irregularities (immediately apparent from disruption of the alphabetical acrostic) may obscure even closer structural and stylistic correspondences between the psalm and Prov. 31:10–31. Another kind of parallel to the structural patterns under consideration is suggested by the poetic analyses (largely metrical) of D. N. Freedman, who has detected in Ps. 23, 29, and 137 "an X-like structure within a frame," produced by the use of chiasm in the mid-point of these poetic units, the chiasm being flanked by symmetrical poetic elements. See "Pottery, Poetry, and Prophecy: An Essay on Biblical Poetry," *JBL* 96 (1977): 13.

24. What is suggested here is something along the lines of N. M. Sarna's observations concerning the juxtaposition of originally independent literary units "on the basis of association of ideas, words, or phrases." See "Psalm 89: A Study in Inner Biblical Exegesis," *Biblical and Other Studies*, ed. A. Altmann, Philip W. Lown Institute of Advanced Judaic Studies, Brandeis University, Studies and Texts 1 (Cambridge: Harvard University Press, 1963), 30.

31:10–29) the symmetry is, again, one of "equal and opposite," but in the different sense of two components of equal length, identical content, and common phraseology echoing, and so reinforcing, each other's praise of the excellent wife from opposite sides of an intervening poetic unit.

Most significantly, both poems artfully exploit chiasm as a means of articulating and highlighting their own particular kinds of symmetry. In the first poem the chiasm (v. 4, *yyn—škr*; v. 6, *škr—yyn*) occurs within the two symmetrical components themselves, accentuating the conceptual contrast between them. In the second, the chiasm (v. 19, *šlḥ yd—kp*; v. 20, *kp—šlḥ yd*) occurs in a self-contained poetic unit intruding between the two symmetrical components, accentuating their conceptual balance or equivalence. In both poems, however, the symmetry of chiasm epitomizes and, in effect, integrates the various other manifestations of internal and external symmetry seen to be operative in each. The juxtaposition of the two poems of Proverbs 31, as it now stands in the Hebrew text, and however it may have come about, has effected a most happy and fitting union. Indeed, Lemuel's mother has been provided with a most appropriate daughter-in-law, in more ways than one.

32

WISDOM AS WIFE:
PROVERBS 31:10–31

Thomas P. McCreesh

The poem on the ʾēšet ḥayil, the "good wife" or "worthy wife," from chapter 31 of the Book of Proverbs is a significant key to understanding the Book of Proverbs as a whole. On the surface the poem is deceptively simple and transparent. Its contents closely resemble the concerns and practical advice of the preceding twenty or so chapters of individual sayings. It might appear to be no more than a longer contribution to the same themes. But further study reveals more.

The poem functions as a summary, a coda, for the whole book. Its placement at the end of the book, organized as an alphabetic acrostic (the only such acrostic in the book), points to it as a separate conclusion to the work. A similar technique is used at the end of the Book of Sirach where another alphabetic acrostic (51:13–30) concludes the work. Similar poems of praise in the wisdom tradition (but which do not close a book) are also acrostics: Psalm 112 and its praise of the just man and Psalm 119 with its long praise of the

From *Révue Biblique* 92, 1 (1985): 25–46. Used by permission.

law. There are still other summaries to the biblical books which are not acrostics. The Book of Ecclesiastes sums up its thoughts in the last chapter with the famous allegory on old age (12:1–7) and then concludes with a repetition of the opening words of the book (12:8). Hosea 14:2–9 functions in much the same manner for that book. In addition, the final verse of Hosea (14:11) is another independent coda.[1] Like these, then, Proverbs 31:10–31 draws together the major themes, motifs, and ideas of the book in a final, summarizing statement about wisdom under the image of an industrious, resourceful, and selfless wife. It is the final piece in a symbolic framework that unifies the whole book, including the individual sayings.[2] In turn, the symbolic framework presents a coherent statement about the nature of wisdom.

We will begin with a look at the traditional interpretation of our poem. In the words of R. B. Y. Scott these verses portray:

> . . . the virtues and accomplishments of an ideal wife and mother, mistress of the household of a prominent man.[3]

She is a model of behavior for the Israelite wife and mother. Most of the commentaries follow this general line of interpretation.[4] Certainly such a woman as this would be invaluable seeing the innumerable tasks she manages and the many enterprises in which she successfully engages!

The husband in verse 11 is described as completely trusting his wife's abilities and judgment. Her ability to work so skillfully with the wool and the flax refers, as one commentator puts it, to the ". . . woman's unfettered artistic freedom."[5] Her rising early, "while it is yet night" (v. 15), describes her ability to run a household competently and efficiently.[6] The numerous tasks this woman performs—and they are many: business dealings, selling her homemade clothing, buying and running a vineyard, religious duties such as feed-

1. F. I. Anderson and D. N. Freedman, *Hosea* (Anchor Bible, 24), New York, 1980, 643, 647.

2. The symbolic framework of the book and the role of the women in it has already been described for chapters 1–9 of Proverbs by J. N. Aletti, *Séduction et Parole en Proverbes I–IX*, in *VT* 27 (1977): 129–44. In this article the author refers to the significance of the poem in chapter 31 for this symbolism in note 31. . . .

3. *Proverbs. Ecclesiastes*, Anchor Bible 18, New York, 1965, 22.

4. C. H. Toy, *A Critical and Exegetical Commentary on the Book of Proverbs*, International Critical Commentary (Edinburgh, 1970), 542; C. T. Fritsch, *The Book of Proverbs*, The Interpreter's Bible 4, Nashville and New York, 1955, 954; A. Robert and A. Feuillet, *Introduction à la Bible*, 2d ed., Tournai, 1959, I, 637; O. Eissfeldt, *The Old Testament. An Introduction*, 3d ed., translated by P. R. Ackroyd, Oxford, 1965, 476; E. Sellin and G. Fohrer, *Einleitung in Das Alte Testament*, 10th ed., Heidelberg, 1965, 352; J. T. Forestall, *Proverbs*, in the Jerome Biblical Commentary, New York, 1968, I, 505; W. McKane, *Proverbs: A New Introduction*, London, 1970, 665–70; R. N. Whybray, *The Book of Proverbs*, Cambridge Bible Commentary, Cambridge, 1972, 184.

5. McKane, op. cit., 667.

6. Ibid., 668.

ing the poor and needy, teaching and kindly counsel—all illustrate her ". . . capacity for sustained work."[7] The value of the wife in this interpretation is in direct proportion to her competence and willingness to do many varied tasks. An underlying sentiment in this interpretation seems to be that she does not embarrass the husband who is so prominent "when he sits among the elders of the land" (v. 23). Is it possible that only such a role-model as this has been canonized for all time? Is it possible to consider this portrait, whether representative of the reality or idealized, and based, as it is, on the socioeconomic structures of a particular period in the history of ancient Israel, as determinative of the domestic division of labor for all time? It can hardly be the case!

The very emphasis of the poem on the woman's many tasks presents us with one of the unusual features of the poem: the husband is left with little or nothing to do! An older commentator remarked about this poem:

> . . . [the husband] goes after his calling, perhaps a calling which, though weighty and honorable, brings in little or nothing. . . .[8]

The husband's "weighty and honorable" profession among the elders at the city gates (v. 23) pales in significance when contrasted with the whirlwind of activity and achievement that is his wife.

Some have tried to explain this away. P. Joüon[9] mentions the suggestion of A. B. Ehrlich[10] that the role of the husband is one of full devotion to the study of the Law. This is why the management of all the other affairs of the household are left to the wife. Is the value of the wife, then, to be measured by the ways in which she frees her husband for study? This theory is a conjecture based on what the poem does *not* say. In fact, however, verse 11 seems to suggest, by the very juxtaposition of the two cola, that whatever the husband's "gain" is (v. 11b), it is the result of the trust he has placed in his wife and all her activities (v. 11a). The association of the two ideas in the one verse is significant, and the "gain" is not specified, as if to suggest all possibilities. The only personal "gain" the husband achieves in the poem is the recognition he receives from sitting with the elders (v. 23). But it is interesting to note that this verse immediately follows a description of the wife's work in "fine linen and purple" (v. 22). This kind of clothing is not for the poor, but only for people like those who sit at city gates! Is the husband's position and the wife's

---

7. Ibid.
8. F. Delitzsch, *Biblical Commentary on the Proverbs of Solomon,* vol. 6 of the *Commentary on the Old Testament,* translated by J. Martin and M. G. Easton, Grand Rapids, Michigan, 1976, II, 327–28.
9. *Les temps dans Proverbes 31, 10–31 (La Femme Forte),* Bib., III, 1922, 349, note 3.
10. *Psalmen, Sprüche und Hiob,* in vol. 6 of *Randglossen zur Hebräischen Bibel,* Leipzig, 1981, 176.

work again being associated, albeit by way of suggestion? Ultimately, the husband does not have the place of honor in the poem. It is with the wife that the poem concludes, voicing the praise given her by both husband and children (vv. 28–29).

The poem focuses quite deliberately on the wife almost to the exclusion of everyone else. This is a point worth nothing. It is not simply that the poem is concerned to portray only the woman, but that by this very portrayal the role of the husband and of others is correspondingly reduced. Everyone is served, helped, and ministered to by the wife: her own household (vv. 12, 15, 21, and 27) and even the poor and needy (v. 20). She not only acquires all the necessary household provisions, but she distributes them, and uses them to manufacture clothing for sale, as well as for her family. The entire domestic operation of the household is in her hands. Even the money with which she purchases the vineyard (v. 16b) is her own. Thus, she appears to be completely self-sufficient, rather wealthy, and also spends herself and her resources totally for others. Nowhere does her husband contribute to any of this.

What I am suggesting is that this particular portrait of a busy, industrious wife is intentionally one-sided because it is meant to describe not just any wife, not even the ideal wife, but a very special, unique wife. This wife is at the heart and source of everything that happens within her domain. Nothing is foreign to her, nothing is beneath her dignity, nothing is beyond her. This wife is primarily a symbol.

This symbolism and its relationship to the early part of Proverbs is suggested in the words of André Barucq from his commentary on Proverbs:

> Ce portrait peut être mis en parallèle avec celui de la Sagesse personnifiée de 9 1–6. Les deux femmes sont des maîtresses de maison expertes. Celle de *Pr* **31** n'invite pas chez elle. Son activité est toute au profit des siens: son mari et ses domestiques. C'est une forme de sagesse.[11]

---

11. *Le livre des Proverbes*, in *Sources Bibliques*, Paris, 1964, 231. The *Bible de Jérusalem*, Paris, 1973, 931, note *c*, observes that this poem may have been understood allegorically by the scribes as a description of personified Wisdom and points to v. 30b as a basis for this suggestion. The MT for this verse is: *'iššâ yirat yhwh hî' tithallāl*. The form *yirat* would be unusual as a feminine adjective modifying *'iššâ* (one would expect *yᵉrē'at*), but Aquila, the Syriac, the Targum, and the Vulgate interpret it this way: "A woman who fears the Lord, she is to be praised." Normally, *yirat* would be the construct of the substantive *yirâ*, "fear." In this sense, the MT can be taken in two ways. First, *yirat yhwh* could be in apposition to *'iššâ* so that the MT bears witness to a rereading of the poem in which the woman is identified with the "fear of the Lord": "The woman, the fear of the Lord, she is to be praised." This would affirm an early sapiential interpretation of the woman, for the "fear of the Lord" is the first stage of wisdom (Prov. 1:7; 9:10; 15:33). On the other hand, the substantive *yirat* might also be taken as the object of praise by the woman. This requires the verb *tthll* to be interpreted in the ordinary reflexive sense of "boast, glory in," with the preposition *bᵉ* understood before *yirat*: "The woman, she is to glory in the fear of the Lord."

This latter understanding of the substantival use of *yirat* appears to be behind the LXX rendition of this verse. In its double translation of v. 30b, the LXX does not place the woman and "fear of the Lord" in apposition, nor even in parallel. The first part of the translation, *gunē gar*

The woman of chapter 31 is found settled down and busy on behalf of her husband, children, and servants. The household in this chapter is fully established so that the wife's attention can be directed totally toward all of its manifold concerns. On the other hand, Wisdom, in the first part of the book, searches for any who will heed her words. To those who do so she promises (1:33):

> ". . . he who listens to me will dwell secure,
> and will be at ease, without dread of evil."[12]

In chapter 8 she cries out (vv. 4–5):

> "To you, O men, I call,
> and my cry is to the sons of men.

---

sunetē eulogeitai, may well recall the original Hebrew behind the present MT: "for a wise woman is to be praised" (cf. H. P. Rüger, *Zum Text von Prov. 31, 30*, in *Die Welt des Orients*, V, 1969–1970, 96–99). The second part of the translation places "fear of the Lord" as the object of the woman's praise—*phobon de Kyriou hautē aineitō*, "but let her praise the fear of the Lord." The LXX, therefore, does not give any direct support to a sapiential interpretation of the woman, but it does witness to a substantival understanding of *yirat*.

The rabbinic literature witnesses to both the adjectival and substantival understanding of *yirat*. There are two places in the *Babylonian Talmud* where Prov. 31:30b is quoted. The first reference quotes *yirat* adjectivally: "And the daughters of Jerusalem came forth and danced in the vineyards while saying, 'Young man, raise your eyes and look at what you are selecting for yourself. Do not set your eyes on beauty; set your eyes on family. Grace is a deception and beauty a vanity; a woman who fears the Lord, she is to be praised'" (*b. Ta'an.* 26b). The second quote treats *yirat* as a substantive: "'Grace is a deception,' this refers to Joseph, 'and beauty a vanity,' this refers to Boaz; 'the fear of the Lord, this is to be praised,' this refers to Palti son of Layish. Another interpretation: 'Grace is a deception,' this refers to the generation of Moses; 'and beauty a vanity,' this refers to the generation of Joshua; 'the fear of the Lord, this is to be praised,' this refers to the generation of Hezekiah. Another interpretation: 'Grace is a deception,' this refers to the generation of Moses and Joshua; 'and beauty a vanity,' this refers to the generation of Hezekiah; 'the fear of he Lord, this is to be praised,' this refers to the generation of R. Judah son of R. Ila'i . . . ." (*b. Sanh.* 20a). Another example is found in *Exod. Rab.* 1.15, where *yira* is clearly an adjective: "And the midwives feared God.' Concerning them it is said: 'A woman who fears the Lord, she is to be praised' (Prov. 31:30). And they did not act according to the command given them by the king of Egypt." In the last example, from *Qoh. Rab.* III. 14, the *yirat* again occurs as an adjective, but the emphasis of the passage is on *yirat*, and not on the woman: "R. Jeremiah said, 'Great is that fear [of God], for Solomon did not conclude the two books which he wrote without fear, as it is written in the book of Proverbs: 'Grace is a deception and beauty a vanity; a woman who fears the Lord, she is to be praised;' and in this book it is written: 'The end of the matter; all has been heard. Fear God.'" As with the LXX, therefore, none of these examples directly support a sapiential understanding of the woman, either. But they do show that the rabbinic tradition is aware of more than one way of interpreting *yirat*.

Recent authors have been aware of sapiential allusions in the poem as well. H. Ringgren, *Sprüche/Prediger*, in *Das Alte Testament Deutsch*, 16/1, Göttingen, 1962, 121, calls the woman in chapter 31 even more clearly an example of that kind of wisdom which enables people to succeed in life. E. Jacob, *Sagesse et Alphabet, A propos de Proverbes 31. 10–31*, in *Hommages à André Dupont-Sommer*, edited by A. Caquot and M. Philonenko, Paris, 1971, 288, says that the sapiential tradition itself invites us to see a figure of wisdom behind the diverse activities of the woman.

12. Unless otherwise noted the translation of biblical texts is taken from the RSV.

> O simple ones, learn prudence;
>   foolish men. pay attention."

Then in chapter 9, having just built a house and prepared a feast, Wisdom extends an even further invitation—those who would heed her call are to enter her house (vv. 4–6):

> "Whoever is simple, let him turn in here!"
>   To him who is without sense she says,
> "Come, eat of my bread
>   and drink of the wine I have mixed.
> Leave simpleness, and live,
>   and walk in the way of insight."

Her gaze and call are directed outward. Do not the two portraits complement one another? The portrait of Wisdom inviting those who heed her call to make their home with her in chapter 9 is completed by the portrait of the woman settled down with her own in chapter 31. And the security and peace promised by Wisdom in 1:33 is amply portrayed in 31:10–31.

If the portrait in chapter 9 is that of Wisdom searching for companions, the portrait of chapter 31 must symbolize Wisdom finally settled down with her own. These portraits, as well as others in Proverbs, form a coherent picture of Wisdom and present us with a framework for understanding the nature of wisdom as it is viewed by the author/editor of Proverbs. It is our intention, however, to concentrate on the poem in chapter 31 and illustrate more fully the wisdom dimension of that portrait since this aspect has not been fully analyzed and developed previously. Finally, the relationship of this poem to the rest of the book will be sketched briefly.

The first feature to note in the poem is one that has drawn considerable attention in the past. This is its construction as an alphabetic acrostic. This feature has been blamed by some for the somewhat haphazard and unnatural arrangement of the verses.[13] For instance, the money used to buy the vineyard in verse 16 comes presumably from the sale of the clothing noted seven verses later in verse 24. The mention of the woman spinning, verse 19, comes after her manufacture of cloth is noted in verse 13; and the whole process from purchase of wool and flax to finished garments is described in widely separated verses—13, 19, and 24.[14] This lack of logical sequence is attributed to the extrinsic order demanded by the acrostic principle. It does seem unusual, however, to say that a device for organizing material causes disorder! Was the poet looking for the kind of order that we find lacking? Rather than arrange his ma-

---

13. McKane, op. cit., 665–66; Toy, op. cit., 542; Whybray, op. cit., 184.
14. McKane, op. cit., 275.

terial in a natural, even climactic sequence, it may be that he has left it as a list of discrete and separate actions whose *cumulative* effect is to impress with its manifold and variegated nature. The poet wants to leave us with the picture of a woman capable of many different things, as well as being independent, resourceful, and wealthy.

Furthermore, organization can be discerned after studying the number of word repetitions that occur. There are fifteen cases where a word repeats at least once—a remarkable feature in a poem of only twenty lines. Some of the repetitions mark interesting changes or developments in meaning as well. A case in point is the use of *kap*, "palm, hand," and *yād*, "hand." *Kap* is repeated three times, *yād* twice. *Kap* is the first to occur in verse 13b, where it describes the woman working in wool and flax. Verse 16 picks up *kap* again but in the context of the money produced by the work of the woman's hands, *mippᵉrî kappeyhā*, "the fruit of her hands," which enabled her to buy and plant a vineyard. A synonym, *zᵉrōaᶜ*, "arm," is in the following verse (17) to comment on the woman's activity: *wattᵉʾammēṣ zᵉrōᶜôteyhā*, "and makes her arms strong." Verse 19b repeats *kap* again to describe the woman's manufacture of clothing and uses *yād* for the first time.

At this point a chiasmus occurs between verses 19 and 20 centered on the words *kap* and *yād*, and includes the repetition of the verb *šlḥ*, "send."[15] A remarkable transformation of meaning is accomplished. In verse 20 *kap* and *yād*, now switched in positions to form the chiasmus, no longer refer to the woman's craftsmanship and industriousness in practical, household affairs, but to her moral stature as one who acts on behalf of the poor. The chiasmus is illustrated as follows:

v. 19 *yādeyhā šillᵉḥāh bakkîšôr*

A

wᵉkappeyhā tāmᵉkû pālek

B

v. 20 *kappāh pārᵉśāh leᶜānî*

B′

wᵉyādeyhā šillᵉḥāh lāʾᵉbyôn

A′

After this, *kap* is no longer repeated but *yād* occurs once more in the last verse of the poem. Here the final transformation of meaning takes place as the woman, instead of using her hands for others, is now going to be the recipient of "the fruit of her hands." Thus, against the background of the repetition of *kap* and *yād*, the poem has moved from portraying the woman in practical,

15. Murray H. Lichtenstein, *Chiasm and Symmetry in Proverbs 31*, in *CBQ* 44 (1982): 202–11.

household affairs, to a consideration of her charity and concern for others, to a final look at the praise her deeds will bring her.

This chiasmus also marks the middle of the poem, placed between two nine-verse units (vv. 10–18 and 21–29) and followed by an independent, two-verse coda (vv. 30–31). In addition, the beginning of the first nine-verse unit, and the end of the second is linked by an inclusion formed with the words *ḥyl* (vv. 10 and 29) and *b*ᵉ*lh* (vv. 11 and 28).[16] The repetition of *ḥyl* emphasizes the incomparable worth of the woman celebrated in the poem. The question posed in verse 10 underlines the difficulty in finding such an *ʾēšet ḥayil*; but by verse 29 it is clear that she has surpassed all the others who have displayed *ḥyl*. The repetition of *baᶜal*, "husband," marks the switch from noting the husband's trust in his wife (v. 11) and his own renown among his peers (v. 23), to his own praise of his wife at the end of the poem (v. 28b). Thus, the inclusion frames these lines of the poem thematically as well as stylistically.

The coda (vv. 30–31) forms a coherent unit around the repetition of the verbal root *hll*, "praise," a third person singular form in verse 30 (*tithallāl*), and a third person plural form in verse 31 (*wiyhalᵉlûhā*). But that these two verses form a concluding summary to the poem is even more evident from the number of words and roots they repeat from the rest of the poem. The first verse of the coda (v. 30b) uses *ʾšh*, recalling the very first phrase of the poem (v. 10a) and the only time that root is repeated. The word *yirat* in verse 30b harkens back to the verbal root *tîrāʾ* of verse 21a. Herein there is an implied contrast between those things about which the woman has no fear, namely, how well she has provided for her household (v. 21), and the only fear she does have, the "fear of the Lord" (v. 30b). The first line of the coda, therefore, emphasizes the woman's moral virtues and is linked to the beginning of each of the poem's two nine-verse units.

The second verse of the coda (v. 31) is almost entirely composed of repeated words and roots and concentrates on the woman's practical virtues. The initial imperative *tᵉnû*, "give," echoes *nātᵉnâ* from verse 24b. In the latter instance, it is the woman who gives to others from her productivity; in the last verse, she will be given a reward for her labors. The next word, *mippᵉrî* also occurs in verse 16b. There the woman's labor (*mpry kpyh*) plants a vineyard which will presumably support her household. But, again, in verse 31a the woman's labor will redound to herself. The *yādeyhā* of verse 31a is repeated from vv. 19a and 20b, as described above.

In the second half of the verse, the verb *wiyhalᵉlûhā* not only echoes the previous verse (*tithallāl*), where both verbs describe the praise given the woman, but it also echoes the same verb in verse 28b (*wayᵉhalᵉlāh*) where the husband praises his wife. The following phrase *baššᵉᶜārîm*, "at the gates," is

---

16. Lichtenstein, op. cit., 205–8.

repeated from verse 23a and marks the change from the husband's being among the renowned elders "at the gates" of the city, to the wife's being extolled at the same city gates. Finally, the last word of the verse, *ma^{ca}seyhā*, "her works," is echoed in verses 22a and 24a by verbal forms of the same root. Again, the verbs describe the woman's labor for the sake of others, from which labor will ultimately come her own reward (v. 31b). In an almost mechanical way, consequently, these two verses summarize the thematic movement of the poem from concentration on the woman's praiseworthy deeds to a consideration of the praise and reward the woman herself deserves. At the same time, these verses refer to both the moral and practical aspects of the woman's inestimable value—exactly as the chiasmus (vv. 19–20) does, but in the opposite order.

The whole structure of the poem can thus be diagrammed as follows:[17]

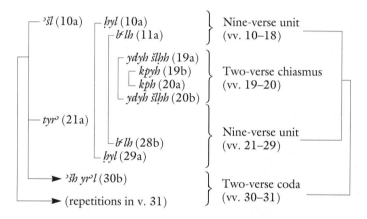

The poem, in effect, is carefully linked together structurally and thematically.

Other word repetitions emphasize the general thematic movement. The root *lbš*, "clothe, be clothed," first occurs in verse 21b (*lābuš*) where it speaks of the protection afforded by the woman's homemade clothing. The word is repeated in the following verse (*l^{e}bûšāh*) with emphasis on the fine, even luxurious quality of her own household's clothing. Its last occurrence is in verse 25a (*l^{e}bûšāh*) where a complete change of theme occurs. Now the woman's clothing is her own dignity and strength, an emphasis on her moral fibre. The same transformation of meaning occurs with the word for "strength," *^cōz*, which is also repeated in verse 25 from verse 17a.

The word for food, *leḥem*, is used twice. The first time, in verse 14b, it alludes to the woman's industriousness and great versatility which is revealed in her procuring "food from afar" for her household. The second occurrence is

17. I utilize here the analysis and diagrams of Lichtenstein, op. cit., 207–8.

in the phrase *leḥem* *aṣᵉlût,* "bread of idleness," from verse 27b, a bread of which the woman does not partake. Since one of the great contrasts in the Book of Proverbs is between *ḥākam,* "the wise person," and *āṣēl,* "the lazy one," this allusion in the poem marks the woman not merely as industrious, but as a woman of wisdom. She acts in a manner that reflects the activity of the wise. The woman's sagacity is also emphasized in verse 26 by a chiasmus which involves the repetition of synonymous, rather than identical terms:

$$pîhā\ patᵉḥāh\ bᵉḥokmāh$$
$$\text{A} \qquad\qquad \text{B}$$
$$wᵉtôrat\ ḥese\ ᶜal\ lᵉšônāh$$
$$\text{B}' \qquad\qquad \text{A}'$$

The very words of the chiasmus itself, which are applied here to the woman, are drawn from the common wisdom vocabulary of the sayings.

One important word is *bêt,* "house, household." The first time the word occurs (v. 15b) it refers to the food the woman can provide for her household, food which the previous verse has just described as procured "from afar." *Bêt* appears again, twice, in verse 21 and there it refers to the woman's well-made clothing which provides sufficient comfort and security for her charges. This repetition is preceded by the chiasmus of *kap* and *yād* in verses 19–20, described above. Both of these poetic devices (the chiasmus and the word repetition) highlight this section as the midpoint of the poem. And there is more. The first occurrence of *bêt* in verse 21 looks back to its appearance in verse 15b, because both words have the same form, *lᵉbêtāh.* The second occurrence of the word in verse 21 matches the form of the word in verse 27, *bêtāh.* Thus, the repetition looks backward and forward, drawing the two halves of the poem together.

The next and final occurrence of *bêt* is in verse 27. The first half of that verse goes: *ṣôpîyāh hᵃlîkôt bêtāh,* "she looks well to the ways of her household." It has the appearance of a summary statement about all that the woman does, particularly in the light of the second half of the verse: *wᵉleḥem ᶜaṣᵉlût lōʾ tōʾkēl,* "and does not eat the bread of idleness." The "bread of idleness," as has already been noted, is a wisdom theme. The repetition of *bêt,* therefore, also marks the thematic progress of the woman from industrious provider to solicitous sage.

Clear contrast and not development in thought marks two cases of repetition. When the verb *qûm,* "rise," is first used in verse 15a it refers to the woman's ceaseless industry, rising even at night to work. Its repetition in verse 28a describes the woman's sons and husband now rising to praise her for her works.

Thus, despite an initial appearance of being somewhat haphazardly arranged, with various themes picked up, then dropped, only to be picked up again, the poem, upon closer inspection, does manifest clear organization: word repetition and chiasmus, involving the development/contrast of a theme, and emphasis, indicates the natural divisions of the poem. The poem is not a mere ". . . technical and administrative . . ." program for house-wives.[18] It moves from a consideration of ordinary, practical abilities to moral and spiritual virtues. It moves from a view of the woman as being the center and source of activity concerned for others to another view which regards her as the center and object of the concern and praise of others. It presents a picture where the good the woman does for others will be cause for praise and blessing to fall on her own head. In this gradually unfolding progress of thought and significant shifts in emphasis and viewpoint the poem is presenting more than a housewife for our consideration.

The symbolic value of the wife is particularly revealed in the poem's choice of words and phrases. In the very first verse the question concerning the wife, *mî yimṣāʾ*, "who can find," has striking overtones. The question itself is rhetorical and most probably expects a negative response. Other examples of an interrogative particle used with the verb *mṣʾ* confirms this. The example closest to Proverbs 30:10a is found in Proverbs 20:6b. The whole verse goes:

> *rob ʾādām yiqrāʾ ʾîš ḥasdô*
> *wᵉʾîš ʾᵉmûnîm mî yimṣāʾ*

> Many a man proclaims his own loyalty,[19]
> but a faithful man who can find?

Clearly, the contrast between self-proclaimed virtue and the kind that is truly reliable and genuine implies that the latter type is nearly impossible to find. The unvoiced answer to the second colon would be like this: "Practically no one (can find such a person)." In Ecclesiastes 7:24 the question is posed with regard to knowledge about everything that exists: *mî yimṣāʾennû*, "who can find it out?" Presumably, no one. Another question about wisdom is found in Job 28:12, the beginning of the famous poem on wisdom: *wᵉhaḥokmāh mēʾayin timmāṣēʾ*, "And wisdom—where can it be found?" The answer here is "nowhere, except with God," as the rest of the poem illustrates (especially vv. 23–27). In these three examples the implication is that whatever is being sought (a trustworthy person; wisdom) it can hardly be found.

18. Margaret B. Crook, *The Marriageable Maiden of Prov. 31:10–31*, in *JNES* 13 (1954): 137–40.

19. The translation given here follows the MT. But the versions (Pesher, Targum and Vulgate) also suggest *yiqqārēʾ* instead of MT *yiqrāʾ* and *ḥesed* or *ḥāsîd* for MT *ḥasdô*. These readings, however, and translations based on them, do not compromise the implied negative response in the second colon.

The sense of this type of rhetorical question is the force and heightened expression it produces. What is being questioned is beyond price, incomparable, unique, inexpressible.[20] It is, indeed, often impossible to grasp, or find—but not always. Pharaoh, after Joseph interprets his dreams, remarks (Gen. 41:38): *h^animṣāʾ kāzeh ʾîš ʾ^ašer rûaḥ ʾ^elōhîm bô*, "Can we find such a man as this, in whom is the Spirit of God?" The question would seem to imply that this kind of person is too hard to find. Yet the Pharaoh immediately appoints Joseph to the task of overseeing the food supplies. The force of his rhetorical question simply lends greatness and stature to Joseph. There was no one like him in Egypt.

The rhetorical question about the *ʾēšet ḥayil*, therefore, expects the response, "No one can find such a woman!" Yet, paradoxically, this idea is counterbalanced by the rest of the poem which presumes that such a woman is worth pursuing! The question is really meant to stress the woman's incomparable value (as does the synonymous second colon, 10b) but acknowledges at the same time that such value is found only with difficulty. Thus, the opening line of the poem does not necessarily indicate an unattainable ideal, but a very extraordinary individual whose significance and value is worth grasping.

The *mî yimṣāʾ* phrase might have one other possible meaning. In Judges 14:18 Samson explains why his riddle was solved:

> *lûlēʾ ḥ^araštem b^{eʿ}eglātî*
> *lōʾ m^eṣāʾtem ḥîdātî*

> "If you had not plowed with my heifer,
>   you would not have found out my riddle."

What is of interest here is the use of the verb *mṣʾ* with *ḥîdāh*, "riddle" in the sense of solving a riddle (the same meaning occurs in v. 12). Could the poet of Proverbs 31:10a be suggesting that the woman is not only incomparable, but a riddle whose identity is to be solved, discovered? Given the fact that this poem occurs in a section which contains proverbs quite different from all the others in the book, such as the riddle (30:1–4), the various numerical sayings (30:15–16, 18–19, 21–23, 24–28, 29–31), and the warnings (30:5–6, 10, 11–14, 17, 32–33; 31:1–9), this poem would not be out of place as another riddle. It is already unique in the book due to its alphabetic structure. An

---

20. C. J. Labuschagne, *The Incomparability of Yahweh in the Old Testament*, Leiden, 1966, 16–28, demonstrates this with regard to similar rhetorical questions concerning God. There are other rhetorical questions of this type, introduced by the interrogative pronoun *mî*, which use other verbs besides *mṣʾ*. These, too, imply the same kind of negative response that lends emphasis, drama, or a heightened sense of importance, even tension, to the context. Some examples are: Isaiah 44:7; Jeremiah 15:5; 49:19; Psalms 76:8b; 90:11; Job 9:4b, 12, 19b; 12:9; 13:19a; 14:4; 17:3b; 21:31; 25:3b; 26:14c; 34:13; Proverbs 20:9; 24:22b; Ecclesiastes 3:21, 22b; 6:12; 7:13b; 8:4b.

opening verse of Proverbs (1:6) has already hinted at the contents of the book, including *dibrê ḥᵃkāmîm wᵉḥîdōtām,* "the words of the wise and their riddles." The wise and their sayings have already been referred to in 22:17 and in 24:23. But the last two chapters of the book are each given a title which designates the contents as "the words of (a wise man)." Chapter 30 contains "the words of Agur" and he begins with a riddle. Chapter 31 presents "the words of Lemuel" and he concludes with the riddle about the *ʾēšet ḥayil.* These last two chapters, then, may well be what were projected in chapter 1 as "the words of the wise and their riddles"! The unraveling of the riddle about the *ʾēšet ḥayil* leads to the discovery of Wisdom.

The phrase *ʾēšet ḥayil* is equally important. How is the woman to be described? Various translations are offered: a wife of value, valor, strength, graciousness. The basic meaning for *ḥayil* is "power, strength," usually military, with derived meanings of wealth, ability, valor, and sexual power.[21] If *ḥayil* is a virtue, then, it is not for the weak and shy. This is a woman of strength, courage, and ability. Outside the Book of Proverbs the phrase *ʾēšet ḥayil* occurs only once, in Ruth 3:11. It is a phrase used by Boaz to describe the heroine on the occasion when Ruth lies with him to claim him as her kinsman. Ruth had acted with courage, loyalty (to her husband's memory), and daring. They are characteristics that would fit the wife of Proverbs quite well.

But the association of the wife of Proverbs 31 with Ruth, actually, may be more than accidental. Several similarities between the two women are quite striking.

1. Both are paradigms of loyalty and fidelity. Ruth leaves behind her native home and religion for Naomi's; the woman of Proverbs 31 gives ceaseless attention to her family and her household's needs.
2. Both act with tremendous resourcefulness. The one provides a livelihood for herself and her mother-in-law and secures heirs to carry on the family name; the other manages her own house and family with ingenuity and prudence.
3. Both women are portrayed in terms of their marriages, homes, and families. The story of Ruth culminates in her marriage to Boaz and the birth of a son. In effect she builds a house for herself, Naomi, and Boaz.[22] The people and elders who pronounce a blessing over Ruth (4:11) evoke the memory of Rachel and Leah, "who together built up the house of Israel." All three women are renowned, therefore, precisely for having "built up their houses." In Proverbs 31, the

21. Art. *ḥajil* (Eisling) in *ThWAT,* II, col. 904.
22. "House" in this context is not only the physical building, but refers particularly to the posterity of the family; art. *bayit* (Hoffner) in *ThWAT,* 1, cols. 629–38; cf. Deuteronomy 25:9; 1 Samuel 2:35; 2 Samuel 7:27; 1 Kings 11:38.

woman is portrayed as already settled down with her husband and children in her house, a house which, as was suggested above, she was earlier looking forward to securing for herself (9:1–6).

4. Finally, both women are praised for what they do. Boaz calls her blessed and declares her to be an *ʾēšet ḥayil* (3:10–11). In Proverbs 31:28 the woman's children bless her, and in the following verse, the husband declares that she surpasses all the other women who have displayed *ḥayil*.

The comparison with Ruth, consequently, serves to delineate some of the more striking characteristics of the portrait in Proverbs 31:10–31. Furthermore, the allusion to other biblical women around whom so much activity is centered, and on whom depends the survival and continuity of a family (and a race), strengthens the view that the woman of Proverbs 31 is to be seen in the same light. Proverbs 12:4a contains the only other use of the phrase *ʾēšet ḥayil*, where such a woman is deemed *ʿᵃṭeret baʿlāh*, "the crown of her husband." The saying seems to give a hint of what is to come in chapter 31 and provides, in advance, an apt image with which to characterize the portrait drawn there.

There may be an interesting contrast intended here between the wife of 31:10–31 and the woman referred to in 31:3a, centered around the various uses of *ḥayil*. In the latter verse the mother of Lemuel warns her son, *ʾal tittēn lannāšîm ḥêlekā*, "Give not your strength to women." The *ḥayil* here, presumably, is the man's sexual power which he is not to squander or waste on loose women. This is a clear reference to the women, frequently described in Proverbs, who cause infidelity, ignorance, sorrow, and ultimately death.[23] These women are not described as having *ḥayil* themselves, in any sense of the word, but must seek it from others. On the other hand, the woman to be sought is the one who has *ḥayil* —strength, ability, valor, and wealth—and uses it selflessly and totally for others. The women without *ḥayil* only destroy; the woman with *ḥayil* creates, builds up, strengthens, nurtures, and protects. The Book of Proverbs closes, consequently, with the same theme with which it began: a contrast between the women whose ways lead to death, and the woman Wisdom who promises life (chap. 9). In chapter 31, however, the balance is tipped overwhelmingly in favor of the latter.

The word *ḥayil* provides still more allusions. The notion of "wealth" for *ḥayil* is not foreign to the context of our poem and could be alluded to here as well. The woman trades in faraway places (v. 14b), is able to buy a vineyard (v. 16), recognizes a profit from her merchandizing (v. 18a), and sells cloth-

---

23. Cf. Proverbs 2:16–19; 5:3–6, 20; 6:24–26; 7:6–27; 9:13–18; 11:22; 12:4b; 19:13b; 21:9, 19; 22:14; 23:27–28; 25:24; 27:15.

ing (v. 24). This accords well with what we have been told about Wisdom earlier (8:18, 21):

> "Riches and honor are with me,
>   enduring wealth and prosperity . . .
> endowing with wealth those who love me,
>   and filling their treasuries."

And one of the proverbs also asserts that the means by which a house is well-built and richly furnished is Wisdom (24:3–4):

> By wisdom a house is built,
>   and by understanding it is established;
> by knowledge the rooms are filled
>   with all precious and pleasant riches.

Although what the wife does in providing for her household may not appear to be "riches" and "enduring wealth," two other words used in the poem do seem to stress the value and abundance of her provisions. The first of these is *šālāl* in verse 11b where it describes the "gain" the husband will receive from his wife. The ordinary meaning of *šālāl*, however, is "booty, spoil," and its usage in this context seems quite unusual. Perhaps the word is intended to indicate varied and abundant riches, such as would be represented by the booty taken in war.[24] The other word is *ṭerep*, in verse 15b, used to describe the food with which the woman supplies her household. The word normally refers to the prey of animals—most often the lion—who get it by attack and slaughter; it is also used several times as a metaphor for military conquest.[25] At the very least, this word represents provisions acquired only after the exercise of great strength, prowess, and ingenuity and would seem to commend the extraordinary ability of the wife in providing for her household even against great odds. Both *ṭerep* and *šālāl*, therefore, illustrate in a very dramatic way the wife's ability to provide for those in her charge.[26] Her abilities and knowledge are suggested as ranging over many diverse areas of life, public as well as private. The *ḥayil* of this woman is of no ordinary kind.

There are other wisdom allusions in the poem. The wife, again in the first verse, is compared to *pᵉnîmîm*, variously translated as "pearls, corals" or simply "jewels"—"She is far more precious than jewels." The same word, reading the *Qere*, is used to describe wisdom in Proverbs 3:15, *yᵉqārāh hîʾ mip-*

---

24. Cf. Deuteronomy 20:14; Joshua 7:21; Judges 5:30; 8:24–25; 1 Samuel 30:19–20; Ezekiel 38:13.

25. Cf. Genesis 49:9; Numbers 23:24; Isaiah 5:29; 31:4; Nahum 2:13–14; 3:1.

26. The war context for many of the uses of *šālāl* and *ṭerep* could suggest a comparison between the wife and such famous women in the OT as Deborah and Judith who fought for Israel. But this would be difficult to reconcile with the domestic setting of the poem in Proverbs 31.

p^{e}nîmîm, "She is more precious than jewels. . . ." Proverbs 8:11, considered to be a gloss based on 3:15, also reads, *kî tôbāh ḥokmāh mipp^{e}nînîm*, "for wisdom is better than jewels." Wisdom is further compared to precious jewels in 21:15, 8:19, and 16:16. It seems clear that the poet applies to the wife in chapter 31 what has been said of wisdom.

Another interesting example is the description of the husband in verse 11:

> *bāṭaḥ bāh lēb ba'lāh*
> *w^{e}šālāl lō' yeḥsār*

The heart of her husband trusts in her,
   and he will have no lack of gain.

This is reminiscent of the sentiments urged upon the student of wisdom in chapter 4, verses 6, 8, and 9:

> "Do not forsake her, and she will keep you;
>   love her, and she will guard you. . .
> Prize her highly, and she will exalt you;
>   she will honor you if you embrace her.
> She will place on your head a fair garland;
>   she will bestow on you a beautiful crown."

Even more telling in this regard is the saying at Proverbs 28:26, *bôṭēaḥ b^{e}libbô hû' k^{e}sîl*, "He who trusts in his own mind is a fool." The same words are used in this saying as are applied to the husband—the verb *bāṭaḥ*, "trusts" and *lēb*, "heart, mind." The husband, however, is precisely the one who has not trusted his own heart, but has entrusted it to another, namely—in the sense of this saying—to Wisdom.

The wife and Wisdom parallel in yet other ways. Both laugh (*sḥq*) at the future. In 1:26 Wisdom promises to laugh at the doom that is to overtake those who do not listen to her:

> *gam '^{a}nî b^e'êd^{e}kem 'eśḥāq*
> *'el'ag b^{e}bō' paḥd^{e}kem*

I also will laugh at your calamity;
   I will mock when panic strikes you.

The future is threat and destruction only for those who do not heed Wisdom. Wisdom herself is secure, and so is relaxed as only a spectator at another's misfortune.[27] The wife has the same posture with regard to what will come; she

---

27. McKane, op. cit., 275.

is secure, so she can only laugh as well (v. 25b), *watǐshaq l^eyôm ʾah^arôn,* "and she laughs at the time to come." With the prophets the days to come were full of threat and punishment; in Wisdom's company there is nothing to fear, as she states in 1:33:

> ". . . he who listens to me will dwell secure
>   and will be at ease, without dread of evil."

The reference in verse 12 of the poem to the wife dealing out good and not evil could certainly be said of Wisdom, although nowhere in the text of Proverbs is such a statement explicitly applied to Wisdom. Another line in our poem has an echo in one of the proverbs. The wife is described in verse 15 as even rising at night to work and verse 18b picks up this theme: *lōʾ yikbeh ballayelāh (Q) nērāh,* "Her lamp does not go out at night." The wife's activity is ceaseless, day and night. A possible allusion to Proverbs 13:9 gives this theme further meaning. The saying goes:

> ʾôr ṣaddîqîm yǐsmaḥ
>   w^enēr r^ešāʿîm yidʿāk

> The light of the righteous rejoices,
>   but the lamp of the wicked will be put out.

The word for "lamp" is *nēr* in both texts. It may be that the wife's lamp does not go out because she is to be considered as among the just, working with and for the just. This, too, is the role of Wisdom.

When describing how the wife obtains supplies in verse 14 the poem uses an interesting simile:

> hāy^etāh kāʾŏnîyôt sôḥēr
>   mimmerḥāq tābîʾ laḥmāh

> She is like the ships of the merchant,
>   she brings her food from afar.

The image highlights both the activities of this woman and her resourcefulness. But considering the wisdom context of this poem the simile recalls the figure of Solomon, the wise king, who was also the only one in Israel's history to successfully build a merchant fleet (with the help of King Hiram of Tyre).[28] Thus, the wisdom represented by Solomon also seems to be associated with this wife. Such an allusion, of course, would only be appropriate in a book at-

---

28. Cf. 1 Kings 9:26–28 = 2 Chronicles 8:17–18; 1 Kings 10:22 = 2 Chronicles 9:21.

tributed to Solomon (1:1), and where two collections of sayings within the book also bear his name (10:1; 25:1).

The picture of the wife drawn in chapter 31, consequently, inclines heavily toward the symbolic. The one-sided attention given to the wife, the concentration on her many activities, even to the exclusion of others and their contributions, underlined by the use of word repetition, and the numerous allusions to wisdom or to a wisdom activity, strongly favor this interpretation.

Having illustrated the wisdom motifs behind the portrait of the wife in chapter 31, it is time now to turn briefly to the introductory discourse of Wisdom in chapters 1, 8, and 9. A brief look at these chapters will help us begin to define their relationship with chapter 31.

An outstanding feature of Wisdom in the first nine chapters of Proverbs is her call. This call begins each of her discourses in chapters 1, 8, and 9. The setting for the call is the same in each chapter. It is very public: "in the street" and "in the markets" (1:20); "on the heights" and beside "the way" and "paths" (8:2); and she also takes her stand at the city gates (1:21b; 8:3). In chapter 9 the maids of Wisdom issue the call from the heights overlooking the town (9:3). The ones addressed in each case are the same also: the simple (*petî*—1:22a; 8:5a; 9:4a), the fool (*kᵉsîl*—1:22c; 8:5b) or the senseless one (*ḥᵃsar lēb*—9:4b). These are the inexperienced, the uninstructed, the uninitiated, whom Wisdom calls to be students, her followers, her companions. The appeal of Wisdom, therefore, is for anyone who has not had her instruction, and so she addresses herself to all. And any who are without her need her.

In chapter 9 Wisdom's call becomes an invitation (9:4). It is issued through her servants, from her house, Wisdom's house, which we hear of now for the first time. The house of her rival Folly, the adultress, has already been mentioned several times (2:18; 5:8; 7:8). But Wisdom, who up to this point has been little more than a voice, has just finished describing her origins (chapter 8), and now presents herself, in her own house, as a young woman seeking marriage. Her words in 9:5, recalling similar language in the Song of Songs (5:1), take on the aura of a lover's invitation: "Come, eat of my bread and drink of the wine I have mixed." The slaughtering of the beasts, the mixing of the wine, the setting of the table (9:2), all seem to betoken a great, marriage-like feast. Wisdom's rival, finally identified as Folly in 9:13, also extends the same invitation (9:16). But she is an adultress, one whose ways and words are deceptive and lead only to death. The picture of the two rivals has become a little clearer, as a result, by the time they extend their invitations in chapter 9. The invitations, consequently, involve more than mere learning and instruction, but, from the context in which they are extended, point to a choice between a faithful, lifelong companion, and a fickle, faithless, ultimately destructive relationship. How does one make the choice and respond to the invitations?

What follows in the succeeding chapters are the individual proverbs, the brief, two-cola sayings which make up the bulk of the book. This is where Wisdom is to be found and understood. The nature of Wisdom as demanding choice and response is reflected in the myriad choices represented by these sayings. The "wise man and the fool," "the lazy and the industrious," "the wicked and the just," "heeding instruction and correction" or "mocking them," "speaking truthfully or lying," "working profitably or squandering goods," "seeking love or nursing hates"—these are the choices to which wisdom wants to invite all. The fact that the proverbs are not organized coherently under some theme or by some system of ethics is based on a refusal to see life as a neat system. The Wisdom presented here is more than a mere list of prescriptions, or a list of guideposts for a happy life. There is a Wisdom which is discovered and can only be discovered in the very process of pursuing it. That process calls for choices which determine the direction of our lives and even who we are. Wisdom presents these proverbs, which illustrate this full array of human behavior and its consequences, as signs on the road which either lead to her or away from her. Wisdom, in other words, is gained by experience—learning and doing.

It is only through the process of discovery, discernment, choice, response, communication, and responsibility that one can reach Wisdom. So, too, it is only after one has apprenticed himself to Wisdom and studied her proverbs that one can finally recognize the distinctive features of Wisdom in the valuable, industrious wife, busy in her home—placed, of course, at the end of the proverbs, at the end of the book!

It is interesting to note at this point that the wife is called an ʾēšet ḥayil in direct contrast, possibly, to Folly who, at 9:13, is called an ʾēšet keŝîlût, a "woman of foolishness, of stupidity." The latter is also called hōmîyāh, "noisy, boisterous." She is too obvious, too readily and clearly identifiable with her smooth lips and honeyed words now to be missed. By the end of the book we hear no more of Folly or of her house. Because it is no more. As we were warned in 7:27:

> Her house is the way to Sheol,
>> going down to the chambers of death.

The ʾēšet ḥayil, Wisdom, however—who can find her? It takes more understanding and experience to discover her.

Now at the end of the book, however, we can see her: self-sufficient, selfless, about the many different tasks in which she guides and helps us. The poem's marked concentration of attention on the wife and on all that she does, the development of various themes emphasizing her virtues as well as her practical prudence and ingenuity, and the remarkable similarities between the portrait of the wife and various descriptions of Wisdom, indicate that the poem in chapter 31 is the book's final, masterful portrait of Wisdom. She was presented in chapter 9 as the young marriageable woman seeking lovers who would accept the gifts and life she could offer. Now that time of courtship, of learning, is over. In chapter 31 Wisdom is a faithful wife and a skilled mistress of her household, finally settled down with her own. This ingenious symbolic framework of the Book of Proverbs presents a consistent picture of Wisdom. She is not some lofty, remote ideal for those initiated into her mysteries, but a practical, ever-present, faithful guide, and lifelong companion for all who choose her way. Her origins are with God (8:22–30) and her teaching wins blessings from God (8:35). But her home is in this world. This is the way Wisdom herself wanted it. Even while she was beside the Creator, rejoicing in his presence, she was also, in her own words from 8:31:

> rejoicing in his inhabited world
> and delighting in the sons of men.

SELECT BIBLIOGRAPHY

Books

Aitken, Kenneth T. *Proverbs*. Philadelphia: Westminster, 1986.

Alden, Robert L. *Proverbs: A Commentary on an Ancient Book of Timeless Advice*. Grand Rapids: Baker, 1983.

Arnot, William. *Studies in Proverbs: Laws from Heaven for Life on Earth*. 1858. Reprint. Grand Rapids: Kregel, 1978.

Boström, Lennart. *The God of the Sages: The Portrayal of God in the Book of Proverbs*. Stockholm: Almqvist & Wiksell International, 1990.

Bridges, Charles. *A Modern Study in Proverbs*. Revised by George F. Santa. Milford, Mich.: Mott Media, 1978.

Bryce, Glendon E. *A Legacy of Wisdom: The Egyptian Contribution to the Wisdom of Israel*. Lewisburg, Penn.: Bucknell University Press, 1979.

Buzzell, Sid. "Proverbs." In *The Bible Knowledge Commentary, Old Testament*, edited by John F. Walvoord and Roy B. Zuck. Wheaton, Ill.: Victor, 1985.

Cohen, A. *Proverbs*. Soncino Books of the Bible. London: Soncino, 1946.

Collins, John J. *Proverbs and Ecclesiastes*. Knox Preaching Guides. Atlanta: John Knox, 1980.

Dahood, Mitchell J. *Proverbs and Northwest Semitic Philology*. Rome: Pontifical Biblical Institute, 1963.

Delitzsch, Franz. *Biblical Commentary on the Proverbs of Solomon*. Translated by M. G. Easton. 2 vols. Grand Rapids: Eerdmans, 1950.

Draper, James T. *Proverbs: The Secret of Beautiful Living*. Wheaton, Ill.: Tyndale House, 1977.

Eims, LeRoy. *Wisdom from Above for Living Here Below*. Wheaton, Ill.: Victor, 1978.

Farmer, Kathleen A. *Who Knows What Is Good? A Commentary on Proverbs and Ecclesiastes*. ITC Series. Grand Rapids: Eerdmans, 1991.

Garrett, Duane A. *Proverbs, Ecclesiastes, Song of Songs*. New American Commentary. Nashville: Broadman, 1993.

Goldberg, Louis. *Savoring the Wisdom of Proverbs*. Chicago: Moody, 1990.

Helmbold, Andrew K. "The Relationship of Proverbs and Amenemope." In *The Law and the Prophets,* edited by John H. Skilton. Nutley, N.J.: Presbyterian and Reformed, 1974.

Hubbard, David A. *Proverbs.* The Communicator's Commentary. Dallas: Word, 1989.

Jones, Edgar. *Proverbs and Ecclesiastes.* Torch Bible Commentaries. New York: Macmillan, 1961.

Kidner, Derek. *The Proverbs: An Introduction and Commentary.* Tyndale Old Testament Commentaries. Chicago: InterVarsity, 1964.

Larsen, Paul E. *Wise Up and Live!* Glendale, Calif.: Regal, 1974.

Lawson, George. *Exposition of Proverbs.* 1829. Reprint. Grand Rapids: Kregel, 1980.

McKane, W. *Proverbs.* Old Testament Library. Philadelphia: Westminster, 1960.

Mouser, William E., Jr. *Walking in Wisdom: Studying the Proverbs of Solomon.* Downers Grove, Ill.: InterVarsity, 1983.

Murphy, Roland E. "Proverbs." In *Wisdom Literature: The Forms of the Old Testament Literature,* vol. 13. Grand Rapids: Eerdmans, 1981.

Nel, Philip Johannes. *The Structure and Ethos of the Wisdom Admonitions in Proverbs.* New York: Walter de Gruyter, 1982.

Oesterley, W. O. E. *The Book of Proverbs.* New York: E. P. Dutton, 1929.

Perdue, Leo G. *Wisdom and Creation: The Theology of Wisdom Literature.* Nashville: Abingdon, 1994.

Perowne, T. T. *Proverbs.* Cambridge Bible for Schools and Colleges. Cambridge: At the University Press, 1916.

Plaut, W. Gunther. *Book of Proverbs: A Commentary.* New York: Union of American Hebrew Congregations, 1961.

Ross, Allen P. "Proverbs." In *The Expositor's Bible Commentary,* vol. 5. Grand Rapids: Zondervan, 1961.

Scott, R. B. Y. *Proverbs-Ecclesiastes.* Anchor Bible. Garden City, N.Y.: Doubleday, 1965.

Swindoll, Charles R. *Living on the Ragged Edge.* Waco, Tex.: Word, 1985.

Toy, Crawford. *A Critical and Exegetical Commentary on the Book of Proverbs.* International Critical Commentary. Edinburgh: T. and T. Clark, 1899.

van Leeuwen, Raymond C. *Context and Meaning in Proverbs 25–27.* Atlanta: Scholars, 1988.

Westermann, Claus. *Roots of Wisdom: The Oldest Proverbs of Israel and Other Peoples.* Louisville: Westminster John Knox, 1995.

Whybray, R. N. *The Book of Proverbs.* Cambridge Bible Commentary. Cambridge: Cambridge University Press, 1972.

———. *Wealth and Poverty in the Book of Proverbs.* Sheffield: JSOT Press, 1990.

———. *Wisdom in Proverbs: The Concept of Wisdom in Proverbs 1–9.* London: SCM, 1965.

Articles

Blocher, Henri. "The Fear of the Lord as the 'Principle' of Wisdom." *Tyndale Bulletin* 28 (1977): 3–28.

Brueggemann, Walter. "A Neglected Sapiential Word Pair." *Zeitschrift für die alttestamentliche Wissenschaft* 89 (1977): 234–58.

Bryce, Glendon E. "Another Wisdom 'Book' in Proverbs." *Journal of Biblical Literature* 91 (1972): 145–57.

Donald, Trevor. "The Semantic Field of 'Folly' in Proverbs, Job, Psalms, and Ecclesiastes." *Vetus Testamentum* 13 (1963): 286–92.

Fensham, F. Charles. "Widow, Orphan, and the Poor in Ancient Near Eastern Legal and Wisdom Literature." *Journal of Near Eastern Studies* 21 (1961): 129–39.

Gluck, J. J. "The Figure of 'Inversion' in the Book of Proverbs." *Semitics* 5 (1977): 24–31.

Habel, Norman. "The Symbolism of Wisdom in Proverbs 1–9." *Interpretation* 26 (1972): 131–57.

Hildebrandt, Ted. "Proverbs 22:6a: Train Up a Child?" *Grace Theological Journal* 9 (1988): 3–19.

———. "Proverbial Pairs: Compositional Units in Proverbs 10–29." *Journal of Biblical Literature* 107 (1988): 207–24.

Kidner, F. Derek. "The Relationship between God and Man in Proverbs." *Tyndale Bulletin* (1961): 4–9.

Kitchen, K. A. "Proverbs and Wisdom Books of the Ancient Near East: The Factual History of a Literary Form." *Tyndale Bulletin* 28 (1977): 69–114.

———. "Some Egyptian Background to the Old Testament." *Tyndale Bulletin* 5–6 (1960): 4–18.

Lichtenstein, Murray H. "Chiasm and Symmetry in Proverbs 31." *Catholic Biblical Quarterly* 44 (April 1982): 202–11.

McCreesh, Thomas P. "Wisdom as Wife: Proverbs 31:10–31." *Révue Biblique* 92 (1985): 25–46.

Ruffle, John. "The Teaching of Amenemope and Its Connection with the Book of Proverbs." *Tyndale Bulletin* 28 (1977): 29–68.

Scott, R. B. Y. "Wise and Foolish, Righteous and Wicked." In *Studies in the Religion of Ancient Israel*. Supplements to *Vetus Testamentum*, vol. 23. Leiden: Brill, 1972.

Trible, Phyllis. "Wisdom Builds a Poem: The Architecture of Proverbs." *Journal of Biblical Literature* 94 (December 1975): 509–18.

Waltke, Bruce K. "Lady Wisdom or Mediatrix: An Exposition of Proverbs 1:20–33." *Presbyterion: Covenant Seminary Review* 14 (spring 1988): 1–15.

———. "The Authority of Proverbs: An Exposition of Proverbs 1:2–6." *Presbyterion: Covenant Seminary Review* 12 (fall 1987): 65–78.

———. "The Book of Proverbs and Ancient Wisdom Literature." *Bibliotheca Sacra* 136 (July–September 1979): 221–38.

———. "The Book of Proverbs and Old Testament Theology." *Bibliotheca Sacra* 136 (October–December 1979): 302–18.

Williams, James G. "The Power of Form: A Study of Biblical Proverbs." *Semeia* 17 (1980): 35–58.

Yee, Gale A. "An Analysis of Proverbs 8:22–31 According to Style and Structure." *Zeitschrift für die alttestamentliche Wissenschaft* 94 (1982): 58–66.

Subject Index

415

SCRIPTURE INDEX